Sunset

Annuals & Perennials

BY THE EDITORS OF SUNSET BOOKS AND SUNSET MAGAZINE

SAXON HOLT

Primary colors are evident in red-and-yellow perennial colum-bine (Aquilegia) *and blue annual forget-me-not* (Myosotis).

Sunset Publishing Corporation ■ Menlo Park, California

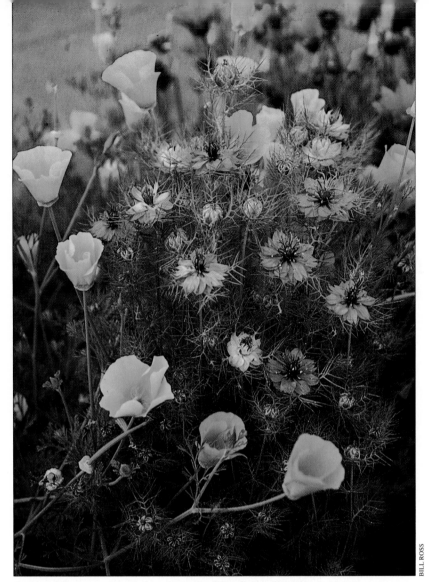

BILL ROSS

Spring performers: annuals love-in-a-mist (Nigella) *and California poppies* (Eschscholzia).

Violet speedwell (Veronica), *yellow yarrow* (Achillea), *and pale mauve sea lavender* (Limonium), *all perennials, weave a tapestry of varied colors, forms, and textures.*

SAXON HOLT

For Garden Color and Beauty

Under separate covers, the *Sunset* books *Annuals* and *Perennials* have dazzled gardeners with possibilities for creating beautiful garden and patio color. Now we've combined all the information about these two groups of tried-and-true performers in one handy volume.

The two titles have parallel formats. First, the plants are defined—annuals in one case, perennials in the other. Next, you learn how to use these plants effectively in the garden, with charts and lists to guide your selections. The following chapter provides the details of growing, from soil preparation through planting and care. Finally, you'll find an encyclopedic listing of over 100 annuals and 140 perennials, including detailed descriptions as well as a discussion of the conditions and care each plant needs to perform well.

Cover: A study in contrast, both in colors and shapes, features brilliant yellow sunflowers *(Helianthus)*, purple clary sage *(Salvia sclarea)*, purple coneflower *(Echinacea purpurea)*, and a dot of dark blue monkshood *(Aconitum)*. Cover design by Susan Bryant. Photography by Cynthia Woodyard.

Editorial Director, Sunset Books:
Bob Doyle

Fifth printing July 1998

Contents

Annuals

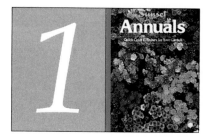

Learn everything you need to know about growing and choosing annual flowers, starting with basic suggestions for combining annuals attractively in the garden. Nearly 20 pages of lists and charts highlight choices for specific needs, whether you're looking for winter color, good cut flowers, or successful selections for hot sun or cool shade. Advice on growing annuals covers site selection, soil preparation, planting (from seed or young plants), watering, fertilizing, and pest control. An A-to-Z listing describes over 100 worthy annuals.

Perennials

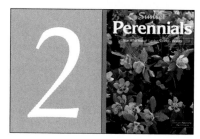

Our primer on perennials offers all the information you need, from selection through culture. Learn how to use perennials effectively in the garden, with illustrated planting plans providing inspiration. Plant lists let you select for seasonal color, low or high water use, shade tolerance, container gardens, and more. A separate chapter tells all about growing: site selection, soil preparation, planting, care, and propagation. An A-to-Z encyclopedia discusses more than 140 perennials, giving individual descriptions and cultural needs for each.

Sunset

Annuals

BY THE EDITORS OF SUNSET BOOKS AND SUNSET MAGAZINE

*Planted in profusion, summer annuals dress up entry steps,
offering a colorful welcome.*

Sunset Publishing Corporation ■ **Menlo Park, California**

Pansy (Viola wittrockiana) 'Jolly Joker'

Research & Text
Lance Walheim

Contributing Editor
Mary E. Harrison

Coordinating Editor
Linda J. Selden

Design
Joe di Chiarro

Illustrations
Lois Lovejoy
Jane McCreary

Calligraphy
Sherry Bringham

Editorial Director, Sunset Books:
Bob Doyle

Photographers

Scott Atkinson: 36, 38, 41, 42, 45; **Liz Ball/ Photo/Nats:** 50 top, 51 top; **Glenn Christiansen:** 7; **Priscilla Connell/Photo/ Nats:** 50 top middle, 62 bottom; **John R. Dunmire:** 67 top left; **Thomas E. Eltzroth:** 29 top, 55 top right, 61 bottom, 62 top left, 74 bottom, 81 top right, 88 top left; **Derek Fell:** 51 bottom middle, 51 bottom, 54 left, 58 left, 59 right, 62 top right, 64 top, 76 top left and bottom, 85 left, 92 top right; **Saxon Holt:** 2, 4, 8, 10, 11, 12, 15, 16, 17, 18, 19, 20, 21, 22 right, 23 bottom right, 24, 29 bottom, 30 left, 31, 32 bottom, 33 bottom, 34, 35, 39, 52, 54 right, 55 top left and bottom, 58 right, 59 middle, 60 top right and bottom, 63 top, 64 bottom, 65, 66, 67 top right and bottom, 68 top right and bottom, 69, 70 top and middle, 71, 72 bottom, 74 top left, 75 left, 77, 78 top right and bottom, 79, 80 top right and bottom, 81 top left, 82 middle, 83, 85 right, 86, 87 top left, 88 bottom left, 90, 91 top, 92 top left, 94 top; **Horticultural Photography:** 27 bottom, 57, 61 top, 73 bottom, 75 right, 78 top left, 81 bottom, 82 top, 84 top left and right, 87 bottom, 88 top right, 89 bottom; **Robert E. Lyons/Photo/Nats:** 51 middle; **Ells Marugg:** 56 bottom; **Robert and Linda Mitchell:** 50 bottom middle, 51 top middle, 87 top right; **Norman A. Plate:** 1, 25, 40, 59 left, 63 bottom; **Bill Ross:** 14, 23 top and bottom left, 25 top, 26 left, 27 top, 72 top left, 80 top left, 88 bottom right, 94 bottom; **Teri Sandison:** 72 top right; **David M. Stone/Photo/Nats:** 91 bottom; **David Stubbs:** 50 bottom; **Michael S. Thompson:** 22 left, 30 right, 32 top, 56 top left, 60 top left, 68 top left, 73 top, 76 top right, 89 top, 92 bottom left, 93 top left and bottom; **Darrow M. Watt:** 28, 33 top, 56 top right, 70 bottom, 74 top right, 82 bottom, 84 bottom, 93 top right; **Russ A. Widstrand:** 26 right.

Cover: This mixed planting of annual phlox (*Phlox drummondii*) shows just one example of the vibrant color flowering annuals can bring to home gardens. Cover design by Susan Bryant. Photography by Bill Ross.

Gardening with Color

Flowering annuals are extremely rewarding plants to grow. They can turn your garden into a vibrant tapestry of color or, used with restraint, provide just enough accent to make everything else in your landscape look fresher and more interesting.

But using annuals successfully takes thoughtful planning. This book will show you how to mix and match colors, how to achieve the longest possible season of bloom, and how to select just the right annuals for particular planting sites. We also explain how to care for annuals— from seed to transplant to full bloom.

As a group, flowering annuals comprise an amazingly diverse group of plants. To help you explore this diversity, we describe more than 100 species in the last chapter, Annuals A to Z.

For carefully checking our manuscript, special thanks go to Tilly Holtrop of Goldsmith Seeds, Gilroy, California; Roslyn Doss of Park Seed Company, Greenwood, South Carolina; and Jim Nau of Ball Seed Company, West Chicago, Illinois. We'd also like to extend thanks to Nona E. Wolfram-Koivula of All-America Selections, Downers Grove, Illinois and Burlingame Garden Center. Finally, we thank Marcia Williamson for her careful editing of the manuscript.

Contents

Viola

The Versatile Annuals

*G*arden color is what most people expect from flowering annuals. And it's true: no other group of plants can so quickly create a tapestry of bold or subtle colors, and at so little expense. Annuals are garden color, in every hue and tone imaginable. But besides being colorful, annuals are also versatile. They represent a huge, incredibly diverse class of plants that can play a variety of roles in the garden.

Cosmos

Lobelia, phlox, salvia, and sweet alyssum (Lobularia) yield a stunning combination of annual color and texture.

5

What Is an Annual?

Botanically, an annual is a plant that completes its life cycle in a year or less. The seed germinates, the plant grows, flowers, sets new seed, and dies—all in one growing season. The seeds set by many annuals will fall to the ground and, conditions permitting, germinate at some time in the future, usually the following winter or spring. These volunteers, as they are often called, can be left in place to flower, but they are likely to differ in habit or flower color from their parents.

Annuals are usually compared to perennials, which are defined as nonwoody plants that live for more than two years. Depending on how well they are adapted to where they are being grown, perennials can usually be counted on to bloom year after year, with bloom improving as plants mature.

Between annuals and perennials are biennials, which complete their life cycle in two years. The first year, they develop foliage; the second year, they bloom, set seed, and die.

Even though in a botanical sense annuals, perennials, and biennials fit into neatly defined categories, the distinctions that separate them are often blurred in nurseries and home gardens. Many tender perennials (such as geraniums, primroses, and verbenas), which will bloom year after year in mild-winter climates, are treated like annuals where winters are cold. Because they are quick to bloom, they can also be treated like annuals in mild-winter areas. In other words, even though they might bloom again the next year, the plants are discarded at the end of the season to make room for others. (In that sense, any plant that blooms within a year after you buy it could be considered an annual.)

Some biennials, including hollyhocks and Canterbury bells, can also be treated like annuals. If you buy nursery transplants and set them out early enough, they will bloom the first season. In essence, the nurseryman has provided the first growing season.

Cool-season Annuals Versus Warm-season Annuals

Annuals can be considered cool-season or warm-season plants, depending on their hardiness and ability to grow in cool soils.

Cool-season annuals (such as pansies, primroses, and calendulas) usually do best in the cool soils and mild temperatures of fall and spring. They are hardy to varying degrees (some are technically perennials), with most withstanding fairly heavy frosts. With the onset of hot weather, cool-season annuals are usually quick to set seed and deteriorate. In areas with short or cool summers, many cool-season annuals perform well all summer long. In addition, some varieties have been bred for greater heat tolerance and can bloom longer into warm weather. Where winters are mild, many cool-season annuals can be planted in fall for winter and early-spring bloom.

Warm-season annuals (such as marigolds, zinnias, and impatiens) grow and flower best in the warm months of late spring, summer, and early fall. Since most are sensitive to frost, they are planted after the average date of the last spring frost. Their bloom season usually ends with the first frost of fall.

Varieties, Hybrids & Strains

Seed companies, plant breeders, and growers have gone to great lengths to provide the highest-quality flowering annuals. Through careful breeding and vigilant selection of superior types, annuals are constantly being improved. These improvements include more and earlier bloom, wider color range, improved plant habit and vigor, and resistance to disease and insects.

The results of these improvements are offered to you as named varieties, such as 'Apricot Brandy' celosia or 'Royal Carpet' alyssum. Annual varieties are usually F-1 hybrids, which means they result from the cross-pollination of two specific plants, and are designated with single quotes. This pollination usually takes place under controlled conditions, such as in a greenhouse, so the results are uniform.

Some annual seed is produced through open pollination, meaning that the parent plants are grown in fields and the flowers are pollinated naturally, by wind or insects. Since you can never be sure exactly which plants were the parents, there is always a chance for variability among annuals grown from seed produced by open-pollinated plants. However, many open-pollinated plants do come "true to type," meaning that seeds grown from them will result in plants that are identical or very similar to the source of the seed. A strain, such as State Fair zinnias, is a group of plants that share similar growth characteristics but are variable in some one respect, usually flower color.

If you decide to save seeds or let your annuals reseed themselves, you need to be aware of another important distinction between F-1 hybrids and open-pollinated varieties. Seed collected from F-1 hybrids is not likely to produce plants identical to the parents. Unless pollination is controlled, the next generation will probably be significantly different in flower or plant form. Seed collected from open-pollinated plants is more likely to resemble parent plants.

All-America Selections

Each year the All-America Selection (AAS) organization judges new annual and vegetable varieties for exceptional performance. Nearly 100 varieties are planted at more than 50 trial gardens throughout the United States and Canada. Each annual is evaluated by impartial experts for its overall garden merit, local adaptation, length of bloom season, and vigor. On average, four varieties are given medals as outstanding performers. You'll find AAS award winners called out in many seed catalogs, in nurseries, and in the "Annuals A to Z" section of this book (pages 53 to 94). These plants can be counted on for superior bloom or outstanding garden performance.

Using This Book

Begin your experience with flowering annuals with an understanding of how to use them in the garden. "Designing with Annuals," starting on page 10, gives basic suggestions on how to combine and contrast colors and plant textures. The seasonal color charts help you plan for the longest possible period of bloom. Lists of annuals for specific growing conditions (such as for sun or shade) and with particular growth habits (such as low-growing or tall) help you select plants that fit your garden conditions and landscape needs. And lists of annuals with special characteristics (such as distinctive flower fragrance) encourage you to fashion a colorful landscape that expresses your own personal style.

The chapter "How to Grow Annuals," beginning on page 37, provides all the basics on culture: choosing a planting site, preparing the soil, germinating seed, growing healthy transplants, providing adequate water and nutrients, and controlling pests.

But the heart and soul of this book begin on page 53, where the plant encyclopedia opens. There you'll find full descriptions of more than 100 annuals, with all the information you'll need to successfully grow each one.

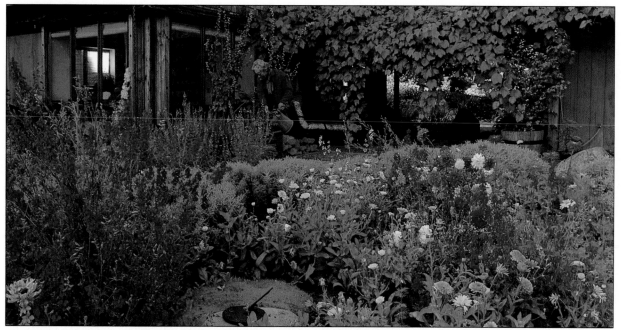

An artistically designed planting of annuals, including calendulas, zinnias, larkspur (Consolida), nigella, and hollyhocks (Alcea), creates a meadow of casual-looking color.

Annuals in the Garden

*F*lowering annuals are the workhorses of the flower garden. No other single group of plants can, in such a short time, so dramatically affect how a garden looks and feels. Flowering annuals can create interest in a dull green landscape or spotlight the best features of an exciting one. They can make a garden seem more relaxing or a front entry more inviting. They stimulate the senses, directing the eye from place to place, or making a cool spot seem warmer or a hot one more comfortable and appealing.

Antirrhinum majus

Annuals splash a riot of color across what was once a green garden. The boldly colored flowers include marigolds (Tagetes), salvia, petunias, and phlox.

9

$\mathcal{D}$esigning with Annuals

A well-timed mixture of cool-season annuals contrasts rich-toned snapdragons (Antirrhinum) with cool whites of sweet alyssum (Lobularia) and chrysanthemums.

The impact of annuals has much to do with their vibrant colors. But the most effective plantings are more than eye-catching splashes of color. They make use of texture, plant habit, and flower form, and rely on subtle complements and contrasts to create a specific look or mood.

Success depends to a certain extent on experience. But if you're new to gardening with annuals, you can still expect many more pleasant surprises than disappointments. Plant choices are many, and expanding every year; there is always something new. As you explore the possibilities, try keeping a garden journal to record varieties and flower combinations you especially liked, and to note where they were planted and when they bloomed. You'll soon build your own fund of knowledge with which to ensure future success.

Following a few simple guidelines will help you use flowering annuals most effectively.

Timing. When a plant flowers depends on many things, including the nature of the plant itself (see pages 53 to 94), your local climate, the planting site, and the weather. Some of these factors you can't control, and some you can. Still, annuals are usually grouped by the season in which they flower: spring, summer, fall, or, in mild-winter areas, winter. And that is the best place to start when planning a flower garden. But if you want to establish a long period of color, it's also important to think about how your garden will swing from one season to the next.

When spring annuals finish flowering, will you pull them all out and replant with new summer annuals, leaving several weeks when nothing will be in bloom? Or will you gradually work young summer annuals in among the flowering spring annuals so they'll be coming into bloom as the others finish? How will that affect your color scheme? What about planting spring- and summer-flowering annuals in separate places?

There are many ways to keep a garden in bloom month after month. You can purchase blooming plants in 4-inch pots or gallon cans so seasonal changes are barely noticeable. You can also plant young annuals in containers and keep them in a staging area until they are looking their best.

The important thing is to have a well-thought-out plan, especially if you'll be buying seeds and starting them yourself. Remember, if you want pansies in bloom in April, you may have to order seed 3 months in advance and sow it 8 to 10 weeks before transplant time.

Matching cultural needs. Some annuals grow best in sun, some in shade. Some bloom vigorously with constant moisture, and others take to soil on the dry side. Some annuals respond to regular fertilizer applications, and others will not bloom if the soil is too rich in nitrogen.

It's easiest to meet cultural needs by planting a bed with one type of annual. If you are mixing different plants, make sure they have similar cultural requirements.

Staggering heights. Keep the short plants in front and the taller ones toward the back. If you put the tall plants in front, you won't be able to see the smaller ones behind them. But don't be too dogmatic about it. For example, if a planting is to be made up entirely of lower-growing annuals (for instance, a border lining a walkway), weaving low-growing campanula through slightly taller salvia or dusty miller would result in a more interesting sight to stroll by or view directly from above.

Spacing and numbers. The assertion that "there is strength in numbers" very definitely applies to flowering annuals. If you want impact, use the spacings recommended in the chapter "Annuals A to Z" (pages 53 to 94), and fill the area to be planted. The result will be a brilliant mass of solid color, with little open soil left for weeds or debris.

A sixpack of Peter Pan zinnias stretched out in a 12-foot-long row looks strangely sparse. Six sixpacks (36 plants) properly spaced in the same area yield a satisfying concentration of vibrant color.

Plant habit and flower texture. Blending and contrasting colors are obviously important to successful flower gardening, but so are mixing and matching plant habits and flower textures. Compare the visual impact of a 10-foot-high sunflower with that of a ground-hugging cascading lobelia. One is an assertively upright sentry, with large, bold leaves and a platterlike circular flower. The other is diminutive, with delicate bloom and an outward-reaching habit. This comparison may be a bit extreme, but it points out how individual plants can contrast in character without reference to color.

Blending annuals with different habits gives each stronger impact. The spires of fairy primrose are more stately when fronted by the bold faces of pan-sies. The feathery foliage of dusty miller beautifully complements the mounding habit and trumpetlike flowers of petunias. The ever-moving, ribbonlike foliage and spiked seedheads of annual grasses lending graceful movement as well as subtle color to a landscape make a beautiful accent among refined Transvaal daisies. And an even carpet of sweet alyssum can form a perfect foil for the flat flower clusters of sweet William (*Dianthus*).

Proper spacing and a well-planned transition of heights from front to back creates a successful border of ageratum, marigolds (Tagetes), and salvia.

Using Color

Color is what gardening with annuals is all about. Like a painter, a gardener can use annuals in bold or subtle strokes, choosing bright hues or muted tones. The colors are at your fingertips: all you need to do is plant them out.

When pairing different colors, don't shy away from your favorite combinations. A garden should reflect the tastes of the gardener. And don't forget that there is beauty in simplicity. An all-white garden can be a wonderfully cool place to be in midsummer; a planting entirely composed of red zinnias can be a visually stimulating focal point in an otherwise green landscape.

Understanding the Color Wheel

The color wheel picture on the facing page is a rainbow spectrum in a circle. It shows the interrelationships of colors and illustrates color principles that you can reliably apply to planning a flower garden.

Primary. Red, yellow, and blue are called primary colors. All other colors can be produced by various mixtures of these three. Conversely, no mixture of

Generous waves of yellow and orange marigolds (Tagetes) are set off wonderfully by spikes of blue salvia.

other colors will produce pure red, yellow, or blue. These three colors are spaced equally around the color wheel.

Complementary. Colors directly across the wheel—red and green, for example, or blue and orange—are said to be complementary. If you combine annuals of complementary colors, they contrast with each other. Color contrasts—such as blue lobelia in front of a large planting of yellow marigolds—can lead the eye to a certain area: think of a large green tree underplanted with red impatiens.

But proportion is important. Contrasting colors can easily be overused and become visually disruptive. Large plantings of contrasting annuals set side by side—such as orange marigolds next to blue ageratum—can look both boring and slightly disquieting. The same marigolds highlighted with just a flash of ageratum make a much more pleasing sight.

Harmonious. Colors that lie between any two primary colors are said to harmonize with one another. This simply means they are graduated mixtures of those two primary colors. For example, the transition from yellow to red—through yellow-orange, orange, and red-orange—is accomplished by gradually adding more red to yellow. The closer the two colors are in the spectrum, the more harmonious they are.

Gardens planted with harmonious colors can be very attractive, particularly if you want to bring a sense of unity to a landscape without overpowering it.

Warm versus cool. The spectrum divides into two easily recognizable halves: warm colors and cool colors. The warm tones center around orange, the cool ones around blue. The dividing line would be drawn between green and yellow–green on one side and red and red–violet on the other.

The warmth or coolness of colors can affect the emotions of those viewing them. Annuals with warm orange and red flowers could make a hot patio or deck seem even hotter. The same patio planted with blues, violets, and whites can seem cooler and more inviting. A woodsy garden planted in cool blues and violets is extremely subdued and relaxing.

Warm colors also have their place. They have particular impact when viewed from a distance. Red cosmos planted near the rear of a garden immediately attract the eye, while light blue larkspur would not be nearly as noticeable.

Color value: light to dark. Not only does the color wheel show relationships between one color and another, it also shows that a single color has a range of different values from light to dark. Each pure spectrum color in the wheel is identified by name. These colors become lighter in value toward the center of the wheel, as they are diluted with more and more white. Toward the outside of the wheel, as the amount of white decreases, each color becomes darker in value with the addition of black.

No matter how value may vary from light to dark, the color retains the same contrasting and harmonious relationships with others on the wheel. For example, full blue with pale peach is just a variation of the blue-and-orange contrast.

Value affects how a color relates to white. Colors with lighter values harmonize with white, while those with darker values contrast. To illustrate the point, imagine dark red geraniums edged with white violas compared to light pink geraniums edged with the same violas. One look is bold and boisterous, the other soft and subdued.

Never underestimate the power of white flowers.

White reflects more light than any other color. White flowers can brighten the darkest area—even a patio on a moonlit night.

Gray. As the great moderator of color, gray deserves special mention. And when it comes to annuals, gray means dusty miller.

The color gray results from a mixture of any two complementary colors, so it can be employed to tie together otherwise-contrasting colors. Imagine a bed of blue salvia mixed with orange marigolds. Then envision the same colors surrounded by an edging of dusty miller. The contrast still exists, but is subdued by the presence of the gray-leafed plant.

Playing with Color

Now that the color lesson is over, it's time to have fun and let yourself go. You can get ideas for color combinations anywhere: from paintings, public parks, botanical gardens, even other people's gardens. Or try taking your favorite bicolored flower and using its component hues to plan additions and combinations. With all the "instant color" available in nurseries today, you can even check your palette of blooming plants before you buy.

Color Wheel

Color wheel shows primary colors (yellow, red, blue) spaced equidistant around the circle, with the transitional colors that connect them. The pure hue of each color is labeled, the shade of each color is made by the addition of black, and the tint comes when white is added.

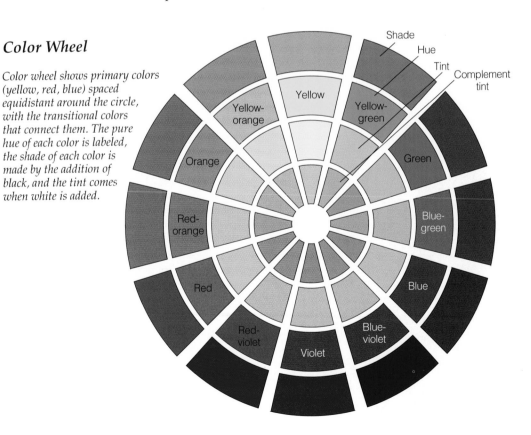

Flower Color by the Seasons

Knowing when an annual blooms and the colors in which it blooms is the key to effectively planning a flower garden. On the following pages are lists of popular annuals according to season of bloom. Also marked are the flower colors each plant has to offer.

Spring performers: nigella and California poppies (Eschscholzia)

Spring

NAME OF PLANT	RED	PINK	YELLOW	ORANGE	BLUE	PURPLE	WHITE	MULTICOLORED	GREEN
Annual grasses									■
Antirrhinum	■	■	■	■		■	■	■	
Arctotis	■	■	■	■		■	■	■	
Brachycome		■			■		■		
Brassica	■	■				■	■	■	■
Calceolaria	■	■	■					■	
Calendula			■	■			■		
Cheiranthus	■	■	■	■		■			
Chrysanthemum			■				■	■	
Clarkia	■	■	■			■	■		
Coleus	■	■	■	■		■	■	■	■
Consolida	■	■			■	■	■		
Cynoglossum		■			■	■			
Dianthus	■	■	■				■	■	
Dimorphotheca	■	■	■	■			■		
Eschscholzia	■	■	■				■		
Felicia					■				
Gazania	■	■	■	■		■	■	■	
Iberis	■					■	■		
Lathyrus	■	■		■	■	■	■	■	
Linum	■	■					■		
Lobularia	■					■	■		
Lychnis		■			■	■	■		
Matthiola	■	■	■			■	■	■	
Myosotis		■			■		■		
Nemesia	■	■	■		■	■	■	■	
Nemophila					■		■		
Nicotiana	■					■	■		■
Nigella		■			■	■	■		
Papaver	■	■	■	■			■	■	
Pelargonium	■	■		■		■	■	■	
Petunia	■	■	■		■	■	■	■	
Primula	■	■	■	■	■	■	■	■	
Reseda							■		■
Schizanthus	■	■	■			■	■		
Senecio	■	■			■	■	■	■	
Trachymene					■				
Tropaeolum	■		■	■			■		
Viola	■		■	■	■	■	■	■	
Wildflowers	■	■	■	■	■	■	■	■	■

(Continued on page 16)

*Wispy blue forget-me-nots (Myosotis) combine with lightly
fragrant sweet alyssum (Lobularia) to celebrate springtime.*

Summer

NAME OF PLANT	RED	PINK	YELLOW	ORANGE	BLUE	PURPLE	WHITE	MULTICOLORED	GREEN
Abelmoschus	■	■						■	
Ageratum		■			■	■	■		
Alcea	■	■	■	■		■	■		
Amaranthus	■		■						
Ammi							■		
Ammobium							■		
Anchusa					■				
Annual grasses									■
Antirrhinum	■	■	■	■		■	■	■	
Arctotis	■	■	■	■		■	■	■	
Begonia	■	■					■		
Brachycome		■			■	■			
Browallia					■	■	■		
Bupleurum			■						
Calceolaria	■	■	■					■	
Calendula			■	■			■		
Callistephus	■	■	■			■	■		
Campanula		■			■		■		
Capsicum	■		■	■					
Carthamus			■	■					
Catharanthus	■	■				■	■		
Celosia	■	■	■	■		■			
Centaurea		■	■		■	■	■		
Chrysanthemum			■				■	■	
Clarkia	■	■	■			■	■		
Cleome		■	■			■	■		
Coleus	■	■	■	■		■	■	■	■
Convolvulus	■	■			■	■	■		
Coreopsis	■		■	■				■	
Cosmos	■	■	■	■		■	■		
Crepis	■	■					■		
Cuphea	■								
Dahlia	■	■	■	■		■		■	
Dianthus	■	■	■			■	■		
Diascia		■							
Dyssodia			■						
Eschscholzia	■	■	■				■		
Euphorbia							■	■	■
Felicia					■				
Gaillardia	■		■	■				■	
Gazania	■	■	■	■		■	■	■	
Gerbera	■	■	■	■			■		
Gilia					■				
Gomphrena	■	■		■		■	■		
Gypsophila	■	■					■		
Helianthus			■	■				■	
Helichrysum	■	■	■	■			■		
Heliotropium					■	■	■		
Helipterum	■	■	■				■		
Iberis	■	■				■	■		
Impatiens	■	■		■		■	■		

Among summer pastels: blue salvia and pink lychnis

NAME OF PLANT	RED	PINK	YELLOW	ORANGE	BLUE	PURPLE	WHITE	MULTICOLORED	GREEN
Ipomoea	■	■			■	■	■		
Kochia	■								■
Lathyrus	■	■		■	■	■	■	■	
Lavatera	■	■					■		
Limonium	■	■	■	■	■		■		
Linaria	■	■	■	■	■	■	■	■	
Linum	■	■					■		
Lobelia	■	■			■		■		
Lobularia	■	■				■	■		
Lychnis		■			■	■	■		
Mimulus	■		■	■	■			■	
Mirabilis	■	■	■	■			■	■	
Moluccella									■
Nemesia	■	■	■	■	■	■	■	■	
Nicotiana	■	■				■	■		■
Nierembergia					■	■	■		
Papaver	■	■		■			■	■	
Pelargonium	■	■		■		■	■	■	
Pentzia				■					
Petunia	■	■	■	■	■	■	■	■	

NAME OF PLANT	RED	PINK	YELLOW	ORANGE	BLUE	PURPLE	WHITE	MULTICOLORED	GREEN
Phlox	■	■				■	■	■	
Portulaca	■	■	■	■			■		
Proboscidea		■				■	■		
Rudbeckia	■		■	■				■	
Salpiglossis	■	■	■			■	■	■	
Salvia	■				■	■	■		
Sanvitalia			■	■		■			
Scabiosa	■	■			■	■	■		
Schizanthus	■	■	■			■	■		
Tagetes	■		■	■			■	■	
Talinum		■							
Thunbergia			■	■			■		
Tithonia				■					
Torenia	■	■			■	■	■		
Trachymene					■				
Tropaeolum	■		■	■			■		
Verbena	■	■			■	■	■	■	
Viola	■		■		■	■	■	■	
Wildflowers	■	■	■	■	■	■	■	■	■
Zinnia	■	■	■	■		■	■	■	■

(Continued on next page)

'Old Mexico' zinnia blooms in bright shades of yellow, orange, and red throughout summer.

...Flower Color by Season

Fall

NAME OF PLANT	RED	PINK	YELLOW	ORANGE	BLUE	PURPLE	WHITE	MULTICOLORED	GREEN
Abelmoschus	■	■						■	
Ageratum		■			■	■	■		
Amaranthus	■		■						
Annual grasses									■
Begonia	■	■					■		
Brassica	■	■				■	■	■	■
Calendula			■	■			■		
Catharanthus	■	■				■	■		
Chrysanthemum			■				■	■	
Coleus	■	■	■	■		■	■	■	■
Cosmos	■	■	■	■			■	■	
Cuphea	■								
Dahlia	■	■	■	■		■	■	■	
Dyssodia			■						
Euphorbia							■	■	■
Gaillardia	■		■	■				■	
Gerbera	■	■	■	■			■		
Gomphrena	■	■			■		■	■	

NAME OF PLANT	RED	PINK	YELLOW	ORANGE	BLUE	PURPLE	WHITE	MULTICOLORED	GREEN
Impatiens	■	■		■		■	■	■	
Ipomoea	■	■			■	■	■		
Kochia	■								■
Lobelia	■	■			■		■		
Lobularia	■	■				■	■		
Mirabilis	■	■	■				■	■	
Pelargonium	■	■		■			■	■	
Petunia	■	■	■	■	■	■	■	■	
Phlox	■	■				■	■	■	
Portulaca	■	■	■	■			■		
Salvia	■					■	■	■	
Sanvitalia			■	■			■		
Scabiosa	■	■				■	■		
Tagetes	■	■		■			■	■	
Torenia	■	■			■	■	■	■	
Verbena	■	■			■	■	■	■	
Wildflowers	■	■	■	■	■	■	■	■	
Zinnia	■	■	■	■		■	■	■	■

Most summer annuals, like these petunias and marigolds, bloom until the first frost.

Winter

NAME OF PLANT	RED	PINK	YELLOW	ORANGE	BLUE	PURPLE	WHITE	MULTICOLORED	GREEN
Antirrhinum	■	■	■	■		■	■	■	
Brassica	■	■				■	■	■	■
Calendula			■	■			■		
Chrysanthemum			■				■	■	
Dimorphotheca	■	■	■	■			■		
Linaria	■	■	■	■	■	■	■	■	
Lobularia	■	■				■	■		
Lychnis			■			■	■		
Nemesia	■	■	■			■	■	■	
Primula	■	■	■	■	■	■	■		
Schizanthus	■	■	■			■	■		
Senecio	■	■			■	■	■	■	
Tropaeolum	■	■	■	■			■		
Viola	■		■	■	■	■	■	■	
Wildflowers	■	■	■	■	■	■	■	■	

When planted in fall, cool-season annuals such as calendula, sweet alyssum (Lobularia), and linaria will bloom during winter in mild-winter climates.

Pansies (Viola) offer mild-winter gardens a rainbow of color.

$\mathcal{W}$here & How to Use Annuals

Each annual has its own cultural needs of sun or shade, moist soil or dry. Each also has a unique growth habit that makes it appropriate for certain garden situations. Grouping plants with similar needs and selecting ones that fit well in a particular location or with your style of gardening are important steps in planning a successful flower garden. Here and on the following 15 pages are lists of annuals grouped by cultural needs, growth habits, and specific uses to help you make the right choices.

This sunny summer combination stars red zinnias, white cosmos, and yellow sunflowers (Helianthus) and marigolds (Tagetes).

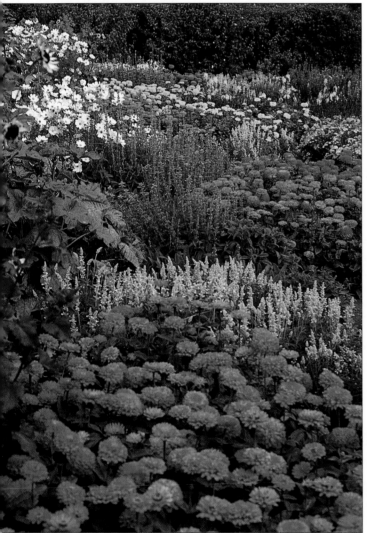

Annuals for Full Sun

These are annuals that flower best when planted where they can receive at least 6 hours of direct sunlight a day. Many can be grown in areas with light shade for a portion of the day, but they may bloom less, become more leggy and less compact, or be subject to mildew.

Abelmoschus *(Silk flower)*
Ageratum *(Floss flower)*
Alcea *(Hollyhock)*
Amaranthus *(Love-lies-bleeding)*
Ammi *(White lace flower)*
Ammobium *(Winged everlasting)*
Anchusa *(Summer forget-me-not)*
Annual grasses
Antirrhinum *(Snapdragon)*
Arctotis *(African daisy)*
Brachycome *(Swan River daisy)*
Brassica *(Flowering cabbage and kale)*
Bupleurum
Calendula
Callistephus *(China aster)*
Campanula *(Canterbury bells)*
Capsicum *(Ornamental pepper)*
Carthamus *(Safflower)*
Catharanthus *(Madagascar periwinkle)*
Celosia *(Cockscomb)*
Centaurea
Cheiranthus *(Wallflower)*
Chrysanthemum
Clarkia
Cleome *(Spider flower)*
Consolida *(Larkspur)*
Convolvulus *(Dwarf morning glory)*
Coreopsis
Cosmos
Crepis *(Hawk's beard)*
Cuphea *(Firecracker plant)*
Cynoglossum *(Chinese forget-me-not)*
Dahlia
Dianthus
Diascia *(Twinspur)*
Dimorphotheca *(African daisy)*
Dyssodia *(Dahlberg daisy)*
Eschscholzia *(California poppy)*

Flowering in mixed colors, zinnias, purple cockscomb (Celosia), and blue salvia stand up to heat and bright sun.

Euphorbia *(Snow-on-the-mountain)*
Felicia *(Blue marguerite)*
Gaillardia *(Blanket flower)*
Gazania
Gerbera *(Transvaal daisy)*
Gilia *(Blue thimble flower)*
Gomphrena *(Globe amaranth)*
Gypsophila *(Baby's breath)*
Helianthus *(Sunflower)*
Helichrysum *(Strawflower)*
Heliotropium *(Heliotrope)*
Helipterum *(Strawflower)*
Iberis *(Candytuft)*
Ipomoea *(Morning glory)*
Kochia *(Summer cypress)*
Lathyrus *(Sweet pea)*
Lavatera *(Tree mallow)*
Limonium *(Statice)*
Linaria *(Toadflax)*
Linum *(Flax)*
Lobelia
Lobularia *(Sweet alyssum)*
Lychnis
Matthiola *(Stock)*
Mirabilis *(Four o'clock)*
Moluccella *(Bells-of-Ireland)*
Nemesia

Nemophila *(Baby blue eyes)*
Nicotiana *(Flowering tobacco)*
Nierembergia *(Cup flower)*
Nigella *(Love-in-a-mist)*
Papaver *(Poppy)*
Pelargonium *(Geranium)*
Pentzia *(Gold button)*
Petunia
Phlox
Portulaca *(Moss rose)*
Proboscidea *(Unicorn plant)*
Reseda *(Mignonette)*
Rudbeckia *(Black-eyed Susan)*
Salpiglossis *(Painted-tongue)*
Salvia
Sanvitalia *(Creeping zinnia)*
Scabiosa *(Pincushion flower)*
Tagetes *(Marigold)*
Talinum *(Jewels of Opar)*
Thunbergia *(Black-eyed Susan vine)*
Tithonia *(Mexican sunflower)*
Torenia *(Wishbone flower)*
Trachymene *(Blue lace flower)*
Tropaeolum *(Nasturtium)*
Verbena
Viola *(Pansy and viola)*
Zinnia

Annuals for Shady Gardens

The first step toward growing flowers in shade successfully is to recognize the type of shade you have. Types include filtered shade from a high canopy of trees, dense shade on the north side of a house, morning shade followed by afternoon sun, and afternoon shade preceded by morning sun. And what's shady in spring may be sunny in summer. It is fair to say that there are almost as many kinds of shade as there are gardens that are shady. Keeping a record of

Violas and monkey flowers (Mimulus) bloom reliably in partial shade.

what plants work well in the shady parts of your own garden is the best way to ensure success from year to year.

Few plants will grow in very dense shade. However, many sun-loving plants can tolerate shade for part of the day. Here are annuals that will bloom in shade. Those marked with an asterisk (*) are most reliable in dense shade.

Begonia *(Bedding begonia)**
Browallia
Calceolaria
Campanula *(Canterbury bells)*
Cheiranthus *(Wallflower)*
Cleome *(Spider flower)*
Coleus*
Consolida *(Larkspur)*
Cynoglossum *(Chinese forget-me-not)*
Gerbera *(Transvaal daisy)*
Impatiens*
Linaria *(Toadflax)*
Lobelia
Lobularia *(Sweet alyssum)*
Mimulus *(Monkey flower)**
Myosotis *(Forget-me-not)**
Nemophila *(Baby blue eyes)*
Nicotiana *(Flowering tobacco)*
Nigella *(Love-in-a-mist)*
Pelargonium *(Geranium)*
Primula *(Primrose)*
Schizanthus *(Butterfly flower)*
Senecio *(Cineraria)***
Thunbergia *(Black-eyed Susan vine)*
Torenia *(Wishbone flower)**
Viola *(Pansy and viola)*

Potted fairy primrose (Primula) is ideal for a shady entryway.

Annuals for Hot, Dry Places

Most annuals require regular irrigation to bloom consistently. However, some perform better where heat and/or sunlight are intense and watering irregular.

Amaranthus (Love-lies-bleeding)
Annual grasses
Arctotis (African daisy)
Brachycome (Swan River daisy)
Centaurea (Cornflower and dusty miller)
Convolvulus (Dwarf morning glory)
Coreopsis
Dimorphotheca (African daisy)
Dyssodia (Dahlberg daisy)
Eschscholzia (California poppy)
Euphorbia (Snow-on-the-mountain)
Gaillardia (Blanket flower)
Gazania
Gomphrena (Globe amaranth)
Gypsophila (Baby's breath)
Iberis (Candytuft)
Kochia (Summer cypress)
Mirabilis (Four o'clock)
Phlox
Portulaca (Moss rose)
Rudbeckia (Black-eyed Susan)
Salvia
Sanvitalia (Creeping zinnia)
Tagetes (Marigold)
Tithonia (Mexican sunflower)
Tropaeolun. (Nasturtium)
Verbena

Verbena is a reliable bloomer for a hot, dry planting site.

African daisy (Arctotis) does best in dry soils.

Love-lies-bleeding (Amaranthus) and marigolds (Tagetes) thrive in heat.

Annuals for Containers

Growing annuals in containers has many advantages. Most important is that containers are mobile. You can keep them in an out-of-the-way spot while the plants are filling out, then move them to center stage at bloom time. Containers also let you enjoy flowers where there is little space or open soil, such as on patios or decks or in entryways. And containers come in a wide range of sizes, colors, and styles that can complement your plants as well as your garden.

As long as you use a good soil mix (see page 49 for information on container soils), you can grow almost any annual in a container. However, shorter varieties and ones with neat, compact habits and long bloom periods are most satisfactory. You can use one plant per pot, or mix and match colors and plant textures.

Try to mix plants with similar sun requirements and bloom periods. Remember that containers dry out quickly and need to be watered more often than flower beds. Container-grown annuals also need more frequent applications of nitrogen fertilizer (for more information on container care, see page 49).

Try to keep taller plants in the middle and shorter or cascading plants (see the list of annuals for hanging baskets on page 26) near the edge of the container. And space plants a little closer than you would in open ground.

Ageratum (Floss flower)
Annual grasses
Antirrhinum (Snapdragon)
Begonia (Bedding begonia)
Brachycome (Swan River daisy)
Brassica (Flowering cabbage and kale)
Browallia
Calceolaria
Calendula
Callistephus (China aster)
Campanula (Canterbury bells)
Capsicum (Ornamental pepper)
Catharanthus (Madagascar periwinkle)
Celosia (Cockscomb)
Centaurea (Dusty miller)
Chrysanthemum
Coleus
Convolvulus (Dwarf morning glory)
Coreopsis
Cosmos
Cuphea (Firecracker plant)
Dahlia
Dianthus
Diascia (Twinspur)
Dyssodia (Dahlberg daisy)
Felicia (Blue marguerite)
Gaillardia (Blanket flower)

The mounding habit of petunias makes them ideal for growing in containers.

Gazania
Gerbera *(Transvaal daisy)*
Gomphrena *(Globe amaranth)*
Helichrysum *(Strawflower)*
Heliotropium *(Heliotrope)*
Iberis *(Candytuft)*
Impatiens
Kochia *(Summer cypress)*
Lathyrus *(Sweet pea)*
Lobelia
Lobularia *(Sweet alyssum)*
Lychnis
Matthiola *(Stock)*
Mimulus *(Monkey flower)*
Nemesia
Nicotiana *(Flowering tobacco)*
Nierembergia *(Cup flower)*
Papaver *(Poppy)*

Pelargonium *(Geranium)*
Petunia
Phlox
Portulaca *(Moss rose)*
Primula *(Primrose)*
Rudbeckia *(Black-eyed Susan)*
Salvia
Sanvitalia *(Creeping zinnia)*
Schizanthus *(Butterfly flower)*
Senecio *(Cineraria)*
Tagetes *(Marigold)*
Thunbergia *(Black-eyed Susan vine)*
Torenia *(Wishbone flower)*
Tropaeolum *(Nasturtium)*
Verbena
Viola *(Pansy and viola)*
Zinnia

Colorful planter bursts with pink petunias, cascading lobelia, and focal-point marigolds (Tagetes).

Containers brimming with annual color make this garden a dazzler. Petunias, marigolds (Tagetes), lobelia, dusty miller (Centaurea), and dwarf dahlias—to name a few—are all on display here.

Annuals for Hanging Baskets

Hanging baskets bring flowers to eye level, where they can be enjoyed up close. Plants with spreading, mounding, or very compact habits are best suited to this aerial form of gardening. For more information on gardening in hanging baskets, see page 49.

Begonia (Bedding begonia)
Brachycome (Swan River daisy)
Browallia
Campanula
Chrysanthemum
Convolvulus (Dwarf morning glory)
Dianthus
Dyssodia (Dahlberg daisy)
Impatiens
Lobelia
Lobularia (Sweet alyssum)
Mimulus (Monkey flower)
Nemesia
Nierembergia (Cup flower)
Pelargonium (Ivy geranium)
Petunia
Phlox
Portulaca (Moss rose)
Primula (Primrose)
Salvia
Sanvitalia (Creeping zinnia)
Schizanthus (Butterfly flower)
Tagetes (Marigold)
Thunbergia (Black-eyed Susan vine)
Tropaeolum (Nasturtium)
Verbena
Viola (Pansy and viola)

Compact marigolds (Tagetes), pansies (Viola), salvia, and nemesia fill a hanging wicker basket.

The spreading habit of Swan River daisy (Brachycome) makes it grow softly around a hanging container.

Annuals for Edgings

These are neat, low-growing annuals or types that are available in low-growing varieties. For the most part, they stay under 12 inches high and are ideal for growing in front of taller plants, in narrow spaces or along walkways, or near the edges of containers.

Ageratum (Floss flower)
Annual grasses
Antirrhinum (Snapdragon)
Begonia (Bedding begonia)
Brachycome (Swan River daisy)
Brassica (Flowering cabbage and kale)
Browallia
Calendula
Callistephus (China aster)
Catharanthus (Madagascar periwinkle)
Centaurea (Dusty miller)
Chrysanthemum
Coleus
Convolvulus (Dwarf morning glory)
Crepis (Hawk's beard)
Dahlia
Dianthus
Diascia (Twinspur)
Dimorphotheca (African daisy)
Dyssodia (Dahlberg daisy)
Felicia (Blue marguerite)
Gazania
Gerbera (Transvaal daisy)
Gomphrena (Globe amaranth)
Helichrysum (Strawflower)
Iberis (Candytuft)
Linaria (Toadflax)
Lobelia
Lobularia (Sweet alyssum)
Lychnis
Mimulus (Monkey flower)
Nemesia
Nierembergia (Cup flower)
Petunia
Phlox
Portulaca (Moss rose)
Primula (Primrose)
Salvia
Sanvitalia (Creeping zinnia)
Schizanthus (Butterfly flower)
Tagetes (Marigold)
Torenia (Wishbone flower)
Tropaeolum (Nasturtium)
Verbena
Viola (Pansy and viola)
Zinnia

Ground-hugging purple and white sweet alyssum (Lobularia) is a perfect edging. It is grown here with Iceland poppies.

Compact blue ageratum edges silvery dusty miller (Centaurea) with accents of red salvia.

Annuals for Cut Flowers

Whether you grow flowers for cutting in a border mixed with other flowers or design a bed just to supply bouquets, these are the annuals to choose for cut arrangements. For longest-lasting bouquets, cut the flowers in the evening, remove lower leaves, and place stems immediately in water. Some varieties do best with stem ends seared; check the encyclopedia entries. Change the water in the vase frequently.

Sunflowers (Helianthus), shown here in a generous-looking bouquet of mixed varieties, make a bold statement as cut flowers.

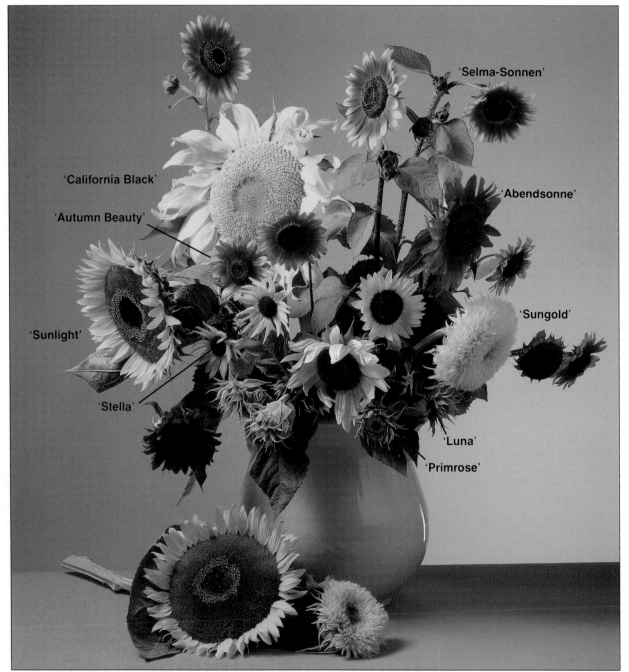

'Selma-Sonnen'

'California Black'

'Abendsonne'

'Autumn Beauty'

'Sungold'

'Sunlight'

'Stella'

'Luna'

'Primrose'

Ageratum (Floss flower, tall types)

Ammi (White lace flower)

Annual grasses

Antirrhinum (Snapdragon)

Browallia

Bupleurum

Calendula

Callistephus (China aster)

Campanula (Canterbury bells)

Carthamus (Safflower)

Celosia (Cockscomb)

Centaurea (Cornflower and sweet sultan)

Chrysanthemum

Clarkia

Cleome (Spider flower)

Consolida (Larkspur)

Coreopsis

Cosmos

Cynoglossum (Chinese forget-me-not)

Dahlia

Dianthus

Eschscholzia (California poppy)

Euphorbia (Snow-on-the-mountain)

Gaillardia (Blanket flower)

Gerbera (Transvaal daisy)

Gomphrena (Globe amaranth)

Gypsophila (Baby's breath)

Helianthus (Sunflower)

Helichrysum (Strawflower)

Heliotropium (Heliotrope)

Kochia (Burning bush)

Lathyrus (Sweet pea)

Limonium (Statice)

Lychnis

Matthiola (Stock)

Moluccella (Bells-of-Ireland)

Myosotis (Forget-me-not)

Papaver (Poppy)

Pentzia (Gold button)

Phlox

Rudbeckia (Black-eyed Susan)

Salpiglossis

Scabiosa (Pincushion flower)

Tagetes (Marigold)

Talinum (Jewels of Opar)

Tithonia (Mexican sunflower)

Trachymene (Blue lace flower)

Viola (Pansy and viola)

Zinnia

China asters (Callistephus) make long-lasting cut flowers.

Zinnias can be mainstays in a cutting garden.

Annuals with Colorful Foliage

Plants with colorful leaves can be stunning by themselves. Or use them to highlight or contrast with other flowering plants in beds or bouquets.

Amaranthus (Love-lies-bleeding)
Ammobium (Winged everlasting)
Begonia (Bedding begonia)
Brassica (Flowering cabbage and kale)
Centaurea (Dusty miller)
Coleus
Euphorbia (Snow-on-the-mountain)
Impatiens (New Guinea impatiens)
Pelargonium (Zonal geranium)

New Guinea impatiens offer interesting leaf texture as well as flower color. Some are variegated.

Painted in shades of green to maroon, coleus leaves mix well with impatiens. It's best to pinch off coleus flowers.

Tall Annuals

These are annuals to use at the back of a border for vertical emphasis, or as background plants. Most grow, or are available in varieties that grow, over 3 feet tall.

Alcea (Hollyhock)
Amaranthus (Love-lies-bleeding)
Annual grasses
Antirrhinum (Snapdragon)
Campanula (Canterbury bells)
Celosia (Cockscomb)
Clarkia
Cleome (Spider flower)
Cosmos
Consolida (Larkspur)
Helianthus (Sunflower)
Lavatera (Tree mallow)
Moluccella (Bells-of-Ireland)
Nicotiana (Flowering tobacco)
Tagetes (Marigold)
Tithonia (Mexican sunflower)
Zinnia

Old-fashioned hollyhocks (Alcea) make a stunning vertical statement, ideal for softening a large wall.

Tall snapdragons (Antirrhinum) provide a perfect background for lower and slightly lighter-toned pansies (Viola).

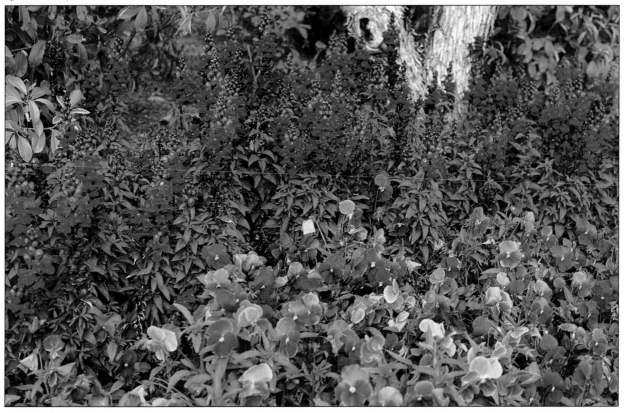

Annuals for Dried Bouquets

Often called everlastings, the flowers or seed heads of these plants will retain their color when dried if you hang them upside down in a cool, dark, well-ventilated place. Many other annual flowers can be dried using silica gels or by pressing.

Ammobium (Winged everlasting)
Annual grasses
Carthamus (Safflower)
Celosia (Cockscomb)
Centaurea (Cornflower)
Crepis (Hawk's beard)
Gomphrena (Globe amaranth)
Gypsophila (Annual baby's breath)
Helianthus (Sunflower)
Helichrysum (Strawflower)
Helipterum (Strawflower)
Limonium (Statice)
Moluccella (Bells-of-Ireland)
Nigella (Love-in-a-mist)
Pentzia (Gold button)
Proboscidea (Unicorn plant)
Scabiosa (Pincushion flower)

Strawflower (Helipterum) retains color intensity when dried.

The dainty flowers of gomphrena and the bold blossoms of cockscomb (Celosia) are old standbys for everlasting bouquets.

Annuals with Fragrant Flowers

When you plant fragrant flowers, you're inviting another one of your senses into the garden, increasing the pleasures it can offer you. These annuals have fragrant flowers—some faintly aromatic, others sweetly alluring. Plants with stronger fragrance are marked with an asterisk (*). Place them along walkways, around decks or patios, near windows, or in any other spot where they can be enjoyed often.

Centaurea (Sweet sultan)
Cheiranthus (Wallflower)
*Dianthus**
Heliotropium (Heliotrope)*
Lathyrus (Sweet pea)*
Matthiola (Stock)*
Mirabilis (Four o'clock)
Nicotiana (Flowering tobacco)
Petunia
Primula (Primrose)
Reseda (Mignonette)*
Tropaeolum (Nasturtium)

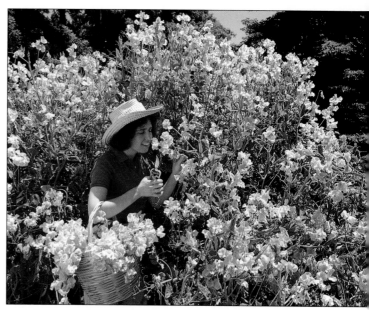

Few flowers can match the wonderfully rich, sweet fragrance of a crowd of sweet peas (Lathyrus).

Stock (Matthiola), fronted by yellow pansies (Viola) here, has strong, spicy fragrance.

Wildflowers & Annuals That Naturalize

In the true sense of the word, a wildflower is a plant that is native to your area—and therefore supremely well adapted to it. But with wildflower mixes on the shelves of almost every garden center today, all a plant really needs to be called a wildflower is to be easy to grow from seed and capable of naturalizing either by reseeding or being perennial.

Wildflower gardens can be effective, especially in a large area that is difficult to maintain. Seed is usually sown over a prepared planting bed in late fall or early spring. Wildflowers can also be interspersed with cultivated plants in beds and borders. But take care to plant species that are suited to your specific area.

There are a number of good resources to help you find which plants are best grown as wildflowers in your area. The National Wildflower Research Cen-ter (2600 FM 973 North, Austin, TX 78725) has a clearinghouse for information on current research and wildflower projects in each state and can supply advice on seed sources, recommended species, and appropriate planting procedures. The Soil Conservation Society of America (7515 Northeast Ankeny Rd., Ankeny, IA 50021-9764) and the Nature Conservancy (1815 North Lynn St., Arlington, VA 22209) also offer information on wildflowers and native plants. Many states have native plant societies that can provide information on regional wildflowers.

On the facing page are annuals that will reliably reseed themselves. In areas where the ground does not freeze, most can be counted on to bloom year after year. They are best used in open areas where neatness or a formal look is not important. Many need regular watering.

Red and pink Shirley poppies (Papaver), orange California poppies (Eschscholzia), and baby blue eyes (Nemophila) form a delicately beautiful spring wildflower meadow.

California poppies (Eschscholzia) and calendulas are two annuals that reseed and bloom year after year.

Brachycome (Swan River daisy)
Calendula
Centaurea (Cornflower)
Cheiranthus (Wallflower)
Chrysanthemum
Clarkia
Consolida (Larkspur)
Cosmos
Dimorphotheca (African daisy)
Eschscholzia (California poppy)
Gilia (Blue thimble flower)

Helianthus (Sunflower)
Lavatera (Tree mallow)
Linaria (Toadflax)
Linum (Flax)
Lobularia (Sweet alyssum)
Mirabilis (Four o'clock)
Myosotis (Forget-me-not)
Nemophila (Baby blue eyes)
Papaver (Shirley poppy)
Phlox
Tropaeolum (Nasturtium)

How to Grow Annuals

CARE FROM SEED TO BLOOM

lowering annuals are the plant world's instant gratifiers. Whether you start them from seed or buy them in bloom, they perform very quickly, with only one season to run their course. Like sprinters, they race from germination to flowering, then set new seed to begin the cycle again. Give these botanic athletes the right exposure, good nutrients, and consistent conditioning, and they'll reward you with a brilliant floral display at the finish.

Impatiens

Nurseries and garden centers provide ideas, seeds, and plants to start you on the road to a colorful garden.

Planting Cycle

Compared with almost all other plants, the life cycle of an annual is very short. Although the name suggests that such plants live a year, in the garden many won't survive even half that long. Once their blooming cycle is over, most will be pulled, whether still living or not, to make room for the next season's flowers.

Because of this abbreviated cycle, gardening with annuals is more exacting than with plants that live for years. If you make a miscalculation growing a flowering shrub, you probably have plenty of time to correct it. But make a mistake with an annual, and you may have struck out.

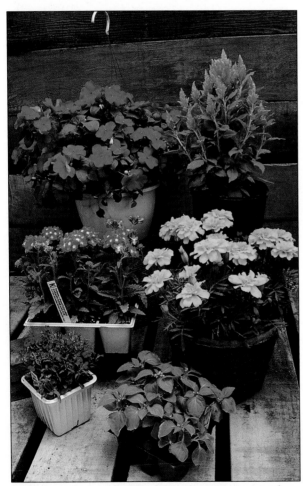

Annuals can be purchased from the nursery in a variety of containers. From front to back: six-packs, 4-inch pots, pressed fiber pots, cell-packs, hanging baskets, and gallon pots.

That doesn't mean annuals are hard to grow; in fact, they are relatively easy. What it does mean is that your success—and, generally, the amount of bloom produced—depends heavily on the care you take in raising or purchasing healthy seedlings; choosing an appropriate planting site; preparing the soil; and providing adequate moisture, nutrients, and pest control. For the best bloom, most annuals need to grow vigorously throughout their cycle. Let them stall from a lack of any of their necessities, and you probably won't have time to set things right.

Where to Plant

Most gardeners know where they want to plant annuals, so the real question becomes which annuals will grow best in that location. Note how much sun your planting area receives and match that exposure and your cultural practices with the needs of plants described in the next section of this book.

There are some planting locations to avoid. Few of the annuals described in this book can thrive in dense shade or in soils heavily infiltrated with roots of trees or shrubs. Sometimes you can prune a tree to let more light reach the ground beneath it. But if the soil is full of greedy roots, consider growing annuals in containers.

Remember, also, to plant your annuals where you'll see them often and be able to enjoy your garden's success.

When to Plant

When to sow seeds or set out annuals depends on your climate, growing season, and plant choice.

Cold-winter climates. In much of the country where winters are snowy or at least freezing, annuals bloom from mid-spring through early autumn. Cool-season or hardy annuals (such as pansies, Iceland poppies, flowering cabbage and kale, and primroses) can be planted in very early spring, almost as soon as the ground can be worked. If you delay planting until the weather has settled into mid-spring warmth, you risk disappointment. These plants need to develop roots and foliage during cool weather in order to bloom vigorously as the days grow warmer.

Most summer-flowering or warm-season annuals (such as marigolds, zinnias, and impatiens) should be planted after any danger of frost has passed. Others (such as amaranthus and celosia) grow best when planted later, after the soil has thoroughly warmed.

Mild-winter climates. Where winters are mild—either frost-free or lightly frosty—late winter and early spring are the best times to plant most cool-season annuals, and mid-spring is the time to plant summer or warm-season annuals.

But there is another season in these mild-winter areas: winter. Plants such as cinerarias, Iceland poppies, pansies, and calendulas, to name a few (see page 19 for others), will bloom in winter and early spring if planted in fall. Timing is important. Plant while the days are still warm enough to encourage growth, but while day length is decreasing. If you plant too soon, annuals will rush into bloom before they have become established. Plant too late, and you probably won't get any bloom until spring.

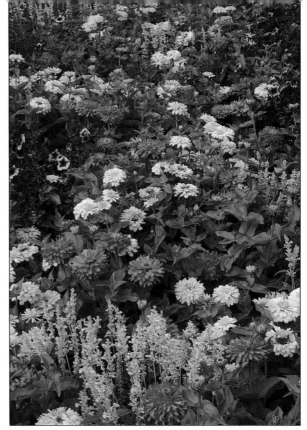

Zinnias weave through salvia and petunias.

Average Hard-Frost Dates* / *Based on U.S.D.A. weather records*

State	Last in Spring	First in Fall	State	Last in Spring	First in Fall	State	Last in Spring	First in Fall
Alabama, N.W.	Mar. 25	Oct. 30	Kansas	Apr. 20	Oct. 15	Ohio, No.	May 6	Oct. 15
Alabama, S.E.	Mar. 8	Nov. 15	Kentucky	Apr. 15	Oct. 20	Ohio, So.	Apr. 20	Oct. 20
Arizona, No.	Apr. 23	Oct. 19				Oklahoma	Apr. 2	Nov. 2
Arizona, So.	Mar. 1	Dec. 1	Louisiana, No.	Mar. 13	Nov. 10	Oregon, W.	Apr. 17	Oct. 25
Arkansas, No.	Apr. 7	Oct. 23	Louisiana, So.	Feb. 20	Nov. 20	Oregon, E.	June 4	Sept.22
Arkansas, So.	Mar. 25	Nov. 3						
			Maine	May 25	Sept.25	Pennsylvania, W.	Apr. 20	Oct. 10
California			Maryland	Apr. 19	Oct. 20	Pennsylvania, Cen.	May 1	Oct. 15
Imperial Valley	Jan. 25	Dec. 15	Massachusetts	Apr. 25	Oct. 25	Pennsylvania, E.	Apr. 17	Oct. 15
Interior Valleys	Mar. 1	Nov. 15	Michigan, Upper pen.	May 25	Sept.15			
Southern Coast	Jan. 15	Dec. 15	Michigan, No.	May 17	Sept.25	Rhode Island	Apr. 25	Oct. 25
Central Coast	Feb. 25	Dec. 1	Michigan, So.	May 10	Oct. 8			
Mountain Sections	Apr. 25	Sept. 1	Minnesota, No.	May 26	Sept.15	S. Carolina, N.W.	Apr. 1	Nov. 8
Colorado, West	May 25	Sept.18	Minnesota, So.	May 11	Oct. 1	S. Carolina, S.E.	Mar. 15	Nov. 15
Colorado, N.E.	May 11	Sept.27	Mississippi, No.	Mar. 25	Oct. 30	S. Dakota	May 15	Sept.25
Colorado, S.E.	May 1	Oct. 15	Mississippi, So.	Mar. 15	Nov. 15			
Connecticut	Apr. 25	Oct. 20	Missouri	Apr. 20	Oct. 20	Tennessee	Apr. 10	Oct. 25
			Montana	May 21	Sept.22	Texas, N.W.	Mar. 21	Nov. 10
Delaware	Apr. 15	Oct. 25				Texas, N.E.	Apr. 15	Nov. 1
District of Columbia	Apr. 11	Oct. 23	Nebraska, W.	May 11	Oct. 4	Texas, So.	Feb. 10	Dec. 15
			Nebraska, E.	Apr. 15	Oct. 15			
Florida, No.	Feb. 25	Dec. 5	Nevada, W.	May 19	Sept.22	Utah	Apr. 26	Oct. 19
Florida, Cen.	Feb. 11	Dec. 28	Nevada, E.	June 1	Sept.14			
Florida, South of Lake Okeechobee,			New Hampshire	May 23	Sept.25	Vermont	May 23	Sept.25
almost frost-free			New Jersey	Apr. 20	Oct. 25	Virginia, No.	Apr. 15	Oct. 25
			New Mexico, No.	Apr. 23	Oct. 17	Virginia, So.	Apr. 10	Oct. 30
Georgia, No.	Apr. 1	Nov. 1	New Mexico, So.	Apr. 1	Nov. 1			
Georgia, So.	Mar. 15	Nov. 15	New York, W.	May 10	Oct. 8	Washington, W.	Apr. 10	Nov. 15
			New York, E.	May 1	Oct. 15	Washington, E.	May 15	Oct. 1
Idaho	May 21	Sept.22	New York, No.	May 15	Oct. 1	West Virginia, W.	May 1	Oct. 15
Illinois, No.	May 1	Oct. 8	N. Carolina, W.	Apr. 15	Oct. 25	West Virginia, E.	May 15	Oct. 1
Illinois, So.	Apr. 15	Oct. 20	N. Carolina, E.	Apr. 8	Nov. 1	Wisconsin, No.	May 17	Sept.25
Indiana, No.	May 1	Oct. 8	N. Dakota, W.	May 21	Sept.13	Wisconsin, So.	May 1	Oct. 10
Indiana, So.	Apr. 15	Oct. 20	N. Dakota, E.	May 16	Sept.20	Wyoming, W.	June 20	Aug. 20
Iowa, No.	May 1	Oct. 2				Wyoming, E.	May 21	Sept.20
Iowa, So.	Apr. 15	Oct. 9						

* Allow 10 days either side of above dates to meet local conditions and seasonal differences.

Improving the Soil

Good garden soil is porous and drains well, but retains sufficient moisture for roots; and it provides ample nutrients to meet the needs of the plants. Preparing such a soil is one of the most important aspects of growing annuals successfully.

Acid or Alkaline? Test Your Soil

Having your soil tested is a sound gardening practice. It can tell you a great deal about your garden's potential. However, it is usually not necessary to test the places where you want to plant annuals unless you suspect a problem. Your local nursery or agricultural extension office can give you general information and advise you on the possible usefulness of a soil test.

Typically, a test reveals the acidity or alkalinity of your soil. This is expressed in pH numbers: pH 7 is neutral, pH greater than 7 is alkaline, and pH less than 7 is acid. Most annuals grow best in neutral or slightly acid soil. As a rule of thumb, high-rainfall areas tend to have acid soils and low-rainfall areas alkaline soils.

Soil tests also point out any deficiencies of major nutrients.

In many states the local agricultural extension office does testing; if not, it can recommend a private laboratory. You can also buy kits through mail-order garden-supply companies and many nurseries that let you test your own soil.

If the test indicates your soil is too acidic, add lime when you prepare for planting. If your soil is too alkaline, add sulfur. Again, your local nursery or agricultural extension office can recommend how much to add. If your soil is deficient in one or more nutrients, add the appropriate fertilizer (see pages 46 to 47) when you prepare the soil.

Well-prepared soil helps ensure a colorful display like this bed of pansies (Viola), stock (Matthiola), sweet alyssum (Lobularia), petunias, and dianthus.

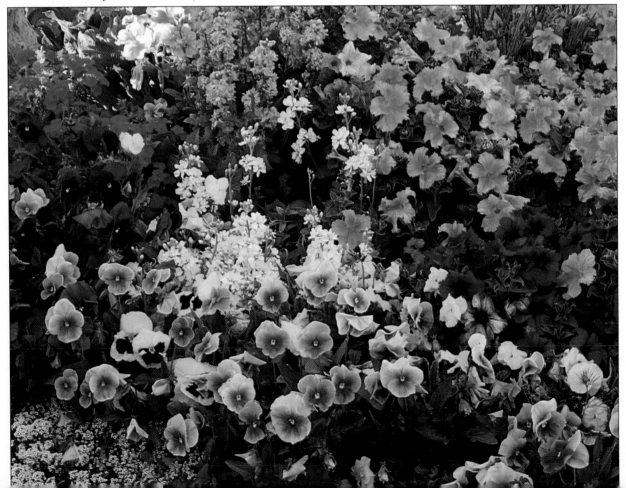

Soil Sense

Garden soils are generally classified as sandy, loamy, or clayey. Sandy soils usually dry out and drain quickly and are often low in nutrients but well aerated. At the opposite extreme, clayey soils take longer to dry and are usually poorly aerated and slow-draining.

In between clayey and sandy soils are loamy soils, made up of a combination of clay and sand particles and organic matter. These are the best to garden in because they hold moisture and nutrients while being well aerated and fast-draining.

Most garden soils fall either toward the sandy or clayey side, but they can easily be improved with the addition of organic soil amendments.

Soil amendments. Many types can help. Peat moss and manures are sold almost everywhere. Compost is available to any gardener willing to take the time to prepare it and can also be purchased packaged in nurseries or in bulk at some waste disposal sites.

Many by-products of regional agriculture and industry are good soil amendments: redwood and fir bark from lumber-producing regions; sawdust; spent mushroom compost; ground corn cobs; apple or grape pomace (the residue from making cider or wine).

If you plan to amend your soil with manure or wood products (bark or sawdust), you'll need to take a few precautions. Fresh manures can actually harm roots: if you use unaged manure, add it to the soil several months before planting. (If you dig in well-aged manure, you can plant right away.)

Wood products need nitrogen to aid their decomposition and will take from the soil whatever nitrogen they need. The result can be nitrogen-deprived plants. Packaged wood products and some that are sold in bulk are usually nitrogen-fortified, so they can be applied directly. But if you use raw or untreated products, add 1 pound of ammonium sulfate for every 1-inch-deep layer of organic material spread over 100 square feet. Scatter the ammonium sulfate over the spread-out organic matter, then dig the mixture into the soil. Wait about a month before planting.

Preparing the Soil

Thorough preparation means adding a 3-inch layer of amendment and repeatedly turning and digging the soil to a depth of at least 12 inches. It's also a good idea to incorporate a complete fertilizer (see page 47) that has a high ratio of phosphorus and potassium—a 5-10-10 formula, for example.

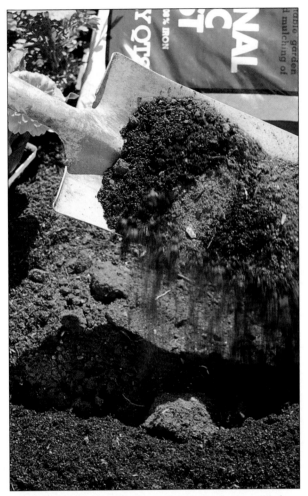

Working ample amounts of organic matter into the soil before planting improves aeration of a clayey soil and moisture-holding capacity of a sandy soil.

Soil is in good condition for digging when it is moist but crumbles easily. Never work a soil that is sticky and saturated with water. You will only compact it—just the opposite of what you're trying to achieve.

For a small area, dig by hand with a spade or spading fork. For a large, open area, use a rotary tiller. If you don't own a rotary tiller, you can rent one at a local rental yard (check in the Yellow Pages of your phone book).

If possible, prepare your soil several weeks before you intend to plant. This will give the amendments time to mellow and settle slightly. You can pull or hoe out any weeds that spring up during this period without having to work around newly set plants. Just before planting, do a final raking to smooth out any humps or hollows.

Seed vs. Transplants

Annuals can be started from either seeds or transplants. Starting from seed takes more time and energy, but it costs less and gives you a much greater variety of plants to choose from. There is also real pleasure to be derived from growing plants all the way from seed to flower.

Starting from seed. Seeds of annuals can either be started indoors in flats or pots (see photo below) or sown directly in the soil where they are to flower. Some annuals are easier to grow from seed than others. Large seeds, like those of nasturtiums, marigolds, and zinnias, germinate quickly and can be started indoors or sown outdoors with little chance of failure. Seed of such annuals as petunias, impatiens, and geraniums are smaller and slower to germinate, and seedlings take longer to reach transplant size. These plants are hardly ever direct-sown. They can be started indoors, but they demand precise growing

conditions and vigilant care. Most people prefer to purchase transplants of annuals like these.

Purchasing transplants. Nursery transplants save you time. And with many plants available in bloom, it's possible to visit a nursery in the morning and have a colorful garden in the afternoon. But instant gratification will cost you considerably more than growing plants from seed.

There is one pitfall to avoid when starting with transplants. Make sure you purchase plants that are healthy and growing vigorously. Plants that have yellowing foliage or are leggy, rootbound, or obviously too big for their pots will be slow to get established in the garden. Most will bloom poorly and require constant watering. When you're shopping for transplants, don't be afraid to slip one or two of each kind gently from their containers to examine the roots. If you see a mass of dense, white, tangled roots

Annual seeds can be started indoors in nursery flats or in purchased ready-to-plant peat pots and pressed peat cubes.

Remove plant by gently pressing on bottom of sixpack. Plant in a diamond pattern, using a precut stick for even spacing.

near the outside of the pot, the plant is rootbound. Look for plants with a fine network of roots, and ones with rootballs in which you can still see soil.

Planting Procedures

Be careful to set plants at the proper depth so their roots can spread into the soil. Planting too deep will cause many annuals to rot at their crown. Annuals planted too shallow will dry out quickly. You also want to be sure the soil is settled and firm around the roots.

Dig each planting hole larger than the plant's rootball. Tip the pot on its side and gently remove the plant from the container (with plastic sixpacks, use your thumb to push up from the bottom). Set the plant in the hole, making sure the top of the rootball is even with the surrounding soil surface. Firm soil around the roots and water well.

$\mathcal{S}$tarting from Seed

Some annuals, like sweet alyssum, marigolds, and zinnias, are easy to grow from seeds sown directly in ordinary garden soil. When the time is right, you simply scatter the seeds, lightly cover them with soil, and keep them moist; they germinate in just a few days. Seeds of other annuals have more precise requirements regarding soil temperature and light, and are best started indoors. This is a good way to get a jump on the season.

All the information you need for starting seeds can usually be found on the seed packet. You can also check details given in the encyclopedia section of this book, starting on page 53.

The steps for starting seeds are shown in the illustrations below. Use a sterile growing medium such as packaged vermiculite or potting soil. Make sure all pots and containers are clean (if necessary, scrub with a dilute solution of bleach). Choose a warm, well-lit spot; a greenhouse is ideal, but a sunny window can also work well. Be sure to sow at the appropriate depth. After sowing, keep the soil evenly moist. Letting the growing medium dry out will kill the seeds, but overwatering is likely to cause them to rot.

Once the seeds have germinated, the seedlings must receive strong light, or they will become leggy. Many nurseries sell supplemental lighting systems. You can also maintain consistent soil temperatures by installing heating cables, also available in most nurseries.

A week or two before the seedlings are ready to be transplanted outdoors, harden them off by taking them outside each day for periods of gradually increasing length. Start in a shady spot for just a few hours; bit by bit, expose them to more sun until they are used to outdoor conditions.

Sow seeds in flats of sterile soil or in the ground. Keep planting medium moist.

If sowing directly in garden soil, thin seedlings to proper spacing.

If sowing in flats, transplant seedlings to larger pots or into the garden when they develop the first set of true leaves.

Water & Mulch

To grow vigorously and bloom profusely, annuals need adequate soil moisture throughout their life cycle—enough water so plants never wilt, but not so much that the soil remains soggy and the plants drown.

How often to water. Frequency depends on a number of factors. Plants need to be watered more often when they are younger and have not yet fully developed their root systems. They also need more frequent irrigation in hot, sunny, or windy weather than in cool, cloudy, or calm weather. Soil texture can also influence how often you need to water, though with properly amended soil, this becomes less important.

Newly planted annuals require special attention. Recently sown seeds may need to be watered more than twice a day in warm weather. Young seedlings or transplants may need water at least once a day. As plants become established, you can gradually water less frequently.

The best advice in setting up a watering schedule is to be a good observer of both the weather and your plants. Watch for any signs of wilting, especially in hot weather. Get down on your hands and knees and stick your fingers into the soil: when the top 2 or 3 inches is dry, it's time to water.

How much to water. Apply enough to wet the entire root zone. For most annuals, this means to at least 12 to 18 inches. Watering deeply encourages deep rooting, and the deeper the roots go, the less vulnerable they will be to moisture fluctuations at the soil's surface. If you water plants daily but only lightly, they'll establish shallow root systems and be vulnerable to sudden drying out. Instead, water deeply, allow the soil to dry partially, then water deeply again.

To check how deeply water is penetrating, probe the soil with a long screwdriver or narrow rod. It will move more easily through moist soil and become harder to push in dry soil.

Watering Techniques

What's the best way to apply the water? You have a number of choices.

Overhead watering. This can be done by sprinklers or with a hand-held hose. Sprinklers provide more efficient coverage, especially for large plantings.

Overhead watering does have disadvantages. Some flowers (such as zinnias and petunias) are more susceptible to disease if their leaves and flowers are constantly wet. (If you overhead-water, do it early in the day so the foliage can dry by nighttime.) Overhead watering can wash the color from some flowers. And it can cause taller plants to tip over.

Furrows. If you're planting long, narrow rows of annuals, you may want to water them by digging or hoeing 6- to 8-inch-deep furrows or trenches along one or both sides of the row. Then let a hose run in one end of the furrow until it is full.

The problem with furrows is that they need constant maintenance—and long ones must have a gentle slope from one end to the other. In a wide bed or border, the furrow can be difficult to maintain once the plants are large.

Drip irrigation. This is the most efficient way to water. Drip emitters (or perforated tubing) deliver water right where you want it without wasteful run-off or damage to plant foliage. A drip system can easily be hooked up to an automatic timer to keep plants on schedule while you are away. Your local nurseryman or irrigation supply store can help you design an appropriate drip layout.

Mulches

Simply stated, a mulch is a layer of organic material on the surface of the soil. Nature provides this in the form of fallen leaves and twigs. Good gardeners observe the value of this cover and take pains to follow nature's lead.

Why mulch? A layer of organic material spread 2 to 3 inches deep between plants (close to the plant's base without covering it) greatly reduces evaporation from the soil beneath. Thus the soil surface remains moist longer and is not subject to cracking when dried by the sun.

A mulch also keeps soil cooler than if it were left

bare. But if applied too early in the season, when soil is cold, it can delay warming of the soil and slow development of plants. Particularly in cold-winter climates, where you need to make the most of the growing season, you shouldn't apply mulch until spring weather has warmed the soil.

Mulches also help in weed control. Most weed seeds cannot germinate beneath a thick layer of organic material, and any that do sprout and grow are easy to pull because of the mulch's loose texture.

In addition, mulches can have aesthetic value. A uniform layer of organic material looks neat and tidy; it also prevents mud from splashing on foliage and low-growing flowers.

Last but certainly not least, a mulch improves the quality of the soil beneath it. Organic matter gradually decomposes and becomes incorporated into the upper inches of the soil, improving its texture and ability to assimilate water. When it's time to change plants in a bed, you can work the soil to further incorporate the mulch and improve soil texture.

Mulching materials. Mulch must be loose or coarse enough for water to penetrate. This rules out anything that compacts into an airless mass when moistened—thin-textured leaves or a thick layer of grass clippings, for example. Beyond this restriction, though, your choices are quite varied. Wood by-products (see soil amendments on page 41) and bark chips are widely used, as is compost. Pine needles are popular where they're available. You can even use grass clippings if you spread them among the plants one thin layer at a time, allowing each layer to dry before adding another.

Some agricultural by-products also make excellent mulches—grape pomace and rice hulls, for example.

When woven through annuals, ooze tubes apply water to roots at a slow, even pace. Water goes only where it's needed; none is wasted. And, since foliage stays dry, chance for disease is reduced.

Nutrients & Fertilizers

To grow vigorously and stay healthy, plants need adequate nutrients, most of which they extract from the soil. But if the soil can't provide enough nutrients, the gardener must step in and apply supplementary fertilizer (popularly termed "plant food").

Newly planted annuals, especially, need a steady and balanced diet to reach a floriferous maturity. Three nutrients—nitrogen, phosphorus, and potassium—are needed in quantity. There are about six minor nutrients that also are important but needed in far smaller amounts. In addition, various trace elements are required—but in minute quantities. The role that each of the three major nutrients plays is described in "A Fertilizer Primer" on the facing page.

Fertilizer Choices

Most gardeners prefer the convenience of a complete fertilizer—one that includes each of the three major nutrients. You can also provide each of the "major three" separately: blood meal to supply nitrogen, bone meal for phosphorus, and ground rock potash for potassium. But before you proceed to the fertilizer section of your nursery, there's more to know about available types.

Dry and liquid. The boxes and bags of fertilizers on nursery shelves contain dry fertilizers. Many are complete fertilizers in granular and pellet form; they dissolve over a period of time after being mixed into the soil or applied to the surface. Some dry fertilizers are single-nutrient types that are also meant to be mixed into the soil or applied to its surface.

Liquid fertilizer and soluble granules are intended to be dissolved in water (according to label directions) and added to the soil. These may also be complete fertilizers or single-nutrient types (in this case, usually nitrogen sources, such as fish emulsion).

When preparing the soil for planting annuals, dry fertilizers are an obvious choice. Many gardeners prefer to continue with dry fertilizers as they are needed during the growing season (see "Timing the Applications" on the facing page) because they are relatively quick to apply, generally less expensive than liquids, and simple to use. If, however, you apply them unevenly or too heavily, you can burn plant foliage.

Liquid fertilizers are deservedly popular for container-grown annuals. If water can reach all the roots confined in a container in a matter of minutes, a liquid fertilizer can act as a quick tonic. Even though nitrogen not taken up by the roots will be leached out by subsequent waterings, it is little extra trouble to mix and use a liquid fertilizer repeatedly during the growing season as you water your containers.

Liquid fertilizers can be just as effective for plants in the ground. Nurseries now carry many ready-to-use products that come in hose-end sprayers. No mixing is necessary; all you do is attach them to your hose, turn on the water, and spray the fertilizer on the plants. Even though you pay a high price for the amount of nitrogen in ready-to-use fertilizers, you gain much in convenience. Liquid fertilizers that contain urea can also supply nitrogen to the plant through its leaves. Called foliar feeding, such supplementation can be a good way to give annuals a quick boost.

Some liquid fertilizers (not fish emulsion) can be applied through drip-irrigation systems or hose-end sprinklers via fertilizer injectors. These allow you to feed while you water. Your local nursery or irrigation supply store can suggest which type of equipment would best suit your system.

Slow-release. Gaining in popularity and availability are various dry fertilizers that are categorically termed slow-, controlled-, or timed-release. In one way or another, these resist or control the leaching out of nutrients by water. One application will slowly but steadily release nutrients with each watering over a specific period of time. The chief benefit of these fertilizers, though, is sustained release of nitrogen—the most-needed major nutrient, and the one that is most easily leached from the soil. And while they cost more than other kinds of fertilizer, you can weigh this against the small amount you use in a given season and the time you save.

The forerunner to these fertilizers was the urea-formaldehyde type (called urea or urea-form), which gave a sustained nitrogen release because it broke down slowly in the soil. Any fertilizer that contains nitrogen in the form of urea (this is stated on the package) yields a more sustained nitrogen release than fertilizers that contain nitrogen in nitrate or ammoniac form.

Directions on the packages of slow-release fertilizers clearly state the amount to use and when to reapply. These fertilizers are equally useful for growing annuals in the ground and in containers. However, many slow-release fertilizers don't begin to release nutrients for a week or two after application. Others release nutrients more slowly in cool weather. To avoid lag times, many gardeners use them in conjunction with light applications of faster-acting fertilizers.

Timing the Applications

For colorful results, most annuals need a steady supply of nutrients from planting time through the bloom period (a few annuals, such as California poppies, asters, and schizanthus, prefer infertile soil). If you add a complete fertilizer when you prepare the soil, there should be enough nutrients to keep the plants growing vigorously for about the first 6 weeks, at which point you should apply a further nutrient boost—dry, liquid, or controlled-release. How often you feed plants thereafter depends on which kind of fertilizer you plan to use.

Liquids should be repeated every 2 weeks (or every 7 to 10 days at half strength). How often you apply a dry fertilizer depends on its strength; the package directions will suggest timing and quantity. As for controlled-release fertilizers, a single application in conjunction with a liquid feeding may be enough in areas where growing seasons are short; use no more than two applications where growing seasons are long.

If you live in an area with very sandy soil, you'll have to water more frequently. This means you'll also have to add nitrogen more often, since frequent watering leaches it from the soil. In such areas, you can keep your annuals growing vigorously by applying liquid nutrients at quarter to half strength with each watering.

A Fertilizer Primer

Most commercial fertilizers are "complete," meaning they contain the three major plant nutrients: nitrogen (N), phosphorus (P), and potassium (K). The percentage of each nutrient is given on the package label; an 8-5-5 contains by volume 8 percent N, 5 percent P, and 5 percent K. For best performance and bloom, a plant needs all three of these nutrients.

Checking the percentages of nutrients (particularly nitrogen) by volume in a container of fertilizer gives you a basis for comparing prices. For example, a 10-pound bag of 10-5-5 fertilizer contains half the nitrogen of a same-size bag of 20-5-5. With all else being equal, the 10-5-5 product should be worth half as much.

Nitrogen is the most important nutrient, used to form proteins, chlorophyll, and enzymes necessary for normal cell function and reproduction. If a plant receives too little nitrogen, leaves turn yellow and growth is stunted. An excess, on the other hand, produces rank, sappy growth vulnerable to insects and disease, and may reduce the number of flowers.

Nitrogen is useful to plants only in its nitrate form; if applied in its organic or ammonium form, the element must be converted to nitrate in the soil before roots can absorb it. But nitrates are water soluble, easily leached beyond the reach of roots. For this reason, plants require nitrogen in greater quantity than phosphorus or potassium, which remain available to plants once they are applied.

Plants use *phosphorus* to form nucleic acids important for early growth and for root and seed formation.

Unlike nitrogen, phosphorus is not water soluble. Instead, it binds chemically to mineral particles in the soil and is then taken up by the roots. It must be applied where the roots are (or where they are to be): dig it into the soil or apply it in deep trenches. If you spread it on the soil surface, it will bind to particles in only the top inch or two of soil—and so will be assimilated by only the shallowest roots.

Potassium helps transport sugars and starches and is necessary for root growth, disease resistance, and fruiting. The water-soluble potassium in fertilizers goes through an intermediate step in the soil to become *exchangeable potassium*, which roots can absorb by contact. Potassium should also be applied at root level.

Maintaining Appearance

Once you have prepared the soil, planted, fertilized, and maintained soil moisture, most of the work is done. There are, however, a few additional practices that can keep your annuals looking their best.

Weeding. Keep weeds pulled or hoed from the very beginning. They rob desirable plants of water and nutrients while making your flower bed look unkempt.

If you are planting large areas or are bothered by particularly troublesome weeds, you might want to consider using an herbicide. *Pre-emergent* herbicides kill weed seeds before they germinate. They can be sprayed over or worked into the soil before or after planting. *Post-emergent* (or contact) herbicides affect growing weeds.

Pinching. Most annuals are bred to be compact and well branched. However, some, including petunias, geraniums, and many chrysanthemums, benefit from pinching (see illustration at right) to promote bushiness. Others, including marigolds and zinnias, will produce better overall bloom if you pinch out the first blossoms that form on young plants. In general, pinching any plant that has become too leggy or too tall will make it bushier and more compact.

Staking. If a plant starts to fall over or becomes too leggy when in bloom, it needs to be staked. Staking is usually necessary only with the tallest annuals, or ones that are not getting enough sun. The illustration at right shows some common methods. The important thing is to support the flowers while concealing the stakes.

Deadheading. Once flowers have faded, a plant puts its energy into ripening its seeds so it can reproduce. This is usually done at the expense of new flower production. In other words, a plant that is ripening seeds produces less bloom.

Removing spent flowers, called deadheading, can do more than keep a garden looking neat; it can prolong bloom. Large-flowered annuals, such as zinnias, are easy to deadhead: just pinch off or cut flowers back to the next branch. With smaller-flowered plants, such as alyssum and verbena, it's easier to shear the flower heads off with pruning shears. Make sure you don't cut back too far: never remove more than a third of the plant. Follow up with a feeding.

Pinching promotes bushiness and more bloom.

Staking keeps tall or leggy plants from falling over.

Deadheading encourages a longer bloom period.

Container Gardening

Gardening in containers and hanging baskets seems to become more popular every year. Particularly with annuals, container gardening lets you bring the flowers into close visual range, where they can really be enjoyed, on patios and decks and in entryways. There is a wealth of handsome containers to choose from. Whether you prefer a rustic oak half-barrel or a stylish ceramic pot, the only requirement is that the container have holes in the bottom for drainage.

On pages 24 to 25 is a list of plants that are ideally suited for growing in containers; on page 26 is a similar list of plants for use in hanging baskets. But before you jump in, realize that some of the basic rules for growing annuals change slightly when you switch to containers.

Soil. Choose a lightweight, sterile potting soil specifically designed for container gardening. A good mixture provides just the right balance of drainage, aeration, and moisture-holding capacity for ideal root growth. Potting soils are sold in bags at nurseries and garden centers, and in bulk from companies that sell topsoil.

If you have a lot of pots to fill, you may want to mix your own potting soil, although thoroughly blending one is quite a bit of work. One of the easier soil formulas calls for mixing ⅔ cubic yard nitrogen-stabilized bark (or peat moss) with ⅓ cubic yard washed 20-grit sand and adding to this 6 pounds of 0-10-10 dry fertilizer and 10 pounds of dolomite or dolomitic limestone.

Don't use ordinary garden soil in containers. No matter how good it is, the results are rarely as pleasing as with potting soil.

Watering. Soil in containers dries out very quickly, and you have to be vigilant in keeping it moist. In hot or windy weather, you might have to water more than once a day.

Inspect your containers often. If they feel light when you lift them, or if the top 2 inches of soil are dry, it's time to water. When you do water, apply enough to wet the entire rootball—enough so that some water runs out the bottom of the pot. This may take several passes with a hose.

If the rootball is really dry, it may shrink away from the edges of the pot, making it very difficult to wet. If water keeps running down the space along the edges, you may have to partially submerge the pot in a tub so it can absorb water from the bottom.

There are two ways you can ease container watering chores. The first is to mix super-absorbent soil polymers in your potting soil. Available in most nurseries, these hold hundreds of times their weight in water, which is still available to irrigate plant roots. Adding polymers to the potting soil lets you stretch the intervals between waterings.

A drip-irrigation system can also go a long way toward easing watering chores, especially when used with an automatic timer. Your local nursery or irrigation supply store can help design a system for containers.

Fertilizer. Potting soils may contain few nutrients, and any nitrogen they have is quickly leached out by watering. Consequently, container-grown annuals need frequent fertilizing. Liquid fertilizers are easiest to use. Start right after planting; repeat at least every 2 weeks.

Another alternative is to mix a timed-release fertilizer into the potting soil before planting.

Hanging Baskets

Growing annuals in hanging baskets is very similar to growing them in containers. The only difference is that hanging baskets, being exposed to the elements on all sides, dry out faster. Unless you are willing to water twice a day in hot weather, install an automatic drip system to keep baskets moist.

Instructions for building and planting a moss-lined hanging basket are illustrated below. Many nurseries carry moss baskets as well as a variety of hanging baskets made of wood, plastic, and clay.

Line the metal frame generously with moist sphagnum moss. Push moss firmly between wires. Plant sides: using your finger, make holes in the sides of the basket and insert each annual. Fill basket with soil. Plant top.

The best way to reduce the chances of pest and disease problems is to keep your garden clean; plant well-adapted species and varieties (resistant to common pests, if possible); and provide the appropriate amounts of light, water, and fertilizer. If pests do strike, take prompt action to thwart them. If disease appears, treat it promptly or remove and destroy affected plants and plant parts.

Below, we list the most common pests and diseases that may affect annuals and suggest some controls and preventative measures. Try physical and biological controls first; if those fail, use packaged controls.

Aphids. Soft, rounded, and up to matchhead-size, aphids may be green, pink to reddish brown, or black. They cluster on new growth, sucking plant juices. Heavy infestations can devitalize a plant, distort growth, and aid in the spread of viruses.

Controls. Aphids are easy to dispatch with a strong spray of water or insecticidal soap. There are also many predators of aphids, including lacewing larvae and ladybird beetles. Or spray with pyrethrins, rotenone, diazinon, or malathion.

Beetles. In this category are various hard-shelled insects that chew holes in foliage and flowers. Grubs (small worms), the larval stage, live in soil. Japanese beetles (see photo) and cucumber or diabrotica beetles (¼ inch, yellow with black spots) are very destructive.

Control. Hand-pick and destroy beetles. Use the biological control, milky spore, for Japanese beetle grubs or hormone traps for adults. Malathion and Sevin are effective chemical controls.

Earwigs. These small, brownish black insects have pincerlike rear appendages. They feed at night on soft leaf and flower tissue, particularly of dahlias.

Controls. Leave rolled, moist newspaper in the garden at night. Earwigs will hide in it in the morning. They can then be disposed of in a bucket of water. Or use earwig baits containing Baygon or Sevin.

Geranium budworms. Larvae of night-flying moths, they attack geraniums, ageratum, nicotiana, and petunias, rendering them bloomless. The small caterpillar eats the unopened buds or flowers, taking on the color of the flower on which it feeds.

Controls. If you see a bud with a small hole in it, pick and step on it or destroy it. That will kill the small larvae. For heavy infestations, spray with the biological control, *Bacillus thuringiensis*, or use pyrethrins, Sevin, or Orthene.

Mites. Tiny spiders appear as specks of red, yellow, or green dust and form silvery webs on the undersides of leaves.

    Controls. Frequent sprays with a strong jet of water will help dislodge them. Adding insecticidal soap to the water is even more effective. Natural predators include lacewing larvae and several species of predatory mites. Kelthane is the most effective chemical control.

Slugs, snails. These destructive garden pests are very common. They feed at night and on cool, overcast days; on warm sunny days, they hide. Both creatures eat leaves.

    Controls. Hand-pick and destroy any you can find. Or place boards out at night, turn them each morning, and crush the pests. They are also attracted to the fermented yeast in beer: place a beer-filled tray in the garden at night, and many will drown in it. There are also copper and salt-impregnated barriers that can be placed around beds. Or use baits containing metaldehyde or mesurol.

Whiteflies. These tiny, white, flying pests feed on undersides of leaves. Nymphs suck plant juices.

    Controls. Spray plants with insecticidal soap or use yellow, sticky traps. There are many natural enemies, including parasitic wasps. Dursban is an effective chemical spray.

Powdery mildew. A white or grayish powdery or mealy coating appears on leaves and flower buds, especially on dahlias and zinnias late in the year.

    Controls. Once established, powdery mildew is difficult to control. It's best to remove and discard infected plants. Benomyl and triforine are preventative sprays with some chance of success if you spray at the first signs of infection.

Rust. Usually appearing first on the undersides of leaves, yellow-orange pustules mature and burst; then wind and splashing water scatter spores. This is a common problem with snapdragons and hollyhocks.

    Controls. Water early in the morning so foliage can dry quickly. Avoid overhead watering. Give your planting area a good winter cleanup. Triforine, chlorathalonil, and wettable sulfur are effective preventative sprays. If an infestation occurs, remove and destroy infected plants or plant parts.

Annuals A to Z

*I*n the following 41 pages, you'll find descriptive profiles of more than 100 flowering annuals. Some, such as marigolds (Tagetes) and zinnias, have been old standbys for decades and can be found in almost any mail-order catalog or retail nursery. Others, such as Dahlberg daisy (Dyssodia) and twinspur (Diascia), are relatively new to American gardens and deserve to be more widely planted. These may be slightly harder to find in nurseries, but are available by mail: see page 94 for catalog sources.

Viola

Bright yellow marigolds (Tagetes) and creeping zinnia (Sanvitalia) edge pinkish red petunias.

53

Using Our Encyclopedia

Our encyclopedia lists the annuals by their botanical names, the most reliable nomenclature. Each Latin name is followed by a common name (or names) and the identity of plant family to which that annual belongs. If you're looking for a plant and only know its common name, refer to the index on pages 95–96.

The information provided on each annual is designed to help you evaluate its suitability to your garden, and to help you grow it successfully. Each entry begins with a thumbnail sketch covering the plant's primary season of bloom, its range of flower colors, the exposure (sun or shade) in which it does best, its height, and the best time to plant. Planting time, indicated by season, assumes you use the most reliable method to start the plants: sowing seeds indoors or outside, or transplanting seedlings purchased at a nursery. However, unless otherwise noted, almost any annual that can be grown from seed can also be started from nursery transplants, if available. Exact planting dates for your region are best determined by checking average frost dates (see page 39).

Following this information is a description of the plant and its flowers, an indication of which varieties are most commonly available, and tips for using it most effectively in a particular site or design.

Finally, each encyclopedia entry gives you the cultural information you need to grow the plant successfully from seed to bloom.

Abelmoschus moschatus

ABELMOSCHUS MOSCHATUS
Silk flower
Malvaceae

Flowers in: Summer to frost
Colors: Red or pink with white centers
Exposure: Full sun
Grows to: 12 to 15 inches
When to plant: Sow seeds outdoors after all danger of frost is past

A relative of okra, silk flower produces abundant five-petaled, 3- to 4½-inch-wide, single flowers resembling tropical hibiscus. It is a bushy plant about 12 to 15 inches tall and as wide, with deep green, deeply divided leaves. It is most floriferous in areas with long, hot summers. Silk flower grows best in good garden soil, heat, and full sun, but will also bloom in partial shade. Flowering 100 days after sowing, it will continue to bloom up to frost or cold weather. It can be grown indoors in a window with bright light. 'Mischief' and 'Mischief Soft Pink' are vigorous hybrids.

Culture. Soak seeds in tepid water for 1 hour before sowing. Plant outdoors, covering the seeds lightly, as soon as the ground is warm. Or start indoors 6 to 8 weeks before transplanting outdoors. Germination takes place in 10 to 14 days. Water regularly.

AGERATUM HOUSTONIANUM
Floss flower
Compositae

Flowers in: Early summer to fall
Colors: Azure blue, lavender blue, white, pink
Exposure: Sun, or filtered shade in hot climates
Grows to: 12 to 26 inches
When to plant: Set out transplants in spring after all danger of frost is past; in mild-winter climates, set out transplants in late summer for fall bloom

Ageratum, originally from Mexico, is a reliable favorite for summer and fall color. Mound-shaped plants produce showy, fluffy blossoms, which offer

Ageratum houstonianum

one of the truest blues in the garden. The tiny tassel-like flowers are borne in dense clusters. Leaves are roundish (usually heart-shaped at the base), dark green, and hairy.

Dwarf varieties such as 'Blue Puffs' and 'Blue Blazer' are attractive upright plants, excellent for edging, bedding, or containers and for mixing with other low-growing annuals such as sweet alyssum, dwarf marigolds, and petunias. Taller varieties are more open in growth and are excellent as cut flowers, lasting a long time in water. 'Blue Horizon', which grows 30 inches high, is one of the most widely available. 'Capri' is a dynamic bicolor of mid-blue with contrasting white centers, growing 12 to 15 inches tall.

Culture. Plant in full sun except in hot-summer climates, where filtered shade is better. Be sure soil is warm before transplanting outdoors. Rich moist soil is ideal, although average soil is adequate provided plants are kept watered. In mild-winter areas, plant in late summer for fall color.

Ageratum is most conveniently grown from purchased transplants. Young plants are tender and slow to develop, but are easy to transplant, even when in bloom. Pinch back after planting out to promote bushiness. Space dwarf varieties 6 inches apart, tall ones 12 to 18 inches. Deadheading helps keep plants looking neat and promotes continued flowering. *Ageratum* is not frost tolerant; the first frost will kill the plants.

Seeds germinate in 5 to 10 days at 60° to 70°F/16° to 21°C and take 6 to 10 weeks to reach transplant size.

Alcea rosea

Ammi majus

ALCEA ROSEA
(ALTHAEA ROSEA)
Hollyhock
Malvaceae

Flowers in: Summer
Colors: White, pink, rose, red, purple, creamy yellow, apricot
Exposure: Full sun
Grows to: 6 to 8 feet; dwarf varieties to 36 to 40 inches
When to plant: Sow seeds indoors in winter to early spring for summer bloom

The stately bloom spikes of hollyhocks have adorned countless gates and doorways. This finest of background plants was originally a short-lived Chinese perennial. It is now generally grown as a biennial, although annual strains bloom the first year from seed if sown in early spring. With good luck, you will get a second year of bloom from the original plants, and the plants often self-seed. Hollyhocks are an old-fashioned favorite that look best against a fence or wall or at the back of a border. Old single varieties can reach 9 feet; newer strains are generally shorter. The erect plants are clothed in big, rough, heart-shaped leaves. Single, semidouble, or double saucer-shaped flowers that are 3 to 6 inches wide and sometimes have frilly edges bloom on spikes from the bottom upward.

Summer Carnival, with double blooms in a wide range of colors, will flower the same summer from spring sowing. Powderpuff has fluffy, 4-inch double blooms on dwarf 4- to 5-foot plants.

Culture. Start seed in January or February in mild-winter areas, in March in other climates, sowing at a depth of ⅛ inch. Germination takes place in about 9 days at 55°F/13°C. Set out plants, or sow seeds directly, in ordinary garden soil as soon as warm weather has arrived. Direct-seeded plants may not bloom until the following year. Set plants 18 to 24 inches apart. Water well. If the site is windy, hollyhocks need staking. Japanese beetles particularly like the leaves of hollyhocks. Rust and anthracnose are common diseases.

AMARANTHUS
Love-lies-bleeding, Summer poinsettia
Amaranthaceae

Flowers in: Summer to frost
Colors: Brilliantly colored foliage ranges from chocolate brown to crimson, bright green, and gold
Exposure: Full sun or partial shade
Grows to: Taller varieties to 4 feet; smaller varieties to 24 inches
When to plant: Sow seeds outdoors in late spring to early summer

Amaranthus are easily grown and a good choice for backgrounds, borders, or to create a point of interest. Although they are coarse, sometimes weedy plants, a few choice cultivars exhibit brilliantly colored foliage or flower spikes, commanding attention from midsummer until frost.

A. tricolor 'Illumination' has heavy stalks of pendant foliage forming a wide 4-foot column, the upper third

Amaranthus

of which is crimson crowned with gold. The popular Joseph's Coat is 24 inches tall, bearing multicolored foliage of yellow, green, and crimson, with lance-shaped leaves. *A. caudatus*, love-lies-bleeding, has erect or cascading spikes of green or shades of red; these can be air-dried for winter bouquets.

Picked when young and tender, the leaves and stems of many species can be cooked like spinach.

Culture. Sow seed outdoors in average garden soil in full sun or part shade after the soil has warmed. Germination usually takes 14 to 21 days. Space smaller varieties 18 inches apart, taller ones 24 to 36 inches.

AMMI MAJUS
White lace flower, Bishop's flower
Umbelliferae

Flowers in: Summer
Colors: White
Exposure: Full sun
Grows to: 34 to 36 inches
When to plant: Sow seeds outdoors in early spring

The round, flat, 5- to 6-inch flower heads of *Ammi majus* look like Queen Anne's lace, but the plants are not as weedy or invasive. The pure white color and airy habit are welcome in borders. Easy to grow and free-flowering, *A. majus* is excellent for cutting.

Culture. This plant resents transplanting; sow seeds where they are to grow. Seeds germinate in 7 to 14 days.

Ammobium alatum

AMMOBIUM ALATUM
Winged everlasting
Compositae

Flowers in: Summer
Colors: Silvery white with yellow centers
Exposure: Full sun
Grows to: 12 to 36 inches
When to plant: Sow seeds outdoors in early spring or in fall in mild-winter climates

Winged everlasting is a half-hardy perennial originally from Australia, now commonly grown as an annual in North America. It is prized for its faintly spicy flowers with glistening silvery white petals and yellow centers. The long, oval, woolly leaves grow in a clump at the base of the plant. The blossoms do not fade with age, making winged everlasting extremely useful in dried arrangements. Its common name refers to the stems, which are stiff, branched, and have raised ridges or "wings."

Culture. Sow seeds outdoors (sandy soil is best) ¼ inch deep as soon as the ground can be worked. In mild climates, seeds may be sown in fall. Plant in full sun, thinning to stand 10 to 15 inches apart. For earlier bloom, start seeds indoors 6 to 8 weeks before last frost and transplant outdoors after all danger of frost is past.

Plants often self-sow. For dried arrangements, cut when the flowers are past bud stage but not fully open. It is best to pick them on a dry, sunny day. Hang them upside down in a shaded, well-ventilated place to dry.

ANCHUSA CAPENSIS
Summer forget-me-not, Bugloss, Cape forget-me-not
Boraginaceae

Flowers in: Summer
Colors: Blue
Exposure: Full sun
Grows to: 9 to 19 inches
When to plant: Start seeds indoors 6 to 8 weeks before last frost; set out plants in spring, after all danger of frost is past

The rich blue, white-centered, somewhat tubular flowers of summer forget-me-not contrast splendidly with the reds and yellows so prevalent among summer-flowering annuals. Flowers are red in bud, ultimately blue, ¼ inch wide, and clustered on hairy, branching stems. Leaves are bright green and lance-shaped. *Anchusa* is good for edging, or try massing it in beds or borders to dramatize the vivid blue color. It combines particularly well with yellow marigolds and red petunias.

'Blue Angel' is a free-flowering, compact plant (to 9 inches) with intense ultramarine flowers.

Culture. Plants grow readily in any well-drained soil in full sun. Chill seeds 1 week before sowing. Sow ⅛ inch deep. Maintain night temperatures of 70°F/21°C and daytime temperatures of 85°F/29°C; germination takes about 14 to 21 days. Transplant seedlings outdoors 6 to 12 inches apart, and keep them well watered. After the first flush of bloom, cut plants back to within 6 to 8 inches of the ground;

Anchusa capensis

Annual grasses

they will rejuvenate quickly and be more beautiful than ever. Fertilize lightly if at all.

ANNUAL GRASSES
Gramineae

Flowers in: Spring to fall
Colors: Green, silver, gold, plum
Exposure: Sun
Grows to: 12 to 36 inches, depending on variety
When to plant: Sow seeds indoors in late winter in short-season areas, outdoors in early spring elsewhere

Plum-hued, waving grasses; silvery, slender grasses; tall, majestic grasses—all of these deserve a spot in a garden. Grown for their seed heads rather than their leaves, annual grasses lend a charming mistiness when interplanted with flowers. Low sorts are excellent for bordering tall plants that look better with their bases covered. Taller types add a vertical elegance or create a focal point. Annual grasses are also wonderful mixed with flowers in containers. Some grasses are useful to cut for winter bouquets, and others are attractive planted in beds by themselves.

There are many species to choose from. Cloud grass, *Agrostis nebulosa*, is a fine, hairlike grass, giving a hazy effect. Growing 18 inches tall, it blooms in early summer and then dies back. Quaking or rattlesnake grass comes in two forms: *Briza maxima* grows 18 inches tall, while *B. minor gracilis* is shorter, reaching a height of about 12 inches. Both have flat, drooping, oval or heart-shaped spikelets that dangle from wiry stems and resemble rattle-snake rattles. Quaking grass is best used in a cutting garden, as it is a bit ungainly for more tailored borders. It also dies back after "blooming" in early summer. Brome grass, *Bromus brizaeformis*, is similar to quaking grass but grows taller, to a height of 24 inches. Job's grass, *Coix lacryma-jobi*, grows 24 to 36 inches high and produces curious pearly gray seeds that hang from leaflike sheaths. It will do best in a moist spot in the garden. Each seed is about the size of a cherry pit, and is hard.

Love grass, *Eragrostis interrupta*, closely resembles cloud grass when planted in masses. Spikelets are small and dancing. Squirrel-tail grass, *Hordeum jubatum*, is of interest because of its short, feathery heads of bloom, which reach 24 to 36 inches high. Hare's-tail grass, *Lagurus ovatus*, is a short-growing plant with downy white 1- to 1½-inch-long tufts at the tips of the stems. It is useful as a low edging for other annuals and grows 12 to 18 inches tall. It is also long-lasting in winter bouquets because the flower heads will not shatter with age. *Zea*, or striped maize, can be attractive in bold masses. Its green leaves are striped with yellow, white, red, or pink. It grows 24 to 36 inches high and should be planted at the same time as corn. Striped maize is attractive planted in medium-sized pots and grouped on a patio or terrace.

Culture. In general, the annual grasses are easy to grow. Most grow quickly, and should be sown outdoors in early spring or started indoors 6 weeks earlier in areas with shorter growing seasons. In mild-winter climates, most can be sown outdoors in fall or winter. One of the trickier aspects of growing annual grasses is that, until they bloom, they look like grassy weeds. Label them carefully so you don't pull them out by mistake.

A way to avoid having flower beds that look as though they are full of weeds is to sow annual grasses seeds in 6-inch pots or flats. Once the grasses have come up and have nicely filled in, knock them from the containers, cut the root mass into small pieces (like lawn plugs), and transplant them into the garden.

Grasses require room to develop. Plant them at least 12 inches apart. The smaller grasses look better when planted in substantial drifts of the same species. Seed can be collected for following seasons.

To gather for winter bouquets, pick grass with flowers that have not yet opened completely, cutting the stems as long as you can. Strip excess leaves, tie stems together, and hang upside down in a cool, dry, airy room. They should air-dry in 2 to 3 weeks.

ANTIRRHINUM MAJUS
Snapdragon
Scrophulariaceae

Flowers in: Winter to spring in mild-winter climates, spring to summer in other areas
Colors: Reddish purple, lavender, crimson, red, white, yellow, bronze, orange, pink, and combinations
Exposure: Full sun
Grows to: Tall varieties to 36 inches; intermediate to 18 inches; dwarf to 12 inches
When to plant: Set out transplants in early spring in cold-winter climates, in fall in mild-winter areas

Snapdragons are fantastic in form and color, come in a great range of heights, and bloom abundantly. They are an excellent choice for sunny borders and cutting. The common name is easily understood by anyone who has pinched the throat of the flower and watched the hinged blossom open and close. Native to the Mediterranean region (in mild climates, they are perennials and bloom from early winter until summer), snapdragons are usually treated as annuals. They are available in three height ranges: tall, intermediate, and dwarf. Tall and intermediate forms provide colorful vertical accents. Dwarf kinds are useful for edgings, in pots, and in rock gardens. For most gardens, snapdragons of medium height are best, since they produce stems long enough for cutting but are not tall enough to require staking.

The flowers, to 1½ inches long, are borne in terminal racemes blooming from bottom to top. A single plant may produce 7 or 8 blossom spikes in the course of the season. Foliage is medium green, lance-shaped, and somewhat sticky.

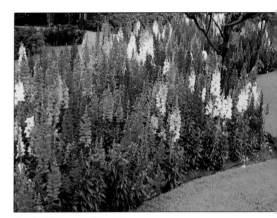

Antirrhinum majus

Of the tall kinds, the Rocket and Madame Butterfly hybrids produce strong plants and magnificent flowers. Among intermediates, the Sonnet series produces a good color range, and the Liberty series has shapely spikes of large, brightly colored flowers. The dwarf Little Darling and Floral Carpet hybrids are vigorous and colorful. The Sweetheart series has double azalea-type flowers.

Culture. Snapdragons are most easily grown from purchased transplants, as seeds must be started indoors up to 3 months before setting out. If growing from seed, start in a coldframe or indoors where night temperatures are 45° to 50°F/7° to 10°C and day temperatures do not exceed 65°F/18°C. Seeds germinate in 1 to 2 weeks. Young plants don't grow in hot weather. Keep plants in vigorous growth, watering and feeding regularly. Avoid overhead watering, which can spread rust spores, but don't let plants dry out. It is advisable to change snapdragon planting locations from one year to another to discourage rust.

Space tall and intermediate plants 15 inches apart, dwarf plants 9 inches apart. Pinch tips to encourage bushy growth and abundant flowering.

As the flowers mature, use them freely for bouquets. Cut flower stalks when half of the flowers are open, cutting to within 4 inches of the base of the plant. This will encourage the plants to produce additional stems that will bloom later in the season and will delay the onset of rust. Stake taller varieties when they have 4 or 5 sets of leaves.

ARCTOTIS
African daisy
Compositae

Flowers in: Spring into summer
Colors: White, yellow, orange, red, purple, pink, and bicolors
Exposure: Full sun
Grows to: 12 to 24 inches
When to plant: Sow seeds outdoors in early spring in cold-winter climates, in fall in mild-winter areas

These colorful, easy-to-grow annuals form a wonderful carpet of color when direct-sown. Showy daisylike flowers bearing a contrasting ring of color around the central eye are borne on slender stems. Elongated leaves are lobed, rough, and hairy or woolly. African daisy does especially well in coastal gardens. The flowers, which close at night and on cloudy days, are good for cutting, although they last only a few days in water.

Arctotis hybrids are most commonly available and grow 1 to 1½ feet tall. The 3-inch flowers come in white, pink, red, purplish, cream, yellow, and orange, usually with a dark ring around the nearly black eye spot. In mild climates, plants make growth in winter and early spring and bloom from spring into early summer, with scattered bloom later. They will self-sow, but tend to revert to orange. Plants may survive as perennials in mild climates, but bloom best in their first year.

A. stoechadifolia grandis is a bushy annual to 2½ feet with gray-green, slightly hairy leaves. The 3-inch-wide, satiny white daisies have a yellow ring

Arctotis

surrounding a deep steel-blue central eye, haloed with light yellow and tinted lavender-blue on the reverse.

Culture. Plant seeds outdoors as soon as the soil can be worked in spring; or, for early bloom, start indoors in winter, planting to a depth of ⅛ inch. Germination takes about 8 days. Thin to stand 10 to 12 inches apart in sandy soil. Flowering begins approximately 11 weeks after sowing. Avoid excessive use of fertilizers, especially those high in nitrogen. Full sun is essential. African daisies do best with minimal watering.

BEGONIA SEMPERFLORENS
Bedding begonia
Begoniaceae

Flowers in: Late spring, continuing until frost
Colors: Shades of red and pink, and white; leaves are bright green or bronzy red
Exposure: Partial sun to shade
Grows to: Most 6 to 12 inches, a few to 16 inches
When to plant: Set out transplants after all danger of frost is past

Bedding begonias (or wax or fibrous begonias, as they are sometimes called) are native to South America. They are a large group of hybrids and cultivars that grow 6 to 12 inches tall and bloom continuously outdoors in summer. The blooms grow close together, often covering the glossy bronzy red or green foliage. They are superb for window boxes, hanging baskets, beds, and borders, and can also be grown as house plants. Blossoms may be single or double; some have large flowers, some clusters of smaller blooms.

Bedding begonias can be lifted in fall and potted as house plants, where they will bloom indefinitely in a window with bright light. Cuttings started from house plants in spring root readily to provide specimens for the summer garden.

Pizzazz is a series of uniform, early-blooming, green-leafed plants that hold up well to weather. The Cocktail series features dwarf plants with bronze foliage and flowers in a wide range of colors.

Begonia semperflorens

Culture. Since begonias take 12 to 16 weeks to grow from seed, it is much easier to start with nursery transplants. Set transplants outdoors in rich, moisture-retentive soil after all danger of frost is past. Provide shade from the afternoon sun, especially in hot climates, but avoid deep shade, which will make the plants grow leggy and set fewer flowers. Bronze-leafed varieties do better in full sun than the green-leafed ones. In fact, they darken with more light.

Seeds germinate in 2 to 3 weeks at 70° to 80°F/21° to 27°C and should be kept above 50°F/10°C at night.

BRACHYCOME IBERIDIFOLIA
Swan River daisy
Compositae

Flowers in: Spring into summer
Colors: Blue, pink, white
Exposure: Full sun
Grows to: 9 to 12 inches high and 12 inches wide
When to plant: Sow seeds outdoors after all danger of frost is past

Covered with a profusion of delicately fragrant blue, pink, or white flowers with dark eyes, Swan River daisies are excellent for massing in mixed beds and borders. Their soft hues are good complements to warmer-colored annuals like zinnias and marigolds. However, they are best adapted to cool-summer areas and burn out quickly in warm weather. Leaves are small and delicate, toothed, and dark green. The plant grows in a bushy, mounded habit

Brachycome iberidifolia

Brassica

BROWALLIA SPECIOSA
Lovely browallia, Amethyst flower
Solanaceae

Flowers in: Late spring through summer
Colors: Blue, violet, and white
Exposure: Partial shade
Grows to: 12 to 36 inches
When to plant: Sow seeds indoors 8 to 10 weeks before last frost

Browallia produces a neat mound-shaped plant covered with brilliant blue, violet, or white flowers related to, and resembling, small petunias. Blue-flowering types have a contrasting white eye or throat. The one-sided clusters of velvety blooms are ½ to 2 inches long and as wide. *Browallia* blooms profusely for a long period in warm, moist, shady beds and borders. Where summers are short, it may not bloom until late summer or fall. Its leaves are lance-shaped, delicate, and bright green.

B. speciosa is most commonly grown. A sprawling plant with larger flowers to 2 inches in diameter, it lives over as a perennial in mild-winter climates. It is excellent for containers and hanging baskets because its mounding habit makes it drape over edges. 'Blue Bells Improved' is a compact variety with lavender blue flowers. 'Silver Bells' has pure white flowers and a trailing habit. The Troll series, including blue and white forms, produces compact, bushy plants well suited for growing in pots.

B. americana is branching, 1 to 2 feet high, with glossy roundish leaves; it is

that is suitable for growing in containers and hanging baskets.

Flowers may be cut for use in small vases, where they combine daintily with sweet alyssum. Use in rock gardens, as an edging, or in raised beds.

Culture. Sow seeds directly in ordinary garden soil, covering lightly; or, for earliest bloom, sow indoors in early spring. Germination takes about 8 days. Pinch the plants at 2 inches to induce bushiness. Thin to stand 5 to 6 inches apart. Flowering begins about 13 weeks after sowing and continues for 6 weeks or more in cool weather. Successive sowings result in a longer bloom period. The plants are fragile. Place short, brushy twigs among them to keep them from being beaten down by weather.

BRASSICA
Flowering cabbage & kale
Cruciferae

Flowers in: Early spring and fall, into winter in mild-winter climates
Colors: Grown for colorful foliage: green or white leaves with white, pink, rose, or purple markings
Exposure: Full sun
Grows to: 12 to 18 inches
When to plant: Best when started in mid to late summer to mature in the fall, since plants are most colorful in cool weather

Flowering cabbage and kale are excellent cool-weather bedding plants, providing magnificent rich foliage color late in the season. Looking a lot like their edible cousins, but without form-

ing tight heads, they yield textured rosettes of coarse foliage. Outer leaves are mostly smooth, often bluish green. The inner leaves are either off-white or deeply tinged with pink, rose, red, or purple, with color intensifying toward the center.

Flowering kale differs from flowering cabbage by being slightly looser in the head and more heavily fringed at the leaf edges. Cabbage forms lower-growing, flattened plants with broad heads.

Ornamental cabbage and kale produce a solid mass of color when planted as an edging or in a bed. They also grow well in containers and combine wonderfully with other fall and winter flowers, such as chrysanthemums and pansies. Their colored leaves set off gold and russet shades in fall arrangements. The foliage is also edible, though usually bitter-tasting, and makes a stunning garnish for all sorts of salads.

Culture. Plants are very similar to their edible cousins. When seed is started in midsummer and transplants are set out in late summer, heads mature beautifully in the cool months of fall. Colors actually intensify with light frosts. In mild-winter climates, plants will look good into winter. When planted in spring, ornamental cabbage and kale form looser heads and tend to bolt quickly as weather warms.

Start seeds 6 to 8 weeks before transplanting outdoors. Seeds germinate in about 10 days at 65° to 70°F/18° to 21°C. Space plants 15 to 18 inches apart in full sun. Protect seedlings from cabbage worms and aphids.

Browallia speciosa

Bupleurum griffithii

... *Browallia speciosa*

easily grown and a pleasing border plant. Violet or blue tubular flowers ½ inch long and across are borne among leaves. 'Sapphire' is a free-flowering dwarf variety with dark blue flowers with white eyes.

Culture. Start *browallia* seeds indoors, uncovered, at 65°F/18°C, 8 to 10 weeks before the last frost. Germination takes 12 to 21 days. Plant 9 to 12 inches apart in fertile, evenly moist soil in partial shade. Fertilize regularly. Pinch frequently to promote bushiness and continued bloom. If cut back and potted up, *browallia* will bloom again indoors in winter.

BUPLEURUM GRIFFITHII
Umbelliferae

Flowers in: Summer
Colors: Yellow
Exposure: Sun or partial shade
Grows to: 12 to 18 inches
When to plant: Sow seeds indoors 6 to 8 weeks before last frost

This plant is enjoying new popularity in European floral markets as a filler for arrangements. *Bupleurum* has leaves like a eucalyptus and yellow flowers like a euphorbia. Its abundant fan-shaped branches provide a striking backdrop for any flower form or color. It's easy to grow and quickly yields lots of material for cutting.

Culture. Germination takes 20 days at 70°F/21°C. Plant out in ordinary soil in sun or partial shade. Water bupleurum regularly.

CALCEOLARIA
Slipper flower, Pocketbook plant
Scrophulariaceae

Flowers in: Spring to summer
Colors: Yellow, red, maroon, and pink—often with spots
Exposure: Partial shade
Grows to: 12 to 18 inches
When to plant: Set out plants in spring, after the danger of frost; in fall in mild-winter climates

Calceolarias are tropical American, tender perennials sometimes grown as half-hardy annuals. All have showy and interesting flowers with two lips. The upper lip is small and the lower one large, inflated, and slipperlike. They grow best outdoors in Western coastal areas or cool high-altitude gardens, as plants suffer in heat.

C. *crenatiflora* (C. *herbeohybrida*) is the species best known and usually called pocketbook plant. It grows 12 to 18 inches high and produces yellow, pink, red, and maroon flowers that often are speckled. It is usually grown by florists as an indoor pot plant and is difficult to grow from seed. The hybrid Anytime series is more heat tolerant. It does well in containers or planted in a mass outdoors.

Culture. It's easiest to start with nursery transplants, if you can find them. Otherwise, start seeds indoors 12 weeks before the last spring frost. In mild-winter areas, sow in midsummer for fall transplanting. Sow seeds, uncovered, at 70°F/21°C. After germina-

Calceolaria

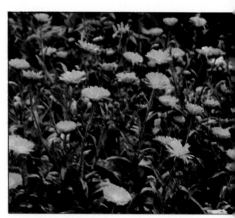

Calendula officinalis

tion (in about 16 days), transplant to small pots and continue growing, with 50° to 60°F/10° to 16°C night temperatures. Plants grow best in moderately rich, slightly acid soil with regular watering. Cut back after flowering, and your plants may bloom again.

CALENDULA OFFICINALIS
Pot marigold
Compositae

Flowers in: Spring and early summer in cold-winter climates; fall through spring in mild-winter areas
Colors: White, cream, orange, yellow, and apricot shades
Exposure: Full sun
Grows to: 12 to 30 inches
When to plant: Sow seeds outdoors in early spring, in fall in mild-winter climates

Few annuals are easier to grow or flower more abundantly than these scentless Mediterranean natives. They have a bushy, upright habit and rich, harmonious flower colors. The 2- to 4-inch flowers are daisylike and range from white through cream and lemon to bright yellow, apricot, and orange. They bloom over a long period, provided faded flowers and seed heads are removed. Foliage is light green, hairy, and brittle. *Calendulas* are ideal for containers or as massed bedding plants, and are long-lasting cut flowers. The flower petals are edible, with a slightly tangy taste. Use fresh petals in salads, soups, and egg dishes; dried petals can be used all year in soups and rice.

Bon Bon, Fiesta, and Gypsy Festival strains offer dwarf plants 10 to 12 inches high with early bloom. The Princess series has black-centered flowers. Radio has quilled petals.

Culture. *Calendulas* thrive in full sun, rich soil, and cool weather. Sow seeds ½ to 1 inch deep as soon as the ground can be worked in spring. Or start seeds indoors 6 to 8 weeks before transplanting. Seeds germinate in 10 days. Thin or space plants to 12 to 15 inches apart. A second sowing in early summer gives a good autumn bloom. In mild-winter climates, sow again in late summer or early fall for winter and spring color. Protect plants from slugs and snails.

CALLISTEPHUS CHINENSIS
China aster
Compositae

Flowers in: Summer
Colors: White, creamy yellow, pink, red, blue, and lavender or purple (often with yellow centers)
Exposure: Full sun or light shade
Grows to: 6 to 30 inches
When to plant: Sow seeds outdoors in spring after all danger of frost is past

Asters are rather difficult to grow, since they dislike transplanting and are subject to several diseases. Still, they are treasured by gardeners for their brilliant colors and usefulness as cut flowers. Their botanical name is from the Greek, meaning "beautiful crown."

Callistephus chinensis

Asters are available in many different flower forms: daisylike, chrysanthemumlike, pincushion-type, peony-flowered, ball or quilled, curled, incurved, and with crested centers. They are branching, erect plants with hairy stems. Leaves are dark green and serrated or deeply lobed. Asters bloom for 4 to 7 weeks. You can extend their flowering season by planting early-, mid-, and late-season varieties or by planting successively through spring. In a border, they are outstanding massed in solid colors. Planting a mixture of colors provides a glowing rainbow in the garden.

Asters are unexcelled for cutting, with long stems and handsome foliage; a light, fresh scent; and a wide range of colors. And they are long-lasting. Unlike most annuals, asters quit blooming when they are cut. Whole plants can be dug up for indoor arrangements, as their branching habit makes each plant a bouquet in itself.

Pot 'n Patio is a dwarf series, to 6 inches, with double flowers available in single colors or a mixture, and is ideal for edgings and patio containers. It can also be grown indoors in a sunny window, and will bloom without supplemental light. The Matsumoto series offers medium-tall plants to 24 inches, bred for disease resistance and heat tolerance, featuring double flowers with yellow centers. Serene is a pompon version of Matsumoto. Seastar has large flowers with thin, curled petals, making a beautiful and unusual flower on 30-inch plants.

Culture. Asters are particularly susceptible to fusarium wilt, which causes young and old plants to turn yellow and wilt. Avoid the disease by planting wilt-resistant strains. Plant seeds outdoors, barely covering them, in rich, well-drained soil. Seeds germinate in 8 to 10 days. For a succession of bloom, start a few plants indoors several weeks before the last frost date. Space tall varieties 12 inches apart, dwarf varieties 6 to 8 inches. Stake tall kinds early. For show quality blooms, pinch out flowering shoots to allow 6 flowers per plant.

To avoid fusarium wilt, do not plant asters in the same bed year after year; and don't plant them in heavy clay

Campanula medium

soils, which tend to get waterlogged. Asters are also susceptible to the virus called aster yellows, carried by leafhoppers. Keep plants some distance from calendulas and remove nearby weeds, which can be hosts to insects and disease. Asters can be covered during the early part of the season with polyester row cover or cheesecloth to keep out disease-bearing insects. Remove and destroy plants infected with wilt or yellows.

CAMPANULA MEDIUM
Canterbury bells
Campanulaceae

Flowers in: Early summer
Colors: Predominantly blue, also pink, rose, lavender, and white
Exposure: Full sun in cooler climates; light shade in hot-summer areas
Grows to: 30 inches
When to plant: Set out transplants in early spring, in fall in mild-winter climates

Campanula is a large genus, the majority of which are biennials and perennials. The most common annual, *C. medium*, is originally a biennial, from which annual forms have been developed. Annual types are generally shorter, but the attractive, bell-shaped flowers are quite similar. The fine blue colors are particularly welcome in a border, and show off to advantage when fronted with colorful short-growing annuals such as Shirley poppies. The erect, pyramid-shaped spires of 2-inch-long flowers make unusual, long-lasting cut flowers.

(Continued on next page)

Capsicum annuum

. . . *Campanula medium*

Another member of the genus that is sometimes treated as an annual is *C. isophylla*. Plants in the F1 hybrid Stella series, offered in blue and white with 1-inch, star-shaped flowers and heart-shaped leaves, are excellent in containers. Planted in hanging baskets, they produce with their tidy habit a globe that is completely flower-covered all summer. Give them extra light, and you can force them to flower indoors in the winter.

Culture. Because plants take 6 months to flower from seed, transplants purchased from a nursery will provide earliest bloom. They transplant easily, even when in bloom. Space 12 inches apart in the garden. Plant in deep, moist loam or humus-enriched soil. Shade roots with other plants or mulch.

CAPSICUM ANNUUM
**Ornamental pepper,
Christmas pepper**
Solanaceae

Flowers in: Summer
Colors: Yellow, orange, red fruits
Exposure: Full sun to partial shade, sunny window
Grows to: 8 to 10 inches
When to plant: Set out transplants after soil has warmed in spring

Ornamental pepper is unusual and decorative in the garden or in a container outdoors. The well-branched plants produce a mound of dark green leaves that are oval and pointed. Small white flowers are dainty and rather insignificant. The small round or cone-shaped peppers grow upright above

the foliage and ripen from whitish green to yellow to orange and red. All of these colors are present at the same time as the individual ¾-inch fruits ripen. Ornamental peppers are good as an edging, mixed with marigolds or purple-leafed basil, or as a container or house plant. Grow outside during summer and bring indoors in the fall as an ornamental holiday plant.

'Holiday Cheer' is an All-America Selection with round fruit. 'Treasure Red' has tapered fruit.

Culture. Treat them like tomatoes and peppers, sowing seeds indoors at 75° to 80°F/24° to 27°C, 6 to 8 weeks before last frost; or purchase plants from a nursery. Seeds germinate in 5 to 8 days. Space plants 8 inches apart in average soil.

CARTHAMUS TINCTORIUS
Safflower, False saffron
Compositae

Flowers in: Summer
Color: Cream to orange shades
Exposure: Full sun
Grows to: 12 to 36 inches
When to plant: Sow seeds outdoors after all danger of frost is past

Carthamus, a native of Egypt, was once extensively cultivated for the yellow dye extracted from its flowers. Easily grown, the erect plants have serrated or spiny leaves (a spineless version is also available). The thistlelike 1½-inch-wide blooms are useful as cut flowers, fresh or dried. They provide a hard-

Carthamus tinctorius

Catharanthus roseus

to-find orange color for dried arrangements. The dried flower petals are sometimes used in place of true saffron, which they resemble in color and flavor (hence the common name).

Culture. Plant in average soil. Plants need little water, once established.

CATHARANTHUS ROSEUS (VINCA ROSEA)
Madagascar periwinkle
Apocynaceae

Flowers in: Late spring to fall
Colors: Shades of pink, rose, lavender, and white
Exposure: Full sun to light shade
Grows to: 20 inches
When to plant: Set out transplants after soil has warmed in spring

Catharanthus, often called annual vinca, is a veritable workhorse in a sunny garden. Erect, mounded plants or creeping, low-growing dwarfs are in constant bloom, producing single phloxlike flowers in harmonious colors. The glossy, dark green, oblong leaves complement the blooms nicely. Vinca is a free-flowering tender perennial grown as an annual. One of its greatest assets is that it blooms all summer. It is attractive edging a border, makes a lovely ground cover in a bed of lilies, and is graceful trailing from a window box. As easily grown as alyssum, it also self-sows. Pot up plants before the first frost and bring them indoors.

Among the upright vincas, the Cooler series, bred for cooler climates, offers earliest blooms and withstands summer heat. Its 7-inch plants bear large, brilliant flowers with overlapping, rounded petals. They are excellent in borders or in pots. 'Pretty-in-Pink', 'Pretty-in-Rose', and 'Pretty-in-White' are All-America Selections. Growing from 14 to 20 inches tall, they produce large flowers and create a colorful show throughout summer. The Carpet series of creeping periwinkles grows 3 inches tall, spreads 24 inches across, and provides color all season. These are beautiful cascading from hanging baskets.

Culture. Since seeds must be sown early indoors for earliest bloom, it's most convenient to start with transplants purchased at a nursery. Plant in average soil, 8 to 12 inches apart. Water and fertilize regularly to promote vigor. If growing from seeds, germinate at 78° to 80°F/26° to 27°C for 3 days, then 75° to 78°F/24° to 26°C for remainder of the 7- to 15-day germination period.

CELOSIA ARGENTEA
Cockscomb, Chinese woolflower
Amaranthaceae

Flowers in: Summer
Colors: Brilliant shades of yellow, orange, pink, red, and purple
Exposure: Full sun
Grows to: 12 to 36 inches
When to plant: Sow seeds outdoors in spring after the soil has warmed

Celosia is grown for its striking (sometimes considered grotesque) flower heads, which come in various forms. The flowers are vividly colored and so should be used with discretion. They are best massed together or planted near other brightly colored annuals. *C. argentea plumosa* has blossoms resembling ostrich plumes. The feathery stalks are an unusual formal accent and can be interesting in arrangements. *C. argentea cristata* has velvety, crested flowers that resemble the vivid combs of roosters. Both *celosias* have long, narrow, lance-shaped leaves that are often bronze-colored or have red margins. Dried, the colorful, dense flower heads make good additions to winter bouquets. Both varieties thrive

in the heat of summer. Dwarf forms, especially the feathery ones, are useful in window boxes and containers. Place dwarf types in front of tall, branching varieties to create a colorful display.

Of the medium- to tall-growing celosias, the self-branching, 24-inch-high Century series of *C. a. plumosa,* available in single colors or a mixture, provides an early, colorful display. 'Century Red' is handsomely framed by bronze foliage, as is All-America Selection 'New Look', which grows 14 to 16 inches tall. Another award winner, 'Pink Castle', bears flowers of a beautiful rose-pink color on 12-inch by 12-inch plants. *C. a. cristata* 'Toreador' and 'Fireglow' feature intense red flower heads on 18- to 20-inch-tall plants.

In the dwarf range, *C. a. plumosa* Kimono offers an exciting mixture of uniform plumes in a broad range of colors on extra-dwarf 5- to 6-inch plants. *C. a. cristata* Jewel Box Mixture, to 5 inches tall, has large, comb-shaped blooms in a rich blend of colors; its neat, compact habit makes it ideal for bedding and containers.

Culture. Grow in rich garden soil. Plants respond well to feeding. They thrive in heat but not in cold, so do not sow or transplant too early. Keep the seedbed evenly moist, as seeds are sensitive to dry conditions. Seeds germinate in 8 to 10 days. Thin to stand 9 to 12 inches apart. In a nursery, look for young plants, as older transplants can suffer shock that inhibits flower production. To dry, cut the flowers and

Celosia argentea

Centaurea cyanus

hang them upside down in a dry, airy place. Strengthen *C. a. cristata's* stems with florist's wire to support the heavy flower heads.

CENTAUREA
Bachelor's button or Cornflower, Dusty miller, Sweet sultan
Compositae

Flowers in: Summer
Colors: *C. cyanus* and *C. moschata:* Blue, pink, rose, purple, yellow, and white; *C. cineraria* is grown for its silver foliage
Exposure: Full sun
Grows to: *C. cyanus* to 36 inches, *C. moschata* to 24 inches, *C. cineraria* to 12 inches
When to plant: Depends on variety (see below)

Centaurea is a diverse genus which includes the annuals commonly known as bachelor's button or cornflower, sweet sultan, and dusty miller.

C. cineraria is a silver-leafed plant called dusty miller—as are other silver-foliaged plants, such as the perennial *Senecio cineraria* and the annual *Chyrsanthemum ptarmiciflorum. C. cineraria's* felty, white, divided foliage makes it an elegant edging plant; the silver color softens and contrasts with bright flowers. It prefers relatively dry soil and tolerates heat, making it an excellent container plant. The cool hue of dusty miller complements hot-colored flowers such as geraniums, salvia, and petunias. It adds texture and interest in mixed plantings in window boxes or patio containers. It is also good foliage material for cut-flower arrangements. In mild-winter climates, it can be grown as a perennial and will send up 14- to 18-inch-tall stems of golden yellow blossoms in the spring. 'Silver Dust', 8 inches tall, has finely cut foliage and can be pruned to maintain a bushy shape.

C. cyanus is the popular bachelor's button or cornflower, a bushy plant with grayish, lance-shaped foliage and dense, thistlelike flower heads. It gives a lacy effect to a border and blooms prolifically, peaking in spring to midsummer. Excellent for cutting, its longlasting, richly colored blossoms are unsurpassed in a summer bouquet. The traditional flower for boutonnieres, cut blossoms last for some time without water. Deadhead the old blooms to keep them in flower, or make successive sowings to prolong the bloom season. The plants self-sow, but the seedlings often revert to inferior flower forms. Birds are attracted to the seed heads. Try interplanting blue varieties with yellow- or orange-colored annuals such as California poppies or *Gazania*. Plant the tall and medium-tall varieties in the back or middle of a border. Dwarf forms are suitable for containers.

C. cyanus 'Blue Boy' has rich blue flowers and grows to 30 inches. Polka Dot Mixed is a charming dwarf, to 18 inches, with a bushy habit.

C. moschata, sweet sultan, has finely fringed, 3-inch-wide flowers with a delicate fragrance. It favors cool climates. 'The Bride', growing to 24 inches tall, has fragrant, pure white flowers that are excellent for cutting.

Culture. C. cineraria is slow-growing, and best purchased as transplants or started early indoors. Plant 8 to 9 inches apart outdoors after all danger of frost is past. C. cyanus is easily grown from seed; sow in the fall for the earliest possible start, or as soon as the ground can be worked in spring. Thin to 12 inches apart. Taller kinds should be staked. Sow seeds of C. moschata where they are to grow, as it resents transplanting. Thin to 8 to 12 inches apart. It's at its best in cool weather and must be planted in the garden in early spring to succeed. Flowering slows down in hot weather, but returns with cooler fall temperatures.

Cheiranthus cheiri

CHEIRANTHUS CHEIRI
Wallflower
Cruciferae

Flowers in: Spring or late summer
Color: Tones of yellow, orange, red, burgundy, purple, and brown
Exposure: Full sun or partial shade
Grows to: 12 to 24 inches
When to plant: Set out transplants in very early spring for spring bloom; for late-summer bloom, sow seeds outdoors in early spring. In mildwinter areas, sow seeds outdoors in fall

Wallflowers have long been cherished by gardeners in Britain, where the cool, damp climate favors them. They can be grown in this country in similar climates, such as the Pacific Northwest and the coastal Northeast, where they often live on as perennials. Wallflowers have showy, sweetly fragrant clusters of single or double flowers and an erect, bushy habit. Their 3-inch-long leaves are narrow and pointed. The richly colored ½- to 1-inch-wide blossoms make splendid cut flowers. Plant a few beneath a window or near a doorway so their sweet fragrance can waft through the house. They thrive along south-facing rock walls or foundations, where the soil and shelter suit them. Try planting them as companions for spring-blooming bulbs such as tulips.

Culture. Plant in moist soil with good drainage. Early-flowering varieties will bloom about 5 months after sowing. Seeds germinate in 5 to 21 days at a temperature of 54°F/12°C.

CHRYSANTHEMUM
Compositae

Flowers in: Spring, summer, and fall; winter in mild-winter climates
Colors: White and shades of yellow—some with red or purple zoning
Exposure: Full sun
Grows to: 4 to 24 inches
When to plant: Sow seeds outdoors or set out transplants in early spring, in fall in mild-winter climates

This important genus, usually thought of for its fall-blooming perennial varieties, includes several valuable annuals as well. All are excellent for spring and summer borders; many are incredibly free-flowering. They make fine, long-lasting cut flowers.

C. carinatum, tricolor chrysanthemum, is an erect, tall plant (up to 2 feet) with single or double ray flowers and a contrasting zone of purple, red, or yellow surrounding a dark purple eye. The foliage is deeply cut. 'Polar Star' is bright and charming, with white daisylike flowers and yellow zoning.

C. coronarium, crown daisy, is a bushy plant to 24 inches tall covered with 2-inch flowers, typically in shades of yellow. A native of southern Europe, it has pale green, deeply cut leaves. 'Primrose Gem' is a low-growing bush, 12 to 18 inches tall. Its flowers have golden centers set off by a double row of soft yellow petals.

C. multicaule and C. paludosum, mini-marguerites, are both small, well-branched annuals that prefer cool weather. They grow to 12 inches and

Chrysanthemum paludosum

produce masses of 1½-inch daisylike flowers, excellent for edging, window boxes, and hanging baskets. 'Yellow Buttons', just 4 to 7 inches tall, is a vigorous plant with bright yellow, single flowers. 'White Buttons', to 7 inches, is covered with flowers with white petals surrounding yellow centers.

C. ptarmiciflorum, silver lace (one of several plants known as dusty miller), has finely cut silver foliage and grows 8 inches tall.

Culture. Plant in average soil. Seeds germinate in 8 to 20 days at 68°F/20°C. Thin to stand 12 inches apart. Pinch young plants to promote bushiness. Plants do not tolerate heat well. Stake taller varieties. Remove spent blossoms to prolong bloom period.

CLARKIA
Onagraceae

Flowers in: Spring to early summer
Colors: Shades of white, yellow, red, pink, rose, and lavender
Exposure: Full sun
Grows to: 12 to 48 inches
When to plant: Sow seeds outdoors in early spring or in the fall in mild-winter areas

The clarkia family includes several beautiful Western wildflowers and hybrids. Natives of western North and South America, they were named for Captain William Clark of the Lewis and Clark expedition. Clarkias grow best in cool climates, thriving in mountainous areas of the West. They do not tolerate heat. Their showy flowers are attractive in borders or in beds. Clarkia stems are wiry and slender, and will be prostrate unless staked. They make good cut flowers, as they last several days in water.

C. amoena (Godetia amoena), commonly called godetia or farewell-to-spring, is a native of the west coast of North America. Its flowers grow in spikes above tapered, dark green leaves on 20- to 36-inch plants. Dwarf forms grow to 12 inches. The satiny single or double cup-shaped flowers are 2 inches across. In mild-winter climates, sow in fall for spring bloom.

C. concinna, red-ribbons, is native to California, and grows to 18 inches tall. The feathery pink-to-lavender flowers have deeply lobed petals, resembling ribbons. The bushy plant has small, oblong leaves.

C. pulchella grows to 15 inches tall. Single and double white, lavender, or carmine flowers are triple-lobed at the tips. The slender plant has reddish stems and narrow, pointed leaves. Single flowers are deeply toothed to a clawlike base. This clarkia works well near the front of a border.

C. unguiculata (C. elegans), clarkia or mountain garland, grows up to 4 feet tall. It is the most widely grown of the clarkias. Single or double 1- to 2-inch flowers grow in spikes above reddish stems and oval, lance-shaped leaves. The spring-blooming flowers, in scarlet, salmon, carmine, white, purple, rose, or creamy yellow, are effective massed. The frilly, double-flowered kinds are most widely available as seeds.

Culture. As clarkias do not like transplanting, sow seeds where they are to flower, in sandy soil without fertilizer. Soil needs to be cool (55°F/13°C) for germination, which can take from 5 to 20 days. Thin to stand 9 inches apart (space *C. unguiculata* 6 inches apart, as it blooms better when somewhat crowded). Keep soil moist until plants bloom.

Clarkia unguiculata

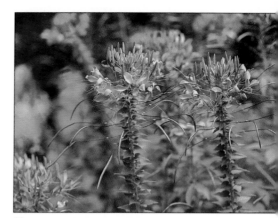

Cleome

CLEOME
Spider flower
Capparaceae

Flowers in: Summer to fall
Color: Shades of pink, purple, white, and yellow
Grows to: 5 feet
Exposure: Full sun or light shade
When to plant: Sow seeds outdoors after soil has warmed

An airy mass of *cleome* provides a colorful and unusual background at the back of a border. This plant (*C. spinosa*) can provide a quick-growing screen or hedge, and it blooms from summer until hard frost. Its bushy, somewhat coarse spikes are topped with clusters of single flowers. Stamens that are 2 to 3 inches long protrude from each flower, giving a distinctive airy effect. Long, narrow, pointed seed pods form below the flowers, like spider legs. The compound leaves are made up of leaflets arranged like fingers on a hand.

A member of the caper family, spider flower has a peculiar lemony odor that some find disagreeable. The plants tend to be leggy and leafless at the bottom, but this can be remedied by planting shorter-growing annuals in front of them. Thorns develop where flowering branches join the hairy main stem, so be careful when cutting for indoor bouquets. Cut flowers will continue opening for about a week indoors. Named varieties such as 'Helen Campbell' (white-flowered), 'Rose Queen', 'Ruby Queen', and 'Queen Mixed' display improved colors.

(Continued on next page)

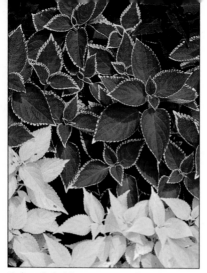

Coleus hybridus

. . . *Cleome*

C. lutea is a Western wildflower with yellow flowers and pale green leaves.

Culture. This plant is easily grown from seed. Chill seeds overnight and plant in average soil. Seeds germinate in 10 to 14 days, growing best with 85°F/29°C days and 70°F/21°C nights. Space at least 24 inches apart. Stake to hold upright. Keep plants on the dry side to prevent them from getting leggy. Spider flowers self-sow and can become invasive.

COLEUS HYBRIDUS
Labiatae

Flowers in: Flowers insignificant
Colors: Foliage is green, chartreuse, yellow, buff, salmon, orange, red, purple, and brown—often with several colors on each leaf
Exposure: Filtered sun to light shade
Grows to: 24 inches
When to plant: Set out transplants in spring after the danger of frost

This Java native is grown for its vibrant, multicolored leaves. A member of the mint family, it has variegated coloring and toothed or ruffled foliage that can offer an uninterrupted display of color in a garden or container. *Coleus* is actually a tender perennial treated as an annual. It has small blue flower spikes, but these should be pinched out early to maintain the plant's bushy shape. A mass of coleus adds considerable color to a lightly shaded border. Placement makes a difference in coloration, as too much sun can bleach out foliage color, while too much shade can also mute color.

The Wizard series has large, heart-shaped leaves and grows just 12 to 14 inches tall. The well-branched plants are superb in baskets and containers. Wizard is available in a wide range of color combinations. 'Volcano' grows to a similar size, with luminous scarlet leaves and a spreading habit. Among small-leafed kinds, Carefree offers a mixture of deeply lobed leaves on 10-inch bushy plants. Saber produces a mixture of long, vivid, saberlike leaves. Fiji is a fringe-leafed coleus that grows to 10 inches tall. 'Poncho Scarlet' has a cascading effect that is superb in hanging baskets. Its elongated stems hold broad, rainbow-type leaves of deep scarlet edged with chartreuse.

Culture. Coleus plants are easily grown from seeds, transplants, or cuttings. For garden use, start seeds indoors 10 weeks before the last frost. Seeds germinate in 10 days at 70° to 75°F/21° to 24°C, uncovered. Purchased seedlings from a nursery can offer an early start. Space plants 12 to 20 inches apart; pinch often to promote bushiness. Cuttings root easily in sand or water. In fall, make cuttings of the most attractive plants to use as house plants over the winter. Then make new cuttings in spring to plant outdoors.

CONSOLIDA AMBIGUA (DELPHINIUM AJACIS)
Larkspur, Annual delphinium
Ranunculaceae

Flowers in: Spring and early summer
Colors: White, blue, lilac, pink, rose, salmon, and carmine
Exposure: Partial shade
Grows to: 4 feet
When to plant: Sow seeds outdoors in fall or as soon as ground can be worked in spring

Prized because of its resemblance to the stately perennial delphinium and for its ease of culture, larkspur is indeed an asset to most flower gardens. Native to southern Europe, the upright plants have ferny, deeply cut foliage. Some forms of larkspur bear long, full, hyacinthlike spikes of blossoms with few side branches. Others are well-branched and carry dense blossom clusters along their branches. Larkspurs provide excellent foliage and bloom for the middle and back of a border. Their pastel colors are set off to advantage against a dark background such as evergreens or a planting of *Perilla*. Dwarf varieties can provide intense color for the front of a border. The bloom season is rather short where summers are hot. Larkspurs are excellent for cutting.

'Dwarf Blue Butterfly' is a compact plant that grows to 14 inches tall, with 1½-inch-diameter flowers in a deep, intense blue. Giant Imperial produces upright 4-foot-tall plants with excellent-quality blue, carmine, lilac, pink, salmon, rose, and white blooms. The Dwarf Hyacinth Flowering series offers neat 12-inch-tall plants with spikes of tightly knit flowers in pink, violet, lilac, denim blue, and white.

Culture. Prepare a fertile, well-drained seedbed. Chill the seeds for 7 days to improve germination. Broadcast where plants are to grow (larkspurs resent transplanting) in late fall or very early spring. Lightly cover and tamp seeds in with the palm of your hand. Seeds germinate in 10 to 20 days. Provide plenty of moisture as the plants grow. Taller varieties benefit from staking.

Consolida ambigua

Convolvulus tricolor

CONVOLVULUS TRICOLOR
Dwarf morning glory
Convolvulaceae

Flowers in: Summer
Color: Blue, purple, lilac, red, pink, and white, with a band of white around the yellow throat
Exposure: Full sun
Grows to: 6 to 12 inches
When to plant: Sow seeds outdoors in spring after the soil has warmed; in short-growing-season areas, start seeds indoors 6 weeks before last frost

Convolvulus tricolor has 1½-inch-wide funnel-shaped blossoms, very similar to morning glory flowers. Like morning glory, this is a daytime bloomer, with the flowers closing at night. A native of southern Europe, it flowers continuously in dry, sunny locations, forming a neat mound up to 12 inches tall and with greater spread. It provides intense color and a good foundation at the base of taller plants and also excels in a rock garden. The mounding habit of dwarf morning glory makes it an excellent choice for containers, window boxes, and hanging baskets. 'Blue Ensign' has brilliant blue flowers on a compact, 6-inch-tall plant that spreads to 15 inches wide.

Culture. Nick each seed coat and soak seeds overnight in water before sowing. If sowing indoors, plant in peat pots to minimize root disturbance when transplanting. Germinate seeds at 60° to 65°F/16° to 18°C. The plant grows best in warm weather.

COREOPSIS TINCTORIA
Annual coreopsis, Calliopsis
Compositae

Flowers in: Summer
Colors: Yellow, orange, maroon, bronze, and shades of red, often with a contrasting band of color surrounding the purplish brown centers
Exposure: Full sun
Grows to: 24 inches
When to plant: Sow seed outdoors as soon as ground can be worked in early spring

Annual coreopsis has daisylike blooms that dance on the breeze above lacy, finely cut foliage. Its flowers are similar to those of perennial coreopsis. It resembles cosmos in growth habit. The plant is good massed in a sunny bed, as it tolerates heat. The common yellow form is pretty planted among cornflowers. Dwarf and double varieties are also available. It will bloom freely throughout summer, and often self-sows. The flowers are ideal for cutting.

Culture. Plant in average soil. Seeds germinate in 7 to 14 days. Space 6 to 8 inches apart, since plants bloom best when crowded. Stake taller varieties for support; their stems are wiry and slender.

Coreopsis tinctoria

Cosmos bipinnatus

COSMOS
Compositae

Flowers in: Late spring to early fall
Colors: Yellow, orange, red, white, pink, and bicolors
Exposure: Full sun to partial shade
Grows to: 24 inches to 7 feet
When to plant: Sow seeds outdoors in spring after any danger of frost

With its graceful flowers and airy, feathery foliage, cosmos is an invaluable addition to a border, and very easily grown. Its rapid growth and tall habit make it a good background for intermediate and dwarf annuals and perennials. Modern varieties are earlier-blooming than the original autumn-blooming Mexican natives. The serrated flower petals may be daisylike, or may be crested, doubled, or quilled around yellow centers. The graceful 1- to 2-inch-wide blossoms make excellent cut flowers, and the foliage can also serve well as a filler for bouquets.

C. bipinnatus has flowers in white, pink, rose, lavender, purple, crimson, and bicolors. Make several successive sowings to assure a good supply of flowers, which will continue blooming until frost. The long, thin, branching stalks at the plant's base tend to look leggy, so set plants toward the back of a border, with short-growing annuals in front of them. Sensation is a bushy series with mixed blooms of rose, crimson, white, and pink; it blooms 10 weeks from seed. 'Imperial Pink' has single blooms of a deep rose-pink on strong, branching, 3- to 4-foot plants. 'Candystripe' has cool white

Crepis rubra

. . . Cosmos

flowers splashed with crimson. 'Sonata' offers snowy white flowers on plants only 24 inches tall.

C. *sulphureus*, yellow or Klondike cosmos, grows to 7 feet with bold yellow, golden orange, or scarlet-orange flowers. It can become weedy-looking, especially toward the end of the season. The Ladybird series provides free-flowering plants with semidouble blossoms on dwarf, compact, 12-inch plants. It is available in single colors of orange and yellow and as a mixture that includes scarlet. 'Sunny Red', an All-America Selection, has single scarlet flowers that soften to orange as they mature.

Culture. Sow seeds in well-drained average soil. Germination takes 5 to 7 days. Plants grow best in soil that is dry and not very fertile. Stake taller varieties to keep them upright. Space 12 inches apart. Remove spent flowers to keep plants blooming. Cosmos often self-sows.

CREPIS RUBRA
Hawk's beard
Compositae

Flowers in: Early summer
Colors: Pink, red, and white
Exposure: Full sun
Grows to: 15 to 18 inches
When to plant: Sow seeds outdoors in fall in mild-winter climates; elsewhere, sow as soon as ground can be worked in spring

This bushy Mediterranean native puts on a colorful show despite its small size. Slender flower stems rise above clumps of smooth, pale green, serrated or deeply lobed leaves. The 1½- to 2-inch-wide dandelionlike flowers are followed by clusters of soft, silvery hairs. The dried seed heads, if cut before they mature, can make a feathery addition to dried arrangements. The blossoms are not good for cutting, as they close in the afternoon. Hawk's beard is useful as an edging plant and handsome in a rock garden. 'Rubra' has pale pink to reddish flowers, while the cultivar 'Alba' has white flowers.

Culture. Seeds germinate in 10 days at 70°F/21°C. Hawk's beard thrives in poor soil. Thin plants to 4 inches apart.

CUPHEA IGNEA
Firecracker plant, Cigar plant
Lythraceae

Flowers in: Summer and fall
Color: Red
Exposure: Full sun or light shade
Grows to: 12 inches
When to plant: Set out transplants after soil has warmed in spring

Firecracker plant is a novelty, providing an unusual color accent in gardens or in containers. A native of Mexico, it has bright red ¾-inch-long tubular flowers, with black and white markings on the tip suggesting a burnt ash. Red is the most commonly available flower color, though some varieties have lavender, lilac, pink, or purple blossoms. The flowers grow on compact, bushy plants. The dark green, lance-shaped leaves are 1 to 1½ inches long and appear on reddish stems.

Cuphea ignea

Cynoglossum amabile

A tender perennial grown as an annual, firecracker plant prefers warm weather. It makes a colorful display when massed toward the front of a border. Or try it in containers mixed with the silvery foliage of dusty miller or variegated vinca. Cuttings are easily rooted in fall for use in indoor window gardens.

Culture. Firecracker plant flowers 4 to 5 months after sowing, so purchasing nursery-grown transplants is advantageous. Space plants 9 inches apart in average soil. Seeds germinate in 7 to 14 days at 68°F/20°C.

CYNOGLOSSUM AMABILE
Chinese forget-me-not
Boraginaceae

Flowers in: Spring to early summer
Colors: Blue, pink, and white
Exposure: Full sun to light shade
Grows to: 15 to 18 inches
When to plant: Start seeds indoors 4 weeks before last frost for earliest bloom, or sow seeds outdoors in early spring (in fall in mild-winter climates)

The fresh blue color of Chinese forget-me-not adds a cool accent among early-blooming warm-colored annuals such as orange *Dimorphotheca* and pink or rose *Dianthus*. The plant's habit is somewhat weedy. Its foliage is soft, hairy, and a grayish green. The ¼-inch-wide, star-shaped flowers are held in graceful tall sprays, most commonly of a deep or sky blue color.

The plant easily reseeds itself; in fact, volunteer seedlings can become a nuisance. The seeds cling to clothing and animal fur. 'Firmament' bears multitudes of sky blue flowers. 'Blue Showers' was bred especially to be used as cut flowers.

Culture. It's easily grown in average soil. Seeds germinate in 2 to 3 weeks at 68°F/20°C. Thin to stand 9 inches apart in groups of three or more plants. Deadhead to reduce the number of volunteer seedlings and promote flowering on side branches.

DAHLIA
Compositae

Flowers in: Summer to fall
Colors: Every color except blue
Exposure: Full sun for at least half the day
Grows to: 12 to 20 inches
When to plant: Sow seeds indoors 6 to 8 weeks before last frost, or purchase nursery-grown transplants for planting out in spring

Gardeners may be most familiar with the tall-growing tuberous dahlias that produce huge blossoms. Many are unaware that the smaller dwarf dahlias can be grown from seed as annuals that will, in the first year, produce a mass of bloom. Annual dahlias are actually tender perennials from Mexico. These early-flowering dwarf plants bloom profusely with brilliant 2- to 3-inch blossoms in many forms. Foliage is dark green or bronze. Plants look showy in a mixed border, and are ef-

Dahlia

fective massed together. Their vibrant display of color is almost unmatched by any other midsummer- or fall-blooming plant. Early-blooming 'Piccolo' produces single, 2½-inch, daisylike flowers on compact 8- to 10-inch plants, with a wide color range, including bicolors. The Figaro Improved and Sunny series offer 14- to 20-inch plants with double flowers, Figaro in mixed colors, Sunny in single colors of red or yellow. Extra-early Redskin has attractive bronze foliage with double flowers in mixed colors on 20-inch plants, and is an All-America Selection.

Culture. Seeds germinate in 10 to 20 days with daytime temperatures of 70° to 75°F/21° to 24°C. Plant in moist, fertile soil, spacing plants 24 to 30 inches apart. Over-fertilizing can promote foliage development at the expense of flowers. For larger, showier blossoms, pinch out side buds and leave only the buds at the top of the plant to bloom. Prune back lightly in midsummer to prolong the blooming season. Provide plenty of water during dry weather. As the plants are well-branched and sturdy, they do not usually require staking. Cut flowers will last longer if the cut stem ends are dipped into boiling water. Plants may winter over in mild-winter climates. Tubers can be dug and stored over the winter. It is best, however, to replace dwarf dahlias each year to assure vigorous bloom.

Earwigs are a common pest.

DIANTHUS
Pink, Carnation
Caryophyllaceae

Flowers in: Spring and summer
Colors: Shades of red and pink; also white, yellow, and mahogany
Exposure: Full sun
Grows to: 8 to 18 inches
When to plant: In mild-winter climates, sow seeds outdoors in fall. In other regions, start indoors at least 8 to 10 weeks before last frost

Dianthus is best known for its biennial and perennial species. Annual varieties are available in a number of flower forms and colors. The flowers have distinctive fringed or toothed petals,

Dianthus chinensis

and most are fragrant. The plants are equally successful in the ground or in containers. Dwarf forms are suitable for rock gardens.

D. caryophyllus is known as the hardy carnation. It is similar to florists' carnations, but has smaller blossoms and a spicier fragrance; the flowers add scent as well as color to arrangements. It is not hardy in cold-winter climates. The Knight series flowers within 5 months from seed, with strong, 12-inch stems supporting a continuous supply of blooms, available in shades of red, orange, yellow, and white. The blossoms are fragrant and the plant is heat tolerant. The Trailing Carnations Mix has a pendulous habit, and its pink and red blossoms bring a graceful cascade of color to window boxes and hanging baskets.

The China pink (*D. chinensis*) grows in clumps with single flowers borne atop strong, short stems. The faintly fragrant flowers are often splashed with contrasting colors. It is an excellent edging at the front of a border. 'Pink Flash' is very early-flowering, and the blooms lighten from mid-pink to pastel pink as they mature. The plants grow to 12 inches tall. Princess, a compact 8- to 10-inch-tall strain, blooms throughout summer. It is available in five colors. The Telstar series includes All-America Selection 'Telstar Picotee', producing crimson flowers with white fringes on 8- to 10-inch plants. The Parfait series is named for its festive layering of rich color. The 2-inch-wide flowers, borne in abundance, have an eye pattern of a deeper color. 'Strawberry Parfait' is scarlet;

Diascia barberae

Dimorphotheca sinuata

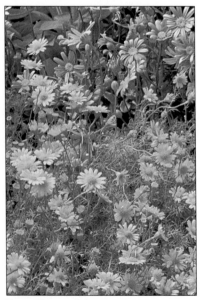
Dyssodia tenuiloba

... *Dianthus*

'Raspberry Parfait' is royal crimson. Magic Charms, an All-America Selection winner, produces abundant flowers (in five colors) on compact, vigorous plants. Both carnations and pinks have clumps of slim, pointed, silver-green leaves.

D. barbatus, sweet William, is usually grown as a biennial; but if started indoors in late winter, it will bloom the first year. It has broad, lance-shaped leaves of medium green. Its flowers are borne in clusters atop short stems. 'Wee Willie' blooms just 6 to 8 weeks from seed and grows 3 to 6 inches tall.

Culture. Chill seeds of *D. caryophyllus* for 1 to 2 weeks before sowing to improve germination. Leave seeds of *D. caryophyllus* uncovered; lightly cover seeds of *D. chinensis* and *D. barbatus*. Seeds germinate in 5 days at 70°F/21°C.

When seedlings are large enough to handle, transplant outdoors and grow at 50° to 55°F/10° to 13°C. Space plants 8 to 10 inches apart in well-drained soil. Pinch young plants to promote bushiness. For larger carnation flowers, remove all but one flower bud per plant.

DIASCIA BARBERAE
Twinspur
Scrophulariaceae

Flowers in: Summer
Colors: Rose-pink, deep pink, and coral
Exposure: Full sun; partial shade in hot-summer areas
Grows to: 12 inches
When to plant: Start seeds indoors 6 to 8 weeks before last frost or sow seeds outdoors after all danger of frost is past

This South African native is aptly named: the plant's flowers have two curving, hornlike spurs on the backs of the lower petals. Flowers are ¾ inch across and have yellow throats blotched with green. They appear in clusters at the ends of slender stems. The toothed leaves are small, glossy, and dark green. A fine choice for a rock garden, twinspur is easily propagated from cuttings. 'Pink Queen' produces 6-inch clusters of rose-pink flowers on 9- to 12-inch plants.

Culture. Seeds germinate in 15 days at 60°F/16°C. Twinspur flowers about 14 weeks after seeds are sown. Set plants out in spring in average soil, spacing them 6 inches apart. After the first flush of bloom, cut stalks back to the mound of foliage to encourage additional blossoms.

DIMORPHOTHECA
Cape marigold, African daisy
Compositae

Flowers in: Winter and early spring in mild-winter areas, summer in other climates
Colors: Shades of orange, red, pink, and white
Exposure: Full sun
Grows to: 12 inches
When to plant: Sow seeds outdoors in early spring in cold-winter climates, in fall in mild-winter areas

These valuable plants are free-blooming and provide broad masses of brilliant color during warm weather (they are not suited to cool coastal climates). *D. sinuata* (sold as *D. aurantiaca*) is perhaps the most familiar annual in this genus. The daisylike flowers come in a number of colors, most with contrasting dark centers. The spreading plants are useful as a ground cover, as an edging for a border, and as a filler among low-growing shrubs. The flowers are not useful for cut arrangements because they close at night and on cloudy days.

The hybrid 'Starshine' is a neat, mound-shaped, 12-inch-tall plant, covered with 2- to 3-inch-wide blooms in delicate shades of carmine, pink, rose, and white. Plants spread to 18 inches across. 'Tetra Goliath' has 3½-inch-wide flowers of vibrant orange on 12-inch plants. It thrives in summer heat.

D. pluvialis, the Cape marigold, has white flowers that are tinged with purple on the undersides of the petals. 'Glistening White' is a dwarf form, with flowers that are 4 inches across.

Culture. Seeds germinate in 7 to 14 days at 60° to 70°F/16° to 21°C. Plants are easy to grow in well-drained soil with full sun. Thin to 18 inches apart. Successive sowings will prolong the bloom season. *D. sinuata* reseeds itself in warm-winter areas.

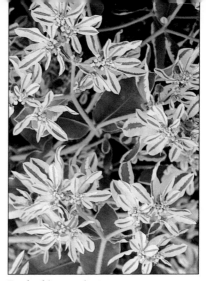

DYSSODIA TENUILOBA
Dahlberg daisy, Golden fleece
Compositae

Flowers in: Summer to fall, extending to early winter in mild-winter climates
Colors: Yellow
Exposure: Full sun
Grows to: 12 inches
When to plant: Set out plants in spring after all danger of frost is past; in mild-winter climates, set out plants in fall or very early spring

With its sprawling habit and haze of fernlike foliage, the Dahlberg daisy is a perfect choice for hanging baskets and containers. It is also a good choice for edging a border or adding a spot of color in a rock garden. Finely divided, dark green foliage is clothed in golden yellow flowers up to ½ inch across. Native to Texas and Mexico, the plant grows well in hot-summer climates.

Culture. It is easiest to purchase plants from a nursery, as seeds can be difficult to start and plants can take 4 months to flower. Seeds germinate, uncovered, in 10 to 16 days at 65° to 70°F/18° to 21°C. Plants grow best in sandy, well-drained soil. Space them 6 inches apart in the garden. Deadhead to promote flowering. Plants may live over in mild-winter climates, but they become straggly as they get older.

ESCHSCHOLZIA CALIFORNICA
California poppy
Papaveraceae

Flowers in: Early spring to summer
Colors: Shades of gold, orange, red, pink, and white
Exposure: Full sun
Grows to: 8 to 24 inches
When to plant: Sow seeds outdoors in fall or very early spring

This is the state flower of California, where it grows wild on hillsides and along roads. Its silky, brilliantly colored flowers dance above lacy foliage. It is easily grown and rewards even the most inexperienced gardener with myriads of satiny flowers that are up to 2 to 3 inches across. Foliage branches from the base of the plant and the leaves are finely cut and blue-green.

California poppy is wonderful for naturalizing, for covering sunny hillsides, or for planting in a dry rock garden. The flowers are short-lived when cut for arrangements; to use them at all, cut them while still furled. Grown in a border, California poppies must be deadheaded regularly or they will go to seed, with the foliage turning a straw color. Birds are attracted to the seed.

'Aurantiaca Orange King' grows 12 inches high and is early- and long-flowering, with intense orange single flowers. Thai Silk Mix offers uniform 10-inch plants with bronze-tinted foliage and 1½-inch semidouble fluted-and wavy-edged blooms in bright shades of red, pink, orange and gold. It is also available in a mixture of pink shades. 'Dalli' is a compact grower just 8 to 10 inches tall, and has stunning scarlet flowers with yellow throats and fluted petals.

Culture. Prepare the seedbed in fall. The plants do best in cool weather; early sowing, either in the fall or as soon as ground can be worked in very early spring, is advised. Seeds germinate in 7 to 14 days. Thin seedlings to 6 inches apart. The plants do not transplant well. In warm-winter climates, California poppies self-sow and come up year after year.

Eschscholzia californica

Euphorbia marginata

EUPHORBIA MARGINATA
Snow-on-the-mountain
Euphorbiaceae

Flowers in: Summer to fall
Colors: Foliage is a silvery green splashed with white
Exposure: Full sun to part shade
Grows to: 18 to 36 inches
When to plant: Sow seeds outdoors as soon as ground can be worked in spring

Grown for the attractive green-and-white coloration of the foliage, snow-on-the-mountain fills in attractively in the middle or back of a border. The oval, light green foliage is striped and margined with white on the upper leaves, with some of the topmost leaves nearly all white. The cool colors of the plant contrast well with brightly colored annuals. As the base of the plant is bare, it's a good idea to front it with shorter annuals. It provides complementary background for a mass of California poppies or dwarf zinnias. To use it in a flower bouquet, dip the cut ends of stems in boiling water or sear them over a flame; then arrange flowers in warm water in vases. 'Summer Icicle' is a dwarf variety, growing 18 inches tall with striking foliage. 'White Top' is uniform and erect, and grows to 36 inches tall.

Culture. Plant in average soil. Seeds germinate in 7 to 14 days. Thin plants to 12 inches apart. Transplant warily. Be careful when working with this plant, as its milky sap can irritate skin, eyes, and open cuts.

Felicia

Gaillardia

FELICIA
Blue daisy, Blue marguerite, Kingfisher daisy
Compositae

Flowers in: Spring to summer
Colors: Blue
Exposure: Full sun
Grows to: 18 inches
When to plant: Set out purchased plants in spring in cold-winter climates; plant in fall in mild-winter areas

Felicias are South African shrubby perennials, grown as annuals in cold-winter climates, with blue daisylike flowers. The low-growing plants have hairy leaves that are dark green, oval, and roughish. *F. amelloides*, the blue daisy or blue marguerite, has 1- to 3-inch-wide blossoms, blue with yellow centers, on plants growing to 18 inches tall. The plant will spread to 4 to 5 feet wide unless it is cut back. Keep it in shape by cutting often for flower arrangements (though flowers may close at night and on cloudy days). Its spreading habit makes it effective when planted at the top of a retaining wall or in a balcony planter from which it can cascade. 'George Lewis', 'Midnight', and 'Rhapsody in Blue' all have very dark blue flowers. 'Astrid Thomas' is dwarf, with medium blue flowers that remain open at night. There is also a white-flowered variety. 'San Luis', 'San Gabriel', and 'Santa Anita' have medium blue flowers that are 2½ to 3 inches across. The kingfisher daisy (*F. bergeriana*) grows just 6 inches tall and is a true annual. It flourishes in warm southern climates.

Culture. Purchased nursery-grown transplants can provide earlier bloom, as the plants require 3 to 4 months to bloom from seeds. Plant in well-drained soil. Provide water during dry weather. Pinch out the main shoot and side shoots when the plants are young to encourage compact growth. Shear plants back by a third when most of the flowers have gone to seed. They will quickly rebloom. Plant kingfisher daisies 6 to 12 inches apart in a sheltered, sunny spot.

GAILLARDIA PULCHELLA
Blanket flower
Compositae

Flowers in: Early summer to frost
Colors: Yellow, red, orange, and bicolors
Exposure: Full sun
Grows to: 24 inches
When to plant: Sow seeds outdoors after all danger of frost is past

Blanket flower provides sunny, vivid color in the garden and in cut arrangements. The warm-colored, sun-loving plants are especially appreciated when other flowers have been ruined by frost. Double and semidouble blooms rise on long, leafy stems above narrow, deeply cut, downy foliage. They are showy when massed together, and also are suitable for wildflower plantings. Since they grow well in dry soil, *gaillardias* are excellent choices for window boxes and containers. 'Red Plume', an All-America Selection, has a uniform dwarf habit and an extended

flowering season. The 12- to 14-inch plants are covered with brick red double blooms that are 1½ to 2 inches across, held well above the foliage. 'Yellow Sun' produces a dense mound of foliage with bright yellow, 2-inch, ball-shaped blooms and makes an excellent companion to red plume.

Culture. Sow seeds in well-drained soil. Seeds germinate in 14 to 21 days. Plants will not develop well in cold or heavy soils. Space 12 inches apart. Deadhead to encourage continued bloom.

GAZANIA RIGENS
Treasure flower
Compositae

Flowers in: Spring to early summer
Colors: Yellow, gold, cream, orange, pink, and bronzy red
Exposure: Full sun
Grows to: 12 inches
When to plant: Start seeds indoors 4 to 6 weeks before last frost; or purchase nursery-grown transplants to set out in spring after soil has warmed

These gaily colored perennials (grown as annuals in cold-winter climates) are best suited to desert gardens and are widely grown in the Southwest. The bright daisylike blossoms are up to 4 inches across, carried on stalks that rise 6 to 12 inches from the base of the plant. The shimmering petals surround dark centers, and the undersides of the petals are purplish. The 6- to 9-inch-long dark green leaves are sometimes lobed, are variable in shape,

Gazania rigens

and are felty on the undersides. Plants grow well in sites exposed to wind. The flowers close in overcast weather and at night, and so they are not good for cutting. Where the climate suits them, they make an attractive, free-blooming ground cover. They are dazzling when massed together. 'Moonglow' has bright yellow double blossoms that stay open even on dull days. The Chansonette Mixture has a good range of colors and is early-blooming and extra-compact. The 10-inch plants have 3-inch flowers in clear, bright colors. The Daybreak series is available in single colors of orange, yellow, bronze, and a mixture. 'Sunshine' has huge, 5-inch flowers with as many as 4 or 5 sharply defined blossom colors and silvery foliage on compact 6-inch plants. Carnival Mixed has mixed colors and gray-green foliage on 12-inch plants.

Culture. *Gazania* grows best where summer temperatures are in the 80°sF/27°C and 90°sF/32°C. It does not grow well where nights are cool or humidity is high. Space plants 8 to 12 inches apart in well-drained soil. Plants can be lifted in fall for colorful indoor display. If growing from seeds, cover the seeds lightly and then shade the flats to exclude all light. Maintain a temperature of 70°F/21°C. Seeds sown in mid-January should begin blooming in April.

GERBERA JAMESONII
Transvaal daisy
Compositae

Flowers in: Early summer and fall
Colors: Shades of pink, red, orange, yellow, and white
Exposure: Full sun; partial shade in hot-summer areas
Grows to: 8 to 18 inches
When to plant: Set out transplants in spring after soil has warmed

The Transvaal daisy is surely the most refined of the daisylike flowers. Its flower colors are deep, and all its forms—single, double, crested, and quilled—are elegant. It is grown as an annual in most climates, as a perennial in mild-winter climates. The plants spread slowly to form clumps of 9- to 10-inch-long lobed, medium green

leaves with woolly undersides. The flowers, with slender ray petals, rise above the foliage on erect or gracefully curving stems; they look handsome at the front of a border and make superior cut flowers. The Happipot strain is a dwarf, compact mixture 8 to 10 inches tall with red, rose, pink, salmon, orange, yellow, and cream blooms. The Skipper strain has smaller leaves and shorter flower stems and is suited to small container plantings or for use as an edging. The Tempo series offers dwarf plants in single shades of orange-scarlet, orange, rose-pink, scarlet, and yellow.

Culture. Transvaal daisies are somewhat difficult to grow from seed, and it is best to purchase transplants from the nursery. Plant in well-drained, fertile soil, being careful not to bury the crown. Space 12 to 15 inches apart. Protect from snails and slugs. Transvaal daisies prefer warm weather, but need afternoon shade and frequent watering where summers are hot and dry. However, plants will succumb quickly in poorly drained or soggy soils. If you are growing from seed, be sure to start with fresh seeds. Allow 4 to 6 weeks for germination at 70° to 75°F/21° to 24°C. When cutting flowers for arrangements, slit the bottom inch of the stem before placing in water.

Gerbera jamesonii

Gilia capitata

GILIA
Blue thimble flower, Bird's eyes
Polemoniaceae

Flowers in: Summer to early fall
Colors: Blue to violet
Exposure: Full sun
Grows to: 24 inches
When to plant: Sow seeds outdoors after all danger of frost is past

Gilia is a large genus comprising annuals, biennials, and perennials that are native to the American West and related to phlox. The annual forms are charming plants, covered with a profusion of small, showy flowers.

G. capitata, the blue thimble flower, is most widely available and withstands hot weather better than other species. Its tiny pale blue to violet blue flowers are held in dense, rounded clusters resembling pincushions. The finely cut foliage gives a lacy effect. While the flowers are small, they are so numerous that they make the whole plant beautiful. *G. tricolor*, bird's eyes, is a branching plant with finely cut leaves. Its pale- to deep-violet ½-inch flowers have yellow throats with purple spots; they are carried singly or in small clusters. Both species are good choices for a border, a rock garden, or a wildflower garden.

Culture. Plant in dry to average soil. Thin to 6 inches apart. Support taller varieties with brushy twigs. Plants are shallow-rooted, so provide water during extended dry periods. They grow best in cool-summer climates. Seeds germinate in 15 days at 68°F/20°C.

Gomphrena globosa

GOMPHRENA
Globe amaranth
Amaranthaceae

Flowers in: Summer to fall
Colors: Red, pink, white, orange, and purple
Exposure: Full sun
Grows to: 10 to 24 inches
When to plant: For earliest bloom, start seeds indoors 6 weeks before last frost; or sow outdoors, after all danger of frost is past

The cloverlike blossoms of globe amaranth are valued for fresh and dried bouquets, as well as for their handsome show in the garden. The mound-shaped plants are erect and well-branched, with oblong leaves of medium green. The small, dense flower heads are borne on long-stalked stems.

G. globosa has white, pink, lavender, red, or purple flowers. G. haageana has orange blossoms. The colors of globe amaranth are not especially harmonious and are best complemented by white flowers such as annual Gypsophila or white Ageratum.

Plants grow well in hot weather. The dwarf varieties make colorful edging plants, and taller varieties provide excellent cut flowers to use fresh or dried (they hold their color well when dried). 'Strawberry Fields' is the first true red Gomphrena, and 'Lavender Lady' blooms in a luscious lavender color. Both grow to 24 inches tall and produce a continuous bonanza of 1½-inch flowers. The Buddy series offers compact, 10- to 12-inch plants that bloom until frost; they are available in deep purple or white.

Culture. Soak seeds in water overnight before sowing. Seeds germinate in 10 to 14 days at 72°F/22°C. Plant in ordinary soil, thinning to 6 to 8 inches. Taller varieties benefit from staking. To dry blossoms, pick when blooms are thoroughly mature and hang them upside down in a shaded spot.

GYPSOPHILA ELEGANS
Annual baby's breath
Caryophyllaceae

Flowers in: Summer
Colors: White, pink, and red
Exposure: Full sun
Grows to: 18 inches
When to plant: Sow seeds outdoors in spring; for continuous bloom, sow again every 3 to 4 weeks from late spring into summer

Annual baby's breath has a multitude of dainty flowers that give the plant a misty, hazy effect. The single flowers are ½ inch or more across. The upright plant has lance-shaped leaves up to 3 inches long. Because the plants live for only 5 to 6 weeks, succession sowing is required to prolong the blooming season. This makes annual baby's breath somewhat of a chore to grow in a border. If you are willing to go to the trouble, try it as an airy blanket in front of gladiolus and other summer-blooming bulbs. It may be most suitable in a cutting garden; it makes an excellent addition to cut-flower arrangements. 'Covent Garden' has the largest white flowers. 'Kermesina' bears deep rose-colored blooms on plants that are 2½ feet tall.

Gypsophila elegans

Helianthus

Culture. Grow in average soil (rich soil will produce luxuriant growth that is easily beaten down in rainstorms). The genus name refers to the plant's preference for limestone (alkaline) soils. In areas where soils are strongly acidic, add lime before planting.

Scatter seed and tamp in firmly. Seeds germinate in about 10 days. Thin to 8 inches apart. Allow soil to dry between waterings. Early plantings may reseed themselves and bloom during the same season. When making successive sowings, harvest whole plants for indoor bouquets and replant with fresh seeds. To dry flowers for everlasting bouquets, hang upside down in a cool, dark place.

HELIANTHUS ANNUUS
Sunflower
Compositae

Flowers in: Summer
Colors: Creamy white, yellow, orange, maroon, and bicolors
Exposure: Full sun
Grows to: 24 inches to 12 feet
When to plant: Plant seeds outdoors after all danger of frost is past

Sunflowers are vigorous, erect, fast-growing plants with some of the largest flower heads any gardener could want to grow. The single and double flowers, which range from 4 to 24 inches across, are decorative no matter what their size. The plants are somewhat coarse, with rough, hairy stems and oval, coarsely serrated leaves. The central disk flowers are purplish brown, and are followed by edible seeds that are much-favored by birds. Tall sunflowers are effective in gardens with plants of similar height. They can be used as a hedge or fast-growing screen. The newer dwarf forms provide an impressive display when massed in large numbers.

'Sunbright' grows to 7 feet tall; its flowers have bright yellow, 4- to 6-inch petals. 'Giganteus' bears huge golden flowers that are 12 inches across on 10-foot plants. It is a good seed producer. Large-flowered Mix grows to 5 feet, with 6-inch flowers in yellow, red, and bronze, providing an impressive background of sparkling color. 'Luna' has 4- to 5-inch flowers in a delicate shade of yellow with rich chocolate centers. 'Italian White' has crisp, cream-colored, 4-inch flowers with a gold zone and black eye. 'Sunspot' is a breeding break through, with 10-inch yellow flowers on 24-inch-tall plants. It yields a bounty of seeds.

Culture. Plant in average soil. Seeds germinate in 10 days. Thin to 18 inches apart. Tall varieties should be staked, as the flower heads become heavy when seeds are formed. To save seeds for winter bird food, remove heads as soon as the seeds have matured. Otherwise, the birds will help themselves.

HELICHRYSUM BRACTEATUM
Strawflower
Compositae

Flowers in: Summer
Colors: Yellow, orange, red, pink, and white
Exposure: Full sun
Grows to: 12 to 36 inches
When to plant: Plant seeds outdoors in spring in areas with long growing seasons; in areas with shorter growing seasons, start seeds indoors 4 to 6 weeks before last frost

The papery flowers of strawflower hold their color indefinitely when dried. They are also beautiful in fresh arrangements. The tiny flowers in the center of the blossom are surrounded by stiff, colored leaves called bracts. Straplike, medium green leaves are 2 to 5 inches long. The taller varieties can offer a colorful accent, but they become leggy, require staking, and are

Helichrysum bracteatum

best planted at the back of a garden. Dwarf varieties provide bright color for rock gardens. The Bikini series has compact 12-inch-tall plants covered with brilliant 2-inch flowers; it is available in pink, gold, white, and a bright red. Bright Bikinis Mixture has a blend of dark red, bright yellow, red, hot pink, and white. Pastel Mix offers 2-inch flowers in soft tones that blend well with other flower colors. *H. subulifolium* 'Golden Star' has dainty, 1½-inch, lemon yellow flowers on mounded 15-inch-tall plants.

Culture. Strawflowers thrive in dry areas and on hillsides. Sow seeds in well-drained, average soil. Seeds should germinate in 7 to 10 days at 70° to 75°F/21° to 24°C. Thin to 12 inches apart. To dry, pick flowers that are fully open; hang them upside down in a shady spot.

HELIOTROPIUM ARBORESCENS
Heliotrope, Cherry pie
Boraginaceae

Flowers in: Summer
Colors: Purple, white, and deep blue
Exposure: Full sun
Grows to: 8 to 24 inches
When to plant: Set out transplants in spring after soil has warmed

Once experienced, the rich, romantic scent of old-fashioned heliotrope is never forgotten. The fragrance is sweet and vanillalike, without being cloying. The handsome, branching plants have dark green, rough-textured foli-

Heliotropium arborescens

age that complements lighter-colored foliage. Leaves are lance-shaped and deeply veined. The flowers grow in large, dense clusters. The plants are perennial in their native Peru and other mild-winter areas, but are grown as annuals in much of cold-winter North America.

Heliotrope makes a decorative display in borders as well as in cut-flower arrangements. It is set off to advantage by companion plantings of lighter colored flowers such as sweet alyssum or marigolds. Massed plantings provide more perfume. If you grow heliotrope in containers, you can place the pots where its fragrance can be best enjoyed.

'Mini Marine' is very fragrant; deep purple flower clusters that are 8 to 12 inches across provide a rich display in early summer. The compact, bushy plant grows 8 to 10 inches tall, and is good as a winter house plant. 'Marine' grows to 18 inches, with royal purple flowers. 'Black Beauty' and 'Iowa' bear deep purple flowers.

Culture. Purchase nursery-grown transplants to set out in spring, spacing them 12 inches apart. Plant in rich, fertile soil. Place containers with heliotrope in spots with afternoon shade. Avoid overwatering, as the fragrance is intensified when growing conditions are on the dry side. Cuttings root easily in water or moist loam. Plants may be lifted and brought indoors, but require cool, moist growing conditions. Seeds germinate in 7 to 21 days at 70° to 80°F/21° to 27°C, and must be started 10 to 12 weeks before setting out.

Helipterum roseum

HELIPTERUM ROSEUM (ACROCLINIUM ROSEUM)
Strawflower
Compositae

Flowers in: Summer
Colors: Yellow, pink, rose, carmine, and white
Exposure: Full sun
Grows to: 12 to 24 inches
When to plant: Plant seeds outdoors in spring after the danger of frost is past

Helipterum is another easily grown annual everlasting that is commonly called strawflower (see also *Helichrysum*). A wildflower in Australia, it has double daisylike flowers. The narrow, pointed, medium green leaves are numerous toward the tops of the stems. Flowers hold their color for long periods. The ray petals are thicker, with a brownish or greenish tinge toward the

Iberis

base. Use flowers dried, in winter arrangements.

H. roseum grandiflorum has harmonious hues of rose, carmine, and white on distinctly larger flowers.

Culture. Plant in average soil. Thin seedlings to 9 inches apart. To dry flowers, cut when the blossoms are fully open and hang them upside down in a shady spot.

IBERIS
Candytuft
Cruciferae

Flowers in: Spring and summer
Colors: White, pink, red, purple, and lavender
Exposure: Full sun, partial shade in hot summer areas
Grows to: 12 to 24 inches
When to plant: Sow seeds outdoors in early spring; in mild-winter climates, sow in fall for early-spring flowering

The flowers of candytuft cluster in showy spikes or globes. Rocket candytuft (*I. amara coronaria*) has fragrant white blossoms up to 1 inch across in dense hyacinthlike clusters on stems that grow 12 to 24 inches tall. It is dramatic in a border or in cut flower arrangements.

Globe candytuft (*I. umbellata*) has tiny flowers in flattened cones; it grows 7 to 12 inches tall. Sometimes confused with sweet alyssum, globe candytuft is also a useful edging plant and is a good-looking addition to a rock garden. In addition to white, globe candytuft is available in intense shades of red and purple.

Both candytufts have dark green leaves that are narrow and lance-shaped. Both are most floriferous where summer nights are cool. 'Mount Hood' rocket candytuft produces fragrant, pure white blooms on 24-inch stems. The Flash series (*I. umbellata*) grows up to 10 inches tall, in a bright blend of rosy colors.

Culture. Plant in average soil. Seeds germinate in 7 to 14 days. Thin to 6 to 9 inches apart. In hot-summer areas, plant in light shade and provide plenty of water during periods of heat and drought.

Impatiens

IMPATIENS
Garden balsam, Busy Lizzy
Balsaminaceae

Flowers in: Early summer to fall
Colors: White; shades of red, pink, orange, lavender; and bicolors
Exposure: Full sun to shade, depending on species
Grows to: 8 to 30 inches, depending on species
When to plant: Set out transplants in spring when all danger of frost is past

Impatiens includes annuals and, in some areas, tender perennials grown as annuals. The name refers to the tendency of the seed pod, when barely touched, to split open and "impatiently" shoot out its seeds.

Impatiens wallerana, the most widely grown kind of *impatiens*, is invaluable in shady gardens. The plants provide mounds of bright color throughout the season. The flowers, borne on short stems, are 1 to 2 inches wide, single and double, in vivid as well as pastel hues. The dark green coloring of the broad, pointed leaves is a perfect foil for the blossoms. *Impatiens* are excellent accent plants among shade-loving perennials such as hosta and ferns, and are useful in small beds ringing the trunks of mature shade trees. Planted in single or mixed colors, they make beautiful edgings for shaded borders. Their base-branching habit quickly produces a carpet of color. They are tender perennials, grown as annuals in cold-winter climates, and will reseed themselves in mild-winter areas. The Dazzler series is compact, growing 8 to 10 inches tall, in a dozen luminous, fade-resistant colors. The Super Elfin strain has large blooms in 16 colors on uniform, compact plants. The Shady Lady series includes some excellent garden performers. The Blitz series has the largest flowers, available in 7 colors, and is suited for hanging baskets. In the Showstopper series, noted for its large blooms, 'Showstopper Pink and White' is a charming bicolor, and 'Showstopper Flair' offers a spectacular display of pale pink blooms with hot pink centers. This series is also good for hanging baskets. Accent has strong, early-blooming plants with 2-inch flowers in 15 single colors and 5 bicolors called Accent Star. 'Mega' bears large flowers displaying bright orange-and-white stars. Among the double impatiens, the Duet series has full blossoms combining white with red, orange, scarlet, or deep rose. The compact Rosebud series is good for hanging baskets and containers, and comes in 7 colors. This series must be propagated from cuttings, and is not available in seed form.

New Guinea hybrid *impatiens* have handsome bronze, green, or variegated leaves, striped with cream or red, and extra-large single flowers. This species generally requires more sun than the common *impatiens*. These plants are also tender perennials grown as annuals and are good choices for containers. The Spectra strain combines bronze, green, and variegated foliage with large blooms of white, pink, carmine, rose, light lavender, deep orchid, coral, red, and scarlet on 10- to 14-inch plants. 'Tango', an All-America Selection, grows to 24 inches tall, with large single flowers in a glowing orange color.

Balsam (*I. balsamina*) grows 24 to 30 inches tall with 1- to 2-inch-wide mostly double flowers. It grows well in sun where summers are cool or in shade in hot-summer areas. Bush-type balsams display their flowers near the tops of the plants. Otherwise, flowers are somewhat hidden, as they are borne amid foliage along the tall, erect main stem. The bright green leaves of this old-fashioned true annual are up to 6 inches long and are pointed and deeply serrated. The flowers do not last long when cut. The Color Parade mix has pastel blooms in orange, rose, white, and pink on 14- to 16-inch plants. This is the type with blooms hidden within the foliage, and is best used for bedding. The double flowers of the dwarf Carambole strain are held well above the foliage. The plants grow to 14 inches tall.

Culture. All the species require plenty of moisture, especially during the heat of summer. *I. wallerana* and New Guinea hybrids are somewhat difficult to grow from seed, and it is best to purchase transplants from a nursery. Space plants 9 to 12 inches apart. *I. wallerana* will grow taller when set close together. If you grow these from seeds, expect germination in 10 to 20 days at 75° to 78°F/24° to 26°C. Light, uniform soil temperature, and moisture are very important when growing *I. wallerana* from seed. Balsam can be started indoors 4 to 6 weeks before last frost, then planted out after all danger of frost is past. Seeds germinate in 8 to 10 days. All species transplant well.

IPOMOEA TRICOLOR
Morning glory
Convolvulaceae

Flowers in: Summer to frost
Colors: Blue, white, pink, red, chocolate, crimson, lavender, and violet
Exposure: Full sun
Grows to: Climber, to 10 feet; dwarf forms to 5 inches
When to plant: Sow seeds outdoors after all danger of frost is past

For fast-growing vining cover and showy blossoms, morning glory is unsurpassed. Its large flowers (3 to 5 inches wide) display rich colors of purple, pink, or blue with a paler tube, sometimes striped or margined with a contrasting color. Flowers of older varieties open only from dawn to mid-morning, but newer varieties stay open most of the day. The plants have large heart-shaped, 4- to 5-inch-long leaves and vining tendrils. Morning glory is eye-stopping grown on trellises, fences, or arbors. 'Heavenly Blue' has intense blue color that lightens toward the center. 'Pearly Gates' has enormous white flowers. The Early Call mix has

Ipomoea tricolor

white, pink, crimson, lavender-pink, light blue, and violet flowers. Dwarf variegated strains have variegated leaves and blooms, with rosy red, pink, chocolate, and sky blue flowers, all with white margins. The plants grow to 5 inches high and 8 inches across.

Ipomoea alba, moonflower, is a climbing plant, up to 10 to 20 feet, that has magnificent, sweet-scented, large white flowers. The blossoms, up to 6 inches across, open in the early evening and close the next morning. Use moonflowers for quick screening on an arbor, trellis, or fence. They can become a nuisance, as they often self-sow.

Ipomoea nil (*I. imperialis*) includes the large-flowered Imperial Japanese strains. 'Chocolate' has huge saucer-shaped flowers in a soft chocolate-pink color. 'Scarlett O'Hara' has rosy red flowers.

Cypress vine (*I. quamoclit*) has narrow, threadlike foliage and small, 1½-inch-long scarlet flowers. Hybrid 'Cardinal Climber' has deeply lobed leaves and a profusion of small, 1- to 2-inch-long red flowers that often attract hummingbirds.

Culture. The seeds are very hard; for good germination, nick seed coats with a file or soak in lukewarm water overnight. Plant ½ inch deep in average soil, 8 to 12 inches apart. Seeds germinate in 7 to 21 days. For earliest blooms, plants may be started indoors, at 70° to 75°F/21° to 24°C, in peat pots. Overwatering and overfertilization encourage excess foliage at the expense of flowers. Morning glories reseed themselves, but these volunteers usually are inferior in bloom color and size.

Kochia scoparia

KOCHIA SCOPARIA
Summer cypress, Burning bush
Chenopodiaceae

Flowers in: Grown for foliage only
Colors: Light green during summer, bright red in fall
Exposure: Full sun
Grows to: 36 inches
When to plant: Start seeds indoors 6 to 8 weeks before last frost

Summer cypress has a dense form and soft, feathery foliage in a pleasing shade of green. It can be sheared to any desired shape or height. It can be used as a formal accent in a border and makes a fine low-growing temporary hedge. It grows well in hot-summer areas, and its erect habit suits it to windy locations. The plant is a good choice for containers mixed with low-growing or trailing plants. Flowers are insignificant. The foliage can be used to good effect in cut flower arrangements. *K. s. trichophylla*, burning bush, has the same growth habit, but its foliage turns scarlet to maroon at the first frost.

Culture. Soak seeds for 24 hours before sowing. Seeds germinate, uncovered, in 10 to 15 days at 50°F/10°C. Set out transplants after all danger of frost is past. Plant in average, well-drained soil, 2 feet apart (or 8 inches apart for a hedge). Growth is slow early in the season and increases with the onset of warm weather. In mild-winter climates, plants reseed themselves and the profusion of volunteers can become a nuisance.

LATHYRUS ODORATUS
Sweet pea
Leguminosae

Flowers in: Spring, continuing into summer in cool-summer climates
Colors: Shades of pink, red, purple, lavender, white, cream, apricot, salmon, maroon, and bicolors
Exposure: Full sun
Grows to: Climbers to 5 feet; bush-type 12 to 36 inches
When to plant: Sow seeds outdoors as soon as soil can be worked in early spring. In mild-winter climates, sow in fall for early-spring bloom. Early-flowering types can be sown in mild-winter climates in late summer or early fall for winter bloom

The lovely, fragrant sweet pea is the quintessential flowering plant in British gardens. In the United States, sweet peas are best grown in similar cool, moist climates, such as the Pacific Northwest and coastal New England. But with proper care and selection of early-blooming cultivars, sweet peas can also be enjoyed, even if briefly, in warm climates.

The sweet pea flower is made up of a large rounded petal (called the banner or standard), two narrow side petals (wings), and two lower petals that are somewhat united (keel). They are held in clusters on long stems, making them excellent for cut flower arrangements. The old varieties were known for their sweet fragrance. Many newer ones have little or no fragrance. Oval leaves, somewhat pointed, are light green to blue-green. The bush types make pretty mounds of color, and soften the front part of a border. In hot-summer areas, plan on replanting spots sweet peas have occupied with warm-weather annuals.

The Early Mammoth strain is an early-blooming climber with exceptionally large and wavy-edged blossoms in a rich mix of colors. The Con-

Lathyrus odoratus

Lavatera trimestris

tinental strain is a well-balanced, very early-blooming mix of shades of red, salmon, blue, lavender, and white. Its erect habit makes plants, which grow to 24 to 30 inches tall, require a minimum of support. 'Little Sweetheart', growing to just 12 inches tall, was bred especially for containers and hanging baskets. It presents a colorful display of red, pink, rose, white, purple, lilac, and blue flowers. The Bijou Mixed strain grows to 15 inches tall and is heat resistant.

Culture. Sweet peas require rich, deeply dug soil. It is best to prepare the soil in fall, digging a trench 24 inches deep, adding a 4-inch layer of compost or manure, and filling with topsoil to make a mounded seedbed. The mounding will improve drainage and permit earlier planting in spring.

Early sowing is important, as sweet peas grow best in cool, moist weather. Immerse seeds in warm water and soak them for 24 hours before sowing. Plant as soon as the soil is workable. Sow 6 inches apart in single rows, or 12 inches apart in double rows; treat the rows with a legume innoculant. Seeds germinate in 14 to 21 days.

Prepare trellis or string supports for climbing types as soon as seeds have been planted (or plant in front of a wire fence). Small brushy twigs can be placed in the rows for early training. Allow for good air circulation all around the support.

Be sure to cut off all seed pods: once a plant starts to set seed, it will cease blooming. To keep your sweet peas in bloom, cut flowers when buds break and use them in indoor bouquets. Provide plenty of water during the growing season, and mulch plants early to preserve moisture and keep roots cool.

Limonium sinuatum

LAVATERA TRIMESTRIS
Tree mallow
Malvaceae

Flowers in: Summer to early fall
Colors: White, pink, and red
Exposure: Full sun
Grows to: 36 inches to 6 feet
When to plant: Sow seeds outdoors in early spring

The satiny hibiscuslike flowers of tree mallow can light up the middle or back of a cool-summer border. Single flowers are up to 3 inches across. The foliage, shaped like maple leaves, is medium to dark green. It can also be used as a fast-growing summer hedge. 'Mont Rose' has rose-pink flowers; 'Mont Blanc' has white flowers. Both grow to 21 inches tall. 'Silver Cup' has 4-inch, chalice-like pink flowers.

Culture. Plants grow best in moist, cool-summer climates. Plant in average soil, spaced 24 inches apart. Seeds germinate in 14 to 21 days. To extend the bloom season, make several successive sowings. Stake tall varieties.

Linaria maroccana

LIMONIUM SINUATUM
Statice
Plumbaginaceae

Flowers in: Summer
Colors: Blue, lavender, white, rose, yellow, apricot, and peach
Exposure: Full sun
Grows to: 10 to 48 inches
When to plant: Sow seeds outdoors in early spring or start indoors 8 to 10 weeks before the last frost

Delicate statice is decorative in fresh and dried bouquets. The small, ⅜-inch papery flowers are borne in flat-topped clusters on many-branched, winged stems. The deeply lobed, lance-shaped leaves form a rosette at the base of the plant. This Mediterranean native is a good choice for Pacific Coast gardens. The Soirée strain blooms early, with richly colored flowers on 24- to 30-inch stems. The Dwarf Biedermeier strain has vivid blooms and grows just 10 to 12 inches tall, making it useful for bedding as well as cutting. Petite Bouquet has compact 12-inch plants in a range of colors.

L. suworowii, Russian statice, has well-branched, curved spikes of bright rose or lilac flowers. The rose-colored variety grows to 18 inches, while the lilac variety is extra-tall, reaching 3½ to 4 feet.

Culture. Plant in average, well-drained soil. Water deeply but infrequently. Seeds germinate in 14 to 21 days at 75° to 80°F/24° to 27°C. Thin to 9 to 12 inches apart. Continued cutting of the flowers encourages prolonged bloom.

LINARIA MAROCCANA
Toadflax
Scrophulariaceae

Flowers in: Early summer to fall; winter- to spring-blooming in mild-winter climates
Colors: Red, rose, pink, lavender, blue, purple, gold, yellow, cream, and bicolors
Exposure: Full sun or light shade
Grows to: 12 to 24 inches
When to plant: Sow seeds outdoors as soon as ground can be worked; in mild-winter areas, sow in fall for winter-spring bloom

Linum grandiflorum

A member of the snapdragon family, toadflax has dainty, brightly colored blossoms on slender spikes. The ½-inch blossoms often have contrasting throats. The medium green foliage is very narrow. Toadflax can provide jewel-like color at the front of a border. The Fairy Lights strain grows to 12 inches and has contrasting white throats. The Northern Lights mixture has bright colors on 24-inch-tall plants.

Culture. Easily grown. Sow in ordinary soil. Seeds germinate in 7 to 14 days. Thin to 6 inches apart.

LINUM GRANDIFLORUM
Flowering flax
Linaceae

Flowers in: Spring into summer
Colors: Red, white, and pink
Exposure: Full sun
Grows to: 12 to 30 inches
When to plant: Sow seeds outdoors as soon as ground can be worked in spring; in mild-winter areas, sow in fall for spring bloom

The glowing flowers of annual flax are delightful in mixed beds and borders. The 1- to 2-inch-wide blooms have five petals and last only a single day. The gray-green leaves are slender and grasslike. 'Bright Eyes' provides bushy, 30-inch-tall plants bearing pure white blooms that are 2 inches across, with bright crimson centers. 'Rubrum' has brilliant blood-red flowers with a satiny sheen on 15- to 18-inch plants.

(Continued on next page)

Lobelia erinus

. . . *Linum grandiflorum*

Culture. Flax is easy to grow but difficult to transplant. Plant in ordinary soil. Sow thickly. Seeds can take 3 to 4 weeks to germinate. Thin to 8 to 12 inches apart. Successive sowings will prolong the bloom season. Plants often reseed themselves, without becoming a nuisance.

LOBELIA ERINUS
Lobeliaceae

Flowers in: Summer to frost
Colors: Blue, white, red, and pink
Exposure: Full sun; partial shade in hot-summer climates
Grows to: 4 to 6 inches
When to plant: Set out transplants in spring after all danger of frost is past

Lobelia can be a very successful choice for hanging baskets and window boxes, from which its richly colored flowers can cascade. Its compact, spreading habit makes it useful for edging and in rock gardens. The dainty, lipped blossoms often have contrasting white or yellowish throats. Small, narrow, green or bronze leaves grow thickly on well-branched stems.

Lobelia blooms best where summer nights are cool. Early-blooming 'Blue Moon' is more heat tolerant than other varieties, and has ½-inch-wide, violet-blue flowers on upright, 5-inch-tall plants. The Fountain series has a lush, cascading habit with light blue, lilac, rose, and white flowers. 'Sapphire' has blue flowers with white eyes on a cascading plant. 'Rosamunde' has carmine-red blooms with white eyes on bronze-foliaged dwarf plants. 'Crystal Palace' has bronze-green foliage with dark blue flowers on 4- to 6-inch plants. 'White Lady' produces snow-white blooms.

Culture. Lobelia grows slowly and can take 2 months from seed to planting-out size. It is easiest to start with transplants from a nursery. Plant *lobelia* in ordinary soil, spacing plants 6 inches apart. Pinch to promote bushiness. After first blooms begin to fade, cut back by half to prolong flowering. *Lobelia* sometimes lives over in mild-winter climates. Provide plenty of water during dry periods. Seeds germinate, uncovered, in 20 days at 70° to 75°F/21° to 24°C.

LOBULARIA MARITIMA
Sweet alyssum
Cruciferae

Flowers in: Spring to hard frost; all year in mild-winter climates
Colors: White, cream, rose, pink, purple, violet, and lavender
Exposure: Full sun to light shade
Grows to: 4 to 6 inches
When to plant: Sow seeds outdoors in spring. For winter bloom, sow in fall in mild-winter areas

The honey-scented flowers of sweet alyssum literally cover the plant throughout the season. Sweet alyssum is one of the best annuals for edging the front of a bed or border. Its low-growing habit makes it a good choice for rock gardens and for planting between flagstones or pavers. It is attractive when planted at the top of a retaining wall or in hanging baskets, where its trailing habit can be used to advantage. It grows rapidly and flowers quickly from seeds; it can be started almost any time during the growing season. Its small green leaves are completely hidden by clusters of tiny, four-petaled blossoms.

'Carpet of Snow' has pure white flowers on 3- to 4-inch plants. 'Oriental Night' has dark violet blooms on spreading plants up to 8 inches across.

Lobularia maritima

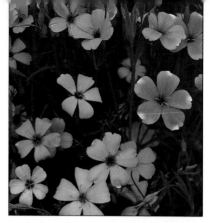

Lychnis coeli-rosa

'Rosie O'Day' has lavender-rose flowers on plants that spread up to 10 inches across. Easter Bonnet and Pastel Carpet strains are beautiful mixtures, the former in shades of purple, rose, lavender and white, the latter a blend of cream, lilac, pink, rose, violet, and white.

Culture. Plant in average soil. Seeds germinate in 8 to 10 days. Thin to 6 to 8 inches apart. (If you are starting seeds indoors, sow seeds, uncovered, in sixpacks since small seedlings are difficult to transplant.) If flowering diminishes, cut plants back by half and fertilize to encourage additional blossoms. Plants sometimes reseed themselves. In mild-winter climates, they will bloom year-round.

LYCHNIS COELI-ROSA
Rose-of-heaven
Caryophyllaceae

Flowers in: Summer; winter to spring in mild-winter climates
Colors: Blue, lavender, white, and pink
Exposure: Full sun
Grows to: 9 to 18 inches
When to plant: Sow seeds outdoors in early spring; in mild-winter areas, sow in fall

Rose-of-heaven is a graceful plant, with upward-facing, saucer-shaped flowers. The single flowers, up to 1 inch across, generally have a contrasting lighter or darker eye. The green or blue-green leaves are long, narrow, and sharply pointed. The plant is good for cutting and bedding and is charming in a container.

Culture. Plant in average soil. Thin to 4 inches apart. Plants bloom early.

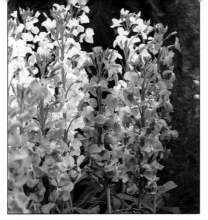

Matthiola incana

MATTHIOLA
Stock
Cruciferae

Flowers in: Spring into summer
Colors: White, cream, apricot, lavender, purple, shades of pink and red, and bicolors
Exposure: Full sun
Grows to: 12 to 30 inches
When to plant: Sow seeds outdoors in early spring; in mild-winter climates, sow in fall for late-winter and early-spring bloom

Few flowers offer the unique fragrance of stocks. Planted next to walkways or windows, their intense, spicy aroma fills the air with heady echoes of cinnamon and clove. The single or double flowers cluster thickly along sturdy flower spikes, and are a reliable backbone for cut-flower arrangements. Foliage is gray-green and lance-shaped. *Matthiola* thrives in cool weather; some newer varieties tolerate heat.

Matthiola incana is the most common species. The Giant Imperials series is widely available in a mixture of colors and grows 18 to 24 inches tall. The Midget series offers uniform, compact, 8- to 10-inch plants with well-formed, fully double flower spikes in vibrant colors, available in single or mixed colors. The Midget series is heat tolerant, although it does best in cool temperatures. The Trisomic Seven-Week series performs well because its double-flowered plants don't set seeds. Dwarf Stockpot can be in full flower 7 to 9 weeks from sowing. 'Beauty of Nice' blooms over a longer period than the early varieties. *Matthiola longipetala bicornis* (night-scented stock) has lilac flowers on 12 to 18 inch stems and a pronounced scent that's most powerful in the evening.

Culture. Choose moderately rich, moist soil in full sun. Sow seeds outdoors as soon as soil can be worked, or start seeds indoors 6 to 8 weeks before average date of last frost. Seeds germinate in 14 to 18 days at 65° to 75°F/18° to 24°C. In beds and borders, space plants 9 to 12 inches apart. Water regularly throughout the growing and flowering period.

MIMULUS HYBRIDUS
Monkey flower
Scrophulariaceae

Flowers in: Summer
Colors: Shades of red, yellow, and orange
Exposure: Partial to full shade
Grows to: 12 to 18 inches
When to plant: Sow seeds outdoors in spring, or set out transplants in spring

The showy, velvety blossoms of monkey flower appear on low-growing, mound-shaped plants. The two-lipped flowers, up to 2 inches across, come in bright colors that are often spotted, and give the impression of a smiling monkey face. Succulent, serrated leaves are light to medium green. Monkey flower can provide warm, bright color at the front of a shady border, and its spreading habit makes it fill out hanging baskets and containers quickly. It grows best in cool, moist climates and is prized in the Pacific Northwest. The Calypso strain has 16- to 18-inch-tall plants with solid and bicolor blooms of gold, wine, and fire-red. The Mystic strain has solid-colored blooms in orange, rose, and yellow on compact, spreading plants. It can tolerate heat better than the other varieties.

Culture. Sow or plant in moist, humus-rich soil. Seeds germinate in 5 to

Mimulus

Mirabilis jalapa

7 days at 60° to 70°F/16° to 21°C. Space 6 inches apart. Plants require plenty of water. Cut back after the first flush of flowers to promote bushiness and continued bloom. Cuttings root easily in sand.

MIRABILIS JALAPA
Four o'clock, Marvel of Peru
Nyctaginaceae

Flowers in: Summer to fall
Colors: Shades of yellow, red, white, and pink
Exposure: Full sun
Grows to: 24 inches to 4 feet
When to plant: Sow seeds outdoors in spring

These old-fashioned plants are called four o'clocks for their flowers' habit of opening in late afternoon. The fragrant, 2-inch-long, trumpet-shaped blossoms, often mottled or striped, close again in morning, but stay open all day on cloudy days. Plants bloom profusely throughout summer. The dark green, 2- to 6-inch-long leaves are borne on erect, well-branched stems. Try this plant in the middle of a border or grow it in containers. The blossoms attract hummingbirds.

Note: All parts of the plant are poisonous.

Culture. Sow in average soil, thinning to 12 to 24 inches apart. Seeds germinate in 10 to 14 days. The plant often reseeds itself and is considered perennial in mild-winter climates. Its tuberous roots can be dug in fall and stored over the winter like dahlia roots.

Moluccella laevis

Myosotis sylvatica

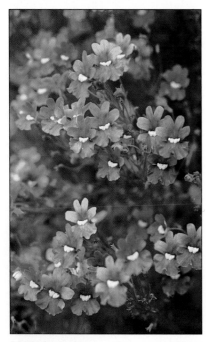

Nemesia strumosa

MOLUCCELLA LAEVIS
Bells-of-Ireland
Labiatae

Flowers in: Summer
Colors: White or pale pink blossoms set in pale green cups
Exposure: Full sun
Grows to: 15 to 36 inches
When to plant: Sow seeds outdoors in early spring; in mild-winter climates, sow seed outdoors in late fall

The unusual spikes of bells-of-Ireland make an interesting addition to a mixed border. Each erect stem bears clusters of tiny fragrant flowers, set inside enlarged calyxes (the outer leaves that appear at the base of most flowers). The calyxes are ornamented with a network of delicate white veins. Leaves of this Mediterranean native are rounded and coarsely toothed. The flowers are charming in bouquets, and can also be dried for use in winter arrangements.

Culture. Sow in loose, well-drained soil while the ground is still cool. Germination is best at about 50°F/10°C and can take 3 to 5 weeks. Thin to 12 inches apart. Seedlings are difficult to transplant. To dry the flowers, pick off the leaves along a stem and hang the stems upside down in a cool, dark, well-ventilated spot. The flowers are wheat-colored when dried.

MYOSOTIS SYLVATICA
Forget-me-not
Boraginaceae

Flowers in: Spring; winter in mild-winter areas
Colors: Blue; also pink and white
Exposure: Light shade
Grows to: 6 to 12 inches
When to plant: Sow seeds outdoors in fall; in cold-winter climates, sow indoors in winter and set out transplants in early spring

Forget-me-not is widely planted in English gardens. The plant's loose sprays of fragrant, pastel flowers make a fine springtime sight when interplanted with tulips. It prefers cool, moist growing conditions, and is best grown in woodland gardens, around the edges of ponds, or along the banks of a stream. Leaves are dark green, narrow, and lance-shaped. The flowers are long-lasting when cut. 'Victoria Blue' forms mound-shaped plants, 6 to 8 inches high, with gentian-blue flowers.

Culture. Plant in moist, fertile soil. Seeds germinate in 8 to 14 days at 68°F/20°C. Thin to 6 to 8 inches apart. Forget-me-not grows best where the spring season is long and cool. Plants die back in the heat of summer, but may reseed and come up in late summer, providing beautiful fall color.

NEMESIA STRUMOSA
Scrophulariaceae

Flowers in: Winter to spring in mild-winter climates; summer elsewhere
Colors: White, yellow, red, pink, lavender, blue, and bicolors
Exposure: Full sun
Grows to: 8 to 18 inches
When to plant: Sow seeds outdoors in fall in mild-winter areas, in spring in cold-winter climates

This South African native thrives in cool-summer climates where nighttime temperatures drop below 65°F/18°C. Its small, cup-shaped, ¾-inch-diameter flowers are carried in clusters 3 to 4 inches deep. The flowers have an enlarged lower lip and resemble snapdragons and *linarias*, plants that are related to them. The jewel-toned blossoms are borne above lance-shaped, serrated leaves. A handsome edging plant, *nemesia* is also good for growing in containers. It is a colorful addition to a rock garden.

'National Ensign' has bright red and pure white bicolored blooms on bushy, compact, 8-inch plants. The Tapestry strain has a rich mix of colors on upright, 10-inch plants. Carnival has brilliant flowers on compact plants.

Culture. Sow in rich, moist, well-drained soil. Germination takes 7 to 14 days at temperatures between 60° and 68°F/16° and 20°C. (For early bloom, start seeds indoors.) Thin to 6 inches apart. Pinch to promote bushy growth, and cut back by half after the first flush of bloom. *Nemesia* blooms best in cool weather.

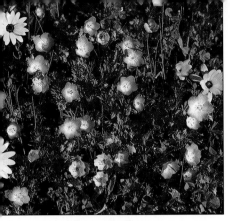

Nemophila menziesii

NEMOPHILA
Baby blue eyes, Five spot
Hydrophyllaceae

Flowers in: Spring
Colors: Blue and white
Exposure: Full sun to partial shade
Grows to: 10 to 12 inches
When to plant: Sow seeds outdoors in early spring; in mild-winter climates, sow outdoors in fall

Baby blue eyes (also called California bluebell) and five spot are dainty, clean-looking California wildflowers. They thrive in the cool Western coastal and mountain climates. Both are trailing plants, growing to 12 inches long, with bell-shaped, single flowers up to 1 inch across. Pale green, hairy, fern-like foliage gives the plants a delicate appearance. Baby blue eyes (*N. menziesii*) has bright blue flowers with pale centers. Five spot (*N. maculata*) has white flowers with a prominent bluish-purple spot at the edge of each of the five petals. The plants form an attractive ground cover among spring-blooming bulbs.

Culture. Plant in moist soil, and supply constant moisture. Seeds germinate in 7 to 12 days. Thin to 6 inches apart. *Nemophila* dislikes transplanting and is quickly killed by heat and humidity. Plants reseed themselves in favorable sites.

Nicotiana alata

NICOTIANA
Flowering tobacco
Solanaceae

Flowers in: Spring through summer
Colors: White, pink, red, purple, and green
Exposure: Full sun to light shade
Grows to: 10 inches to 4 feet
When to plant: Sow seeds indoors 6 to 8 weeks before last frost; set out transplants in spring after all danger of frost is past

Flowering tobacco is an old-fashioned annual grown for its stately elegance and evening fragrance. Newer varieties offer compact plants with rosy flowers that bloom all season and open during the day. Relatives of smoking tobacco, *N. alata* and *N. sylvestris* are tender perennials from South America, grown as annuals in this country; in warm-winter areas they may live over. *N. alata* has soft, sticky, oval leaves that are 2 to 3 inches long. Its tubular flowers, 2 to 3 inches long and 1 to 2 inches across, are borne in clusters on erect stems. For strong, sweet fragrance, especially at night, plant *N. alata* 'Grandiflora', which grows 24 to 36 inches tall, with pure white, night-blooming flowers. Newer varieties of *N. alata* are more dwarf and, generally, not fragrant. The Nicki series is a vigorous grower, to 24 inches, and includes a beautiful red variety. The Domino series is compact, growing 10 to 14 inches tall. It blooms well during summer heat, with flowers in pink, purple, red, green, and white. The Starship series is excellent for mass plantings. It is more compact, with flowers in lemon-lime, red, rose-pink, and white. *N. sylvestris* grows to 5 feet tall, with large, coarse, sticky leaves and long spikes of fragrant, white, tubular flowers 3 to 4 inches long and 1 inch across that open at night. The tall varieties of flowering tobacco work well near windows or at the back of a border. Compact varieties are excellent in beds, border fronts, or containers.

Culture. Seeds germinate, uncovered, in 10 to 15 days at 70° to 75°F/21° to 24°C. Plant in well-drained average soil. Space compact varieties 9 to 12 inches apart, taller varieties 24 inches apart. *N. sylvestris* readily reseeds it-

Nierembergia

self. Newer varieties of *N. alata* are widely available at nurseries as transplants. Tobacco budworm and aphids can be pests; for controls, see page 50.

NIEREMBERGIA
Cup flower
Solanaceae

Flowers in: Summer
Colors: Blue, white, and violet
Exposure: Sun; partial shade in hot-summer climates
Grows to: 4 to 15 inches
When to plant: Sow seeds indoors 8 to 10 weeks before last frost

Sprawling and mounded, cup flower is literally covered with bell-shaped flowers throughout summer. Grown in most areas as an annual, it is a perennial in mild-winter climates. The plants are self-branching, with delicate, threadlike, ½- to ⅔-inch-long leaves. They are effective edging beds, and their spreading, floriferous habit also suits them to use in window boxes or hanging baskets. *N. hippomanica*, known as dwarf cup flower, has white or pale blue flowers. *N. hippomanica violacea* (*N. h. caerulea*), the hardiest member of the genus, has purple flowers with yellow throats. It grows 6 to 15 inches tall. 'Purple Robe' has regal purple, golden-eyed, 1-inch blooms. *N. repens* forms a low-growing mat with white flowers.

Culture. Seeds germinate in 15 to 25 days at 70° to 75°F/21° to 24°C. Seedlings can withstand frost. Set out transplants 2 to 3 weeks before last frost. Plant 6 inches apart in average soil. Cut back after the first flush of flowers to prolong bloom. Plants grow best where summers are cool. Where summers are hot, provide water and shade.

Nigella damascena

Pelargonium hortorum

NIGELLA DAMASCENA
Love-in-a-mist
Ranunculaceae

Flowers in: Spring
Colors: Blue, purple, pink, rose, and white
Exposure: Full sun or partial shade
Grows to: 18 to 24 inches
When to plant: Sow seeds outdoors in fall or early spring

Love-in-a-mist's name says it all. Charming, dainty cornflowerlike blooms are set within fine, feathery foliage, producing a misty show of pastel color. The flowers are followed by puffed-up, pale green seed capsules that add textural interest to dried arrangements. This plant is a beautiful companion to warm-colored dianthus or to poppies. It is not long-lived, and burns up in the heat of summer. The English Court series produces 2-inch-wide double blooms in white, light blue, rose-pink, and deep blue; the green seed pods are accented by prominent purple veins.

The less common *Nigella hispanica* 'Curiosity' has deep blue single flowers with dark centers and maroon stamens, borne on 24-inch plants.

Culture. Sow in well-drained ordinary soil. (For a longer bloom period, sow in fall and in early spring.) Seeds germinate in 7 to 14 days at 60°F/16°C. Thin to 6 to 8 inches apart. Transplanting is tricky. Plants will reseed themselves. To dry seed pods, cut branches when pods are mature and hang them upside down in an airy, shaded spot.

PAPAVER
Poppy
Papaveraceae

Flowers in: Spring through early summer
Colors: Shades of red, pink, orange, yellow, white, and bicolors
Exposure: Full sun
Grows to: 10 to 24 inches
When to plant: Sow seeds or set out transplants outdoors in fall or early spring

The Flanders Field poppy (*P. rhoeas*) or American Legion poppy is the antecedent of today's Shirley poppies, with their wide range of colors. This ancestor is a brilliant red poppy, with dark splotches at the base of the petals, that is grown in the open fields of western Europe. From it have been bred the numerous varieties of Shirley poppy, all bearing silky, translucent petals held in a cup shape. Flowers are 2 inches or more across, and are single or fully double; they dance above the foliage on slender, hairy stems. Leaves are pale green and deeply cut. 'Legion of Honor' has the brilliant crimson flowers and contrasting dark centers of the original form. The Mother of Pearl mix has flowers in delicate hues including gray, soft blue, lilac, peach, dusty pink, white, and speckled and picotee bicolors. All-Double Shirley is a mixture of 24-inch-tall plants with flowers in white, pink, rose, salmon, and scarlet.

Iceland poppy, *P. nudicaule*, is a perennial grown as an early-spring annual in mild-winter climates. It thrives in cool temperatures. The cup-

Papaver rhoeas

shaped, slightly fragrant flowers are up to 3 or 4 inches across. The Wonderland series has giant 4-inch flowers on strong stems and grows to 10 inches tall. It is available in cream, white, orange, pink, and yellow. The Champagne Bubbles series produces strong, bushy, 12-inch-tall plants with flowers in a wide range of colors. The Sparkling Bubbles series includes pastel and other colors on 16-inch plants.

Culture. Sow in well-drained ordinary soil. In mild-winter climates, plant in early fall. Where winters are severe, wait until early spring. Because seeds are tiny, mix them with sand before broadcasting on the seedbed. Seeds germinate in 7 to 14 days. Thin to 6 to 12 inches apart. *P. rhoeas* has a short bloom period, and can be succession-sown in early spring in cool climates. Remove seed heads to prolong flowering. All *Papaver* species are excellent cut flowers; cut when flowers are in bud, and sear stem ends in boiling water or over a flame.

PELARGONIUM
Geranium
Geraniaceae

Flowers in: Spring, summer, fall
Colors: Shades of red, pink, orange, violet, white, and bicolors
Exposure: Full sun to partial shade, depending on variety
Grows to: 8 to 36 inches or more
When to plant: Set out transplants or rooted cuttings in spring

There is hardly any bedding plant as universally popular or well loved as the geranium. These South African natives are actually perennials, but are grown as annual bedding plants where winters are cold. Leaves are generally round or heart-shaped, with scalloped or fluted edges. Several species within the genus are grown as annuals.

Most commonly available, in a wide range of named varieties and easiest to grow, is the zonal geranium (*P. hortorum*). The common name comes from the darker zone of color ringing most leaves of the type. Its flower clusters are flat-topped and individual flowers are single or double. The plants are upright and bushy. With their floriferous nature, these plants are invaluable in patio containers and window boxes, and look especially attractive when mixed with petunias and sweet alyssum.

The ivy geranium (*P. peltatum*) has trailing stems up to 36 inches in length, making it ideal to cascade from hanging baskets. The flowers often have dark markings.

Scented geraniums are available in a variety of fragrances. The foliage carries the scent, which can be detected when a leaf is crushed or rubbed. Among the scented varieties are rose-scented (*P. graveolens*), lemon-scented (*P. crispum*), and peppermint-scented (*P. tomentosum*) kinds.

Of the zonal geraniums, the free-blooming Multibloom strain has a long flowering season and compact growth. Growing just 8 to 10 inches tall, it is suitable for mass plantings and is available in 8 colors. Elite is early to flower and has short stems holding well-rounded flower heads just above the foliage. Orbit is known for its ease of growing, uniformity of habit, and its large round flower heads. Available in 17 colors, it offers the widest color range of any geranium series. 'Orange Appeal' was bred for its appealing orange color. 'Hollywood Star' is among the best bicolors, with rose-and-white blossoms. 'Freckles', a 1991 All-America Selection, has a unique rose spot on the inside of each pink petal. Some cutting-grown zonal geraniums have variegated leaves—like 'Happy Thoughts', with its ball of red flowers atop predominantly white foliage edged in green, and 'Mrs. Parker', which has rose-pink florets above green leaves edged in white.

Of the ivy-leafed geraniums, 'Summer Showers' looks stunning in hanging baskets, with its cascading habit and loose red, pink, and white flower heads borne above foliage resembling that of English ivy. 'Breakaway Hybrid' was bred especially for hanging baskets; it has rounded pink and red flower heads 5 to 6 inches across.

Culture. It is convenient to purchase nursery-grown transplants, since growing from seeds takes a long time. Seeds germinate in 7 to 10 days at 70° to 75°F/21° to 24°C, but require 13 to 15 weeks to come into bloom.

When using zonal geraniums as bedding plants, set them 12 inches apart in fertile, well-drained soil. Keep plants pruned to the desired shape, using the cuttings to start new plants (cuttings root easily in water or moist sand and can then be planted outdoors).

For winter bloom, start young plants in summer and pinch off buds until the plants are brought indoors. For best indoor growth, keep in a sunny window in a relatively humid room (such as a kitchen or bathroom).

Zonal geraniums may also be lifted in fall and overwintered in a cool, unheated cellar. Brush off nearly all the soil from the roots and hang the plants upside down. In spring, cut back the withered stems to 6 to 8 inches and plant outdoors.

The ivy-leafed varieties prefer partial shade. They work well on patios and balconies.

Geranium budworm is a particularly troublesome pest in some areas. See page 50 for controls.

Pentzia

PENTZIA
Gold button
Compositae

***

Flowers in: Summer
Color: Orange
Exposure: Full sun
Grows to: 24 to 30 inches
When to plant: Sow seeds outdoors in early spring

An excellent cut flower for fresh or dried bouquets, gold button bears flattened globes of golden orange, ¾-inch-diameter flowers on dense, bushy plants. When dried, they hold their color indefinitely.

Culture. Broadcast seeds in average soil. *Pentzia* seeds germinate in 5 days at 70°F/21°C. Deadhead spent flowers to prolong bloom. To dry flowers, cut gold buttons when fully open and then hang them upside down in an airy but shaded spot.

PETUNIA HYBRIDA
Common garden petunia
Solanaceae

***

Flowers in: Late spring to fall
Colors: Shades of pink, red, salmon, coral, yellow, cream, blue, purple, white, and bicolors
Exposure: Full sun
Grows to: 8 to 27 inches
When to plant: Set out transplants in spring after all danger of frost is past

Petunias are valued for their large, richly colored flowers and long blooming period. They are suitable for edg-

Petunia hybrida

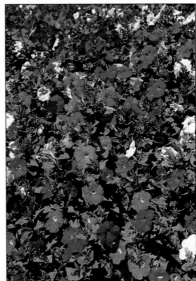

ing beds and borders, interplanting with annuals and perennials in mixed borders, and cultivation in containers or hanging baskets. The plants are adaptable to a wide range of soil and water conditions, and the delicately fragrant flowers are good for cutting. In warm-winter areas of the desert Southwest, petunias can be planted in fall to produce late-winter to mid-summer color.

Single flowers are trumpet-shaped. Double forms resemble carnations. Petunias are generally classed as Grandifloras (those with very large flowers, up to 4½ inches across) or Multifloras (numerous flowers, up to 2 inches across). Botrytis disease can damage blossoms and foliage in humid weather. Multifloras, with their numerous, smaller blossoms, recover more quickly after rainy periods. Hybrids are more expensive because they must be hand-pollinated, but are also more valuable because of their improved colors, uniform growth habits, and ability to stand up to heavy summer rains.

Among the hybrid single Grandifloras, the Ultra series offers extra-compact plants with a spreading habit, available in 13 colors, including the All-America Selection, 'Crimson Star'. The Frost strain, in red, wine-purple, and violet-blue, is eye-catching, with richly textured petals trimmed in white. The Cascade/Supercascade series, with its basal-branching, cascading habit, is excellent for hanging baskets and containers; it comes in 10 colors. The Daddy series has ruffled blooms with brightly colored veins. The Highlight series has a good tolerance to heavy rains but is more susceptible to botrytis disease; its 3-inch blooms are distinctively marked with white throats.

Single Multifloras include the Prime Time series, which is early, compact, and uniform, and is available in 15 colors, including bicolors starred with white. The Plum series has deep and lacy veining on the blossoms; it includes 'Summer Sun', the original true yellow petunia. The compact-growing Celebrity series has flowers in 11 colors, including some with deeply contrasting veins.

Among the double petunias, 'Circus' and 'Purple Pirouette' are both

Grandifloras and All-America Selections, the former with salmon-red and white bicolored blossoms, the latter with bright violet flowers edged in white. The Delight series of double Multifloras offers white, salmon, and red-and-white blossoms.

Culture. Plant in well-drained soil, spacing 7 to 10 inches apart. Because petunias are among the most popular annuals, nurseries carry a wide selection of varieties as young plants. Pinch developing plants to encourage bushy growth. Feed with a complete fertilizer each month, and deadhead regularly to promote continued flowering. As plants become leggy or straggly, cut back to encourage new growth. Smog can produce spots on the leaves of seedlings, especially white-flowered varieties. Tobacco budworm is a pest in some areas; see page 50 for control. Plants can be dug in fall before frost and brought indoors for winter color.

To grow petunias from seed, sow 8 to 10 weeks before last frost. Mix the seed with sand and broadcast on a moist growing medium. Germination takes 10 to 12 days at 70° to 80°F/21° to 27°C. Plants flower 2 to 2½ months from sowing.

PHLOX DRUMMONDII
Annual phlox, Texas pride
Polemoniaceae

Flowers in: Summer to fall
Colors: Red, pink, salmon, purple, white, and bicolors
Exposure: Full sun
Grows to: 6 to 20 inches
When to plant: Sow seeds outdoors after all danger of frost is past; sow in fall in mild-winter and desert climates

This Texas native bears clusters of colorful, slightly fragrant, 1-inch flowers (fine for cutting) atop erect, leafy stems. Bloom continues throughout summer. Dwarf varieties can serve as a flowering ground cover for summer-blooming bulbs. The Palona series is compact and floriferous, growing 8 to 10 inches tall. Available in carmine, crimson, rose, salmon, and white, plants perform well in both cool and moderate climates. The Petticoat strain has 6- to 8-inch-tall plants covered with

Phlox drummondii

star-shaped flowers in white, red, rose, salmon, or pink, with white highlights. Free-flowering 'Brilliant' grows to 20 inches, with white and rose-colored blossoms. The spreading Cecily strain is available in a range of bright colors, many with contrasting eyes.

Culture. Plant in fertile, well-drained soil. Seeds germinate in 10 to 15 days. Space 10 inches apart. Feed monthly with a balanced fertilizer and deadhead to prolong bloom. Cuttings root easily in moist sand or water. Branches of tall varieties can be pegged down to promote growth from lateral buds.

PORTULACA GRANDIFLORA
Moss rose
Portulacaceae

Flowers in: Early summer to frost
Colors: White, cream, yellow, orange, red, and pink
Exposure: Full sun
Grows to: 6 inches
When to plant: Sow seeds outdoors in spring or set out transplants in spring after all danger of frost is past

Portulaca is an old-fashioned favorite that flourishes in sunny, dry areas where few other plants will grow. Silky-petaled, roselike flowers cover the sprawling plants with brilliant

Portulaca grandiflora

color. The reddish, well-branched stems have a trailing habit, and the leaves are narrow, tubular, and succulent. Flowers open fully in sun and close in late afternoon. The plant is an excellent choice for rock gardens, containers, and hanging baskets. The Sundial series is free-flowering and early-blooming. The single flowers of the Wildfire strain are attractive cascading from hanging baskets. The double blossoms of the Afternoon Delight series stay open well into the evening.

Culture. Sow seed in well-drained soil, and keep soil moist until germination. Thin to 8 to 12 inches apart. (To sow indoors, start 6 to 8 weeks before last frost; expect germination in 10 to 14 days at 70° to 80°F/21° to 27°C.) Moss rose often reseeds itself.

PRIMULA
Primrose
Primulaceae

Flowers in: Spring; midwinter in mild-winter areas
Colors: White, pink, red, lavender, purple, blue, yellow, and orange
Exposure: Shade
Grows to: 6 to 18 inches
When to plant: Set out transplants in spring; in mild-winter climates, set out in early fall

Of the more than 600 species within the genus *Primula*, three are often grown as annuals.

The fairy primrose, *P. malacoides*, carries its pink, red, or white blossoms in tiers on slender stems rising from rosettes of soft, pale green oval leaves. The First Love strain has fragrant ¾-inch flowers on strong, wiry, 6- to 8-inch stems. It is a good choice for containers.

P. obconica has clusters of 1½- to 2-inch-wide blooms on long, hairy stems. Its leaves are large, rounded, and hairy (the tiny hairs can cause skin rashes). The Cantata series has flowers up to 2 inches across in a mixture of pearly shades of carmine, pink, blue, apricot, and lavender on bushy 7- to 8-inch plants. Seven separate colors are available in the Juno series. The free-flowering, 12-inch plants have small leaves and early blooms.

P. polyantha has 1- to 2-inch flowers carried in large clusters on stems 12 to 18 inches high. Oval, medium green leaves are pointed and form a rosette. The Pacific Giant series bears flowers up to 2¾ inches across on plants to 12 inches tall.

Culture. These plants cannot tolerate heat. Give them moist, fertile soil. They are difficult to grow from seed, so it is advisable to purchase nursery-grown transplants.

Primula

Proboscidea louisianica

PROBOSCIDEA LOUISIANICA
Unicorn plant, Devil's claw
Martyniaceae

Flowers in: Summer
Colors: Cream, lavender, and pink
Exposure: Full sun
Grows to: Sprawling, to 36 inches
When to plant: In long-summer areas, sow seeds outdoors in spring. In short-summer areas, sow seeds indoors 4 to 6 weeks before last frost

Unicorn plant is grown for its unusual claw-shaped seed pods, which, when dried, resemble birds' feet. It is native to the south central United States. The low, spreading plants have spikes of 2-inch-wide, bell-shaped flowers, the throats of which are blotched with purple or yellow. Leaves are round or heart-shaped, and both leaves and stems are covered with sticky hairs. The green seed pods resemble an elephant's trunk; when they ripen, they split into two or three parts, giving the pod its clawlike appearance. The plant gives off a musky scent that some consider unpleasant.

Culture. To improve germination, soak the seeds for 10 days to loosen seed coats. Seeds germinate in 2 to 8 weeks at 80° to 85°F/27° to 29°C. Plant in rich soil, 4 to 5 feet apart, some distance from other flower gardens (to accommodate the spreading growth habit and strong scent). It grows best in warm weather. To dry pods, cut stems with the pods attached, then hang upside down.

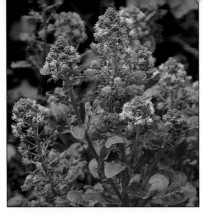

Reseda odorata

RESEDA ODORATA
Mignonette
Resedaceae

Flowers in: Spring
Colors: Greenish white tinged with copper or yellow
Exposure: Sun in cool climates; partial shade in warm climates
Grows to: 12 to 18 inches
When to plant: Sow seeds outdoors as soon as ground can be worked in spring; in mild-winter climates, sow outdoors in late fall or winter

Mignonette is grown for its extraordinarily sweet fragrance. The tiny flowers are borne in dense spikes that loosen as blossoms mature. Plants can be massed for an incredibly fragrant effect. Or interplant them with scentless plants to provide spots of fragrance. Beds or borders near windows and doorways can, in fair weather, perfume the indoors.

Machet, a Dutch strain, has plumes of fringed flowers 12 to 14 inches tall.

Culture. Mignonette grows best in cool weather; flowers dry quickly in heat. Broadcast seeds on the surface of fertile, well-worked soil. Seeds germinate in 2 to 3 weeks at 55°F/13°C. Thin to 10 inches apart. Provide regular, frequent watering. In suitable climates, succession sowing can prolong bloom.

Rudbeckia hirta

RUDBECKIA HIRTA
Black-eyed Susan, Gloriosa daisy
Compositae

Flowers in: Summer
Colors: Yellow, gold, mahogany red, and bicolors
Exposure: Full sun or light shade
Grows to: 8 to 36 inches
When to plant: Sow seeds outdoors in fall or early spring

Easily grown, black-eyed Susans have single or double daisylike flowers; yellow petals surround purplish-brown centers. They flower well in the heat of summer. The plants are short-lived perennials grown as half-hardy annuals. Flowers last well when cut, and cutting promotes continued bloom.

'Double Gold' produces double and semidouble 4½-inch flowers with golden yellow petals and deep brown eyes on 36-inch-tall plants. 'Goldilocks' grows just 8 to 10 inches tall, with double and semidouble blooms of bright gold on compact plants. The hybrid Gloriosa Daisy strain produces flowers up to 6 inches across in shades of yellow, gold, reddish brown, and bicolors, on 36-inch plants. 'Irish Eyes' has 4½- to 5-inch single flowers with yellow petals and unusual clear green centers on 30-inch plants.

Culture. Plant in ordinary soil. Seeds germinate in 14 days. Thin to 12 to 14 inches apart. It often reseeds itself.

SALPIGLOSSIS SINUATA
Painted-tongue, Velvet flower
Solanaceae

Flowers in: Late spring and early summer
Colors: White, yellow, red, pink, purple, and brown
Exposure: Full sun
Grows to: 12 to 36 inches
When to plant: Sow seeds indoors 6 to 8 weeks before last frost

Most successful where summers are cool, painted-tongue provides a brilliant display in beds and borders. The trumpet-shaped flowers have an unusual combination of velvety texture; muted, rich colors; and delicate vein-

Salpiglossis sinuata

ing. They are held in loose clusters on slender, wiry stems. The sticky foliage is lance-shaped and widely notched. Painted-tongue is a good choice for the middle of a border and is complemented by baby's breath or love-in-a-mist. The cut flowers add color, depth, and formal interest to bouquets. Hybrid Casino mixture has a branching habit ideal for bedding, containers, and cutting, and grows 18 to 24 inches tall. 'Kew Blue' grows 12 inches tall, with rich blue flowers accented by striking gold veins.

Culture. Plant seeds in peat pots in a warm, protected location (70° to 80°F/ 21° to 27°C); expect germination in 7 to 10 days. Plant out 12 inches apart in average soil after all danger of frost is past. Pinch young plants to promote bushy growth. Stake taller varieties to keep them upright. The plant is perennial in mild-winter climates.

SALVIA
Sage
Labiatae

Flowers in: Early summer to frost
Colors: Blue, lavender, purple, red, coral, and white
Exposure: Full sun or partial shade
Grows to: 8 to 36 inches
When to plant: Sow seeds indoors 4 to 6 weeks before last frost

Salvia farinacea

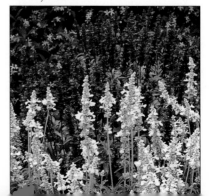

The *Salvia* genus includes a number of perennials, such as culinary sage, and tender annuals. *S. farinacea*, mealy-cup sage, is a perennial grown as an annual in cold-winter climates. Its flowers are carried in tiers on tall, slender stems. Each ½-inch-long blossom is held in a calyx covered with short, whitish hairs, giving the plant a mealy appearance. Silvery foliage forms a mound at the base of the plant. Flowers are good for cutting. The Victoria series has compact 18- to 20-inch plants with medium blue or silvery white flowers. It flowers over a long period and is effective planted in masses.

Gentian sage (*S. patens*) grows to 36 inches tall. The arrow-shaped, 2- to 5-inch-long leaves are covered with short, sticky hairs. Small tubular flowers hang from tall stems. It is evergreen in mild climates, but grown as an annual where winters are severe.

The flowers of *S. viridis* (*S. horminum*), a tender annual, are insignificant, but the leaflike bracts at the top of the plant are colored pink, white, or blue and look attractive in fresh and dried arrangements. 'Claryssa' grows to 18 inches tall with a compact habit.

Scarlet sage (*S. splendens*) has spikes of vividly colored 1½-inch-long tubular flowers that are surrounded by equally colorful calyxes. It will grow well in light shade, especially in hot-summer areas. The flowers do not last long when cut. Their bright colors combine well with white sweet alyssum or silvery dusty miller. The blossoms are attractive to hummingbirds. In addition to the original scarlet color, shades of salmon, lilac, purple, and white are available in both the Empire and Hotline series. 'Red-Hot Sally' has deep red blooms on 10-inch plants. Medium-tall 'Flare' has 18-inch-long red spikes, while 'Bonfire' grows bright red spikes up to 26 inches tall. 'Melba' produces salmon-coral flowers with lighter tips on 8-inch plants.

Culture. Sow seeds on a moist planting medium, with germination in 12 to 15 days at 70°F/21°C (soak seeds of *S. splendens* to speed germination). Plant out after all danger of frost is past. Space 12 inches apart. Water often and feed monthly to keep plants vigorous.

SANVITALIA PROCUMBENS
Creeping zinnia
Compositae

Flowers in: Summer to fall
Colors: Orange, yellow, or white, with purplish brown centers
Exposure: Sun
Grows to: 6 to 8 inches
When to plant: Sow seeds outdoors in spring after the danger of frost is past

The tiny, bright, zinnialike flowers and trailing habit of creeping zinnia make it attractive as an edging for a border, clumped in a rock garden, or cascading from a window box or hanging basket. Masses of small single or double flowers with warm-colored petals and purple or brown centers bloom until frost. Dark green leaves are oval and pointed. 'Mandarin Orange' has vivid orange blooms with dark eyes. The ½- to ¾-inch-wide flowers cover creeping plants that grow 8 inches high and spread up to 16 inches across. 'Gold Braid' has fully double gold blossoms.

Culture. Sow in light, well-drained soil, leaving the seeds uncovered. Seeds germinate in 1 to 2 weeks at 68°F/20°C. Thin to 3 inches apart. Plants thrive in heat and with a minimum of water, once established. However, if allowed to go completely dry, creeping zinnia will stop blooming.

Sanvitalia procumbens

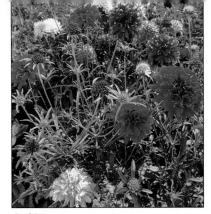

Scabiosa atropurpurea

SCABIOSA ATROPURPUREA
Pincushion flower, Sweet scabious
Dipsaceae

Flowers in: Summer to fall
Colors: White, pink, salmon, red, maroon, lavender, purple, and blue
Exposure: Full sun
Grows to: 24 to 36 inches
When to plant: Sow seeds outdoors in spring; sow in fall in mild-winter climates

Pincushion flower gets its name from the light-colored stamens that protrude from each of many tiny flowers clustered together in a mound; these look like pins stuck into the flower. The 2-inch-wide flower heads rise above a rosette of slender, coarsely toothed leaves. Sweetly fragrant flowers are followed by pale green, cupped seed pods that are covered with bristly reddish hairs, resembling a bottle brush. The Imperial Giants strain includes a deep maroon-purple color that is unusual among annuals, as well as pink, white, salmon, scarlet, deep rose, red, lavender, and blue. *S. stellata* is an annual from southern Europe that is grown for its unusual seed pods; spherical light blue or white flowers turn into papery bronze seed heads of complex design, carried on 6- to 18-inch stems. 'Ping Pong' has small white flowers that are followed by intricate seed heads, each segment centered by a delicate maroon star. The seed heads provide unique accents in dried arrangements.

Culture. Sow in average, well-drained soil. Seeds germinate in 10 to 12 days. Thin to 6 to 8 inches apart. Plants flower best in climates with moderate summer temperatures.

Schizanthus pinnatus

SCHIZANTHUS PINNATUS
**Butterfly flower,
Poor man's orchid**
Solanaceae

Flowers in: Summer; winter and spring in mild-winter climates
Colors: Pink, red, violet, purple, yellow, and white
Exposure: Filtered shade
Grows to: 6 to 24 inches
When to plant: Sow seeds outdoors in spring; in mild-winter climates, sow outdoors in fall

The brilliant, orchidlike blossoms of butterfly flower provide an effective display in containers or at the front of a border. It is best grown in cool-summer areas, and is attractive planted with *Primula malacoides* and cineraria, which flourish in the same climates. Gold-veined flowers cluster on slender, cascading stems. They last well as cut flowers. Dainty fernlike foliage is inconspicuous compared with the blossoms.

The Star Parade strain provides ball-shaped plants that grow 8 inches across and are covered with purple-to-yellow flowers. The Angel Wings strain grows 12 inches high and spreads 10 inches across, with light pink, salmon, carmine, scarlet, lilac, and purple flowers.

Culture. Sow in moist soil. Seeds germinate in 7 to 14 days at 60° to 70°F/ 16° to 21°C. Thin to 12 inches apart. The flowering season is short, but can be extended by succession sowing. Stake taller varieties to keep upright.

SENECIO HYBRIDUS
Cineraria
Compositae

Flowers in: Spring and early summer; late winter and early spring in mild-winter climates
Colors: White, pink, red, yellow, blue, and purple
Exposure: Shade
Grows to: 12 to 15 inches
When to plant: Set out transplants in spring; in mild-winter climates, plant out in fall

Cineraria thrives in cool-summer climates, where its bright colors can light up a shady garden. Velvety flowers, some with contrasting eyes, are held in domed clusters 3 to 5 inches across. The lush green leaves are rounded or heart-shaped, with wavy or toothed margins. The Improved Festival Grandiflora strain produces free-flowering 12- to 14-inch plants with solid and bicolor blooms with distinct eyes. The Multiflora Starlet strain is a compact 8 to 10 inches tall, with florets in red, crimson, copper, rose, white, yellow, and dark and light blue, some with eyes ringed in white.

Culture. Cineraria takes several months to flower from seed, and is most easily grown from purchased transplants. Plant in cool, moist, fertile soil. Water regularly, never letting the plant dry out. Leaf miners, spider mites, slugs, and snails can be problems; for controls, see pages 50–51. Although cineraria is perennial in mild-winter climates, start with new plants each season to get the best

Senecio hybridus

Tagetes

bloom. Plants reseed themselves where the climate suits them. Seeds germinate, uncovered, in 10 to 14 days at 70° to 75°F/21° to 24°C.

TAGETES
Marigold
Compositae

Flowers in: Early summer until frost
Colors: White, off-white, yellow, orange, and orange-red
Exposure: Full sun
Grows to: 6 inches to 4 feet
When to plant: Sow seeds outdoors or set out transplants in spring, after all danger of frost is past

Marigolds are among the most popular flowers in American gardens, producing vibrant color, flowering quickly from seed, and continuing to bloom through the heat of summer. Gardeners today have a wide assortment of marigolds from which to choose, with flowers in almost all the tints and tones of orange and yellow and a good measure of reds, and in many combinations. Flowers come in a pleasing variety of shapes, from single to fully double, and rise well above the foliage. All have vivid beauty and long life when cut. The plants are sturdy and well branched, with attractive, rather finely cut, dark green foliage. The yellow-tinted marigolds fit into any garden design, whether a soft-hued bed or a brilliant color scheme. Use the orange shades more carefully. Most marigolds have a sharp fragrance, but several of the new hybrids have foliage and flowers with no scent.

For use in cut arrangements, strip away most of the foliage from the stems to reduce the pungent scent.

All garden marigolds descend from Mexican species that have been developed and hybridized to produce four separate types. The African, or American, marigold (*Tagetes erecta*) has huge blossoms, 3½ to 5 inches across, on plants that grow 20 to 36 inches tall. Colors, all single, include rich glowing orange, lemon-gold, and sulphur-yellow. The chrysanthemum-flowered varieties have globe-shaped double blooms; carnation-flowered varieties are densely double, with petals waved and rolled. The Perfection series is unsurpassed for mass planting, with a unique petal structure providing weather tolerance. 'Snowdrift' is the best white marigold. The Discovery series has compact plants with super-large, ball-shaped flowers.

So-called French marigolds (*Tagetes patula*) are low-growing (7 to 10 inches), with 1- to 2-inch single or double flowers in many shades of yellow, orange, copper, mahogany red, and combinations. The French marigolds are ideal for foregrounds, bedding, edging, window boxes and other containers, and in small bouquets. As the nights cool, they redouble their efforts, and each individual plant becomes a bouquet in itself. The Boy series, although small-flowered, produces masses of very early blooms with crested centers. The Aurora series offers fully double, compact good looks and dependability, and the new 'Aurora Yellow Fire' presents an unusual color combination of bright yellow and mahogany red. The Janie series has crested flowers with a shapely silhouette; it's the earliest and most floriferous of the French marigolds.

Although French marigolds have long been recommended for nematode control, recent university studies have not confirmed this relationship.

Triploid hybrids are crosses between African and French marigolds, combining African vigor and compact French habit. They bloom early, and because they are unable to set seed, produce scores of 2- to 3-inch blossoms. The Nugget Supreme series offers better germination than others in the class.

Signet or Mexican marigolds (*Tagetes signata pumila*, also known as *T. tenuifolia pumila*) have dainty single flowers. The dwarf, bushy plants feature lacy, fernlike foliage with a delightful lemon fragrance, and are ideal for edging. The flowers are tiny, usually less than 1 inch across, but borne so profusely as to make the plants a solid mass of color for many weeks. The Gem series is available in gold and lemon-yellow. Paprika has bright pimento-red petals edged in gold.

Culture. Marigolds flourish in ordinary garden soil in full sun (be careful not to overfertilize or plant in soil that is very rich in nitrogen, which will produce foliage at the expense of flowers). Seeds are quite large and should be planted ¼ inch deep. They will germinate in about 7 days at 75° to 80°F/24° to 27°C. For extra-early flowers, start seeds 5 or 6 weeks before you set them out, and transfer seedlings to flats or pots as soon as true leaves have formed. Plant outside after the soil has warmed. Space taller varieties 12 to 24 inches apart, dwarf varieties about 6 inches apart. Stake taller varieties early. Remove spent blossoms regularly to encourage continuous flowering.

TALINUM PANICULATUM
Jewels of Opar
Portulacaceae

Flowers in: Summer
Colors: Rosy pink
Exposure: Sun
Grows to: 24 to 30 inches
When to plant: Sow seeds indoors 6 to 8 weeks before last frost

With its airy panicles of tiny blossoms, Jewels of Opar provides a delightful

Talinum paniculatum

Thunbergia

filler for cut flower arrangements. The dense, well-branched plants are covered in glossy, dark green foliage. The blooms, which last only a day, are borne in rapid succession through summer heat and drought.

Culture. Seeds germinate in 5 to 20 days at 68°F/20°C. Plant out in average soil. Space 12 inches apart.

THUNBERGIA ALATA
Black-eyed Susan vine
Acanthaceae

Flowers in: Summer
Colors: White, yellow, and orange
Exposure: Full sun or light shade
Grows to: Climber, up to 10 feet
When to plant: Sow seeds indoors 6 to 8 weeks before last frost

The twining black-eyed Susan vine is studded with flaring 1-inch-diameter tubular flowers. Bright green triangular leaves are 3 inches long. A perennial in mild-winter climates, it is widely grown as a summer annual. The dark-eyed blossoms look decorative on fences and trellises, and dwarf forms are attractive trailing from hanging baskets and window boxes. The Susie series produces vines up to 5 feet long and flowers 1 to 2 inches across. It is a good choice for hanging baskets. *T. gregorii* is similar, without the dark eye in the flower.

Culture. Seeds germinate in 14 to 21 days at 70° to 75°F/21° to 24°C. Set out plants in moist, fertile soil after weather has warmed. Space 12 inches apart.

Tithonia rotundifolia

TITHONIA ROTUNDIFOLIA
Mexican sunflower
Compositae

Flowers in: Summer
Colors: Orange with yellow-orange centers
Exposure: Full sun
Grows to: 30 inches to 5 feet
When to plant: Sow seeds indoors 6 weeks before last frost

The glowing orange, daisylike blooms of Mexican sunflower grow profusely on large, somewhat coarse plants; faintly fragrant, the 3-inch flowers attract butterflies. Deeply veined dark green leaves have serrated edges. Plants grow quickly and may be used as a temporary hedge. Mexican sunflower is heat resistant, and is a good selection for a desert garden. The flowers are handsome when cut. 'Goldfinger' grows 30 to 42 inches tall. Aphids can be a pest; for controls, see page 50.

Culture. Seeds germinate in 10 to 18 days at 70° to 80°F/21° to 27°C. Transplant after all danger of frost is past. Plant in ordinary soil. Space 24 inches apart. Stake to maintain upright habit. Flowers bloom 2 to 3 months after sowing. For cut flowers, sear stem ends in boiling water or over a flame, and condition in warm water.

Torenia fournieri

TORENIA FOURNIERI
Wishbone flower
Scrophulariaceae

Flowers in: Summer to fall
Colors: Blue, lavender, violet, red, pink, and white
Exposure: Partial shade; in sun in cool-summer climates
Grows to: 6 to 12 inches
When to plant: Sow seeds indoors 6 to 8 weeks before last frost

Wishbone flower has small blossoms up to 1 inch across; they resemble miniature gloxinias. The common name comes from the wishbone shape of the stamen in the center of the blossom. Flower petals are often blotched with a contrasting color. Attractive in containers, this plant can also be used as an edging for beds and borders. Lift during fall for indoor bloom. The Clown strain, an All-America Selection, blooms 10 to 14 days earlier than other strains; its globe-shaped plants, which grow 6 to 8 inches tall, produce blooms in white, light blue, dark blue, and rose-pink.

Culture. Seeds germinate, uncovered, in 7 to 15 days at 70°F/21°C. Set out transplants after all danger of frost is past. Plant in moist, fertile soil. Keep watered well. Pinch to promote bushy growth.

TRACHYMENE COERULEA
Blue lace flower
Umbelliferae

Flowers in: Spring; summer in cool-summer climates
Colors: Blue
Exposure: Full sun
Grows to: 24 inches
When to plant: Sow seeds outdoors in spring

Blooms consist of numerous small, sweet-scented, pale blue flowers clustered together in flat-topped umbels. Hairy, much-divided leaves add to the lacy effect. The plant is not particularly showy in garden beds, but is excellent for cutting.

Culture. Sow seeds in average soil. Seeds germinate in 2 to 3 weeks at

Trachymene coerulea

68°F/20°C. Water frequently and provide support for young plants. Blue lace flower is best suited to cool-summer areas.

TROPAEOLUM MAJUS
Nasturtium
Tropaeolaceae

Flowers in: Summer; winter to spring in warm-winter climates
Colors: Cream, yellow, orange, red, and pink
Exposure: Full sun
Grows to: Dwarfs to 15 inches, climbers to 6 to 10 feet
When to plant: Sow seeds outdoors in spring after all danger of frost is past; in mild-winter climates, sow seeds outdoors in fall

Gardeners love nasturtiums for their attractive round foliage and plentiful flowers. Blooms are held on slender stems growing from the axils of the leaves; newer varieties hold the spurred flowers well above the foliage. Young leaves and blossoms have a peppery flavor and are colorful additions in salads. Dwarf varieties are good edging plants for flower and vegetable beds. Climbing varieties may be used to cover trellises or as a ground cover and are also attractive trailing from hanging baskets and window boxes. The Alaska strain has variegated foliage, small leaves, and blooms in cream, yellow, gold, orange, scarlet, mahogany, rose, pink, and apricot on 12- to 15-inch plants. The Whirlybird series has upward-facing flowers on nearly vertical stems. The midsize Double Gleam series, an All-America Selection, has large, fragrant double and semidouble flowers on 36-inch plants. 'Empress of India' has blue-green leaves and single vermilion flowers on 12-inch plants.

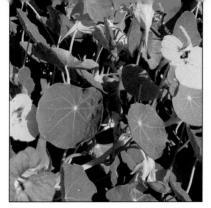

Tropaeolum majus

Canary bird flower (*T. peregrinum*) is a climber growing 10 to 15 feet. Its small yellow flowers have feathery petals. It grows best in cool-summer climates and requires moist soil.

Culture. Plant in average, well-drained soil (rich soil will produce excess foliage at the expense of flowers). Seeds germinate in 14 days. Thin to 12 inches apart. Nasturtiums will live over in mild-winter climates and often reseed themselves. They flower best in cool weather and do not grow well in extremely hot, humid weather. They do not transplant well. Aphids and mealybugs are common pests. For controls, see page 50.

VERBENA HYBRIDA
Garden verbena, Vervain
Verbenaceae

Flowers in: Summer to fall
Colors: White, pink, bright red, purple, blue, and bicolors
Exposure: Full sun
Grows to: 6 to 12 inches
When to plant: Sow seeds indoors 6 to 8 weeks before last frost

Verbena is an old-fashioned favorite among annuals. Its small, richly colored, fragrant flowers are borne in flat clusters 2 to 3 inches wide. The well-branched plants are available in

Verbena hybrida

mounded, trailing, and dwarf forms. Broad, lance-shaped, medium- to gray-green leaves have serrated edges. When in full bloom, plants are a solid mass of color. They are attractive grouped in a border. The trailing forms are useful to create a flowering ground cover and are good choices for hanging baskets. The Amour series has an upright habit and is early to flower. Large, ball-shaped flower heads come in pink, red, purple, white, and rose as well as a mix that includes additional colors. The Springtime series is suitable for hanging baskets and as a ground cover. The Romance strain grows 8 to 10 inches tall, with flowers in scarlet, white, and a mixture. The Showtime series spreads to 18 inches across, in a blend of red, white, violet-blue, rose, and pink. 'Trinidad' has vibrant rose flowers on 10-inch plants. 'Valentine' has clusters of scarlet red blooms with white eyes, up to 3 inches across, on 15-inch plants.

Culture. Chill the seeds 1 week before sowing. Surface-sow on a moistened growing medium. Cover with black plastic until germination begins. Seeds germinate in 3 to 4 weeks at 50° to 75°F/10° to 24°C. Set out transplants after all danger of frost is past. Space 12 to 18 inches apart. Pinch back young plants to promote bushy growth. Deadhead to prolong flowering. Plants can be cut back after the first flush of bloom to encourage fall flower production. Plants may live over in mild-winter climates, but old plants are inferior in growth and flower habit. Verbena is susceptible to rot from excessive moisture.

VIOLA
Pansy, Viola
Violaceae

Flowers in: Early spring to early summer; late winter and spring in mild-winter climates
Colors: White, yellow, orange, red, purple, blue, and bicolors
Exposure: Full sun or partial shade
Grows to: 8 inches
When to plant: Set out transplants several weeks before last frost; in mild-winter climates, set out plants in summer and fall

Viola

The happy faces of low-growing pansies provide brilliant color in cool-season gardens. They are popular for massing with spring-blooming bulbs, and are suitable for containers, hanging baskets, and rock gardens. The velvety flowers of pansies (*V. wittrockiana*) and violas are 2 to 5 inches across and made up of five overlapping petals. They are available in single colors and with contrasting splotches, brightly colored centers, and markings resembling whiskers. Cut flowers make charming small bouquets. Leaves are heart-shaped or oval, sometimes deeply lobed.

The heat-tolerant Crystal Bowl series has 2-inch flowers in 11 clear colors. 'Delft' has 2-inch blooms of porcelain blue and white marked with whiskers and contrasting bright yellow eyes. The Majestic Giant series has huge 4-inch flowers with dark blotches on early-blooming plants, available in 6 colors. The Maxim strain includes All-America Selection 'Maxim Marina', with light blue petals surrounding a dark blue face bordered in white; it resists both heat and cold. 'Padparadja', an All-America Selection, has 2-inch flowers in a unique, clear orange color. The Universal series has a compact, mounded habit, with masses of bloom in 13 colors.

Violas (*V. cornuta*) are short-lived perennials best grown as annuals. The plants grow 8 to 10 inches tall, with flowers 1½ inches across. They are sometimes called horned violets because of the flowers' slender spurs. Their floriferous nature makes up for their smaller flowers, creating a delicate yet colorful show.

Johnny-jump-up (*V. tricolor*) has smaller flowers in a narrower range of colors—usually purple and yellow. They often reseed themselves.

(Continued on next page)

Culture. Pansies and violas must be started 10 weeks before planting out, and so are best purchased as nursery-grown transplants. Alternatively, in cold-winter climates, seeds can be sown in fall in a coldframe and seedlings transplanted in early spring. Seeds germinate in 10 to 21 days at 65° to 70°F/18° to 21°C. Plant in moist, fertile soil; mulch to keep cool and retain moisture. Pansies and violas are most floriferous when nights are cool. Deadhead and cut back leggy plants to prolong bloom. Even heat-tolerant varieties must be replaced in hot-summer climates.

ZINNIA ELEGANS
Garden zinnia
Compositae

Flowers in: Summer to fall
Colors: Shades of white, yellow, orange, red, pink, purple, and bicolors
Exposure: Full sun
Grows to: 6 to 36 inches
When to plant: Sow seeds outdoors in spring, or set out transplants in spring after all danger of frost is past

Zinnias are ever-popular annuals. Easily grown, the plants are available in many heights, flower forms, and colors. They bloom through the heat of summer and provide color in late summer, when most other annuals have finished. These multipurpose plants provide a showy display when massed, and lend color strength when mixed with annuals and perennials in borders.

Dwarf varieties make a colorful edging. The Thumbelina strain has charming small flowers on 6-inch plants. The Short Stuff series produces fully double blooms on 8- to 10-inch plants. The Dreamland series has blooms 4 inches across on 10- to 12-inch plants. 'Rose Pinwheel', bearing rose-pink flowers with yellow centers on 12-inch plants, was bred for mildew resistance. The Peter Pan strain begins to flower when plants are just 6 to 8 inches tall and continues all summer, maturing at a height of 12 to 14 inches. The Border Beauty series has dahlia-type double to semidouble flowers on bushy plants. The Candy

Zinnia Dreamland

Cane series has bright pink, rose, and cerise stripes on white petals, and grows to 17 inches. Hybrid 'Small World Cherry' is an All-America Selection, and one of the most vigorous of all zinnias. The Lilliput strain has vivid, pompon-type blooms on 18- to 24-inch tall plants. Flowers of the Ruffles hybrid series are borne on 24- to 30-inch stems. 'Scarlet Splendor' has

rich, 4- to 5-inch scarlet flowers with semiruffled petals; the plants have a hedgelike habit and require less space than other tall varieties.

Z. angustifolia has compact plants with narrow leaves and flowers 1 inch across; it often lives over in mild-winter climates. 'Classic', with its 1½-inch-wide orange flowers, and 'Classic White', a white-flowering counterpart, have spreading habits and make good choices for hanging baskets. The Persian Carpet strain and 'Old Mexico' variety of *Z. haageana* produce 1½-inch-wide double and semidouble flowers in bright shades of brownish red, yellow, and orange, with pointed petals tipped or bordered with a contrasting color. They are an especially attractive and free-blooming edging.

Culture. Sow in average soil, after it has warmed. Seeds germinate in 7 to 10 days at 70° to 80°F/21° to 27°C. Thin seedlings to 6 to 12 inches apart. Deadhead flowers to prolong bloom. Ground-level watering will help prevent mildew, to which zinnias are susceptible. Feed monthly during the growing season with a complete fertilizer to encourage vigorous growth.

Seed Sources

Seeds of many annuals are sold in nurseries and garden centers. Mail-order catalogs, of which there are many, usually offer a wider selection. Here are three popular mail-order seed companies that offer a large variety of flowering annuals in free catalogs.

W. Atlee Burpee & Co.
300 Park Avenue
Warminster, PA 18974

Park Seed Company
Cokesbury Road
Greenwood, SC 29647-0001

Thompson & Morgan
P.O. Box 1308
Jackson, NJ 08527

Wildflowers

Index

Sunset

Perennials

BY THE EDITORS OF SUNSET BOOKS AND SUNSET MAGAZINE

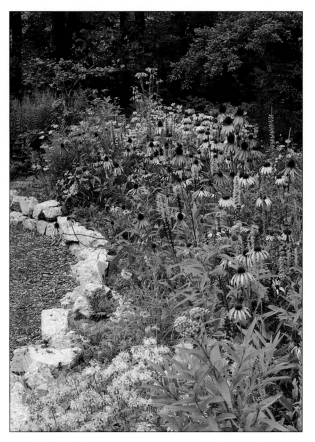

Mingling in harmonious scene are purple coneflower
(Echinacea), *gayfeather* (Liatris), *and beebalm* (Monarda).

Sunset Publishing Corp. ■ Menlo Park, California

Violet speedwell (Veronica), *yellow yarrow* (Achillea), *and pale mauve sea lavender* (Limonium) *weave tapestry of varied colors, forms, and textures.*

Research & Text
Philip Edinger

Coordinating Editor
Suzanne Normand Mathison

Design
Joe di Chiarro

Illustrations
Lois Lovejoy

Calligraphy
Sherry Bringham

Editorial Director, Sunset Books:
Bob Doyle

Photographers

R. Valentine Atkinson: 107 right; **Scott Atkinson:** 30, 32, 42, 43; **Liz Ball/Photo/Nats:** 41 top left, 41 middle center; **Priscilla Connell/Photo/Nats:** 41 top center; **Philip Edinger:** 82 bottom; **Derek Fell:** 7 bottom left and right, 11 bottom, 15 bottom, 28 bottom left, 29, 41 bottom left, center, and right, 52 top, 54 top right, 57 right, 58 top, 71 right, 105 right; **Saxon Holt:** 1, 2, 7 top, 8, 10 left, 11 top left and right, 13 top left, 14 top right and bottom right, 15 top and middle, 24, 28 top right, 34, 46 bottom, 47 right, 49 top right, 50 middle and bottom, 52 bottom left and bottom right, 53, 54 top left, 55 top, 56 right, 58 bottom left, 59 top, 60 top, 61 left, 62 left, 63 right, 66 top right, 67 top right, 69 top, 70 bottom, 71 left, 72 top, 74 top right and bottom, 75, 77, 78, 79 top, 80, 82 top, 84, 85, 87, 89, 91 bottom left and bottom right, 94 left, 96, 97 top, 98, 99 left, 100, 101 top, 102 left, 103, 104 right, 105 middle, 106 top, 108, 109 right, 110; **Horticultural Photography:** 22, 73 bottom, 79 bottom, 83 bottom right, 86 top, 88, 90 right, 95, 105 left, 106 bottom, 109 left; **Dorothy S. Long/Photo/Nats:** 23, 27; **John Lynch/Photo/Nats:** 58 bottom right; **Robert E. Lyons/Photo/Nats:** 41 middle right; **Ells Marugg:** 25, 46 top, 81; **Robert and Linda Mitchell:** 41 middle left; **Don Normark:** 83 bottom left; **Norman A. Plate:** 59 bottom; **Bill Ross:** 28 bottom, 102 right; **David M. Stone/Photo/Nats:** 49 top left; **David Stubbs:** 41 top right; **Michael S. Thompson:** 49 bottom, 50 top, 51, 54 bottom, 55 bottom, 56 left, 60 bottom, 62 right, 65 top, 72 bottom, 83 top, 99 right, 101 bottom, 104 left, 107 left; **Wayside Gardens Co.:** 86 bottom; **Cynthia Woodyard:** 4, 6, 10 right, 13 top right, 14 top left, 44, 47 left, 48, 57 bottom, 61 right, 63 left, 64, 66 top left and bottom, 67 top left and bottom, 68, 69 bottom, 70 top, 73 top, 74 top left, 90 left, 93, 94 right, 97 bottom; **Tom Wyatt:** 13 bottom, 72 bottom.

Cover: Like an earthbound patch of summer sky, blossoms of Music strain columbine *(Aquilegia)* introduce the wonderfully varied world of perennials. Cover design by Susan Bryant. Photography by Saxon Holt.

The Perennial Array

Whether you prefer the tidy simplicity of a daisy, the exotic beauty of a toad lily, the sculptural elegance of an iris, or the unique delicacy of a columbine, you'll find no end to the variety of flower forms among the perennials. No color escapes the perennials spectrum, and some of their flowers display combinations that are the envy of textile designers. In size, you can find large perennials to make grandiose landscape statements as well as small ones to bejewel a handkerchief-size patio.

The four chapters in this book introduce you to the wide world of perennials and show you how to incorporate them effectively in your garden. The chapter on culture provides easy-to-grasp information on all aspects of care, and our extensive encyclopedia presents photographs and detailed descriptions of over 140 favorites and should-be-favorites.

Dedicated amateur growers and professionals alike have contributed to the current state of perennials knowledge. Through this book, they share their collective experience. For valuable assistance with the book's manuscript we thank Ainie Busse of Cokato, Minnesota; Evie Douglas of Snohomish, Washington; John R. Dunmire of Los Altos, California; Marco Polo Stufano of the Bronx, New York; and Dr. William C. Welch of College Station, Texas.

Our thanks go to Pamela Evans for carefully editing the manuscript, to Joan Melim for helping us with the graphic representation of the garden plans, and to Kathy Oetinger for the color wheel.

$\mathcal{C}$ontents

Oenothera
fruticosa

Presenting the Perennials

C ome, . . . meet the perennials. You can visit at any time of year, unless it's freezing outside. And if you can't make it this year, come next year, or the year after.

That's the beauty of perennials: they're here today . . . and here tomorrow. Though you may think of them (and rightly so) as mainstays of spring and summer floral displays, you can—with thoughtful planning and climate permitting—have perennials in flower at any time of the year. Their needs are simple, their rewards great. You should know more about them.

Come into the garden. . . .

The perennials garden invites with its diversity. The countless shapes, sizes, and colors offer an ever-changing prospect—but one that promises return yearly.

Anemone hybrida

The Perennial Question

Longevity distinguishes perennials from annuals. Wherever conditions are suitable, a perennial will grow and flower for at least 3 years. Perennials differ from longer-lived shrubs, on the other hand, in their lack of truly woody stems. Because of this they are sometimes called *herbaceous* perennials (herbaceous meaning "like an herb").

Within this long-lived nonwoody framework are several plant types. One group will die down to the ground at the end of each growing season, then reappear at the start of the next. Peonies *(Paeonia)* and hostas typify this group. Other perennials, such as Shasta daisies *(Chrysanthemum superbum)* and coral bells *(Heuchera)*, go through winter as low tufts of foliage, ready to grow when weather warms. And finally, there are truly evergreen perennials—many daylilies *(Hemerocallis)* and lily-of-the-Nile *(Agapan-*

thus), for example—whose foliage is nearly unchanged throughout winter.

Perennials differ in other ways as well: hardiness, soil preference, moisture need, and sun tolerance immediately come to mind. But to the garden planner, perhaps the most important difference is season of flowering. Although perennials in general reach a floral climax during summer, you have a more than substantial number that are spring flowering, a generous handful that will ornament the autumn garden, and even a few that will cheer the winter landscape, if the climate allows.

No wonder, then, that perennials are so popular: you can fashion any number of different kinds of plantings using perennials as the mainstay. The photographs on these two pages give you a foretaste of perennials' versatility.

From simple understatement to grandiose display, perennials can carry the show from spring into autumn. *Siberian irises and Shasta daisies (Chrysanthemum superbum)* dominate springtime scene *(left); summer floral portrait (top) relies just on daylilies (Hemerocallis) and yarrow (Achillea); making the summer to autumn transition (above) are Joe-Pye weed (Eupatorium),* silver king artemisia *(Artemisia ludoviciana albula),* purple coneflower *(Echinacea), and* thrift *(Armeria maritima). On the facing page, an autumn garden showcases ornamental grasses and spring-fresh* Japanese anemone *(Anemone hybrida).*

Perennials in the Landscape

Perennials have been cultivated as long as gardens have existed. But it was the 18th- and 19th-century European development of flower gardens for pleasure—inspired by an influx of new plant arrivals from around the world—that brought perennials into sharp focus. Selecting from this cornucopia of materials, Victorian England's Gertrude Jekyll designed elaborate perennial borders that even today are recognized as examples of consummate artistry in plant combinations. You'll find her guiding principles in this chapter, along with six original garden plans and helpful lists to guide your plant selection.

*Dianthus
plumarius*

Pocket-size perennial border in contemporary idiom shows artful arrangement of varied colors, shapes, and textures to form a harmonious picture.

9

Designing with Perennials

Contemporary gardeners are influenced in their use of perennials by two established design traditions. One is the careful, studied Gertrude Jekyll perennial border; the other—in some ways opposite—tradition is the more humble "cottage garden."

Gertrude Jekyll's borders offered the ultimate showcase for a wide range of perennial plants. Typically the setting was a 6- to 10-foot-wide bed, fronted by lawn or pavement, backed by a tall hedge or wall, extending in length as far as the gardener desired. Perennials were placed in the border as an artist might compose a painting: in a complex arrangement that considered not only color but also height, leaf texture, plant shape, and time of flowering. The objective was a floral display from spring through autumn in which all plants would complement one another even when not in bloom.

In contrast to such meticulously crafted borders, the cottage garden tradition used freer brushstrokes and a broader plant palette. These eclectic practitioners haphazardly mixed perennials with whatever else they happened to fancy: flowering shrubs, annuals, bulbs, ferns—even vegetables. Guided by an artistic sense, the result would be no less a floral painting than was a Jekyll border—but more like a Grandma Moses "primitive" than a polished Constable.

An all-perennials border still is an effective display for these plants and remains an engaging challenge to one's design abilities. Besides the classic, rectangular border, the "island bed"—situated in a lawn, or even floating in a surround of paving or decking—offers another showcase with the added advantage of being visible (and accessible) from all sides. But gardeners increasingly are choosing perennials to shine as components of mixed plantings, in which they may provide the framework, serve as accent pieces, or function as equal players among flowering shrubs, annuals, and bulbs. By choosing wisely (see page 29), you also can enjoy perennials as container plants.

Classic perennial border principles are easily applied to today's gardens. Combinations of foliage shapes and colors play as important a role as does floral arrangement.

Wayward charm of cottage gardens is captured in exuberant planting that features orange Oriental poppy (Papaver orientale), blue Delphinium, and filmy bronze fennel (Foeniculum vulgare purpureum).

Composing the Picture

Whether you plan an all-perennials garden or a horticultural menagerie, several design tips will help you produce a satisfying "floral painting." They can be summed up in one simple statement: In composing your design, consider the total plant. Don't just focus on color. Though it's the most obvious component of the totality (see page 12), the following elements all work in conjunction with color to give each plant its individuality.

Size. Some plants, of course, are larger than others; even within plants of the same kind, sizes are likely to vary. And the obvious advice is still worth taking: place taller plants toward the back, shorter plants in front; allow more room for the larger plants. That wise counsel notwithstanding, there is a bit more to the size issue. You can use tall plants among shorter ones in the foreground if you need an accent to perk up the flatness. Think of drifts of catmint (*Nepeta faassenii*) and *Coreopsis verticillata* punctuated by a clump of torch-lily (*Kniphofia*). The most effective plantings mix plant sizes for contrast and dramatic effect. A plot with too many small plants looks "fussy" and indistinct; a preponderance of large plants appears crowded and overbearing.

Texture. Leaf size, leaf shape, and plant density combine to produce an overall visual texture. From the threadlike leaf segments of *Coreopsis verticillata* or *Foeniculum vulgare* to the platelike leaves of *Ligularia*; from the simple, swordlike leaves of *Iris* to the elaborately segmented ones of *Columbine*—you have a great range of shapes and sizes with which to compose a varied planting.

Plant density is an associated element, not always directly related to texture. You can have fine-textured yet dense perennials, and coarse or bold-textured ones that are relatively open in structure. A dense plant appears opaque, solid; an open-structured one is translucent.

Forms. Spreading, vertical, rounded, vase shaped—perennials come in a variety of plant shapes. And it is the combination of that variety that spices up the appearance of a planting. Play off the different forms against one another, never letting too much of one dominate the composition. Remember, too, that many perennials change form when they flower, sending flowering stems above and beyond the foliage mass. In composing the picture, consider as well the flower forms and the arrangement of flowers on the stem.

Form and texture combine to enhance visual interest. Top left shows spiky veronica, flat-topped yarrow (Achillea), *and uniquely birdlike columbine* (Aquilegia). *At top right, bold-leafed hosta contrasts with pink, cloudlike blossoms of Jupiter's beard* (Centranthus ruber), *backed by grassy foliage of Siberian iris and* Sisyrinchium striatum. *Simple duet at left combines ornamental grass foliage* (Miscanthus sinensis 'Variegatus') *and Rudbeckia's brash daisy blossoms.*

Working with Color

Perennials offer myriad color opportunities, from vivid to subtle, that can be exploited in any number of ways. Given a knowledge of fundamental color principles, you'll be able to assemble color groupings with the assurance of satisfaction.

Understanding the Color Wheel

The color display shown below arranges the rainbow spectrum in a wheel that clearly shows the interrelationships of the various colors and provides a basis for understanding a number of color principles.

Primary colors are red, yellow, and blue. All other colors are produced by various mixtures of those three. Conversely, no mixture of other colors will give you pure-spectrum red, yellow, or blue. Those three colors are equidistant from one another around the color wheel.

Complementary colors face one another across the wheel—for example, red and green or blue and orange. If you were to mix paints of two complementary colors they would neutralize—or complement—one another, making a shade of gray. If you placed two complementary colors side by side, however, you would create a strong contrast.

Harmonious colors are those that lie between any two *primary* colors and are simply graduated mixtures of those two primaries. Look at the transition from yellow to red—through yellow-orange, orange, and red-orange—and you'll see that the color changes result from a gradual addition of more red to yellow. The closer together on the wheel two colors are, the more harmonious they are.

Warm versus cool colors face off across the color wheel, on either side of a dividing line drawn between green and yellow-green on one side and red and red-violet on the other. The warm tones center around orange, the cool ones around blue.

Color value—light to dark—is evident as you follow any color in the wheel from the perimeter to the

Color Wheel

The color wheel shows the primary colors—red, blue, yellow—spaced equidistantly around the circle, with the transitional colors connecting them. The pure hue of each color is labeled; shades of each color are made by the addition of black; tints are made by adding white.

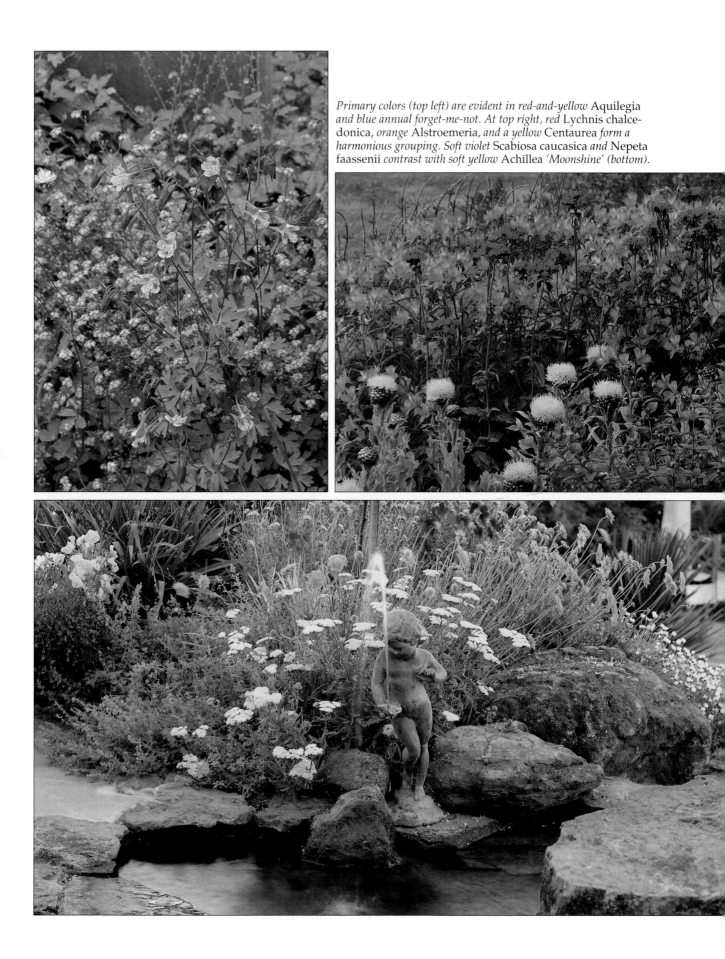

Primary colors (top left) are evident in red-and-yellow Aquilegia *and blue annual forget-me-not. At top right, red* Lychnis chalcedonica, *orange* Alstroemeria, *and a yellow* Centaurea *form a harmonious grouping. Soft violet* Scabiosa caucasica *and* Nepeta faassenii *contrast with soft yellow* Achillea 'Moonshine' *(bottom).*

Working with Color

center. Each pure-spectrum color in the wheel has its name printed over it. You'll see that each color becomes lighter in value toward the center of the wheel, as it is diluted with white, and darker toward the perimeter, with an increasing addition of black.

Color perception is affected by the surface that bears the color, because different surfaces' textures or compositions alter reflectivity. Fabrics illustrate this point clearly. The same value of red will appear bright and metallic in satin (which is highly reflective) but duller, darker, and softer in velvet (which is absorptive).

Color Principles in Practice

Though the subject of color is much more complex than this basic information might imply, you nevertheless can use these basics to plan a garden of pleasing color schemes. Here are some of the possibilities, along with their strengths and weaknesses.

Monochrome. The safest color scheme uses just one color—most frequently seen in "white gardens." One danger of monochrome plantings is monotony, but another hazard—when you get into the warm colors—is unrest. Imagine an all-red garden. To really pull off a monochrome scheme, you have to depend on variation from foliage, texture, and shape.

Contrasts. Color contrasts can provide punctuation, focal points, relief from monotony, and even a sense of exhilaration. You achieve a contrasting scheme when you place complementary colors (opposites on the color wheel) side by side in the garden. In most cases, you'll make the contrasts with flower colors; note, however, that the complement of red is green. Bright red flowers against a green foliage backdrop is as true a contrast as violet delphiniums behind yellow daylilies. Any two, or all three, of the primary colors in combination also make for contrast.

Contrasts of colors at full strength are most effective as accents or foils to quieter, more harmonious schemes (see "Harmonies" on the facing page). When overdone, full-strength contrasts become disquieting and ultimately lose their impact. Equal masses of

Vary color contrast by varying the color values. Here are three versions of the yellow-violet contrast. At top left, full yellow Rudbeckia *combines with light violet* Echinacea; *in the top right photo, the relationship is reversed with light yellow* Achillea *and full violet* Salvia. *The lower right combination features yellow* Kniphofia *and violet* Salvia *at equal, full strength.*

contrasting colors are usually less effective than one color used sparingly as an accent to greater amounts of the other.

But you needn't use colors at full value to achieve contrast. Cream and lavender, for example, have the same contrast as do bright yellow and violet. As the inner bands of the color wheel show, the addition of white to full colors modifies them without changing their complementary relationships.

A third way to manipulate contrasts is to combine contrasting colors at contrasting values. A strong blue with pale peach is just a variation on the blue-and-orange theme. Pink peonies placed against a green hedge is simply a toned-down version of red peonies in the same setting.

Harmonies. Plantings composed of harmonious colors (those that lie between any two primary colors on the wheel) automatically please the eye, because the colors are so obviously related. What such plantings may lack—especially if all the colors are of about the same value—is zest. To bring these plantings to life, you need to introduce some sort of variation in color values within the group, a burst of a complementary color, or a dash of white.

White. Any color's value decreases as white is added to it until the point is reached—represented by the center of the color wheel—at which color is absent and only white is left. White flowers, then, can assort with all colors, but in two different ways. Combined with the lighter values of the various colors, white appears to be harmonious; its absence of color seems closely related to the pale values around it. With colors at full and darker-than-full value, however, white stands out in sharp contrast. Recalling that overuse of contrasts produces unrest, use white sparingly among full colors and their darker values. Or, if you use white as a planting's main color theme, add full-value colors with discretion. Among lighter values, of course, you can use white more lavishly.

Gray. Here is the great moderator among colors. Usually thought of as a cool color, gray—in the form of gray-leafed plants—mingles comfortably with colors on the cool side of the color wheel. But if you remember that gray results from the mixture of any two complementary colors, you'll realize you can use it to tie together two contrasting colors, as well. Imagine first a drift of yellow and violet irises with no other companions, then envision that same planting backed by Silver King artemisia (*Artemisia ludoviciana albula*). The contrast remains but is much softened by the presence of gray.

White can assume several guises in floral combinations. White petals of Shasta daisy (Chrysanthemum superbum) *lighten a warm combination of the yellow daisy centers and coral phlox blossoms. An all-white Shasta daisy, center, makes a cool picture with blue catmint* (Nepeta) *and gray-leafed dusty miller* (Senecio cineraria)—*enlivened by a pointillist contrast of yellow dusty miller flowers. At the bottom, white-flowered* Hibiscus moscheutos *dominates an all-white color scheme.*

Six Perennial Garden Plans

Summer Color for a Mild Climate

"The amount of winter cold a garden will experience plays a large part in plant selection. This cottage garden design contains some favorite combinations enjoyed in the relatively mild-winter gardens in the West.

Perennials predominate, but roses, vines, and a few bulbs add to the floral mix."

Michael Bates, English country garden designer

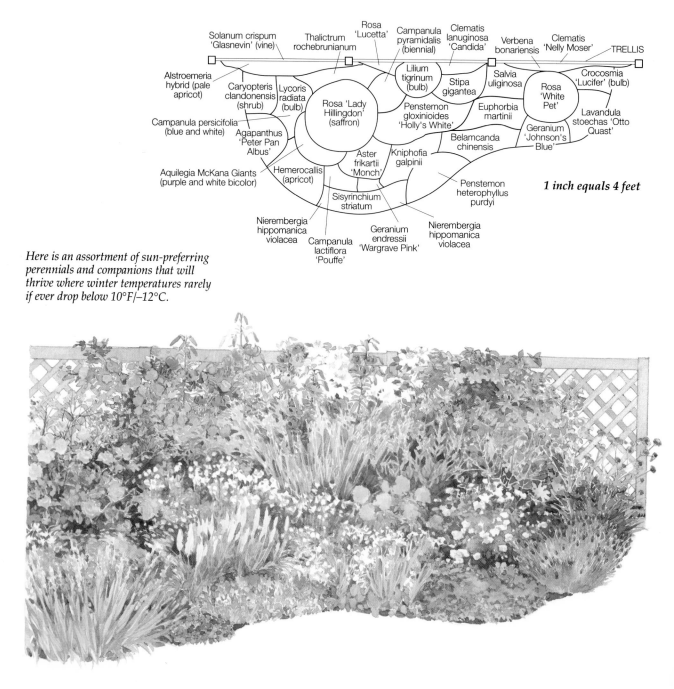

Here is an assortment of sun-preferring perennials and companions that will thrive where winter temperatures rarely if ever drop below 10°F/–12°C.

1 inch equals 4 feet

A Spring-Summer Potpourri

"The gardens that invariably impress you as the most interesting and satisfying are those which successfully meld the various plant groups: trees, shrubs (including roses), perennials, annuals, bulbs, and grasses. This border combines a selection of favorite plants and a soft, informal planting style in a semiformal framework. Two shrubs and a shrub rose give needed structure to the planting."

Michael Bates, English country garden designer

This garden contains an across-the-board assortment of sun-loving spring- and summer-flowering perennials and associated plants with no color restrictions. All plants are hardy to at least –20°F/–29°C.

1 inch equals 4 feet

A Cool Oasis

"Planning a perennial flower bed is much like planning a painting. Colors and shapes blend to create the 'picture' we want. This planting has been inspired by the French Impressionists' paintings—cool, delicate colors with accents of soft whites, creams, and foliage greens. Plants are placed in such a way that colors will drift through one another: there are no sharp edges for the eye's focus. Leaf shapes also are an important design factor."

Joni Prittie, designer and artist

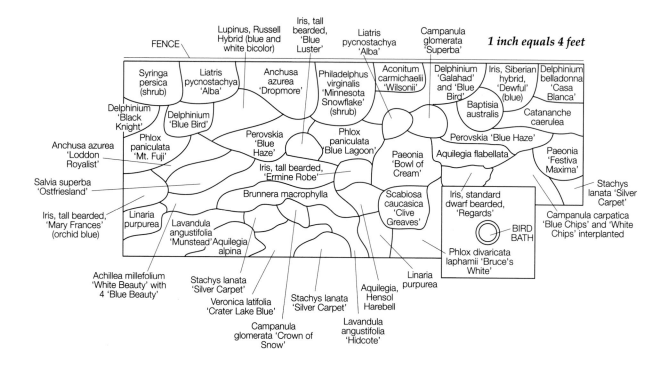

1 inch equals 4 feet

FENCE

Lupinus, Russell Hybrid (blue and white bicolor)
Iris, tall bearded, 'Blue Luster'
Liatris pycnostachya 'Alba'
Campanula glomerata 'Superba'

Syringa persica (shrub)
Liatris pycnostachya 'Alba'
Anchusa azurea 'Dropmore'
Philadelphus virginalis 'Minnesota Snowflake' (shrub)
Aconitum carmichaelii 'Wilsonii'
Delphinium 'Galahad' and 'Blue Bird'
Iris, Siberian hybrid, 'Dewful' (blue)
Delphinium belladonna 'Casa Blanca'

Delphinium 'Black Knight'
Delphinium 'Blue Bird'
Baptisia australis
Catananche caerulea

Anchusa azurea 'Loddon Royalist'
Phlox paniculata 'Mt. Fuji'
Perovskia 'Blue Haze'
Phlox paniculata 'Blue Lagoon'
Perovskia 'Blue Haze'
Paeonia 'Festiva Maxima'

Iris, tall bearded, 'Ermine Robe'
Paeonia 'Bowl of Cream'
Aquilegia flabellata

Salvia superba 'Ostfriesland'
Brunnera macrophylla
Scabiosa caucasica 'Clive Greaves'
Iris, standard dwarf bearded, 'Regards'
Stachys lanata 'Silver Carpet'

Iris, tall bearded, 'Mary Frances' (orchid blue)
Linaria purpurea
Lavandula angustifolia 'Munstead'
Aquilegia alpina
BIRD BATH
Campanula carpatica 'Blue Chips' and 'White Chips' interplanted

Phlox divaricata laphamii 'Bruce's White'

Achillea millefolium 'White Beauty' with 4 'Blue Beauty'
Stachys lanata 'Silver Carpet'
Linaria purpurea

Veronica latifolia 'Crater Lake Blue'
Stachys lanata 'Silver Carpet'
Aquilegia, Hensol Harebell

Campanula glomerata 'Crown of Snow'
Lavandula angustifolia 'Hidcote'

This planting features perennials that prefer full sun; some of the plants start to bloom in late spring, but most bloom in summer. All are hardy to at least −20°F/ −29°C or better.

An Unthirsty Garden

"This water-thrifty planting is planned to be of interest from all sides—and with surprises as you move around it. Its feeling is one of bright summer freshness, including flowers of orange (often a difficult garden color), buff yellow, apricot, periwinkle blue, rose, and white, with silvery and white-felted leaves as moderators."

Joni Prittie, designer and artist

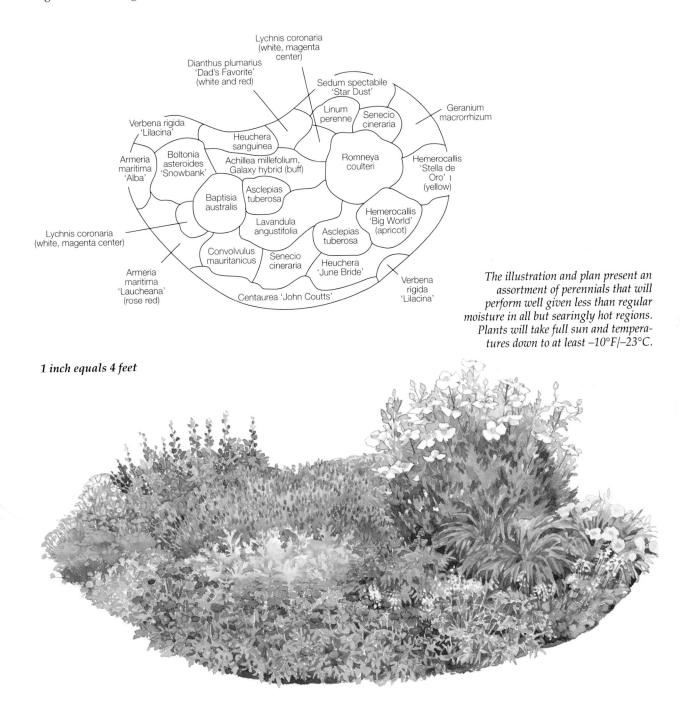

Lychnis coronaria (white, magenta center)

Dianthus plumarius 'Dad's Favorite' (white and red)

Sedum spectabile 'Star Dust'

Linum perenne

Senecio cineraria

Geranium macrorrhizum

Verbena rigida 'Lilacina'

Heuchera sanguinea

Armeria maritima 'Alba'

Boltonia asteroides 'Snowbank'

Achillea millefolium, Galaxy hybrid (buff)

Romneya coulteri

Hemerocallis 'Stella de Oro' (yellow)

Baptisia australis

Asclepias tuberosa

Lavandula angustifolia

Hemerocallis 'Big World' (apricot)

Asclepias tuberosa

Lychnis coronaria (white, magenta center)

Convolvulus mauritanicus

Senecio cineraria

Heuchera 'June Bride'

Armeria maritima 'Laucheana' (rose red)

Verbena rigida 'Lilacina'

Centaurea 'John Coutts'

The illustration and plan present an assortment of perennials that will perform well given less than regular moisture in all but searingly hot regions. Plants will take full sun and temperatures down to at least −10°F/−23°C.

1 inch equals 4 feet

A Splash of Summer Color

"The shape of the lower raised bed resembles a pool, so it is planted with blue-flowered perennials to suggest a sheet of water; bursting from the 'pool' are sprays of white flowers like water jets. The chosen colors are bright and clear—both warm and cool—moderated by gray foliage."

Gary Patterson, landscape designer

Summer conditions—the amount of heat and humidity—determine, in part, the perennials that you can grow. This plan incorporates a number of less particular perennials, suitable for full sun in a dry to moderately humid climate; all are hardy to at least –10°F/–23°C.

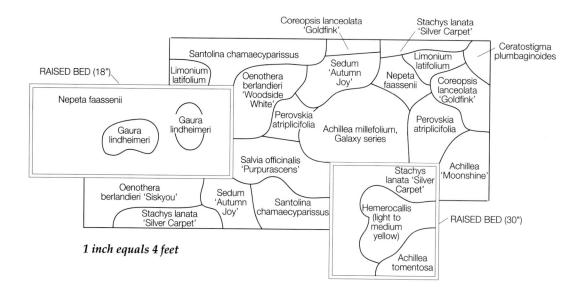

RAISED BED (18")

Nepeta faassenii

Gaura lindheimeri

Gaura lindheimeri

Santolina chamaecyparissus

Limonium latifolium

Oenothera berlandieri 'Woodside White'

Coreopsis lanceolata 'Goldfink'

Sedum 'Autumn Joy'

Stachys lanata 'Silver Carpet'

Limonium latifolium

Nepeta faassenii

Ceratostigma plumbaginoides

Coreopsis lanceolata 'Goldfink'

Perovskia atriplicifolia

Achillea millefolium, Galaxy series

Perovskia atriplicifolia

Salvia officinalis 'Purpurascens'

Achillea 'Moonshine'

Oenothera berlandieri 'Siskyou'

Sedum 'Autumn Joy'

Santolina chamaecyparissus

Stachys lanata 'Silver Carpet'

Hemerocallis (light to medium yellow)

RAISED BED (30")

Stachys lanata 'Silver Carpet'

Achillea tomentosa

1 inch equals 4 feet

Autumn: The Year's Finale

"Though the year's last major bloom period features a more limited choice of perennials, there's no lack of color or abundance. This 'country garden' bed showcases the autumn mainstays—daisies—featuring the expected warm colors but contrasting them with the cool shades of boltonia and aster. Several ornamental grasses, flourishing mature seed heads, remind us that this is the season of harvest."

Gary Patterson, landscape designer

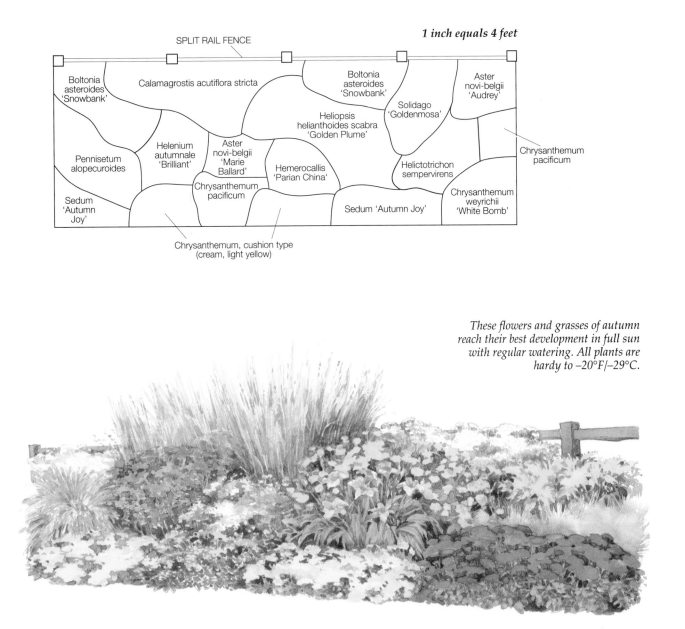

SPLIT RAIL FENCE

1 inch equals 4 feet

Boltonia asteroides 'Snowbank'

Calamagrostis acutiflora stricta

Boltonia asteroides 'Snowbank'

Aster novi-belgii 'Audrey'

Solidago 'Goldenmosa'

Heliopsis helianthoides scabra 'Golden Plume'

Chrysanthemum pacificum

Pennisetum alopecuroides

Helenium autumnale 'Brilliant'

Aster novi-belgii 'Marie Ballard'

Hemerocallis 'Parian China'

Helictotrichon sempervirens

Chrysanthemum pacificum

Sedum 'Autumn Joy'

Chrysanthemum weyrichii 'White Bomb'

Sedum 'Autumn Joy'

Chrysanthemum, cushion type (cream, light yellow)

These flowers and grasses of autumn reach their best development in full sun with regular watering. All plants are hardy to –20°F/–29°C.

The Almost Perennials

These plants—the biennials—march to their own music. Flowering in their *second* year from seed, they're too tardy for inclusion with the annuals. But because typical biennial plants die after flowering, they lack the year-after-year staying power of perennials.

The trick to using biennials in the garden is to always have a supply of new plants coming along—starting a new crop from seed each spring or setting out young nursery-raised stock in summer or autumn. This means a bit of advance planning. You can space the first plants far enough apart so that you can plant next year's plants between them. By following this pattern year after year, you'll have the same biennial flowering each year in roughly the same location. Or you can set out new plants in different spots each year, resigning yourself to a flowerless patch in the garden as the young biennials grow to maturity.

Plant breeders have long worked at pushing biennials into either the annual or perennial category. There are now annual strains of sweet William and hollyhock, for example; and foxgloves are also represented by some truly perennial species and hybrids. But in many cases, the "classic" examples of these plants are still the biennial types, while others—Canterbury bells, for example—are truly one of a kind.

ALCEA rosea. Hollyhock. *Malvaceae.* Hardy to –40°F/–40°C. Few plants are as suggestive of the old-fashioned garden as hollyhocks. Typical blossoms are saucer shaped, about 4 inches across, on towering spikes 7 to 9 feet tall; flowering begins in summer and can last into early autumn. Leaves are large, rounded, and rough-surfaced, carried at ends of slender leafstalks; plants grow as a mound of foliage until flower spikes begin to elongate. Hybrid strains now include shorter-stemmed kinds as well as those with double flowers; colors include yellow, cream, white, pink shades, red, and maroon to purple. Give plants well-prepared soil and regular watering. Rust is their nemesis: choose rust-resistant strains and remove any rusted leaves you find. Watch for slugs, snails.

CAMPANULA medium. Canterbury bells. *Campanulaceae.* Hardy to –30°F/–34°C. Here is another plant that evokes the romance of an old-fashioned cottage garden. From clumps of narrow, lance-shaped leaves rise leafy, vertical stems that bear loose spikes of upward-facing bells to 2 inches across in blue shades, purple, pink, and white. The cup-and-saucer version, 'Calycanthema', has each bell seated on a saucerlike calyx. Flowering period is from mid- or late spring into midsummer. Set out plants in good soil where they'll get full sun in cool- and mild-summer regions, partial shade where summers are hot. Give them regular watering.

DIANTHUS barbatus. Sweet William. *Caryophyllaceae.* Hardy to –30°F/–34°C. With its clumps of narrow leaves and fringe-edged single flowers, sweet William bears an obvious resemblance to its perennial relative, cottage pink (*Dianthus plumarius*). But it takes several departures: leaves are green rather than blue-gray, and the ½-inch flowers come in large, dense clusters. A number of named strains are sold, including some with double flowers; heights range from about 6 inches (Indian Carpet) to 1½ feet. Flowers come in solid colors—white, pink shades, red, and purple—and in striking bicolor combinations, usually with concentric bands of color. Set out in summer, plants will flower the following spring and summer; give them good, well-drained soil and regular water.

DIGITALIS purpurea. Common foxglove. *Scrophulariaceae.* Hardy to –20°F/–29°C. This cottage-garden staple forms clumps of large, furry, tongue-shaped leaves from which emerge tall flowering spikes in spring to early summer. The pendant, thimble-shaped flowers come in mid- to late spring and continue into summer; colors include white, lavender, pink, and purple, usually spotted with a dark purplish color. Various strains are available, including Excelsior, with outward-facing flowers; Gloxiniiflora, with larger, more wide-open blossoms; and 6-foot Shirley. Plant in filtered sunlight to light shade, in good soil receiving regular watering. Watch for slugs and snails. If you leave spent flowering spikes, plants will self-sow.

SALVIA argentea. Silver sage. *Labiatae.* Hardy to –20°F/–29°C. Silver sage gives you highly ornamental foliage to admire while it is building up to the point of flowering. Each plant is a rosette of roundly oval 6- to 8-inch-long gray-white leaves that are covered with silvery, woolly hairs. In the summer of a plant's second year, branched, white, woolly flower stems rise to 3 feet bearing pink- or yellow-tinted white flowers in furry calyxes. Silver sage needs well-drained, average to poor soil and moderate watering.

Digitalis purpurea

Guide to Choosing Perennials

At first encounter, the wealth of perennials may be a bit daunting. How do you make selections from so many plants that differ not only in appearance but also in cultural needs?

This six-page guide addresses that question by organizing this book's perennials into three useful categories. One list shows perennials that rarely if ever need dividing. Three lists highlight common cultural situations: limited water, shade, and moist soil. The remaining lists organize all the perennials by season of bloom—at the same time showing available flower colors for each plant.

Perennials for Permanence

These perennials will remain in place for many years without any decline in performance. Many, in fact, never need dividing.

NAME OF PLANT	HARDY TO
Acanthus mollis	10°F/–12°C
Agapanthus	varies
Alchemilla mollis	–40°F/–40°C
Alstroemeria	5°F/–15°C
Amsonia tabernaemontana	–35°F/–37°C
Anemone hybrida	–20°F/–29°C
Aruncus dioicus	–35°F/–37°C
Asclepias tuberosa	–35°F/–37°C
Baptisia australis	–35°F/–37°C
Cimicifuga	–35°F/–37°C
Crambe cordifolia	–10°F/–23°C
Dictamnus albus	–35°F/–37°C
Echinops	–35°F/–37°C
Eryngium	varies
Eupatorium	–30°F/–34°C
Euphorbia (most)	varies
Gaura lindheimeri	–10°F/–23°C
Gypsophila paniculata	–35°F/–37°C
Helleborus	varies
Hibiscus moscheutos	–10°F/–23°C
Hosta	–35°F/–37°C
Kniphofia	–10°F/–23°C
Ligularia	–30°F/–34°C
Limonium latifolium	–35°F/–37°C
Liriope	–10°F/–23°C
Lythrum salicaria	–35°F/–37°C
Macleaya cordata	–30°F/–34°C
Mertensia	–35°F/–37°C
Paeonia	–50°F/–46°C
Papaver orientale	–40°F/–40°C
Perovskia	–20°F/–29°C
Platycodon grandiflorus	–35°F/–37°C
Polygonatum	–30°F/–34°C
Romneya coulteri	–10°F/–23°C
Tricyrtis	–20°F/–29°C
Trillium	varies

Peonies (Paeonia) are among the most permanent of perennials, often outlasting both garden and gardener. This is the hybrid 'Pillow Talk'.

Needing only moderate water, Perovskia *and* Coreopsis verticillata *make attractive companions.*

Low Water-Use Perennials

Where you cannot (or choose not to) water regularly, consider planting these perennials. A few are heroically drought tolerant, and all will thrive on less-than-regular watering.

NAME OF PLANT	HARDY TO
Achillea	–30°F/–34°C
Anthemis	–30°F/–34°C
Armeria maritima	–35°F/–37°C
Artemisia	varies
Asclepias tuberosa	–35°F/–37°C
Aurinia saxatilis	–35°F/–37°C
Baptisia australis	–35°F/–37°C
Catananche caerulea	–30°F/–34°C
Centaurea	–30°F/–34°C
Centranthus ruber	–20°F/–29°C
Ceratostigma plumbaginoides	–10°F/–23°C
Convolvulus mauritanicus	10°F/–12°C
Coreopsis	–30°F/–34°C
Echinacea purpurea	–35°F/–37°C
Eryngium	varies
Euphorbia	varies
Gaillardia grandiflora	–35°F/–37°C
Gaura lindheimeri	–10°F/–23°C
Gazania	20°F/–7°C
Herbs (most; see pages 84–85)	varies
Limonium latifolium	–35°F/–37°C
Linum	–10°F/–23°C
Lobelia laxiflora	10°F/–12°C
Lychnis coronaria	–35°F/–37°C
Oenothera	varies
Perovskia	–20°F/–29°C
Phlox subulata	–30°F/–34°C
Romneya coulteri	–10°F/–23°C
Rudbeckia	–35°F/–37°C
Salvia	varies
Sedum	–35°F/–37°C
Senecio cineraria	10°F/–12°C
Solidago	–30°F/–34°C
Stachys lanata	–30°F/–34°C
Verbascum	–20°F/–29°C
Zauschneria	0°F/–18°C

Perennials for Shade

In that garden spot with good light but little or no direct sun, these perennials will thrive.

NAME OF PLANT	HARDY TO
Acanthus mollis	0°F/–18°C
Anemone hybrida	–20°F/–29°C
Aruncus dioicus	–35°F/–37°C
Astilbe	–25°F/–32°C
Bergenia	varies
Dicentra	–35°F/–37°C
Digitalis	varies
Doronicum	–30°F/–34°C
Epimedium	–30°F/–34°C
Helleborus	varies
Hosta	–35°F/–37°C
Ligularia	varies
Liriope	–10°F/–23°C
Mertensia	–35°F/–37°C
Polygonatum	–30°F/–34°C
Primula	varies
Pulmonaria	varies
Thalictrum	–20°F/–29°C
Tricyrtis	–20°F/–29°C
Trillium	varies
Viola odorata	–10°F/–23°C

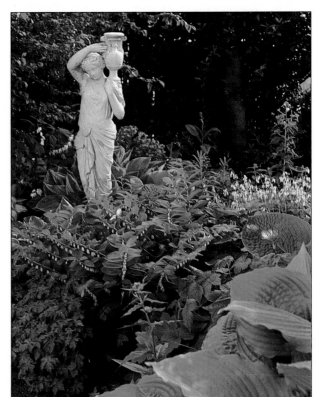

*Good-looking partners in shade are hostas, white-flowered bleeding heart (*Dicentra*), and graceful Solomon's seal (*Polygonatum*).*

Flower Color by Season

Although the year is divided neatly into seasons, flowering times don't sort out quite so precisely. For example, what flowers in mid- to late spring in a mild-winter region may be a highlight of the early summer display in a colder climate, where the growing seasons are more compressed. And a number of perennials begin to flower in one season and continue into the next. These lists, then, place plants in the seasons in which they make a significant display—that's the reason you will encounter some in more than one list.

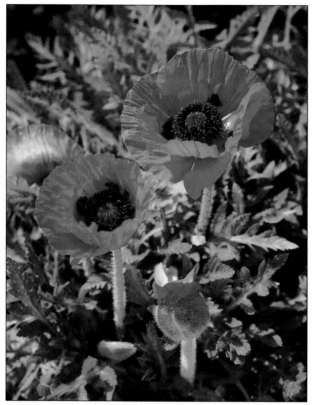

For an arresting late spring color accent, nothing surpasses Oriental poppies (Papaver orientale).

Spring

NAME	HARDY TO	YELLOW/ORANGE	RED/PINK	BLUE/PURPLE	WHITE	MULTICOLORED
Acanthus mollis	10°F/−12°C					■
Alchemilla mollis	−40°F/−40°C	■				
Alstroemeria	5°F/−15°C	■	■		■	■
Amsonia tabernaemontana	−35°F/−37°C			■		
Anchusa azurea	−30°F/−34°C			■		
Aquilegia	varies	■	■	■	■	■
Armeria maritima	−35°F/−37°C		■		■	
Aster frikartii	−20°F/−29°C			■		
Aurinia saxatilis	−35°F/−37°C	■				

NAME	HARDY TO	YELLOW/ORANGE	RED/PINK	BLUE/PURPLE	WHITE	MULTICOLORED
Baptisia australis	−35°F/−37°C			■		
Bergenia	varies		■		■	
Brunnera macrophylla	−35°F/−37°C			■		
Campanula	varies		■	■	■	
Centranthus ruber	−20°F/−29°C		■		■	
Chrysanthemum coccineum	−30°F/−34°C		■		■	
Convolvulus mauritanicus	10°F/−12°C			■		
Dianthus	−30°F/−34°C		■		■	■
Diascia	10°F/−12°C		■			
Dicentra	−35°F/−37°C		■		■	
Digitalis	varies	■	■			
Doronicum	−30°F/−34°C	■				
Epimedium	−30°F/−34°C	■	■		■	
Euphorbia (some)	varies	■	■			
Gaura lindheimeri	−10°F/−23°C				■	
Gazania	20°F/−7°C	■	■		■	■
Geranium	varies		■	■	■	
Geum	−10°F/−23°C	■	■			
Helleborus	varies		■		■	
Hemerocallis	varies	■	■	■		■
Heuchera	−30°F/−34°C		■		■	
Iberis sempervirens	−30°F/−34°C				■	
Iris	varies	■	■	■	■	■
Kniphofia	varies	■	■			■
Linum	−10°F/−23°C	■		■	■	
Lupinus	−30°F/−34°C	■	■	■	■	■
Mertensia	−35°F/−37°C			■		
Nepeta	−35°F/−37°C			■		
Paeonia	−50°F/−46°C		■		■	
Papaver orientale	−40°F/−40°C	■	■			■
Penstemon	varies		■	■	■	■
Perovskia	−20°F/−29°C			■		
Phlox subulata	−30°F/−34°C		■	■	■	
Polygonatum	−30°F/−34°C				■	
Primula	varies	■	■	■	■	■
Pulmonaria	varies		■	■	■	
Romneya coulteri	−10°F/−23°C				■	
Sisyrinchium	0°F/−18°C	■		■	■	
Stachys lanata	−30°F/−34°C		■			
Thalictrum	−20°F/−29°C	■		■	■	
Tradescantia andersoniana	−20°F/−29°C		■	■	■	
Trillium	varies				■	■
Trollius	−30°F/−34°C	■				
Verbascum	−20°F/−29°C	■	■	■	■	
Verbena	10°F/−12°C		■	■	■	
Veronica	−30°F/−34°C		■	■	■	
Viola odorata	−10°F/−23°C		■	■	■	

(Continued on next page)

Summer

NAME	HARDY TO	YELLOW/ORANGE	RED/PINK	BLUE/PURPLE	WHITE	MULTICOLORED
Acanthus mollis	10°F/–12°C				■	
Achillea	–30°F/–34°C	■	■		■	
Aconitum	–30°F/–34°C			■	■	
Agapanthus	varies			■	■	
Alchemilla mollis	–40°F/–40°C	■				
Alstroemeria	5°F/–15°C	■	■		■	■
Amsonia tabernaemontana	–35°F/–37°C			■		
Anchusa azurea	–30°F/–34°C			■		
Anthemis tinctoria	–30°F/–34°C	■				
Armeria maritima	–35°F/–37°C		■		■	
Artemisia lactiflora	–30°F/–34°C				■	
Aruncus dioicus	–35°F/–37°C				■	
Asclepias tuberosa	–35°F/–37°C	■				
Aster (some)	varies		■	■	■	
Astilbe	–25°F/–32°C		■			
Belamcanda chinensis	–10°F/–23°C	■				
Campanula	varies		■	■	■	
Catananche caerulea	–30°F/–34°C			■	■	
Centaurea	–30°F/–34°C	■	■	■		
Centranthus ruber	–20°F/–29°C		■			
Ceratostigma plumbaginoides	–10°F/–23°C			■		
Chrysanthemum (some)	varies	■	■		■	■
Cimicifuga	–35°F/–37°C				■	
Clematis	–35°F/–37°C			■	■	
Convolvulus mauritanicus	10°F/–12°C			■		
Coreopsis	–30°F/–34°C	■				
Cosmos atrosanguineus	15°F/–9°C		■			
Crambe cordifolia	–10°F/–23°C				■	
Delphinium	–35°F/–37°C		■	■	■	■
Dianthus	–30°F/–34°C		■		■	■
Diascia	10°F/–12°C		■			
Dicentra	–35°F/–37°C		■		■	
Dictamnus albus	–35°F/–37°C				■	
Digitalis	varies	■	■			
Echinacea	–35°F/–37°C		■		■	
Echinops	–35°F/–37°C			■		
Erigeron	varies		■	■	■	
Eryngium	varies			■	■	
Eupatorium	–30°F/–34°C		■	■		
Euphorbia corollata	–35°F/–37°C				■	
Filipendula	varies		■			
Gaillardia	–35°F/–37°C	■	■			
Gaura lindheimeri	–10°F/–23°C				■	
Gazania	20°F/–7°C	■	■		■	■
Geranium	varies		■	■	■	
Gerbera jamesonii	15°F/–9°C	■	■			
Geum	–10°F/–23°C	■	■			
Gypsophila paniculata	–35°F/–37°C		■		■	
Helenium	–35°F/–37°C	■	■			
Helianthus	varies	■				
Heliopsis helianthoides	–30°F/–34°C	■				
Hemerocallis	varies	■	■	■		■
Hibiscus moscheutos	–10°F/–23°C		■		■	

NAME	HARDY TO	YELLOW/ORANGE	RED/PINK	BLUE/PURPLE	WHITE	MULTICOLORED
Hosta	–35°F/–37°C			■	■	
Kniphofia	–10°F/–23°C	■	■		■	■
Liatris	–35°F/–37°C			■	■	
Ligularia	varies	■				
Limonium latifolium	–35°F/–37°C			■		
Linaria	–20°F/–29°C		■	■		
Linum	–10°F/–23°C	■		■		
Liriope	–10°F/–23°C			■	■	
Lobelia	varies	■	■	■		
Lupinus	–30°F/–34°C	■	■	■	■	■
Lychnis	varies	■	■		■	
Lythrum salicaria	–35°F/–37°C		■	■		
Macleaya cordata	–30°F/–34°C				■	
Malva	varies		■	■		
Monarda	–30°F/–34°C		■	■		
Nepeta	–35°F/–37°C			■		
Oenothera	varies	■	■			
Penstemon	varies		■	■	■	■
Perovskia	–20°F/–29°C			■		
Phlox	varies		■	■	■	
Physostegia virginiana	–35°F/–37°C		■		■	
Platycodon grandiflorus	–35°F/–37°C		■	■	■	
Potentilla	varies	■	■			
Primula (some)	varies	■	■	■	■	■
Romneya coulteri	–10°F/–23°C				■	
Rudbeckia	–35°F/–37°C	■				
Salvia	varies			■	■	
Scabiosa caucasica	–35°F/–37°C			■	■	
Sedum	–35°F/–37°C		■		■	
Senecio	10°F/–12°C	■				
Sisyrinchium striatum	0°F/–18°C	■				
Solidago	–30°F/–34°C	■				
Stachys	–30°F/–34°C		■	■		
Stokesia laevis	–20°F/–29°C		■	■	■	
Thalictrum	–20°F/–29°C	■		■	■	
Tradescantia andersoniana	–20°F/–29°C		■	■	■	
Tricyrtis	–20°F/–29°C		■	■	■	
Trollius	–30°F/–34°C	■				
Verbascum	–20°F/–29°C	■	■	■	■	
Verbena	10°F/–12°C		■	■	■	
Veronica	–30°F/–34°C		■	■	■	
Zauschneria	0°F/–18°C		■		■	

(Continued on page 28)

Classic cool cohorts—blue hybrid Delphinium *and white* Phlox paniculata—*bring to earth the summer skies of their season.*

Autumn

NAME	HARDY TO	YELLOW/ORANGE	RED/PINK	BLUE/PURPLE	WHITE	MULTICOLORED
Anemone hybrida	−20°F/−29°C		■		■	
Anthemis tinctoria	−30°F/−34°C	■				
Aster	varies		■	■	■	
Boltonia asteroides	−35°F/−37°C		■		■	
Catananche caerulea	−30°F/−34°C			■	■	
Ceratostigma plumbaginoides	−10°F/−23°C			■		
Chelone	−30°F/−34°C		■			
Chrysanthemum (several)	varies	■	■		■	■
Cimicifuga	−35°F/−37°C				■	
Eupatorium	−30°F/−34°C		■	■		
Helenium	−35°F/−37°C	■	■			
Helianthus	varies	■				
Heliopsis	−30°F/−34°C	■				
Hemerocallis (some)	varies	■	■	■		■
Iris (some)	varies	■	■	■	■	■
Physostegia virginiana	−35°F/−37°C		■		■	
Sedum	−35°F/−37°C		■		■	
Solidago	−30°F/−34°C	■				
Stokesia laevis	−20°F/−29°C		■	■	■	
Tricyrtis	−20°F/−29°C			■	■	
Zauschneria	0°F/−18°C		■		■	

Winter

NAME	HARDY TO	YELLOW/ORANGE	RED/PINK	BLUE/PURPLE	WHITE	MULTICOLORED
Bergenia	varies		■		■	
Helleborus	varies		■		■	
Primula	varies	■	■	■	■	■
Viola odorata	−10°F/−23°C		■	■	■	

*Lenten rose (*Helleborus orientalis*) reliably decorates winter landscapes with subtle but elegant blossoms.*

Perennials for Moist Soil

Where soil is always moist—too damp for the "good-drainage" perennials—these plants will prosper. All will also grow in well-watered garden beds.

NAME OF PLANT	HARDY TO
Aruncus dioicus	−35°F/−37°C
Astilbe	−25°F/−32°C
Eupatorium	−30°F/−34°C
Filipendula	varies
Hibiscus moscheutos	−10°F/−23°C
Hosta	−35°F/−37°C
Iris: Japanese, Louisiana, Siberian	varies
Ligularia	varies
Lobelia cardinalis, siphilitica	varies
Lythrum salicaria	−35°F/−37°C
Primula (some)	−20°F/−29°C
Tradescantia andersoniana	−20°F/−29°C
Trollius	−30°F/−34°C

Continually moist soil brings out the best performance in astilbe.

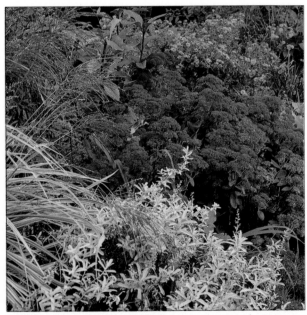

Autumn brings ripening seed heads on ornamental grasses, along with the peak flower display on Sedum spectabile and the New York and New England asters.

Perennials in Containers

Sometimes called "portable color," flowering plants grown in containers are just that and more. When you grow perennials in containers, you can place them in locations that otherwise rule out planting or are unfavorable to growth. You can soften a blank, unplantable expanse of patio, terrace, or deck; or sidestep the constraints of root-riddled soil by placing containers on top of it. Perennials too tender for your normal winter temperatures may grow outdoors in containers and then overwinter in a greenhouse.

A number of perennials are good subjects for container planting and offer you the obvious advantage of carryover from one year to the next. The best choices are those individuals that flower over a long period. Plant sizes and shapes are considerations, too. In most situations, the better-looking container perennials are the smaller, bushier sorts; the large-growing plants—especially those tall and narrow in shape—tend to look ungainly. The list on this page suggests 32 proven container subjects. You may choose to feature just one kind of perennial in a container, to plant an assortment of perennials together, or to fashion a "mixed bouquet" of perennials and annuals.

Preparation and care. Soil holds the key to success in any container planting: you need a medium that roots can penetrate easily, that drains well, but that also retains moisture. Ordinary garden soil, by itself, is too dense for the purpose, though it can be a component of a container mix (see below). If you have just a few containers to plant, you may prefer to buy packaged planting (potting) mix and use it directly from the bag. Compositions of these mixtures vary, but all are "soilless" preparations that ensure good drainage. If you'd rather concoct your own potting mix, a good basic formula combines equal parts good garden soil (not clay), sand (river or

builder's sand) or perlite, and peat moss or nitrogen-stabilized bark.

Container plants must be watered more frequently than plants in the ground, and in hot weather this can mean daily attention. This frequent and thorough watering flushes nutrients from the container soil, so you'll need to apply fertilizer for sustained good growth. The controlled-release types (see page 38) are particularly good for container plants: with each watering, a small amount of fertilizer is released. If you need to administer a quick tonic to a flagging plant, use a liquid fertilizer diluted according to package directions.

Good container choices. The following perennials comprise a broad-

spectrum assortment of colors as well as plant and flower styles.

Achillea	Iberis
Agapanthus	Limonium
Alstroemeria	Liriope
Aurinia	Nepeta
Campanula	Oenothera
Chrysanthemum	Pelargonium
Coreopsis	Penstemon
Dianthus	Potentilla
Diascia	Primula
Erigeron	Salvia
Felicia	Scabiosa
Gaillardia	Sedum
Gazania	Senecio
Geranium	Stokesia
Hemerocallis	Verbena
Hosta	Veronica

Tender ivy geranium (Pelargonium peltatum) is a favorite perennial for container culture in all climates.

A Perennials Primer

A GUIDE TO PLANTING & CARE

Success in the garden can be defined as attaining results that meet or exceed your expectations. The chance of meeting such expectations is greatly increased if you begin your efforts armed with basic knowledge. Therefore, in the following 12 pages you'll learn the fundamentals of perennial culture. First comes the advance work (pages 32–35). Next we address planting and routine care (pages 36–41). Finally, on pages 42 and 43 we show how to rejuvenate perennials as well as increase your supply of favorite plants.

Iris Siberian hybrid

A bountiful display of healthy perennials starts with well-prepared soil, robust plants, and careful planting.

Planning & Groundwork

Success begins with decision. Some gardeners first choose the plants they want to grow and then select suitable places to plant them. But far more gardeners will address location first (the "what will I plant here" question) and then look for appropriate plants. The main point is that any planting site must provide the proper conditions for the plants you choose to place there. Under "proper conditions" come not only sun-or-shade considerations but also soil quality, availability of water, and climatic factors such as heat, cold, humidity, and dryness. Nothing will thwart your plans so much as mismatching plants and growing conditions.

Purchase & Timing

Your nearest nursery or garden center is bound to offer a selection of perennials, generally "best sellers" such as daylilies, irises, oriental poppies, hostas, and columbines. Some retail nurseries go out of their way to stock a broad selection of perennials beyond the time-honored favorites. Most of these retail offerings will be growing in containers of some sort—from small plants in cell-packs to more mature specimens in 1- to 5-gallon "cans."

For the widest range of choice in perennials, though, you must familiarize yourself with the dazzling array presented in the catalogs of perennials specialists. Major suppliers are listed on page 112. These mail-order firms are generalists, offering a broad spectrum of perennials from the favorites to the obscure yet worthy. A few perennials—especially daylilies, irises, and hostas—are so popular that literally thousands of hybrids are available from mail-order nurseries that make those plants their specialties. Perennials received through the mail may be rooted in a bit of soil and encased in a plastic or paper wrap. More often, though, they are shipped essentially bare-root, the roots encased in damp peat moss or other moisture-retentive material within a plastic bag.

To decide when to plant your perennials, follow this general guideline. In spring, plant perennials that flower in summer or autumn; in early autumn, set out perennials that flower in spring. This rule is easy to comply with if you are purchasing from retail nurseries or replanting perennials from your own garden. Mail-order perennials specialists will attempt to send their plants at the best time for your region. However, plants for spring planting that go from cold-climate nurseries to mild-winter customers may of necessity arrive a bit later in spring than is ideal for the warmer region. You may need to give such plants a bit of extra water and shade during their first summer in your garden.

If you set out perennials from containers, it's actually possible to do so at any time of year. How-

Retail nurseries offer hands-on selection: you can evaluate a plant's appearance, even select a plant in flower.

ever, common sense suggests that you at least avoid planting during the heat of summer or, in cold-winter regions, just before the onset of severe winter weather.

Where to Plant

You'll find that a majority of the popular perennials need sunshine and "good, well-drained" soil. The sunshine requirement is straightforward: if a plant needs sun, don't plant it in shade—and vice versa. Each plant's description in the encyclopedia on pages 46 to 110 clearly states its preferred exposure. And you'll notice that climate may influence siting. A number of perennials need a "full-sun" location in areas where summer is cool to mild and "gray days" are the norm but must have partial shade in regions where hot temperatures and intense sun are expected. For these plants, the partial shade is most needed during afternoon hours of the most intense sunlight and temperature. Shade should be as light as possible: from high-branching trees, shadow cast by trees or structures at some distance, or sunlight dappled through latticework, open tree canopies, or shade cloth.

If your soil is "poor"—rocky, gravelly, quite sandy, or lacking in nutrients—and by choice or by circumstance you must take it "as is," you'll have to choose from a rather limited list of perennials that don't demand the best. If your soil—whether good or poor—is infiltrated with tree or shrub roots, you should remove the source of competition, choose another location, or consider growing plants in containers (see page 29). But if you want to revel in the full panoply of a perennial garden, you'll need to know your soil's character and what you can do to enhance its quality.

The Makeup of Soil

If you've ever put in a vegetable garden or planted a bed of annuals, you probably know what "good soil" should be. In brief, it's porous and drains well (so roots won't be waterlogged), yet retains moisture and nutrients well enough for sustained good growth. Most soils can profit from some amount of improvement or conditioning before plants are set out (see page 34). And because perennials will remain planted in the same soil for a period of years, a thorough soil preparation before planting will help ensure their good performance over time. But to learn how to enhance your soil, you first need to understand the composition of soil and discover what sort you have in your garden.

Soil is a complex assortment of mineral particles, decomposing organic matter, microorganisms, air, and water. The size and shape of a soil's mineral particles determine its characteristics—and often serve to name its type. Smallest are *clay* particles, each no more than 1/25,000 of an inch in diameter. At the other extreme are *sand* particles, from 1/12 to 1/250 of an inch in diameter. Between the two fall *silt* particles, at around 1/500 of an inch.

Although gardeners will refer to their "clay soil" or "sandy soil," most garden soils are actually a mixture of particle sizes. But it helps you evaluate your own soil structure if you understand the characteristics of the two extremes. You'll then be able to assess your soil's quality, its needs, and how to manage it.

Clay particles are not only tiny, they are flat or flakelike in shape. A soil composed primarily of clay particles is dense because the particles pack closely together—like a stack of playing cards. There is little pore space between particles, hence water both penetrates and drains through slowly. Clay soils therefore are described as "poorly drained" and, because of their density, "heavy." Their water-holding capacity is very high, due to the immense surface area of the combined particles. Dissolved nutrients are also retained well, making clay soils potentially fertile.

When completely wet, clay soil is sticky and impossible to dig; when dry, it cracks. To test for a claylike soil, pick up a handful of wet soil and shape it into a ball. When you let it go, it won't crumble; and if you squeeze it, some will ooze through your fingers in ribbons.

Sand particles are not only much, much larger than clay particles but also rounded rather than flattened. Hence, they fit together much more loosely (like marbles in a jar), leaving relatively large pore spaces between particles. Water therefore enters sandy soil easily but percolates through it rapidly, taking dissolved nutrients with it. Sandy soils are much less dense than clay soils so are often referred to as "light." These soils are "well drained" in the extreme: plants in sand need watering and fertilizing more frequently than plants growing in other soil types.

To the touch, sandy soil feels gritty; and when you squeeze a handful of wet, sandy soil, the soil ball falls apart when you release it from your grip or poke at it.

Loam is the layperson's one-word term for "good garden soil," having properties that fall between those of clay and sand. Loam drains fairly well—neither too slowly nor too quickly—and dissolved nutrients remain in it long enough to have some sustained effect. Pore spaces are sufficient to admit enough air for healthy root growth.

Part of loam's good character results from its mixture of particle types, from sand to clay. But loam also contains another—and essential—ingredient that makes it more than the sum of its mineral parts: organic matter.

Soil Improvement & Preparation

Organic matter—the decaying remains of once-living plants and animals—is essential to the quality and fertility of all soils. Peat moss and animal manures are two familiar examples. In densely compacted clay soils, the organic matter wedges itself

Special care in preparing your garden soil will be repaid in years of healthy perennial growth.

between particles and groups of particles; this opens the structure so that water, air, and roots can penetrate more easily. In sandy soils, the same organic matter will lodge in the relatively large pore spaces between particles; this slows the rate of water percolation through the soil, retaining moisture and dissolved nutrients longer. Decomposing organic matter also releases small amounts of nutrients, adding to the overall soil fertility. In its final stage of decomposition, organic matter becomes humus, a somewhat sticky substance that both absorbs water and binds together groups of particles. This simultaneously aids water retention and aeration.

In nature, the benefits to soil from organic matter mount up slowly: materials fall to the forest floor and are gradually incorporated into soil as they break down. In the garden, however, you can accelerate the pace of improvement by digging organic matter into your soil before you plant. Because organic materials are eventually consumed by decomposition, even the best soils can benefit from amendment. Dig in the amendments before planting (see "How to prepare soil," facing page) for major improvement. For established plantings, a mulch—as discussed on pages 36 and 38—will provide an ongoing supply of organic matter for surface decomposition.

Organic amendments. A wide assortment of materials is available for use in organic soil amendment. One of the best is homemade compost, but nurseries and garden centers sell packaged items such as peat moss, animal manures, nitrogen-stabilized wood products (such as shredded bark and sawdust), and commercially prepared composts.

If you are planning a large project, look for materials available in bulk, generally sold by the cubic yard. For sources, look in the Yellow Pages under "Soil Conditioners" and "Landscape Equipment and Supplies." Generally these materials are agricultural by-products (ground corncobs, mushroom compost, and apple pomace, for example), lumber by-products, and animal manures.

Most commercially packaged wood-product amendments are labeled "nitrogen-fortified" or "nitrogen-stabilized." Therefore, if you add raw wood shavings or an uncomposted wood product to your soil, you'll need to add nitrogen (see "How to prepare soil" on facing page).

Fertilizers and pH adjustments. The time when you dig in organic amendments to improve your soil is also your best opportunity to add fertilizers that contain phosphorus and potassium. As discussed on page 38 under "Nutrition and Fertilizers," these two

Acid & Alkaline Soils

You can't tell by looking whether your soil is acid or alkaline, but your plants certainly know the difference. It's not simply that some plants prefer, say, vinegar, while others like soda. The degree of acidity or alkalinity primarily affects the nutrient availability; extreme readings in either direction spell poor growth or failure, because basic nutrients are just not available under those conditions. Adding fertilizers to supply the unavailable nutrients is futile: they'll be "tied up" by the soil before plants can use them.

The acidity or alkalinity of a soil is measured in pH, short for potential hydrogen. A pH of 7 is neutral; readings greater than pH 7 are alkaline; and those less than pH 7 are acid. Except for the exceptional plants that require a definitely acid or alkaline soil, pH readings between 6.0 and 7.2 indicate a soil suitable for gardening. As a workable guide, you can assume that high-rainfall, humid-summer regions are likely to have acid soil, and low-rainfall, dry-summer regions to register as alkaline.

A soil test will reveal your soil's pH; some tests will also measure nutrient content (a guide to calculating your fertilizer needs) and the content of organic matter. Many nurseries and garden centers sell soil test kits that will give you an accurate enough reading to spot distinct pH problems. For more precise (and more complete) readings, have a test done professionally. Soil laboratories (look under that heading in the Yellow Pages) will test your soil for a fee; in some states, county or state agricultural extension services will also run tests.

Lime is traditionally used to raise the pH of an acid soil; sulfur is the most effective amendment to correct alkalinity. If a test of your soil indicates the need to raise or lower the pH, check with your county or state agricultural extension office for recommended materials and amounts.

essential elements are really effective only when mixed into the soil at root level.

If a soil test (see "Acid & Alkaline Soils," above) has shown a need to adjust pH by adding lime or sulfur, scatter the prescribed amount over the soil and dig or till it in deeply, along with the organic matter.

How to prepare soil. To give your perennials a hospitable root run, you need to prepare the soil well. Dig it to a depth of about 12 inches, breaking up clods and generally loosening the soil. For a small area, hand-dig with a spade or spading fork for the most thorough preparation. In large (and open) patches, you may prefer the convenience of a rotary tiller. Soil is ready for digging when it is moist but allows lumps to crumble easily. Never try to work a soil that is overwet and sticky: you'll just compact the soil and form bricklike clods.

After the initial digging and loosening, you're ready to add amendments to your soil. Use generous quantities of organic materials—25 to 50 percent of the total soil volume in the cultivated area—and mix them in deeply and thoroughly. A workable rule of thumb is to spread a 3- to 4-inch layer over the surface and dig it throughout the depth you initially prepared.

If the organic amendment you plan to use is a raw, uncomposted material such as sawdust or wood shavings, you'll also need to add nitrogen to the soil. The organisms that decompose organic matter need nitrogen to sustain themselves, but raw wood products (and all other high-cellulose materials) fail to offer enough. Without supplemental nitrogen, the organisms will claim any nitrogen already available in the soil and will have first claim on the nitrogen you add in fertilizers. Even a temporary depletion of that nutrient results in reduced plant growth.

Before you dig a nitrogen-poor amendment into your soil, scatter ammonium sulfate evenly over its surface, using 1 pound of ammonium sulfate for each 1-inch-deep layer of uncomposted organic matter spread over 100 square feet. Then dig it thoroughly into the soil. A year later, scatter half the initial amount of ammonium sulfate over the area; and in the third and fourth years, use a quarter as much.

If possible, prepare your soil at least several weeks before you intend to set out your perennials. This will give soil and amendments some time to "mellow" and to settle slightly. In cold-winter regions, you may want to prepare soil in autumn; by spring it will be in prime condition. Just before planting, you can do a final raking to smooth out the humps and hollows.

Planting & Care

Preparing soil and choosing suitable perennials are the prelude to the real pleasures of planting and growing your selections. The advice in these eight pages applies to plants once you have them—information on all aspects of their "care and feeding," from initial planting to division and rejuvenation.

Planting

All aspects of planting are covered in the illustrations on the facing page. If you have a choice (without unduly delaying planting) pick a cool day. The best situation is a cool, overcast, windless day that will be followed by more of the same for a week or so. Roots then have a chance to explore their new soil before sun, heat, and wind put high demands on them to supply water to their leaves. If you must plant during less favorable weather, shelter newly installed plants from sun and wind for 1 to 3 weeks or until they appear to put on new growth; pay close attention to watering during that period. If pelting rain besieges new plantings, you might shelter plants with boxes for the duration.

Watering

How much and how frequently to water depends on the needs of your particular perennials in conjunction with environmental influences. For best plant performance, the soil should be moistened deeply. Roots are reluctant to extend into dry soil, so you can see that deep watering will encourage deeper rooting. This, in turn, makes plants less vulnerable to moisture fluctuations close to the surface; if most of the roots are in moist soil, brief periods of surface drought are less likely to hamper growth.

How often you'll need to water depends on the type of soil you have—and on the weather. As pointed out on page 33, the more claylike a soil is, the more water it retains and the longer it holds it. And the higher a soil's organic content, the more retentive it will be. Weather influences watering frequency in several ways. Rainfall may take care of some moisture needs during the growing season, reducing your task to supplementation during dry periods. Weather also affects a plant's transpiration rate: the faster a plant transpires, the more water roots will need to replace that lost through leaves. Hot, windy periods accelerate transpiration; cool, still days, on the other hand, retard water uptake and soil evaporation. Length of daylight also affects transpiration by providing more or fewer hours of sunshine (and perhaps wind). Plant size is another factor: smaller plants and young ones not yet established will have small root systems, usually near the surface. These will need more attention than larger, settled-in individuals.

The water needs of most perennials are greatest from the onset of growth through the crescendo of flowering. Following bloom they build up nutrient reserves for the next year's performance before entering a period of dormancy, which ranges from total loss of leaves to a merely static state in which no growth occurs. Once dormant, many perennials need less water; some actually demand a dry period.

Mulches

A mulch is a layer of organic material on the soil surface. Mulches act as an insulating blanket to shield soil from the drying action of sun and wind; at the same time they keep the upper inches of soil at a fairly even and cooler temperature, which aids root growth. They also prevent the soil surface from becoming compacted by watering or eroded by runoff and maintain a texture that water will penetrate easily. Mulches aid in weed control by smothering seeds already present. Any weeds that do germinate can be pulled easily through the loose mulch texture. Because an organic mulch gradually decomposes, it adds to the organic content of the top several inches of soil.

A good mulch should neither compact so tightly that it inhibits water penetration nor be so light or loose that it is carried away by wind. Many of the organic materials you use as soil amendments (see page 34) will serve as mulches. Compost and well-rotted animal manures are traditional favorites that also add small amounts of nutrients to the soil. (Avoid peat moss, though: when it dries it repels water and is easily blown about.) Pine needles are excellent and add a bit of acid as they break down. Ground bark from pine, fir, and hemlock trees is attractive and long lasting, available in textures from a fine grind to 2-inch chunks. Coarse-textured straw may last no more than one growing season, but it is inexpensive

Planting Techniques

1. *Perennials are available in containers—from small pots up to multigallon cans—and bare-root. The bare-root plant may be sold with dry or moist material around its roots.*

2. *With container-grown plants, carefully remove plant from container and observe the root system. If roots are filling the container and crowding its edges, follow step 3.*

3. *When roots of container-grown perennials are congested, take a sharp knife and score root ball in about four places equidistant around root ball. Gently loosen the segments.*

4. *Place any new perennial in a bucket of water for 30 to 60 minutes to keep roots fresh. This restores moisture to bare-root plants and loosens root congestion of pot-bound plants.*

5. *Set root ball (or roots) atop firmed soil mound, spread roots over mound, and fill in soil. Be sure juncture of stem (or leaves) and roots is slightly above soil grade.*

6. *Gently water newly planted perennial to establish good contact between roots and soil. If plant settles below soil grade, insert fingers beneath roots to gently raise it.*

and available virtually everywhere. Local agriculture may generate waste that you can pick up in bulk: ground corncobs, apple and grape pomace, hulls of various nut crops, and tobacco stems are examples.

Several other materials can be used as mulch if you manage them properly. Those ubiquitous grass clippings, if applied in a thick layer, will mat down to become slimy, smelly, and impervious to water. But they work well if you spread a thin layer and let it dry before adding a new thin layer. Sawdust and small wood chips or shavings need nitrogen to decompose. If you buy packaged, nitrogen-fortified sawdust, you can use it right from the bag. But if you use raw sawdust, you'll have to add ½ pound of *actual nitrogen* for each 100 square feet of 1-inch-deep mulch. (To calculate actual nitrogen, multiply the percentage of nitrogen in the fertilizer—always stated on the package—by the number of pounds you apply.)

To mulch effectively, spread a 1- to 2-inch-deep layer between plants or clumps, bringing it close to their bases without covering them. In cold-winter climates, where soil is slow to warm in spring, a mulch spread early in the season will delay soil warming and slow plant development. Wait until growth is well under way before mulching.

Nutrition & Fertilizers

Soil contains the necessary nutrients for plant growth, but not always in sufficient quantities to produce desirable results. Gardeners, therefore, apply fertilizers to cover any known shortfalls (as revealed by a soil test) or to hedge their bets.

Plants need three nutrients in particular for good performance: nitrogen (N), phosphorus (P), and potassium (K)—collectively known as the "major nutrients." Most commercial fertilizers are "complete," meaning that they contain the three major nutrients, always in the amounts listed on the package label. For example, a fertilizer labeled 10-5-5 contains, by volume, 10 percent nitrogen, 5 percent phosphorus, and 5 percent potassium (always in its compound potash, K_2O_5). Of the three, nitrogen is the most likely to be lacking in soil because it is water soluble, hence easily leached from soil by rainfall and watering. It is also the one nutrient used most extensively by plants. Phosphorus and potassium (potash) are, for practical purposes, insoluble, so supplementary amounts must be dug into a plant's root zone to be effective.

Fertilizers are sold in different forms. Dry, granular fertilizers (the most widely used) dissolve when they contact water; you apply them to the soil, scratch or dig them in, and then water to initiate nutrient release. Those that contain nitrogen in the nitrate form will provide it quickly; if you want a more sustained nitrogen release, get a fertilizer in which nitrogen is in *ammonium* or organic form (including nitrogen derived from urea or IBDU). Controlled-release fertilizers are special dry, pelletlike fertilizers encapsulated in permeable membranes. With each watering, small amounts of nutrients leach from the pellets into the soil; depending on the product, nutrients will be released over 3 to 8 months. Liquid fertilizers are soluble fertilizer concentrates to be diluted with water and applied to soil or foliage; they offer a quick tonic to sluggish plants, but there's scant sustained benefit.

To get your perennials off to a good start, add a granular complete fertilizer to the soil before you

Pinching, Deadheading & Cutting Back

Pinch out tips of new growth to induce branching lower on the stem.

Deadhead spent flowers to offset seed production, divert energies to more flowers.

Cut back spent flowering stems, rangy plants, to promote repeat performance.

plant. This is your chance to put supplementary phosphorus and potash into the soil throughout your plants' potential root zones, so choose a formulation that emphasizes the two nutrients—such as 5-10-10 or 10-10-10.

In the years after the initial planting, time fertilizer applications by seasonal growth patterns. The period of greatest nutrient need is during the sustained stretch from first growth of the year through the flowering period; so from late winter to midspring, depending on the climate and when plants start growing, apply a granular complete fertilizer in amounts according to package directions. Choose a formulation that contains 5 to 10 percent of each of the major nutrients, such as 5-10-5 or 10-10-10. In retentive soils, this may suffice for the season; in porous, sandy soils, you may want to give a lighter application midway through the season.

Maintenance

Good grooming puts the finishing touch on a well-cared-for garden. Incorporate the following grooming tips into your yearly upkeep agenda.

Though perennials are not woody plants, some will need "pruning," (see art on facing page). Pinching off tips during the growing period will increase branching, making for a compact, dense plant. "Deadheading"—removing spent blooms—keeps plants looking neat and may prolong flowering. Cutting back all over may induce a second flowering period.

Some perennials lean, topple, or sprawl on their way to flowering; you'll want to provide discreet supports to keep them orderly. The illustrations on this page show a number of time-tested methods.

Seven Staking Methods

To support potentially top-heavy or floppy perennials, choose the sort of staking that suits the plant's growth habit.

Wire fencing cylinder   Bamboo stake and tie

Metal link stakes   Metal stem support

Metal hoop support   Stakes-and-string corset   Brush staking

Planting & Care

Yearly cleanup is a fact of perennial life, the small price we pay for year-after-year performance. At some point after flowering and before the onset of growth the following spring, perennials need to be tidied up. Though mainly cosmetic, such cleanup does deprive certain pests (notably slugs and snails) of refuge. For those perennials that remain green throughout the year, you need only remove old flowering stems and dead leaves. Many perennials, though, are partially to completely deciduous; plants may die down before the onset of winter, or last year's leaves may die back just before the spring growth push.

If you garden where winters are relatively mild, you'll probably want to remove dead leaves and stems in autumn or early winter so the garden will appear tidy. Where winter is colder, perhaps snowy, and winter garden appearance is not an issue, you can delay cleanup until late winter or early spring—being sure to complete the work before growth gets under way in earnest.

Winter Protection

The purpose of winter protection is not to keep plants warm but to keep them cold, without temperature fluctuations. Winter damage (assuming you've chosen plants that will take your normal winter low temperatures) generally occurs to established plants when they're subjected to alternating intervals of freezing and thawing over the course of a winter. This ruptures plant cells, which then decay. Newly planted perennials may be pushed out of the ground by freezing during the freeze-thaw episodes; the exposed roots then may be killed by low temperatures and desiccation. An insulating layer of organic material placed over perennials will moderate the effects of temperature changes.

Snow is a first-rate protective blanket, and some gardeners can count on it to do the job entirely. But wherever snow is erratic, or good snow cover is not assured, cautious gardeners cover their perennials with some sort of organic material that won't pack down into an airtight mass. Traditional choices are evergreen boughs, salt hay, marsh hay, and pine needles.

Once a hard frost has frozen the soil, lay your winter protection in place. Use two layers of evergreen boughs—the top layer at a right angle to the lower layer—or about 6 inches of hay or pine needles. Timing the removal of protection in spring depends on weather. You want to remove the covering before perennials put on much growth, but not so soon that emerging growth will be killed by a late freeze. The safest procedure is to remove protection gradually, in two or three stages.

Rejuvenation

Perennials vary greatly in the length of time they can grow vigorously in one spot without revitalization. Some—like peonies—can remain undisturbed indefinitely, but the majority need periodic rejuvenation to maintain top performance. Typical signs of decline include smaller flowers and shorter stalks; overall reduced vigor; overcrowded clumps, or clumps with bare centers and live plants around the edges; and, finally, few or no flowers.

The individual plant descriptions (pages 46–110) mention for each perennial the best way to rejuvenate or propagate, the time of year to do it, and approximately how long you can expect the plant to remain in place without restorative attention. The photographs of propagation methods on pages 42 and 43 show these procedures. Remember, when rejuvenating your perennials, that the soil will need revitalization, too; refer to the soil preparation advice on pages 34 and 35.

Pests & Diseases

Plant pests and diseases are facts of garden life, but their presence isn't always a call to combat. Take action only if the infestation is extensive in the garden or severe on particular plants. A few chewed leaves here, a few aphids there are no cause for alarm; in many cases, natural predators will do the eradication for you.

If you determine that a problem demands your intervention, choose the least toxic control for your first offensive. This runs the least risk of eliminating beneficial predators along with the problem. The suggested controls for each pest and disease shown on the facing page begin with the least toxic option—usually hand picking or spraying with a jet of water from the hose. Additional controls are listed in their order of increasing toxicity or else target a broader spectrum of pests.

Before you spray with an insecticide or fungicide, be sure plants are well watered a day in advance; a water-stressed plant may be damaged by chemical sprays. The best times of day to spray are early morning and late afternoon, when air is likely to be still. Avoid spraying during the heat of the day, when leaves may be burned by some sprays.

Common Pests & Their Controls

Aphids. Soft, oval, pinhead- to matchhead-size insects are green, pink, red, or black—and sometimes winged. They cluster in colonies on new growth; heavy infestations will stunt growth.

Controls: Hose them off; spray with insecticidal soap, diazinon, malathion, or Orthene.

Beetles. Various hard-shelled insects chew holes in foliage and flowers. Larval phase is grubs (worms) that live in soil.

Controls: Hand pick; use pheromone traps; counter with milky spore disease (for Japanese beetle grubs); spray with Sevin or malathion.

Caterpillars and worms. A diverse assortment of many-legged, crawling larvae of moths and butterflies, they chew leaves and petals.

Controls: Hand pick; spray with *Bacillus thuringiensis*, Sevin, or Orthene.

Slugs and snails. These mollusks are notoriously destructive leaf chewers. They feed at night and on cool, overcast days; on warm, sunny days they hide in dark, moist places.

Controls: Hand pick; scatter metaldehyde or mesurol bait.

Spider mites. Tiny specks of red, yellow, or green appear on leaf undersides in hot weather; silvery webs form in heavy infestations. Leaf surfaces appear stippled.

Controls: Hose them off on 3 consecutive days (or every other day for a week); spray with insecticidal soap or Orthene three times at 7- to 10-day intervals.

Whiteflies. Flying white pests about ½-inch long attach themselves to and feed on the undersides of leaves.

Controls: Hose them off (frequently); spray with insecticidal soap (insecticide sprays are likely to kill natural predators, resulting in an increased whitefly population).

Foliage Diseases & Their Remedies

Botrytis. Soft, tan to brown spots or blotches on flowers and leaves are followed by a covering of coarse, gray mold; fungus is widespread in cool, humid regions.

Controls: Spray with benomyl or mancozeb.

Powdery mildew. A white or gray, powdery or mealy coating on leaves and flower buds, fungus thrives in humid air (but establishes itself only on dry leaves).

Controls: Spray with triforine, benomyl, or folpet.

Rust. Yellow, orange, red, or brown pustules appear on leaf undersides; the powdery spores are spread by wind and water. This fungus is also encouraged by warm days, cool nights, and moisture.

Controls: Spray with folpet or chlorothalonil.

$\mathcal{P}$ropagation Methods

With most perennials, it's a simple matter to start new plants. You may want to do so in order to increase your collection; and you will automatically indulge in some form of propagation when you rejuvenate an established plant. The various methods are presented on these two pages.

You can increase—and rejuvenate—many perennials by digging up their clumps, separating them into single plants or smaller groups, and replanting them.

New plants of quite a number of perennials can be started from stem cuttings or layers; a smaller number can be increased from root cuttings. And of course many perennials may be raised from seed, though seeds taken from hybrid plants may give offspring that vary considerably from the parent.

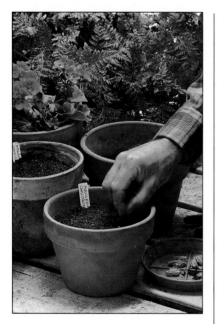

Stem Cuttings

In spring and summer, take 4- to 6-inch cuttings from ends of stems; cut just beneath a leaf (or pair of leaves), remove lowest leaves, and dip cut end in rooting hormone. In a pot of light potting mix (or sand, peat, or perlite mixture), insert cuttings a third to a half their length, then water. For cuttings that wilt easily (as does penstemon, shown here), enclose pot and cuttings in a plastic bag to retain humidity. Many cuttings will root in 2 to 4 weeks—test for rooting by tugging gently. When cuttings are rooted, transplant them to small individual pots; plant out when roots fill pots.

Seeds

Nearly fill a pot or flat with a light potting soil, apply water to firm it, and then scatter seeds over the surface. Cover seeds with a thin layer of potting soil and gently water to ensure contact of seeds with soil. Keep soil moist until seeds germinate. When seedlings show second or third set of true leaves, transplant to small individual pots to grow sufficiently for planting outdoors.

Root Cuttings

Some fleshy-rooted perennials—Oriental poppy, and sea holly, for example—can be increased from root cuttings. Cut pencil- to finger-thick root into 3- to 4-inch segments; make a square cut at top, a slanted cut at bottom to indicate planting end. Insert cuttings completely, top side upward, in a pot of light potting soil. If you have many cuttings, lay them on their sides in a flat of soil; then lightly cover with potting soil. Growth will sprout from the top end (or from several places on horizontal cuttings); when it is an inch or two high, transplant to individual pots to gain in size before planting in the ground.

Layering

Select a low, flexible stem producing healthy growth. Dig a shallow trench into which part of the stem can be buried, then make a shallow cut at a leaf node that will be covered by soil; apply rooting hormone to cut if you wish, then fill in trench. Stake end of stem upright; place stone on soil to keep stem buried. Roots will form where cut was made; staked stem will become new plant. When roots are well formed, cut stem from parent plant and move new plant to desired location.

Iris

Division

Divide perennials that make spreading clumps composed of individual plants (as does *Iris*, shown here) by breaking off or cutting strong parts from older, played out parts. Replant the strong, young plants.

Separate perennials that form tight clumps of individual plants (as does *Hemerocallis*, and *Hosta, Agapanthus*, and others) into single plants or small groups of several plants. Soak clump first to make division easier.

For perennials that form diffuse clumps of leafy stems (as does *Heuchera*, shown here, and *Aster, Chrysanthemum*, and others), pull clumps apart into individual segments. Replant only those that are well rooted.

Hemerocallis (Daylily)

Heuchera (Coral bells)

Perennials on Parade

*T*he world abounds in good garden perennials, and an eager gardening public fuels the demand for production. Each year new perennials make their debut in specialists' catalogs, while retail nurseries add to the diversity of their offerings. In the following 65 pages you'll meet the proven, time-tested favorites as well as a number of fine perennials that deserve wider appreciation. While many of these will be general retail-nursery fare, a few may only be available from perennials specialists; see page 112 for a list of mail-order suppliers.

Well-groomed border features summer display of diverse perennials. Prominent plants are yellow Anthemis tinctoria, *purple* Salvia superba, *lavender-blue* Campanula glomerata, *and steel gray* Eryngium amethystinum.

Achillea 'Moonshine'

Using Our Encyclopedia

*Our perennial descriptions are organized in an easy-reference format. Each entry begins with the plant's botanical name, followed by its common name and the plant family to which it belongs. Some entries contain references to a number of species and hybrids, so the entry appears under the name of the plant genus—*Iris, *for example. Other entries cover only one plant, so they appear listed by genus name followed by the species—*Acanthus mollis, *for example.*

Following the plant and family names, five points of information serve as a quick selection guide: the plant's hardiness to cold; its preferred sun or shade exposure; its moisture needs, expressed in watering frequency; its season of flowering; and its range of flower colors.

Finally, the text offers descriptive profiles of the plants: verbal portraits of flowers, foliage, and plant habits. Each plant's size is indicated, as are any especially strong or weak points. Under "Culture," you'll find information on soil preferences, any special pest or disease cautions, suggestions for periodic rejuvenation, and propagation tips. "Good companions" highlight several other perennials that would be attractive garden associates.

ACANTHUS MOLLIS
Acanthus, Bear's breech
Acanthaceae

Hardy to: 0°F/−18°C
Exposure: Partial shade, sun where cool
Water: Regular to moderate
Flowers in: Late spring, early summer
Colors: White, veined and tinted purple

A thriving acanthus clump looks like an elegant rhubarb, the long-stalked, 2-foot leaves distinctly glossy on the surface and deeply dissected into many lobes. The similarity ends, though, where the 3- to 4-foot flowering spikes emerge, rising up foxglove-fashion and bearing blossoms shaped like large, purple-hooded white snap-

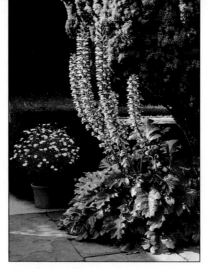

Acanthus mollis

dragons. Each flower nestles above a purplish green bract edged with spiny teeth. The variety 'Latifolius' has even larger leaves and reputedly tolerates a bit more cold.

Culture. In all but mild-summer regions, locate plants where they'll have a bit of shade during the heat of the day to prevent wilting. Growth is robust in good, well-drained soil with regular watering, but plants will survive neglect, poor soil, and some drought.

Although crowded clumps will prosper undisturbed for many years, you may dig and divide them from midautumn through late winter in mild-winter regions; where freezing temperatures are the norm, wait until early spring. A word of warning: root systems are wide spreading, and new plants will sprout from any cut portion of root. When dividing, be careful to remove all roots from the soil; during garden maintenance, avoid cultivating around the roots.

Good companions. *Anemone hybrida, Liriope, Polygonatum.*

ACHILLEA
Yarrow
Compositae

Hardy to: −30°F/−34°C
Exposure: Sun
Water: Moderate
Flowers in: Summer
Colors: Yellow, cream, white, pink, red

Given full sun and periodic division, yarrows can be counted on for good performance and little care. You may envision the "typical" yarrow as having flat clusters of yellow flowers atop tall stems, but a scan of catalogs or a trip to a nursery will reveal a range of choices, including shorter or spreading growth and flowers in cream, pink shades, and red. All have clumps of fairly narrow, elongated leaves, finely dissected and fernlike. Individual flowers are tiny daisies, tightly packed into flattened or slightly rounded heads at the ends of slender (but sturdy), slightly leafy stems. Yarrows are good cut flowers and can be dried for everlasting arrangements.

The tallest yarrows (3 to 5 feet when in flower) are selections and hybrids of *A. filipendulina,* fernleaf yarrow. Widely sold are the brilliant yellows *A. f.* 'Coronation Gold', 3 feet tall, and *A. f.* 'Gold Plate', which has 6-inch heads on stems up to 5 feet.

Most fine yarrows fall in the medium height range: 1½ to 3 feet in flower. At the short end of that range is popular *A.* 'Moonshine', its lemony yellow flowers appearing above silvered gray-green foliage. At the same height, *A. taygetea* produces bright sulfur yellow flowers above gray-green leaves. Common yarrow, *A. millefolium,* has green to gray-green leaves, stems to 3 feet, and white flowers in its basic form; 'Cerise Queen', 'Fire King', and 'Red Beauty' boast flowers in various shades of pinkish red. 'Lilac Beauty' and 'White Beauty' are described by their names. The Galaxy series of hybrids offers a range of colors including pink shades, crimson red, and buff yellow. Sneezeweed, *A. ptarmica,* is an invasive pest in tidy gardens, but double-flowered selec-

Achillea 'Moonshine'

tions 'The Pearl' and 'Angel's Breath' are less aggressive. Their small, narrow leaves and branched, open flower clusters on mounding plants give them an appearance akin to baby's breath (*Gypsophila*).

Three low-growing yarrows can serve as foreground specimens or small-scale ground covers. Greek yarrow, *A. ageratifolia*, forms spreading mats of silvery gray leaves and bears 1-inch clusters of white flowers on 10-inch stems. Silvery yarrow, *A. clavennae (A. argentea)* is of similar size and height but offers pale cream flowers. Woolly yarrow, *A. tomentosa*, is green leafed and yellow flowered; selection 'King George' has cream flowers, whereas those of 'Primrose Beauty' are pale yellow.

Culture. Yarrows grow best in good, well-drained soil but will perform decently in poorer soils with good drainage. Established clumps will tolerate quite a bit of drought, though best results come with moderate watering. After flowering, cut out spent stems. Divide crowded clumps in spring.

Good companions. *Chrysanthemum superbum*, ornamental grasses, *Kniphofia*, *Rudbeckia*, *Salvia*.

ACONITUM
Aconite, Monkshood
Ranunculaceae

Hardy to: –30°F/–34°C; needs some winter chill
Exposure: Sun, light shade
Water: Regular
Flowers in: Summer, fall
Colors: Blue, purple, white

Monkshood is noted for the vivid blue colors it offers the midsummer-to-fall garden palette. Most kinds produce upright spikes of closely set flowers; the taller kinds give the effect of delphiniums and can substitute for them in shaded locations. Individual blossoms feature a helmet- or hood-shaped petal-like sepal, from whence the common name. Attractive clumps of dark green, celerylike foliage grow from tuberous roots. Note: all plant parts are poisonous.

Among the named selections of *A. bicolor*, 3-foot-tall, blue-violet 'Bres-

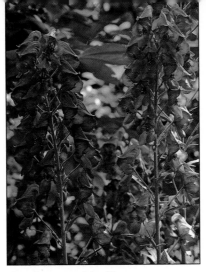

Aconitum carmichaelii

singham Blue' is the most widely sold; 4-foot 'Bicolor' features flowers that combine white and blue. The latest to flower (late summer into fall), *A. carmichaelii (A. fischeri)* lifts its spires of intense blue blossoms 2 to 4 feet high; its more robust variety 'Wilsonii' can reach 6 feet. In this species, the flower "hoods" are tall rather than broad, but in common monkshood, *A. napellus*, the proportions are reversed. In flower, those plants may grow 3 to 5 feet high; blue and violet are the usual colors, though specialists may offer white- and pink-flowered forms.

Culture. Several conditions are necessary for success with monkshoods. Plants need winter chill (temperatures below freezing) and moist, fertile soil. Cool-summer regions coax the best performance. Heat and dryness render them disappointing in much of the South, Southwest, and West. Though plants can remain undisturbed for many years, performance is improved if you dig and divide clumps every 3 to 5 years. Do this in autumn; in coldest regions, carefully mulch transplanted roots the first winter.

Good companions. *Anemone hybrida*, *Astilbe*, *Hosta*, *Thalictrum*.

AGAPANTHUS
Agapanthus, Lily-of-the-Nile
Amaryllidaceae

Hardy to: Varies
Exposure: Sun, partial shade
Water: Regular to moderate
Flowers in: Summer
Colors: Blue, white

Agapanthus

The *Agapanthus* species and hybrids offer refreshing patches of blues and white that are especially welcome during summer's warm days. Though plant sizes vary, and heights range from 1 to 5 feet, all form fountainlike clumps of strap-shaped leaves, from which rise bare stems terminating in spherical clusters of funnel-shaped flowers. Each bloom cluster resembles a burst of blue or white fireworks.

Among the large evergreen kinds, nurseries most frequently stock *A. orientalis*—though it may be offered as *A. africanus* or *A. umbellatus*. From clumps of broad leaves, stems rise 4 to 5 feet high bearing 8- to 12-inch clusters of up to 100 blue or white flowers. The blue shades range from pale to an intense medium hue; choose plants in flower if you are particular about color. The true *A. africanus* (which is sometimes sold as *A. umbellatus*) has narrower foliage (to about 1 inch wide) and flower stalks to 1½ feet high with smaller heads of up to 50 blue blossoms per stem.

The deciduous Headbourne Hybrids come in a range of blues and in white. Nurseries may offer specific named selections or seedling plants of unspecified color. Stems grow to about 2½ feet high with 6-inch flower heads above fairly narrow, rather upright foliage. Distinct among the deciduous types is *A. inapertus*, which has deep blue blossoms in drooping clusters atop 4- to 5-foot stems.

A number of more-or-less dwarf evergreen varieties are good bets for foreground plantings and even small-scale ground covers. 'Peter Pan' gives blue flowers on 1½-foot stems from foliage clumps no more than a foot high. White-flowered 'Peter Pan Albus' is a bit larger overall and is the same as (or very similar to) 'Rancho White'—which may be sold as 'Dwarf White' or simply 'Rancho'. For medium blue flowers on 2-foot stems, choose 'Queen Anne'.

Culture. These are unfussy plants. Though they prefer good, well-drained soil and regular watering, they will prosper in heavy or light soils, and established plants tolerate considerable drought. Plants flower most freely in full sun but will grow easily and flower fairly well in partial shade (though stems there may lean toward the source of light). Where summer is hot, locate plants where they'll be lightly shaded during the heat of the day. Clumps may remain in place for many years—fortunately, because the thick mass of fleshy roots makes division a daunting task! When needed, divide clumps in late winter or early spring. All will survive outdoors to about 10°F/–12°C; deciduous kinds are hardier, perhaps to –10°F/–23°C.

Good companions. Achillea, Chrysanthemum superbum, Coreopsis, Senecio.

ALCHEMILLA MOLLIS
Lady's mantle
Rosaceae

Hardy to: –40°F/–40°C; needs some winter chill
Exposure: Sun, partial shade
Water: Regular
Flowers in: Late spring, summer
Colors: Chartreuse

Alchemilla mollis

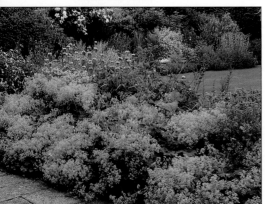

A healthy stand of lady's mantle immediately suggests the adjective "frothy." Each woody-based clump displays a mound of nearly circular, scallop-edged leaves over which spill multibranched flower stems with airy sprays of tiny yellow-green blossoms. The grayed green leaves may reach 4 to 6 inches across, each covered with minute soft hairs. Toothed leaf margins catch and hold dew, while raindrops collect in leaf centers—giving the entire planting a special sparkle. Each plant grows to about 18 inches high, spreading to about 2 feet across. Some catalogs list this plant as *A. vulgaris,* though botanists can argue that *A. vulgaris* is a separate species.

Culture. Good, well-drained but moist soil is the key to success with lady's mantle. Where summer is cool to mild, place plants in sun or light shade. In warm-summer regions, plant in partial shade. Performance usually is disappointing in regions where summer is long, hot, and dry. Plants never need dividing, but where conditions are agreeable, seedling plants will freely appear.

Good companions. Campanula, Digitalis, Geranium, Hosta, Polygonatum.

ALSTROEMERIA
Peruvian lily, Alstroemeria
Liliaceae

Hardy to: 0°F/–18°C
Exposure: Sun, partial shade
Water: Regular
Flowers in: Late spring, summer
Colors: Orange, red, pink, lilac, cream, yellow, white

For a good mental picture of the Peruvian lily, imagine a lilylike plant bearing flowers of a deciduous azalea. From tuberous roots, plants form spreading clumps of upright stems 1½ to 5 feet tall, according to the particular species or strain. Atop these stems come loose clusters of trumpet-shaped flowers in a wide range of colors—including bicolor combinations—often with contrasting dark spots or streaks. The Ligtu hybrids go dormant after flowering, the foliage withering and drying; newer hybrids retain their foliage as long as temperatures remain

Alstroemeria Ligtu hybrid

above freezing—throughout the year in frost-free regions.

Orange-flowered *A. aurantiaca* and its yellow ('Lutea') and red ('Splendens') varieties form wide-spreading clumps (some call it invasive) of 3-foot stems. It has been largely supplanted by hybrid strains of greater color range and more compact growth. The colorful but summer-dormant Ligtu hybrids have been bettered by more recently developed strains (such as the Cordu hybrids) that are virtually evergreen and grow 1 to 3 feet tall in compact clumps. Both named hybrids and unnamed seedlings are available.

Culture. Plant Peruvian lilies in well-drained soil into which you've incorporated organic amendments. The best combination is cool soil temperature and plenty of light. In cool-summer regions, set plants in full sun to partial shade; where summer is hot, be sure that afternoon shade will moderate the heat. Plant so that growing points are about 4 inches beneath the soil surface. A mulch or bed of ground cover annuals will keep soil cool. Although the plants develop thickened storage roots that will tide them over in periods of drought, best growth occurs when soil is regularly watered. You can leave plantings undisturbed indefinitely; but if you want to divide a clump for increase, do it in early spring or autumn while weather is cool.

Good companions. Achillea millefolium and 'Moonshine', Coreopsis, Felicia amelloides.

AMSONIA TABERNAEMONTANA
Blue star
Apocynaceae

Hardy to: –35°F/–37°C; needs some winter chill
Exposure: Sun, partial shade
Water: Regular to moderate
Flowers in: Late spring, summer
Colors: Blue

Bushy, 2- to 3-foot plants have the look of a shrubby willow, but at the end of each stem is a drumsticklike head of star-shaped, pale blue flowers. After flowering ends, the glossy foliage remains attractive through summer. It then puts on its own show when it changes to yellow in autumn. For the same appearance at half the height, choose *A. t. montana*.

Culture. Undemanding blue star needs only average, well-drained soil. Clumps increase steadily in size but seldom need division. You can dig and divide in early spring to increase your planting; but to get new plants, an easier way is to take cuttings during summer.

Good companions. Achillea, Belamcanda chinensis, Coreopsis, Oenothera.

ANCHUSA AZUREA
Italian bugloss
Boraginaceae

Hardy to: –30°F/–34°C
Exposure: Sun
Water: Regular to moderate
Flowers in: Late spring, summer
Colors: Blue

For eye-catching brilliant blue color, you need look no further than Italian bugloss, sometimes sold as *A. italica*. Clumps consist of hairy, lance-shaped leaves (the lowest to 1½ feet long) and flower stems that reach 4 to 5 feet high in some selections. The general effect is that of an oversized forget-me-not (*Myosotis*). On the debit side, the taller kinds can be rangy or floppy and may need staking; as perennials, they are not long lived; and they tend to produce great numbers of volunteer seedlings. If you can accept these liabilities, you'll be rewarded with quantities of unbeatable color.

Amsonia tabernaemontana

'Dropmore' is the classic deep blue selection, flowering in summer on 4- to 5-foot stems. For a bushier, sturdier, 3-foot plant with equally intense color, choose 'Loddon Royalist'. A chunky, 18-inch selection, 'Little John', brings deep blue color to the front of the border.

Culture. Care is simple: provide well-drained soil and enough water to keep plants moist but not saturated. Divide those of choice named selections every 2 to 3 years to keep them sturdy. Otherwise, replace declining plants with young volunteer seedlings.

Anchusa azurea 'Dropmore'

Anemone hybrida

Good companions. Achillea filipendulina, Artemisia, Coreopsis, Hemerocallis.

ANEMONE HYBRIDA
Japanese anemone
Ranunculaceae

Hardy to: –20°F/–29°C; not suited to Gulf Coast and Florida
Exposure: Sun, partial shade
Water: Regular
Flowers in: Late summer, autumn
Colors: Pink shades, white

Japanese anemones are valued for their ability to extend the flowering season after many summer flowers have nearly expended their energies. Dark green, deeply veined leaves consist of three maplelike leaflets at the end of long leafstalks; the low foliage clumps are good-looking from the moment they emerge in spring until frost enforces dormancy. Floating above this on wiry, somewhat leafy stems 3 to 5 feet tall are loose sprays of 2- to 3-inch single or semidouble blossoms that resemble wild roses. This charming appearance masks a tough constitution: established plantings will survive considerable abuse or neglect; healthy ones can spread to the point of invasiveness.

Nurseries may offer a number of named Japanese anemones, such as single white 'Honorine Jobert', single silver-pink 'September Charm', and double raspberry rose 'Prinz Heinrich'. Other related and similar species are sold as "Japanese anemones." These

Anthemis tinctoria

Aquilegia McKana Giant hybrid

Armeria maritima

include *A. hupehensis japonica*, with double, deep rose flowers; pale pink *A. tomentosa*; and white-flowered *A. vitifolia*, which has simple but deeply lobed leaves like those of grapes. The pink-flowered, rampantly spreading plant sold as *A. vitifolia* 'Robustissima' is more likely a form of *A. tomentosa*.

Culture. For top performance, give Japanese anemones good, well-drained but moist soil. They'll grow in light, filtered, or partial shade everywhere; cool- and mild-summer regions offer the option of full sun as well. Plantings never need dividing, though periodically you may need to curb their spread. To take plants for increase, do so in autumn (in mild climates) or in spring just after growth has started; transplants may establish slowly.

Good companions. *Aconitum, Bergenia, Hosta, Physostegia virginiana*.

ANTHEMIS TINCTORIA
Golden marguerite
Compositae

Hardy to: −30°F/−34°C; not suited to Gulf Coast and Florida
Exposure: Sun
Water: Moderate
Flowers in: Summer, early autumn
Colors: Yellow

Cheery yellow, 2-inch daisies come in great profusion on mounding, shrubby plants 2 to 3 feet high and wide. Foliage is pleasantly aromatic, each finely cut leaf light green on the surface, felted in gray on the underside. The typical flower is bright yellow; specialists may offer named selections such as 'Moonlight' (light yellow) and 'Beauty of Grallagh' (nearly orange).

Culture. Golden marguerite is virtually trouble free, needing only a sunny location, well-drained soil, and a moderate amount of water. After the first flush of bloom, cut back lightly; this encourages new flowering growth and offsets seed-setting and its consequent crop of volunteer seedlings. Plants are short lived. You can rejuvenate them by dividing clumps in autumn (in mild climates) or early spring. Even simpler is starting new plants from stem cuttings in spring.

Good companions. *Catananche caerulea, Heliopsis helianthoides, Sedum 'Autumn Joy'*.

AQUILEGIA
Columbine
Ranunculaceae

Hardy to: −35°F/−37°C (species); −20°F/−29°C (hybrids); most not suited to Gulf Coast and Florida
Exposure: Sun, partial shade
Water: Regular
Flowers in: Spring, early summer
Colors: Blue, purple, red, pink, yellow, cream, white; bicolor

Columbines merit all adjectives that suggest grace and charm. The entire plant is delicate and graceful—from the gray-green, maidenhair fernlike foliage to the slender, branching stems that carry flowers seemingly poised for flight. Each blossom consists of five inner petals that form a loose cup, five long and pointed petals that form a sort of saucer for the cup, and (in most kinds) five slender spurs that project backward from the saucer petals. Short-spurred and spurless sorts are available, as well as some with double flowers.

Among tall-growing, long-spurred hybrid strains, the McKana Giants and Spring Song feature a broad range of mixed colors; separate-color strains, such as Crimson Star and Snow Queen, are also available. Shorter-growing strains include Music (1½ feet) and foot-tall Biedermeier and Dragonfly.

Rocky Mountain columbine, *A. caerulea*, is the classic long-spurred, blue-and-white flower on 2- to 3-foot stems. Four-foot golden columbine, *A. chrysantha*, features long-spurred, clear yellow blossoms; its selection 'Silver Queen' is pure white. Western columbine, *A. formosa*, combines yellow and red in flowers on stems to 3 feet; its 2-foot-tall eastern counterpart, *A. canadensis*, also is yellow and red, though pink- and yellow-flowered forms exist. The longest spurs—slender and drooping—are found on yellow-flowered *A. longissima*, which also reaches 3 feet. The similar *A. hinkleyana* succeeds in Gulf Coast gardens.

Among the shorter species are European columbine, *A. vulgaris*, a 2-foot, short-spurred type in blue to purple shades and white. Japanese *A. flabellata* forms a compact, foot-high mound bearing creamy white and lilac-blue short-spurred blossoms. The European *A. alpina* produces short-spurred flowers of blue (or blue and white) on stems to about 1½ feet. Hensol Harebell is a hybrid strain derived from *A. alpina* and *A. vulgaris*; typical flowers are deep blue (though purple, red, pink shades, and white are possible), with curved spurs on stems to 3 feet high.

Culture. Most species hail from high-altitude slopes and meadows in North America, Europe, and Asia. That native habitat gives them a preference for average but well-drained soil and regular watering. Where summer is cool or mild, give plants full sun; in warm-summer climates, plant in filtered sunlight or partial shade. Most columbines are not long-lived perennials: an individual plant lasts about 3 to 4 years. You can dig and divide old clumps in early spring, but usually you'll have better results setting out new plants. If you allow spent flowers to form seed capsules, you'll ensure a crop of volunteer seedlings that will guarantee replacements. If you're growing hybrid strains, the seedlings won't necessarily duplicate the parent plants; seedlings from species (if grown isolated from other columbines) should closely resemble the originals.

Good companions. *Campanula, Iris* (Siberian), *Polygonatum, Primula, Sisyrinchium striatum.*

ARMERIA MARITIMA
Thrift, Sea pink
Plumbaginaceae

Hardy to: −35°F/−37°C
Exposure: Sun
Water: Moderate
Flowers in: Spring; year-round in mild climates
Colors: Pink shades, red, white

From low tufts of narrow, chivelike leaves comes a profusion of bright little flowers clustered in tight pompons at the ends of 6- to 10-inch stems. Though pink is the predominant color, its hues range from pale tints to darkest raspberry. If you care about the particular

shade of pink, buy nursery plants in flower. Specialty nurseries offer named selections such as rosy red 'Dusseldorf Pride' and, for contrast, white 'Alba'. These undemanding plants find their garden niche at border edges, along pathways, among rocks, even as a small-scale ground cover. For a plant of the same appearance but larger—clumps to 10 inches, flower stems to 15 inches—look for *A. pseudarmeria*, which is hardy to −10°F/−23°C.

Culture. Well-drained soil is the key to success with the thrifts. Fertility isn't an issue: they'll thrive in nearly pure sand. With good drainage they will take regular watering, but the safest rule is to water moderately in dry climates, sparingly in moister regions. Clumps spread slowly, need dividing and replanting only when they start to show bare centers. Do this in spring, summer, or autumn in regions where winter lows stay above 20°F/−7°C, or in spring in colder regions.

Good companions. *Iberis sempervirens, Lychnis coronaria, Stachys lanata.*

ARTEMISIA
Wormwood, Artemisia
Compositae

Hardy to: Varies
Exposure: Sun
Water: Moderate
Flowers in: Summer
Colors: Cream-white

With one exception (*A. lactiflora*), you plant the artemisias for beauty of foliage. Their leaves run the gamut of grays, from virtually white through silver to gray-green. Typical foliage is finely divided or dissected, adding a lacelike delicacy to the shimmering lightness. Flowers are insignificant: tiny daisies in loose clusters. Plant choices run from foreground tuffets to shrublike mounds as high as 4 feet.

Southernwood (*A. abrotanum*), hardy to −10°F/−23°C, features finely cut gray-green foliage with a pungent, lemony scent on a spreading, shrubby plant to 3 feet high. Flowers are yellowish white. Common wormwood or absinthe, *A. absinthium*--hardy to −30°F/−34°C—carries its silky, silvery gray foliage on an upright, branching,

Artemisia absinthium

shrubby plant 2 to 4 feet tall. Leaves have a somewhat bitter aroma; flowers are dull yellow. 'Lambrook Silver' is a superior selection that grows 2 to 2½ feet tall. For mild climates (to 10°F/ −12°C), *A. arborescens* offers similar silky, silvery foliage on a shrubby 4-foot plant. A presumed hybrid between this species and *A. absinthium*, *A.* 'Powis Castle' has leaves that are more finely cut on a plant to 3 feet high—useful wherever winter cold gets no lower than about 0°F/−18°C.

Two shrubby species are consistently short growing, useful for gray foreground accents and small ground covers (except in Gulf Coast and Florida gardens). Beach wormwood, *A. stellerana* (one of several distinct plants called "dusty miller"), is hardy to −30°F/−34°C. Broadly lobed, white, hairy leaves cover a spreading plant 1 to 1½ feet high; erect clusters of light yellow flowers rise to about 2 feet. For a dense mound of shimmering silvery gray, look for *A. schmidtiana*, called angel's hair for its leaves' threadlike lobes. Dome-shaped plants reach 1½ to 2 feet high and 1 foot wide. Most widely sold is its foot-tall form, the aptly named 'Silver Mound'. Despite a fragile appearance, *A. schmidtiana* is hardy to −30°F/−34°C.

Two tall-growing wormwoods have stems that die down with the onset of frost. *A. ludoviciana* sends up slender, branching stems of silvery white leaves; lowest leaves are lobed, but those higher on stems are narrow and unlobed. By summertime, when the airy sprays of white flowers are produced, a clump has the densely interlaced effect of tumbleweed. Most common is 'Silver King' (*A. l. albula*), which can reach 3½ feet high; shorter, to about 2 feet, is 'Silver Queen'. Both spread rapidly (especially in light soils) and should be considered invasive unless planted where they can colonize freely or are confined with a root barrier about 8 inches deep.

The second species with annual stems—and the only wormwood to claim beauty of flowers—is *A. lactiflora*, the white mugwort. Elegantly plumed spikes of small cream-white blossoms appear in late summer atop upright stems clad in lobed, dark green leaves. Overall height in flower is 4 to 6 feet. For best performance, give it good soil and regular watering.

Culture. None of the wormwoods, except *A. lactiflora*, is particular about soil fertility, but all need a well-drained soil; as a group they are especially sensitive to wet soil in winter. In the two species whose stems die down to the soil each year, cut spent stems to the ground in autumn or earliest spring. Cut back plants of shrubby kinds fairly heavily just before the growing season in late winter or early spring to keep growth from becoming rangy. Those wormwoods that spread into clumps can be divided for increase; do this in early spring in cold-winter regions, in early spring or autumn where winters are mild. You can start new plants of all wormwoods from tip cuttings in spring or summer.

Good companions. *Asclepias tuberosa, Baptisia australis, Echinacea purpurea, Sedum, Sisyrinchium striatum.*

Aruncus dioicus

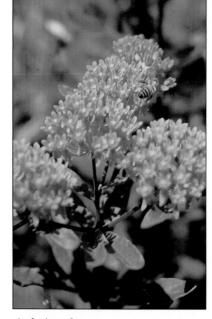

Asclepias tuberosa

ARUNCUS DIOICUS
Goatsbeard
Rosaceae

Hardy to: −35°F/−37°C
Exposure: Sun, shade
Water: Regular
Flowers in: Summer
Colors: White

With its mound of foliage reaching 4 feet high, goatsbeard makes a very shrublike perennial. Rising above the profusion of broad, fernlike foliage, large feathery plumes of tiny cream-white blossoms extend its height to around 6 feet. To visualize it, imagine a giant-size, rather shaggy false spiraea (*Astilbe*). If you'd prefer a half-size version, look for *A. d.* 'Kneiffii'; the same feathery flower plumes top out at 3 feet, above leafy clumps of nearly threadlike leaflets.

Culture. Moist soil—even the spongy moistness of pondside soil—coaxes the best performance, though regular garden watering is sufficient in retentive loam or clay soils. Where summer is cool or mild, you can grow goatsbeard in sun as well as light shade. In hot-summer regions, though, give plants shade throughout the day. Goatsbeard is rarely at its best in regions where summer is hot and dry. In time, plants form hefty clumps but do not need to be divided. You can divide clumps for increase, though, in early spring.

Good companions. *Bergenia, Hosta, Iris* (Siberian), *Ligularia.*

ASCLEPIAS TUBEROSA
Butterfly weed
Asclepiadaceae

Hardy to: −35°F/−37°C
Exposure: Sun
Water: Moderate to little
Flowers in: Summer
Colors: Orange, yellow, red

When its brilliant orange flowers are attracting butterflies, this "weed" seems the very essence of summer. Each spring, many stems grow from a dormant root, reaching 2 to 3 feet high by the time bloom begins. Individual flowers are small and starlike but are grouped together in broad, flattened clusters atop each stem. Lance-shaped leaves to 4 inches long grow along the stems from ground level to the base of each bloom cluster. Though orange is the most usual color, butterfly weed also occurs in other colors. The hybrid seed strain 'Gay Butterflies' contains yellow, orange, red, and pink flowers in addition.

Culture. Plant butterfly weed for permanence: its clumps never need dividing. Choose a deep, well-drained soil; a moisture-retentive soil can lead to root rot. Plants are drought tolerant but best performance comes from moderate watering. The simplest way to increase a planting is to raise new plants from seed. But you can increase a plant by taking root cuttings or by digging deeply (to get virtually all roots) and carefully dividing the clump.

Good companions. *Achillea, Artemisia, Nepeta, Oenothera.*

Aster novi-belgii

ASTER
Aster, Michaelmas daisy
Compositae

Hardy to: Varies; not suited to Gulf Coast and Florida
Exposure: Sun, partial shade
Water: Regular
Flowers in: Spring, summer, autumn
Colors: Blue, violet, crimson, pink, white

Daisy flowers have a near-universal appeal, and the many asters are perfect embodiments of that special wildflower charm. Flowers all follow the same pattern: a central disk (usually yellow) surrounded by one or more rows of ray petals (each petal is actually a separate flower). Leaves are generally narrow and lance shaped. Plants range, however, from low clumpers and spreaders to stalwart, upright 6-footers. The bulk of them (notably the New England and New York asters—the Michaelmas daisies) flower in summer, continuing into autumn. But where the growing season is long, *A. frikartii* will begin in spring. While most of their other daisy kin dot the summer garden scene with shades of yellow, the asters balance out the color scheme with cool and soft colors.

Old favorites, the Michaelmas daisies were the familiar perennial asters to generations of gardeners. Two species—both selections and hybrids—fall under this general name. Both are hardy to –30°F/–34°C. The New England aster, *A. novae-angliae*, is violet-blue in its basic form, rising to 6 feet or more with great, airy flower sprays, its stems clothed in grayish green, hairy leaves. Several pink and nearly red selections are sold; 4-foot 'Harrington's Pink' is especially long flowering and increases less rampantly than most. The similar New York aster, *A. novi-belgii,* is also primarily violet-blue but grows only 3 to 4 feet high and bears smooth foliage. 'Climax' is an especially robust 6-foot variety with telling medium blue blossoms. Many other selections are available in the 3- to 4-foot height range and in an assortment of colors.

Both New England and New York asters have been bred with other aster species to produce plants that are more compact and more resistant to mildew. The result is a number of "dwarfs," including the Oregon-Pacific strain, in the 1- to 2-foot height range. These lack the airy grace of the New England and New York kinds, but they do provide good clumps of color in a wide color range over a long flowering period.

Aster frikartii is a hybrid of *A. amellus* and *A. thompsonii,* a cross that has produced several excellent selections with especially long flowering seasons. The 'Mönch', 'Wonder of Stafa', and 'Jungfrau' are compact, bushy plants in the 3-foot range, bearing clear lavender-blue blossoms. Plants are hardy to –20°F/–29°C and increase at a moderate rate. The parent *A. amellus,* Italian aster, is quite drought tolerant, forming 2-foot bushy clumps of rough, hairy leaves that bear violet blossoms in summer and early fall.

Perennials specialists may offer other species and their hybrids. A. *laterifolius* 'Horizontalis' is a stiff, widely branching plant to about 2 feet. In late summer and autumn it is a mass of small, pink-centered white flowers against a backdrop of narrow, coppery purple leaves. Similar A. *ericoides* has stiff green leaves on a branching shrubby plant to about 3 feet. Small white daisies appear from late summer into autumn; blue-flowered selections are sometimes available. Both species are hardy to –40°F/–40°C. Differing from these in several respects is A. *divaricatus,* also hardy to –40°F/–40°C. Its wiry stems are dark purple, forming loose, sprawling clumps to 2 feet high. It bears heart-shaped leaves; the tiny, white, starlike flowers appear in early autumn. Unlike other asters, it prefers partial shade.

Culture. Care is simple: give asters a place in the sun, reasonably good soil, and regular watering. Well-drained soil is best, as wet soil during winter dormancy can lead to rot. Some kinds (notably the Michaelmas daisies) are particularly susceptible to powdery mildew, a problem minimized by keeping plants well watered. A number of the taller asters tend to flop over by the time blossoming starts: stake them to keep stems erect or pinch stems during the growing period to encourage compactness (though this slightly delays onset of flowering). Especially vigorous kinds (again, notably the Michael-

Astilbe arendsii 'Deutschland'

mas daisies) need to be dug and divided at least every other year. Do this in spring, saving and replanting only the strong plants from a clump's perimeter. Divide and replant any aster when vigor diminishes and the clump's center becomes bare and woody.

Good companions. *Anthemis tinctoria, Boltonia asteroides, Cimicifuga, Hemerocallis, Sedum* 'Autumn Joy', *Solidago.*

ASTILBE
Astilbe, False spiraea, Meadow sweet
Saxifragaceae

Hardy to: –25°F/–32°C; needs some winter chill; not suited to Gulf Coast and Florida
Exposure: Sun, partial shade
Water: Regular
Flowers in: Summer
Colors: Red, magenta, pink, white

In regions whose summers are humid but not extremely hot, astilbes are indispensible in the summer perennial display. Individual flowers are tiny— but carried aloft in great feathery plumes, their effect en masse is spectacular. Most astilbes sold in nurseries and by mail-order specialists are named hybrids of mixed ancestry. Consequently, some have floral plumes that are entirely upright whereas others are more horizontally branched and arching or drooping at the tips. All, though, boast fairly low clumps of handsome fernlike leaves with serrate-edged leaflets. Leafy

Aurinia saxatilis

Belamcanda chinensis

flower stalks reach 1½ to about 5 feet in height, depending on the named selection or species.

A large group of hybrids, *A. arendsii*, is well represented by named selections in nurseries and catalogs. Named selections include all possible astilbe colors on plants that reach 2 to 4 feet in flower. Many of the red-flowered selections have attractive bronzy foliage. Late-flowering *A. taquetii* 'Superba' carries upright plumes to 4 feet high in an eye-catching magenta over somewhat bronzed foliage; it tolerates heat and dryness better than the *A. arendsii* group.

Front-of-the-border positions can be filled by various low-growing kinds. *Astilbe simplicifolia* 'Sprite' features widely branching plumes of pure pink over bronzed foliage, its overall height just 12 inches. *A. chinensis* will actually thrive with only moderate watering. Its selection 'Finale' bears upright, light pink plumes to 18 inches; rosy lilac *A. c.* 'Pumila' has bolt upright flower spikes that rise to 12 inches from a rapidly increasing plant that forms dense, spreading foliage mats.

Culture. Moist but not saturated soil is the key to successful culture. Give astilbes good soil enriched with plenty of organic matter, and then see that they receive moisture regularly. They will thrive—and look superb—at pool or pond margins as long as the soil isn't waterlogged. All grow in full sun (given plenty of moisture) and partial shade; the latter is best if you expect some hot summer weather. Plant in autumn or spring. When bloom production noticeably declines—usually

in 4 to 5 years—dig and divide clumps in early spring.

Good companions. *Bergenia, Chelone, Clematis, Delphinium, Hosta, Iris* (Japanese, Siberian), *Trollius.*

AURINIA SAXATILIS
Basket-of-gold
Cruciferae

Hardy to: –35°F/–37°C; not suited to Gulf Coast and Florida
Exposure: Sun
Water: Moderate
Flowers in: Spring, early summer
Colors: Yellow

These spreading mounds of vivid yellow have been familiar to generations of gardeners as *Alyssum saxatile*. In foreground plantings and in large-scale rock garden schemes, these undemanding mustard relatives are invaluable for brightening the garden during the first major wave of perennial blossoming.

Plants are low-mounding (to about 12 inches) and wide-spreading, with gray to gray-green, narrow, lance-shaped leaves 2 to 5 inches long. Individual flowers are small but are grouped in rounded, 1-inch clusters that cover a plant with brilliant yellow. Several selected forms vary the basic scheme. 'Plena' ('Flore Pleno') has double flowers, while 'Citrina' (also sold as 'Lutea') and 'Silver Queen' tone down the color to pale yellow and butter yellow, respectively. 'Compacta' forms a smaller, tighter-growing clump. Perennials and rock garden specialists may also offer selections with variegated foliage.

Culture. Give plants a sunny location in well-drained soil. Poor soils and

Baptisia australis

those of only moderate fertility suit basket-of-gold perfectly; in good, vegetable garden-type soil, growth is rank and untidy. After flowers finish, shear off spent flower heads; this diverts energy from seed production and forestalls numerous volunteer seedlings. Start new plants from cuttings in spring or summer.

Good companions. *Centranthus ruber, Iberis sempervirens, Iris* (bearded), *Papaver orientale, Phlox subulata.*

BAPTISIA AUSTRALIS
False indigo
Leguminosae

Hardy to: –35°F/–37°C
Exposure: Sun
Water: Moderate
Flowers in: Late spring, early summer
Colors: Blue

False indigo immediately suggests an informal lupine. The shrublike plants, 3 to 4 feet high and wide, are clothed in 3-inch bluish green leaflets grouped clover-fashion, three to each leaf. From this bushy mound come loose spikes of bright to medium blue flowers with the typical wing-and-keel formation of the pea family. If you don't shear off spent flower spikes, attractive dark, elongated seed capsules will follow.

Culture. This is one of those accommodating "plant-and-forget-it" perennials. False indigo needs only a moderately fertile, nonalkaline soil (like many legumes, its roots "fix" nitrogen). Its deep taproot renders it drought tolerant; and once planted, it never needs division. If you need more plants, start them from seed or transplant young volunteer seedlings.

Good companions. *Artemisia, Coreopsis, Oenothera, Sedum, Senecio.*

BELAMCANDA CHINENSIS
Blackberry lily
Iridaceae

Hardy to: −10°F/−23°C
Exposure: Sun, partial shade
Water: Regular to moderate
Flowers in: Summer
Colors: Orange; white, yellow, red, pink, purple *(Pardancanda)*

This old-fashioned favorite provides good foliage contrast to the general run of perennials from spring into autumn. Like its relative *Iris*, it forms clumps of sword-shaped leaves that grow in fanlike sheaves from slowly creeping rhizomes. In summer, numerous 2-inch flowers appear like butterflies alighted on branches of the slender, 3-foot zigzag stems. The six flower segments are a yellow-shaded orange boldly spotted a darker reddish brown; each flower lasts only a day, but new blossoms keep opening for several weeks. As flowers fade, rounded seed capsules develop that, when mature, split open to reveal seed clusters resembling blackberries. You can cut the seed-bearing stems for effective dried arrangements.

The blackberry lily has been bred with the vesper iris (*Pardanthopsis dichotoma*, formerly *Iris dichotoma*) to create the race of bigeneric hybrids *Pardancanda norrisii*, sometimes cataloged as candy lily. The general effect is the same as blackberry lily, but the range of colors is greatly expanded.

Culture. Blackberry lily and its relatives give their best performance in

Bergenia cordifolia

good, well-drained soil with regular watering but will grow reasonably well in average soil with moderate water. In hot-summer regions, give plants a bit of shade. You can increase plantings by dividing clumps; volunteer seedlings of blackberry lily usually produce a supply of surplus plants.

Good companions. *Coreopsis, Cosmos atrosanguineus, Nepeta faassenii, Sedum.*

BERGENIA
Bergenia
Saxifragaceae

Hardy to: Varies; not suited to Gulf Coast and Florida
Exposure: Partial shade, shade
Water: Regular to moderate
Flowers in: Winter, early spring
Colors: Red, purple, pink, white

If bergenias never flowered, they would be worth planting for their handsome foliage alone. Individual leaves are oval to nearly round, leathery, deeply veined, and up to a foot long on equally long leafstalks. Cold weather often brings out bronzed purple tints. Each plant is an informal rosette; thick, creeping rootstocks form gradually expanding clumps. In established plantings, foliage may reach 1½ feet high. Bell-shaped flowers in dense spikes appear among or above the leaves, depending on the species.

Winter-blooming bergenia, *B. crassifolia*, has glossy, rubbery leaves with wavy margins; rising on stems above the foliage, lilac, pink, or rosy purple flowers appear anywhere from midwinter to early spring, depending on climate. Plants are hardy to −30°F/−34°C. The similar heartleaf bergenia, *B. cordifolia*, is equally cold tolerant; its dark pink blossoms appear in midspring, flowering among the glossy, wavy-edged leaves. With its leaf surfaces covered in short, silky hairs, *B. ciliata* is easily distinguished from the latter species. Its new growth is bronze colored; spring flowers are light pink or white. Plants are hardy to −10°F/−23°C, but foliage may be damaged in hard frosts and will die down completely in the coldest areas.

Named hybrids are sold by specialty nurseries. Flower colors run the

Boltonia asteroides 'Snowbank'

full range from magenta purples through pink shades to white, generally on plants similar to *B. cordifolia* and *B. crassifolia* in being cold tolerant.

Culture. Bergenias will grow under such trying conditions as dry shade and poor soil, but they flourish in good soil with regular watering. Where summer is cool, they will grow in full sun; in warmer-summer regions, plant them in filtered sun to full shade. When plantings become crowded or leggy, you can divide and replant in late winter and early spring.

Good companions. *Anemone hybrida, Astilbe, Brunnera macrophylla, Digitalis, Polygonatum, Thalictrum.*

BOLTONIA ASTEROIDES
Boltonia
Compositae

Hardy to: −35°F/−37°C; not suited to Gulf Coast and Florida
Exposure: Sun
Water: Regular to moderate
Flowers in: Late summer, autumn
Colors: White, lavender, pink

It would take a botanist to explain why *Boltonia* isn't an aster. Visually, it might as well be another of the Michaelmas daisies. The wild species makes an upright, fine-textured plant to 7 feet high that becomes top-heavy from the weight of its load of white, lavender, or pink ¾-inch daisies. But the selection 'Snowbank' is truly an improvement, forming a 3- to 4-foot high, self-supporting mound of narrow, bluish green leaves that will be nearly obscured by airy sprays of yellow-centered white flowers during the bloom period. If you want light pink daisies, choose 'Pink Beauty'.

Culture. Plants will grow in a wide range of soils, thriving on spotty care. The boltonias spread rapidly but are not invasive; divide clumps in early spring, about every 3 years.

Good companions. Aster, Chrysanthemum, ornamental grasses, Sedum 'Autumn Joy', Solidago.

BRUNNERA MACROPHYLLA
Brunnera, Siberian bugloss
Boraginaceae

Hardy to: –35°F/–37°C; not suited to Gulf Coast and Florida
Exposure: Sun, partial shade
Water: Regular
Flowers in: Spring
Colors: Blue

In bloom, the confetti shower of dazzling blue blossoms earns this plant the colloquial name of perennial forget-me-not. In early spring, the low, mounded clumps of heart-shaped leaves to 4 inches wide and 6 inches long send up wiry stems bearing light sprays of piercingly blue ¼-inch flowers. As the season progresses, leaves become larger and stems grow taller, reaching 1½ to 2 feet high by the time flowering finishes. For the remainder of the growing year, brunnera maintains a good stand of attractive leafage. This wins it a preeminent place as a filler, small-scale ground cover, or naturalizer in woodland gardens under high-branching shrubs or at border edges. The selection 'Variegata' offers foliage marked in creamy white.

Culture. Although brunnera will succeed even in dry shade, best appearance comes with reasonably good soil and regular (or at least moderate) watering. It is at home anywhere in partial, filtered, or light shade; where summer is cool, you can also plant it in sun. You may divide plants in early spring for increase, but volunteer seedlings usually provide a surplus.

Good companions. Bergenia, Doronicum, Geum, Thalictrum, Trollius.

Brunnera macrophylla

CAMPANULA
Bellflower
Campanulaceae

Hardy to: –30°F/–34°C, except as noted
Exposure: Sun, partial shade
Water: Regular to moderate
Flowers in: Spring, summer
Colors: Blue, violet, white, pink

Campanulas—with their simple bell-like flowers and elegant poise—evoke images of cottage gardens and sentimental Victorian floral sketches. These popular garden subjects range in size from 6-inch ground-covering spreaders to 5-foot flowering sentinels. Although flowers are often bell shaped, they can also be cupped or even flat and star shaped. The prevailing colors are blue, lavender, purple, and white—though an occasional pink individual varies the palette. Aside from the spreading ground cover types, campanulas form clumps, producing rosettes or tufts of leaves from which arise upright flowering stems bearing smaller-stemmed leaves.

Among the campanulas with upright flowering stems, the shortest—averaging about 1 foot high—is *C. carpatica*, the Carpathian or tussock

Campanula persicifolia

bellflower. From low clumps of narrow, bright green leaves come wiry, branched stems that bear cup-shaped, upward-facing flowers. Colors are white or light to dark violet-blue; for specific colors, choose named selections such as 'White Chips' and medium blue 'Blue Chips'. Somewhat taller, generally from 1 to 2 feet, *C. glomerata* is described by its name: clustered bellflower. From clumps of broadly lance-shaped leaves rise stems bearing tight clusters of flaring bells. Blue-violet is the typical color, but named selections offer a range of colors as well as heights. 'Crown of Snow' has white flowers; 'Superba' is a deep violet with stems that may exceed 2 feet; violet-purple 'Joan Elliott' grows to 1½ feet.

Grace and refinement mark the peach-leafed bluebell, *C. persicifolia*. Low clumps of narrow, 4- to 8-inch leaves send up slender, leafy stems 2 to 3 feet high. Each stem bears loose spires of outward-facing, cupped bells in blue, white, or pink carried on short flower stalks. Named selections guarantee specific characteristics: 'Telham Beauty' has 3-inch, lavender-blue blossoms; 'White Pearl' and 'Blue Gardenia' have double flowers. Plants once called *C. latiloba* are now considered forms of the peach-leafed bluebell. They differ in having broader foliage and flowers that are carried directly on the stems.

Tallest of the popular bellflowers, *C. lactiflora* tops out in the 3- to 5-foot range, its upright stems clothed with 3-inch pointed leaves. Rounded to domed flower clusters are almost phloxlike, featuring open, starry bells in blue shades, white, or pink. Plants are hardy to –10°F/–23°C and will tolerate some drought. Named selections include pale pink 'Loddon Anna', 3-foot blue-violet 'Prichard's Variety', and the dwarf, pale blue 'Pouffe', which makes a mound of flowers just over 1 foot in height.

From Yugoslavia come two easy-to-grow, spreading species. The more aggressive of the two is Serbian bellflower, *C. poscharskyana*. Its clumps of heart-shaped leaves (like those of violets) spread by rooting runners to form solid foliage carpets that make a good small-scale ground cover. Soft blue, starlike flowers appear along semiupright stems in late spring. Dalmatian bellflower, *C. portenschlagiana* (sometimes sold as *C. muralis*), is hardy to –20°F/–29°C. The plant is similar to Serbian bellflower but is more compact and slower to spread. Broadly bell-shaped, violet-blue flowers come in small clusters at ends of stems, covering plants from late spring into midsummer. The variety 'Resholt' has larger, darker blue blossoms.

Culture. Plant campanulas in good, well-drained soil. Most need regular watering for best performance, though the Yugoslavian species are somewhat drought tolerant. In cool- and mildsummer regions, you can set out plants in full sun; warm to hot summers dictate planting in filtered sunlight or partial shade. Dig and divide crowded clumps in early spring where winters are cold, in either autumn or early spring in mild-winter regions.

Catananche caerulea

Good companions. Alchemilla mollis, Aquilegia, Heuchera, Hosta, Iris (Siberian), Thalictrum.

CATANANCHE CAERULEA
Cupid's dart
Compositae

Hardy to: –30°F/–34°C
Exposure: Sun
Water: Moderate
Flowers in: Summer, early autumn
Colors: Blue, white

Individual plants of cupid's dart are undeniably wispy, but grouped together they give a lovely, grasslike effect. Very narrow, upright gray-green leaves may reach a foot long, above which float clear blue, 2-inch cornflower-style flowers on threadlike stems; white-flowered forms are also available. Each flower is composed of numerous narrow petals, clasped together by silvery, strawlike bracts. Flower arrangers know cupid's dart as one of the best driers for everlasting arrangements.

Culture. Cupid's dart asks for no more than well-drained soil of average fertility and moderate watering during the growing season. It is quite drought tolerant and will not survive if soil is kept moist. Plants are rather short lived. You can divide clumps to rejuvenate them, but volunteer seedlings usually make replacements available.

Good companions. Anthemis, Armeria, Lychnis coronaria, Oenothera, Sisyrinchium striatum.

CENTAUREA
Knapweed
Compositae

Hardy to: Varies
Exposure: Sun
Water: Moderate
Flowers in: Summer
Colors: Purple, pink, yellow

Perhaps the best-known *Centaurea* is an old favorite annual, the cornflower or bachelor's button, *C. cyanus*. Among perennial kinds, some are grown for flowers, others for decorative foliage.

Centaurea dealbata

Among the showy-flowered species, the most generally available is *C. hypoleuca* 'John Coutts' (sometimes listed as a variety of *C. dealbata*), which is hardy to –30°F/–34°C. Spreading clumps are a profusion of foot-long, deeply cut leaves—soft green on the upper surfaces but gray-white beneath. On stems to 2 feet high come the 3-inch thistlelike flowers, each one a dark lilac rose with a prominent white center.

Culture. Plants grow vigorously in moderately fertile, well-drained soil. Clumps spread easily and should be divided every 3 to 4 years, if needed, to renew them and curb their spread. The true *C. dealbata*, Persian cornflower, is similar, but its stems of purplish pink to lavender flowers are not always held upright. It, too, is hardy to –30°F/–34°C.

Good companions. Achillea 'Moonshine', Coreopsis verticillata, Salvia farinacea, Sedum 'Autumn Joy'.

CENTRANTHUS RUBER
Jupiter's beard, Red valerian
Valerianaceae

Hardy to: –20°F/–29°C
Exposure: Sun, partial shade
Water: Moderate to little
Flowers in: Spring, summer
Colors: Red, pink, white

The phrase "trouble free" perfectly describes Jupiter's beard. So easy is it, in fact, that you'll encounter it as a pretty roadside weed in the far western states. Bushy clumps of upright stems reach about 3 feet high, each stem bearing pointed, 4-inch, grayish blue-green leaves. Tiny flowers appear in elongated, fluffy clusters at stem ends; the red and pink forms furnish bright but softened color, while the white form is especially clear.

Culture. Though its deep, fleshy roots enable it to survive in poor soils with little water, Jupiter's beard improves in appearance given good, well-drained soil and at least moderate watering. After the first flush of bloom, cut off spent flower heads to promote a second flowering. This also forestalls prodigious seed setting that—particularly in moderate climates—can lead to an overabundance of volunteer seedlings. Seedlings, though, are the simplest means of getting additional plants (and at least a small quantity are inevitable). To propagate specific colors, root basal cuttings during spring and summer.

Good companions. *Aster frikartii, Chrysanthemum superbum, Hemerocallis, Iris* (bearded, spuria), *Nepeta.*

CERATOSTIGMA PLUMBAGINOIDES
Dwarf plumbago
Plumbaginaceae

Hardy to: –10°F/–23°C; not suited to Gulf Coast and Florida
Exposure: Sun, partial shade
Water: Moderate
Flowers in: Summer, early autumn
Colors: Blue

Here is another of the "summer blues," valued for bringing nature's coolest color to the garden at the warmest

Centranthus ruber

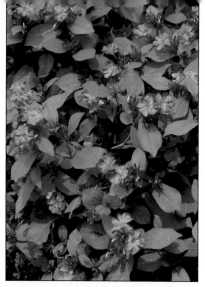

Ceratostigma plumbaginoides

time of year. Bronzed green, 3-inch oval leaves are borne on wiry stems to 1 foot high; phloxlike, ½-inch flowers of intense medium blue form clusters at stem tips. Frost calls a halt to the flower display but contributes a new color by changing foliage to bronzy red. Clumps spread by underground stems to form drifts that make an effective small-scale ground cover.

Culture. Although dwarf plumbago grows well in good soil, it will also prosper in soil that is only moderately fertile. Good drainage is the basic need. Most rapid growth and longest flowering period occur where the growing season is long. Each year, cut old stems to the ground sometime between late autumn and early spring, before growth begins. When vigor declines or clumps show bare patches, dig plantings just as growth begins, divide, and replant healthy rooted segments.

Good companions. *Coreopsis, Oenothera, Sedum spectabile* and 'Autumn Joy', *Stachys lanata, Zauschneria.*

Pond Plant

CHELONE
Turtlehead
Scrophulariaceae

Hardy to: –30°F/–34°C
Exposure: Sun, partial shade
Water: Regular
Flowers in: Late summer, autumn
Colors: Pink, lilac

When you see an individual blossom, you'll understand this perennial's common name—if you can imagine a pink turtle. From spring into summer,

turtlehead is a clump of good-looking foliage: glossy, elliptical leaves with serrated margins. As flowering season nears, leafy, branching stems rise 2 to 3 feet, bearing crowded spikes of the distinctive flowers at the terminal and branch tips. Of the two species generally available, bright pink *C. lyonii* is the more common as well as the taller, reaching 3 feet or a bit more. In hot-summer regions, give it partial shade. More heat- and sun-tolerant is rosy purple *C. obliqua,* which reaches 2 to 3 feet in bloom. For white blossoms, look for *C. glabra* or *C. obliqua* 'Alba'.

Culture. To succeed with turtleheads, give them plenty of moisture. They're ideal for perpetually damp soil and pond margins, though they will thrive in normal garden soil among other plants that need regular watering. Divide plants in spring whenever clumps become crowded; otherwise, to increase plants, take cuttings in summer.

Good companions. *Aconitum, Anemone hybrida, Astilbe, Cimicifuga, Geranium, Hemerocallis.*

CHRYSANTHEMUM
Chrysanthemum
Compositae

Hardy to: Varies
Exposure: Sun
Water: Regular
Flowers in: Spring, summer, autumn
Colors: Pink, red, bronze, orange, yellow, cream, white

What other perennial is so closely and firmly identified with autumn? The

Chelone lyonii

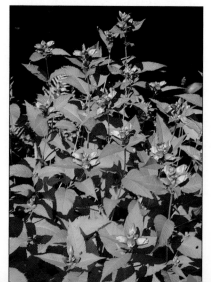

familiar florists' chrysanthemum, *C. morifolium*, enlivens the garden scene during that season, coloring it with the reds, golds, oranges, and bronzes that mirror the tints of the changing autumnal foliage. Yet these plants are just one representative of a large and varied group of familiar spring- and summer-flowering daisies that includes feverfew, Shasta daisy, and the tender marguerite. There's even one individual grown not for flowers but for its decorative foliage.

C. arcticum, the arctic daisy, is extremely cold tolerant—to –50°F/ –46°C—but needs some winter chill and won't thrive in the summer heat and humidity of the deep South. Wide-spreading clumps may reach a foot high, clothed in glossy green, lobed leaves to 3 inches long. Single, yellow-centered white daisies to 2 inches across cover the plant in mid- to late autumn; flowers turn pinkish as they age. Where the growing season is short, plants may be frost damaged before they have a chance to flower. From this species were developed the Northland daisies, a group of taller-growing hybrids with single flowers 3 inches or more in diameter in shades of pink, rosy purple, and yellow.

C. coccineum (once known as *Pyrethrum roseum*) is the familiar painted daisy, hardy to –30°F/–34°C. Three-inch long-stemmed daisies on slender stems come in pink shades, red, and white; bushy plants reach 1½ to 3 feet tall when in flower, featuring bright green, finely divided leaves. Flowering starts in midspring where winters are mild, in late spring in colder regions. If you cut plants back severely after flowering, you'll get a repeat bloom in late summer. Best performance is in regions with warm to hot summer weather. Superior named varieties in specific colors are good choices when available. Divide plants in summer, about every 3 years.

C. morifolium encompasses all the varied plants collectively known as florists' chrysanthemum (or just plain "mums")—reliably hardy to –10°F/ –23°C in the open garden, to about –20°F/–29°C with protection. They're the mainstay of the autumn-blooming perennial show—both in garden borders and in containers—not only because

Chrysanthemum coccineum

cause of their ease of culture and profusion of bloom but also because they are the most varied and versatile of chrysanthemums, available in many flower forms, colors, plant and flower sizes, and growth habits.

Countless named selections are sold by specialty growers and general perennials suppliers, while both named and unnamed plants are widely sold in small pots when in flower. Chrysanthemum specialists recognize a number of specific flower forms among exhibition varieties. But for garden purposes, you'll be more concerned with overall aspect: flowers range from 1 to 6 inches across; are single, semidouble, and double; and come in various forms from basic daisy to pompon to shaggy or quilled. The lower-growing, smaller-flowered kinds with a bushy, compact habit are the best for general garden display. The large-flowered exhibition types usually are rangy growers that need frequent pinching to promote compact growth and staking to remain upright. Climate, too, will influence your choice. Within the hardiness range, the shorter your growing season, the more important it is to select early-flowering sorts.

The small-flowered cushion and pompon mums are generally low-growing (usually under 1½ feet), bushy plants that will remain compact and leafy without any special attention. The taller, decorative mums need their growth pinched back several times during the growing season to promote branching and offset top-heaviness. When any stem reaches 5 inches long, nip out the tip; this will

force branching below the pinch. Continued into summer, this makes for a dense, leafy plant that will produce flowers from the end of each branch. In cold-winter regions where frost comes early, stop pinching in early summer; in less severe climates (where lows seldom dip below 0°F/–18°C), continue pinching into August. After flowering has finished, cut down stems to about 8 inches; in coldest regions, you can leave cut stems over plants as a bit of winter protection. When growth begins the next year, cut the remains of the stems to the ground.

Clumps become crowded quickly, so you'll need to divide about every other year. The best time is early spring, just as growth is beginning. Or you can wait several weeks until growth is 4 to 6 inches high, then take cuttings; these will root quickly and become good-size flowering plants by autumn. Where winters are reasonably mild, you can set out newly acquired plants in autumn or spring; in colder regions, plant in spring.

C. pacificum, often listed as "gold and silver," is a low-growing foliage plant with a pleasing but incidental floral display. Leaves cluster in rosettes toward stem ends, each leaf a jagged-edged green oval sharply outlined in white. Branching, dense plants reach about 1 foot high, spreading as widely as 3 feet. In midautumn, clusters of yellow flowers appear at branch tips, each one a pea-size daisy minus the petals. Plants are hardy to –20°F/ –29°C.

C. parthenium—feverfew, but sometimes called by its old name, matrica-

Chrysanthemum morifolium

ria—is either a carefree perennial or a semiweed, depending on your point of view. Plants are hardy to –30°F/–34°C, forming clumps of lobed, rather feathery, bright green leaves having a pungent, peppery scent. In summer, leafy stems elongate to 2 to 3 feet, producing large clusters of single white daisies less than an inch across. When in flower, plants may need some staking to remain upright unless you pinch them back in midspring. Plants usually maintain good condition no more than 2 years, but an ample supply of volunteer seedlings will be available as replacements if you let spent flowers form seeds. Otherwise, you can take spring cuttings to start new plants or divide clumps annually. Named selections offer variations on the basic theme. 'Silver Ball' has completely double white flowers; 'Golden Ball' has yellow flower heads with no petals. 'Tom Thumb White Stars' is a low-growing, compact sort. The showiest plant is 'Aureum' (often sold as 'Golden Feather'), which has bright chartreuse foliage and white flowers.

C. rubellum is the usual catalog name for the plants properly known as *C. zawadskii latilobium*. Hardy to –30°F/–34°C, they flower from mid- or late summer into early autumn on bushy plants to about 2½ feet high that spread by rhizomes into broad clumps. Finely divided foliage is a backdrop for single daisy flowers 2 to 3 inches across. Bright pink 'Clara Curtis' and buff yellow 'Mary Stoker' are two widely sold varieties. Grow plants in full sun; otherwise, give them the same care as Shasta daisies, below.

C. superbum (sometimes listed as *C. maximum*) is the Shasta daisy so familiar in summer-flowering perennial schemes. Plants are hardy to –20°F/–29°C, though some protection is wise where temperatures fall below –10°F/–23°C. From robust clumps of linear, tooth-edged leaves rise leafy flower stalks in late spring and early summer, each bearing one to several showy white daisies.

The original Shasta daisies featured single 3- to 4-inch flowers with big yellow centers on stems 2 to 4 feet high; popular varieties 'Alaska' and 'Polaris' are good examples. Current

Chrysanthemum superbum

named selections include variations on the original theme. Semidouble- and double-flowered types include 'Esther Read' as well as 'Marconi' and 'Aglaya', which have fringed or quilled petals. 'Wirral Supreme' and 'Thomas Killen' have tufted centers that give the appearance of doubleness. 'Canary Bird' and 'Cobham Gold' have creamy white flowers on plants under 2 feet tall. Among low-growing kinds, single white 'Snowcap' grows just 1 foot high. Other dwarfs are found in the seed strains 'Little Miss Muffet' (semidouble) and 'Snow Lady' (single). Perennials specialists will offer named selections; retail nurseries may carry seed-grown strains identified by name, amount of petallage, or height.

Shasta daisies grow best in full sun where summers are cool to mild. In hot, dry regions, give plants filtered sunlight to partial light shade. Regular watering in good, well-drained soil produces best results. Plants increase quickly, the clumps needing division about every other year. In all areas, early spring is the best time to divide and reset plants. Where winter is mild, you may divide in autumn as well.

C. weyrichii is a foot-high, front-of-the-border plant that spreads by rhizomes into broad clumps or drifts of finely cut foliage. Plants are hardy to –35°F/–37°C. In early autumn, single daisies to 2 inches across appear. 'White Bomb' has white daisies that age to pale pink; 'Pink Bomb' is light pink from start to finish. Give plants

full sun and well-drained soil; divide about every 3 to 4 years.

Culture. Despite their different appearances, all *Chrysanthemum* species and hybrids appreciate good, well-drained soil and plenty of water during the growing season. Descriptions for each type contain specific cultural advice. New plants of florists' chrysanthemum, feverfew, arctic daisy, *C. pacificum*, and *C. weyrichii* can be started from spring cuttings.

Good companions. *Hemerocallis, Monarda, Nepeta, Physostegia, Sedum spectabile* and 'Autumn Joy', *Solidago*.

CIMICIFUGA
Bugbane
Ranunculaceae

Hardy to: –35°F/–37°C; needs some winter chill; not suited to Gulf Coast and Florida
Exposure: Sun, partial shade
Water: Regular
Flowers in: Summer, autumn
Colors: White

Statuesque when in flower but delicate in texture, the bugbanes offer height without massiveness. Clumps of coarsely fernlike, dark green leaves may reach 2½ feet. From these foliage mounds rise slender, branched stems that terminate in elongated "foxtails" of small, bristly flowers consisting only of stamens.

One of the tallest bugbanes is the North American black snakeroot, *C. racemosa*, which easily reaches 6 feet during its midsummer flowering. Its

Cimicifuga racemosa

Clematis integrifolia

white flower groups are erect, in contrast to the arching plumes of *C. simplex,* the Kamchatka bugbane. This species flowers in autumn atop 4-foot stems; its selected form 'White Pearl' has especially large flower spikes. Also autumn blooming, *C. ramosa* 'Atropurpurea' may carry its flowers on 7-foot stems above clumps of purplish foliage.

Culture. In all areas you can treat bugbanes as woodland-edge plants: give them partial or filtered shade, good, organically enriched soil, and plenty of water. Where summer is cool or mild, you can plant in full sun as well. Consider these to be "nearly permanent" perennials: clumps will grow for many years before becoming so crowded as to need division. If you need to divide for increase (or because of crowding), do it in early spring where winters are cold, in autumn in milder-winter climates.

Good companions. Aconitum, Anemone hybrida, Chelone, Hosta, Ligularia, Monarda, Physotegia virginiana.

CLEMATIS
Clematis
Ranunculaceae

Hardy to: −35°F/−37°C; most not suited to Gulf Coast and Florida
Exposure: Sun, partial shade
Water: Regular
Flowers in: Summer
Colors: Blue, white

Although the showy vining *Clematis* hybrids get the lion's share of public attention, discerning gardeners cherish their no-less-attractive perennial kin. The perennial kinds have the effect of small shrubs, bearing their flowers clustered at ends of stems. A tendency toward lax or sprawling growth is easily remedied by discreet staking.

Clematis heracleifolia davidiana bears fragrant, violet blue, hyacinthlike flowers in clusters both at stem ends and on branches from upper portions of the stems; spent flowers later produce decorative silky, silvery seed heads. Plants grow 2 to 4 feet high, bearing leaves composed of broadly oval leaflets 3 to 5 inches long. *C. integrifolia* bears nodding, lily-shaped, milky blue to violet flowers individually on a wiry-stemmed plant with 2- to 4-inch elongated leaves. Stems are both upright and sprawling, to about 3 feet with support. This species will succeed in Gulf Coast gardens.

White-flowered *C. recta* has small, star-shaped, fragrant flowers that make a great, foamy display in many-branched clusters at the ends of stems. Bloom is followed by attractive seed heads composed of threadlike, silvery segments. Foliage is fairly fine textured, each leaf containing up to nine elongated leaflets to 2 inches long. Young foliage of the variety 'Purpurea' is reddish purple. Stems tend to be upright, about 3 to 5 feet, but may sprawl a bit without staking. Grow this clematis among leggy-based shrubs that can provide some support.

Culture. Success with clematis depends on attention to specific but easy-to-satisfy soil requirements. Plants need a well-aerated but moist soil; this translates to good drainage and regular watering. Incorporate generous quantities of organic matter prior to planting. And make sure that soil remains cool during the growing season, either by mulching or by shading it with "living mulch" foliage of non-competitive annuals or perennials. Once plants are established, you can leave them in place indefinitely. Before growth starts in spring, cut back the semiwoody stems to 1 foot or less. If you want to increase a plant, carefully dig and divide a clump in early spring or take cuttings during spring.

Convolvulus mauritanicus

Good companions. Anemone hybrida, Astilbe, Chelone, Dictamnus albus, Hosta, Iris (Siberian).

CONVOLVULUS MAURITANICUS
Ground morning glory
Convolvulaceae

Hardy to: 10°F/−12°C
Exposure: Sun
Water: Moderate
Flowers in: Late spring, summer, autumn
Colors: Blue

In flower, this is a scaled-down version of the familiar vining morning glories, but its 1- to 2-inch funnel-shaped blossoms appear on a spreading plant suitable for foregrounds and small-scale ground cover. Many-stemmed plants mound to about 1½ feet high and spread to 3 feet, the stems clothed in broadly oval, inch-long, softly hairy grayish green leaves.

Culture. Ground morning glory will grow in a variety of soils, from light sand to clay. Plants in well-drained soils will accept regular watering, though moderate watering is sufficient; those growing in heavy, slowly draining soils should be watered moderately or less. Cut back plants heavily in late winter or early spring; divide crowded plantings then, too.

Good companions. Achillea, Coreopsis, Gaura lindheimeri, Lobelia laxiflora, Oenothera.

Coreopsis grandiflora 'Sunray'

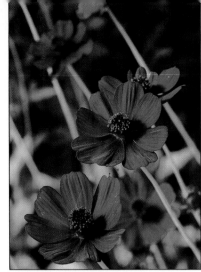

Cosmos atrosanguineus

COREOPSIS
Coreopsis, Tickseed
Compositae

Hardy to: –30°F/–34°C, except as noted
Exposure: Sun
Water: Moderate
Flowers in: Summer
Colors: Yellow

Sunny yellow daisies decorate easy-to-grow plants from late spring into early autumn, the flowers airily poised atop wiry stems. Leaf texture varies from finely cut and filmy to narrow and linear; plant height ranges from ankle high to several feet.

The munchkin of this tribe is *C. auriculata* 'Nana'. Clumps of spoon-shaped leaves grow up to 6 inches high, spreading by stolons into solid patches. Yellow-orange, 2-inch single flowers rise just above the leaves on individual wiry stems. For a slightly larger plant of similar appearance, choose *C. lanceolata* 'Goldfink'; its clumps of linear leaves reach 8 to 10 inches high, the bright yellow single daisies hovering just above the leaves.

Taller plants are found especially among named selections of *C. grandiflora*. Double-flowered 'Sunray' carries its 2-inch flowers at 1½ to 2 feet; semidouble 'Early Sunrise' grows to the same height and begins flowering several weeks earlier than other coreopsis. Seed-raised plants of the two similar species *C. grandiflora* and *C. lanceolata* grow to 2 feet high or a bit more, are profuse and long flowering. Under good garden conditions, *C.*

grandiflora becomes top-heavy and sprawls; unless you routinely remove spent blossoms, you'll get a yearly supply of volunteer seedling plants. For guaranteed good garden characteristics, look for the named selections.

A filmy delicacy distinguishes *C. verticillata* from the other coarser-textured species and varieties. The common name, threadleaf coreopsis, accurately describes the texture of these bushy, mounding plants that grow from 1 to about 2½ feet high depending on the variety. The 2-inch flowers appear from summer into autumn, sometimes nearly obscuring the foliage. Bright yellow 'Zagreb' is the shortest, at 12 to 18 inches; 'Golden Shower' and 'Grandiflora' reach 2 to 2½ feet. 'Moonbeam' offers soft, pale yellow blossoms on a 1½- to 2-foot plant. Clumps of *C. verticillata* break dormancy late, spread by underground stems into sizable colonies unless periodically curbed or divided.

Culture. All coreopsis are trouble-free plants, thriving even in relatively poor soil and, once established, persisting with relatively little water. *C. auriculata* 'Nana', *C. lanceolata* 'Goldfink', and *C. verticillata* may not thrive in Gulf Coast gardens. Plant them in well-drained soil and for best appearance water moderately. Rapid growth and spread may call for frequent division and replanting—as often as every 2 to 3 years. To prolong flowering, remove spent blossoms.

Good companions. Asclepias tuberosa, Convolvulus mauritanicus, Nepeta, Penstemon, Salvia, Sisyrinchium striatum.

COSMOS ATROSANGUINEUS
Chocolate cosmos
Compositae

Hardy to: 15°F/–9°C; not suited to Gulf Coast and Florida
Exposure: Sun
Water: Regular
Flowers in: Summer
Colors: Brownish red

Chocolate lovers take note: these flowers are not only chocolate colored, they are chocolate scented as well! From tuberous roots, this plant breaks dormancy late in the spring growing season but grows rapidly into a lax mound to 2 feet high. Leaves are deeply lobed (in the style of tomato foliage) and bright green, a good contrast to the nearly black-centered maroon single daisies that appear all summer long on wiry stems.

Culture. Chocolate cosmos is an attractive conversation piece for foreground planting in good, well-drained soil. If you want to divide mature clumps for increase, carefully dig and separate the tuberous roots in spring before growth begins. You can also start new plants from cuttings rooted during summer.

Good companions. Achillea, Belamcanda chinensis, Coreopsis, Diascia, Gaura lindheimeri, Linaria.

CRAMBE CORDIFOLIA
Colewort
Cruciferae

Hardy to: –10°F/–23°C
Exposure: Sun
Water: Regular
Flowers in: Summer
Colors: White

Impressive is the word for colewort—rather like an elephant bearing a floral offering! Leaves reaching 2 feet long are broadly heart shaped with lobed, wavy edges, borne on long leafstalks. From this bold pile of foliage stems rise to at least 6 feet, intricately branched and rebranched, bearing a filmy cloud of small, starlike flowers—in effect like a floating clump of baby's breath (*Gypsophila*). Give one plant

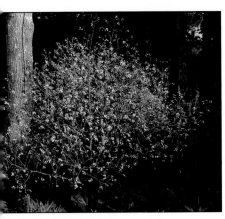

Crambe cordifolia

plenty of room: when in flower, it may occupy a space 4 to 6 feet across.

Culture. Plant colewort in an averagely fertile, well-drained soil, preferably one that is deep and well dug so that roots can penetrate deeply. This is one of the "permanent" perennials: plant it where you will enjoy it year after year.

Good companions. *Acanthus mollis, Boltonia asteroides, Euphorbia corollata, Gypsophila paniculata.*

DELPHINIUM
Delphinium
Ranunculaceae

Hardy to: –35°F/–37°C; not suited to hot-summer regions; needs some winter chill
Exposure: Sun, partial shade
Water: Regular
Flowers in: Summer
Colors: Blue, purple, pink, white, cream; bicolor combinations

Stately, aristocratic delphiniums automatically suggest English gardens, whether of manorial estates or thatch-roofed cottages. For generations they have been essential components of the classic perennial border as well as of the more plebeian cottage garden. It would be wrong to say delphiniums are easy; they need special care, even where the climate is well suited to them. But the rewards are worth every extra effort: elegant spires of rounded blossoms in cool colors that include some of the most penetrating blue shades available to the summer garden. Some of the hybrids have flow-ers of two or even three colors, the center petals (sometimes called a "bee") offering a white, black, or gold contrast to white, blue, and lilac-pink outer petals. Large leaves, lobed and fanlike, resemble maple foliage.

The tall, "typical" delphiniums are complex hybrids of *D. elatum*, reaching 5 to 7 feet tall under optimal conditions. The Pacific strain (variously listed as Pacific Hybrids, Pacific Giants, and Pacific Coast Hybrids) is available as seed-raised, mixed-color plants and in named series that are seed grown to produce specific colors. Included are the Arthurian Round Table series such as 'Astolat' (lilac, dark bee), 'Black Knight' (violet, black bee), 'Galahad' (white), 'Percival' (white, black bee), and 'King Arthur' (violet, white bee). Other Pacific hybrids series are 'Blue Bird' (midblue), 'Blue Jay' (medium to dark blue), and 'Summer Skies' (light blue, white bee). Pacific hybrids are the strain to try if your summer temperatures may be warmer than the ideal.

The other notable strain of tall delphiniums is the Blackmore and Langdon strain developed in England. These hybrids are generally available in mixed-color assortments that encompass the full range of blue shades, purple, and white.

The tall strains have shorter counterparts that trade majestic height for the ability to remain upright with less staking. Examples are 'Blue Fountains', 'Blue Springs', 'Magic Fountains', and 'Pennant'—all mixed colors. These grow 2½ to 3 feet high. The mixed-color 'Connecticut Yankee' strain represents a different ancestry: plants are bushy with many flower stems that rise to 2½ feet over finely dissected foliage.

The *D. belladonna* group includes plants that reach 3 to 4 feet high when in flower. Compared to the tall *D. elatum* hybrids, these are less upright and spirelike—stems are branched, flowers are less crowded together—while plants are a bit more adaptable and longer lived. Separate-color strains include light blue 'Belladonna', dark blue 'Bellamosa', and white 'Casa Blanca'.

Culture. True to their image, delphiniums grow best in an "English" climate

Delphinium

with cool to warm (not hot), humid summers such as are found in the Pacific coast fog belt, the Pacific Northwest west of the Cascades, and—where winters permit—the northern and coastal regions of New England. Success diminishes where summers are hotter, drier, or both. In marginal areas, pay special attention to exposure and water, sheltering plants from the hottest sun and safeguarding against dryness.

Delphiniums need soil that is cool, moist but well-drained, slightly acid to slightly alkaline—and the richer the better. Incorporate quantities of organic matter into the soil well before planting. In the preferred climates, plant in full sun; where hot summer is a possibility, plant where sunlight will be dappled during the heat of the day. Tall kinds are especially top-heavy when in bloom; minimize the risk by planting in wind-sheltered locations, and be prepared to support stems that can lean or topple simply from the weight of the blossoms. Keep slug and snail bait at the ready: these plants are a delicacy.

During the flowering season, cut off spent blossom spikes just below the lowest flower; new growth then will begin from the plant's base. When new basal shoots are about 6 inches tall, cut out the old blossoming spike entirely and apply a complete fertilizer around the plant. The new stems should give a second flowering in late summer or early autumn.

Even with the best care, modern delphinium hybrids tend to be short-lived perennials. You can divide

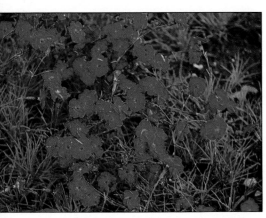

Dianthus plumarius 'Brympton Red'

clumps and set out individual plants in rejuvenated soil, or you can take basal cuttings of favorite plants in spring. But most gardeners find it easier to start fresh with young seedlings or cutting-grown plants from a nursery. You can treat delphiniums as annuals by planting them in autumn (in mild-winter regions) or early spring (in all regions) to flower in summer. This is the best plan in areas that have hot summers and/or mild winters.

Good companions. *Chrysanthemum superbum, Heliopsis helianthoides, Hemerocallis, Iris* (Siberian), *Monarda.*

DIANTHUS
Pink
Caryophyllaceae

Hardy to: –30°F/–34°C, except as noted; not long lived in Gulf Coast and Florida gardens
Exposure: Sun
Water: Moderate
Flowers in: Spring, summer
Colors: Red, pink, white; bicolor combinations

Clove-scented pinks are living garden history. The earliest written record of them is several hundred years before Christ; much later they again turn up in the writings of Chaucer and Shakespeare. Medieval monks grew them, as did Elizabethan nobles. By the end of the 1700s, people of humbler station were both growing pinks and raising new varieties; Scottish weavers in Paisley were in the vanguard of a development that became a horticultural vogue for nearly 100 years. Even today, specialists carry a few named pinks that stem from that period.

Cottage pinks, beloved of the Paisley weavers, are selections of *D. plumarius.* Other popular kinds are maiden pink, *D. deltoides,* Cheddar pink, *D. gratianopolitanus* (*D. caesius*), and the Allwood pinks or border carnations—hybrids between cottage pinks and the large, florist-type carnation *D. caryophyllus.* These are all similar, differing chiefly in size. Plants form dense mats or mounds of very narrow (almost grasslike), gray-green to blue-green foliage. Needlelike stems rise above leaves, each bearing one to several fragrant flowers that are circular in outline and single, semidouble, or double. Petals frequently have fringed margins; decoratively edged and "eyed" flowers are common. Spring into early summer is the main flowering period, though some types and particular individuals will continue through summer or repeat flowering as weather cools.

The *D. plumarius,* or cottage pink, offers a varied assortment of flower colors and patterns on stems 10 to 18 inches high above 6- to 8-inch foliage mounds; individual blooms may reach 1½ inches across. Specialists offer many named selections, including some truly historic individuals such as the 17th-century 'Dad's Favorite' (red-edged white, double), 'Fair Folley' (white and raspberry, single), and 'Pheasant's Eye' (red-centered white, semidouble).

The 20th-century Allwood pinks, sometimes designated *D. allwoodii,* are similar in size and habit (though some have slightly larger blossoms) but differ in one detail: they will continue to flower throughout the summer if you remove spent blooms.

Maiden pink, *D. deltoides,* is more cold tolerant (hardy to –40°F/–40°C) and will grow well in light shade. Plants spread into broad, loose mats of green leaves to about 6 inches high; ¾-inch flowers hover above the foliage, making a nearly solid cover in full bloom. You can buy named selections and mixed-color seed strains that cover purple, red, pink shades, and white. Bright scarlet 'Zing' and rose red 'Zing Rose' are widely grown.

Cheddar pink, *D. gratianopolitanus,* is hardy to –20°F/–29°C. Plants make a ground-hugging mat of blue-gray leaves, with single pink flowers less than an inch across appearing on stems 6 to 10 inches high. The double, light crimson 'Tiny Rubies' is a smaller-growing selection reaching just 4 inches high. Several other equally small named individuals are derived at least in part from the Cheddar pink but bloom from spring into autumn if you keep spent flowers picked. 'Rose Bowl' has cherry pink flowers on 6-inch stems; 'Spotty' is similar, but its petals are spotted with white; 'Little Joe' is crimson.

Culture. All pinks need a light, even gritty soil that drains well. This is especially important in winter: damp soil then can be fatal. Pinks will not grow well in strongly acid soils, preferring neutral to slightly alkaline conditions. Where winter is fairly mild—no colder than about 10°F/–12°C—you can set out new plants in late summer or autumn. In colder regions, early spring is the better time. Cool to mild summer weather is ideal for pinks; in hot-summer regions, they may be more satisfactory with a bit of shade in the afternoon. Remove spent flowers as they fade, breaking off stems at nodes where new growth is starting. Regardless of their stated hardiness, it's a good practice to give plants a light cover of evergreen boughs wherever winter lows will reach –10°F/–23°C.

After several years, individual plants start to decline, producing fewer and smaller flowers from less vigorous growth. To rejuvenate a planting, replace played-out plants with young, cutting-grown starts. You can easily root stems in a sandy rooting mix or light garden soil, taking cuttings of new growth that hasn't flowered—either tip cuttings about 6 nodes in length, or heel cuttings of similar length. You can also layer stems that spread along the ground.

Good companions. *Campanula, Convolvulus mauritanicus, Iberis sempervirens, Iris* (bearded), *Lychnis coronaria, Phlox subulata, Stachys lanata.*

Diascia 'Ruby Field'

DIASCIA
Twinspur
Scrophulariaceae

Hardy to: 10°F/–12°C; not suited to hot, humid summer climates
Exposure: Sun
Water: Regular
Flowers in: Spring, summer
Colors: Pink

Among the masses of flowers, it may take a close look to spot the two small "twin" spurs on the backs of the tubular but open-faced blossoms. Although individual flowers are just ½ to 1 inch long, grouped together in elongated clusters they provide fairly dense wands or carpets of color. Plants are somewhat upright to spreading, depending on the species or variety, with small oval to spade-shaped leaves on many slender stems that emerge from a central clump.

The semiupright plants of *D. rigescens* may spread to 2 to 3 feet across, their relaxed stems turning upward to bear spikes of bright coppery pink blossoms. More distinctly upright, to 1½ feet high and equally wide, *D. integerrima* features spires of rose pink flowers. The spreading, carpetlike habit of salmon pink *D.* 'Ruby Field' recommends it as a small-scale ground cover as well as a low accent plant.

Culture. Plant twinspur in average, well-drained soil. All kinds are low growing, suitable for edge-of-the-border plantings; and because of their need for good drainage, they're espe-

cially appropriate at the margins of raised beds and in the foreground of rockeries. Cut back old stems between growing seasons. Plants may live for only a few years, but it's easy to keep a new supply coming from spring or summer cuttings.

Good companions. *Aster frikartii, Campanula, Cosmos atrosanguineus, Iris* (bearded), *Stachys lanata, Veronica.*

DICENTRA
Bleeding heart
Fumariaceae

Hardy to: –35°F/–37°C; not suited to mild-winter/hot-summer areas
Exposure: Filtered sunlight, partial shade
Water: Regular
Flowers in: Spring, summer
Colors: Pink shades, red, white

Heart-shaped flowers with projecting tips hang from stems like jewels from a necklace. In combination with the finely dissected, almost feathery foliage, the effect created is one of exceptional grace and delicacy.

Eastern and western North America are home to two similar low-growing species. From the East, fringed bleeding heart, *D. eximia,* forms fluffy clumps of blue-gray foliage to 18 inches high; bare stems rise just above leaves bearing deep pink flowers from midspring into summer. A form with white flowers is generally offered as *D. e.* 'Alba' or 'Snowdrift'. Western bleeding heart, *D. formosa,* has blue-green foliage to about 1 foot high, the pale to deep rose flowers clustered on slim stems 6 to 8 inches above the leaves. In contrast to fringed bleeding heart, this species will spread widely (but not invasively) under favorable conditions. The uncommon selection 'Sweetheart' has white flowers, while the form *oregana* is shorter growing with pink-tipped cream blossoms.

Nurseries offer several superior hybrids of the above two species, though exact ancestries are uncertain. 'Bountiful'—perhaps no more than a selection of *D. eximia*—has rosy red flowers over rich blue-green leaves. Cherry pink 'Luxuriant' carries its blossoms up to 20 inches over 10-inch, dark blue-green

foliage; it is the best choice for marginal warm- to hot-summer/mild-winter areas. Sun-tolerant 'Adrian Bloom' has carmine red blossoms carried over distinctly blue-gray foliage.

Common bleeding heart, *D. spectabilis,* is the "classic" bleeding heart with branched flower stems carrying nearly horizontal sprays of pink-and-white pendant blossoms. When in flower, the plant can reach 3 feet high, the soft green leaves rising up the flowering stems. 'Pantaloons' and 'Alba' are selections with pure white blossoms. After the late spring flowering, plants begin to die down and are dormant by midsummer. If this would leave a bare patch in your planting scheme, grow summer-maturing perennials close by to disguise the gap.

Culture. Bleeding heart revels in woodland conditions. Give it light, well-drained soil enriched with organic matter; roots need to be cool and moist but not soggy. Most prefer filtered sunlight to partial shade, but in cool regions *D. spectabilis* and the hybrid 'Luxuriant' will succeed in full sun. All but *D. spectabilis*—one of the "permanent" perennials—may need dividing after several years. Do this in earliest spring before growth is really under way: both roots and new shoots are brittle.

Good companions. *Bergenia, Digitalis, Epimedium, Helleborus, Hosta, Mertensia, Primula, Trillium.*

Dicentra spectabilis

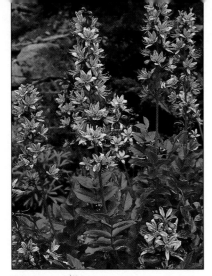

Dictamnus albus

DICTAMNUS ALBUS
Gas plant, Burning bush, Fraxinella
Rutaceae

Hardy to: −35°F/−37°C; needs winter chill; not suited to Gulf Coast and Florida
Exposure: Sun, partial shade
Water: Regular to moderate
Flowers in: Late spring, summer
Colors: Pink, lilac, white

Think of this long-lived perennial as a shrub. It forms bushy clumps 2½ to 3 feet high, its glossy, citrus-scented, 3-inch pointed leaflets remaining handsome throughout the growing season. Loose spires of blossoms appear at branch tips, each flower resembling a wild azalea with narrow petals and prominent stamens. Pink is the basic color, but specialty nurseries offer lilac purple *D. a.* 'Purpureus' and the white 'Albiflorus'. The common names "gas plant" and "burning bush" derive from the plant's lightly flammable quality: in warm, humid weather, volatile oils from the immature seed capsules will briefly ignite if you hold a lighted match near flower clusters.

Culture. Give gas plant well-drained, moderately fertile soil. Plants may be a bit slow to establish, but—like shrubs—they can remain in place indefinitely. You can start new plants from root cuttings, but growing from seed is usually simpler.

Good companions. Geranium, Hemerocallis, Iris (bearded, Siberian), Potentilla, Sedum spectabile and 'Autumn Joy'.

DIGITALIS
Foxglove
Scrophulariaceae

Hardy to: Varies; not suited to Gulf Coast and Florida
Exposure: Partial shade
Water: Regular
Flowers in: Late spring, summer
Colors: Pink, yellow

The classic cottage-garden foxgloves—stately 6-foot spires of pendant, thimble-shaped flowers—are biennial plants (see page 22). For truly perennial sorts, you sacrifice a bit of the majesty and the color range, though you retain all the charm. The perennial species possess the typical foxglove clumps of bold, gray-green, hairy leaves and vertical flower spikes, but height is reduced to about 3 feet. The hybrid *D. mertonensis* bears "gloves" of a dark, warm pink that has been variously described as coppery rose and crushed strawberry. It is hardy to −20°F/−29°C. Even though a hybrid, it will come true from seed—an easy way to increase your planting. Yellow foxglove, *D. grandiflora* (sometimes listed as *D. ambigua*) has pale yellow flowers lightly spotted brown in their interiors; this species is hardy to −30°F/−34°C.

Culture. All foxgloves are at their best in filtered sun to light or partial shade; where summers are cool you can plant in sun. Give plants good soil that will be moist but not saturated. Set out plants in early spring; divide established clumps at the same time. To coax a second flower display, cut out the spent spikes. But if you want seeds to start new plants, leave a flowering stem or two as a seed source.

Good companions. Alchemilla mollis, Campanula, Dicentra, Hosta, Thalictrum.

Digitalis mertonensis

Doronicum plantagineum

DORONICUM
Leopard's bane
Compositae

Hardy to: −30°F/−34°C
Exposure: Partial shade
Water: Regular
Flowers in: Early spring
Colors: Yellow

The leopard's banes pick up the yellow banner of daffodils and carry it further into the spring season. By midsummer, when the many other yellow daisies are in full cry, these plants will have finished their yearly cycle: foliage will have died down, not to reappear until the following year. Because of this, leopard's banes are best used in a strictly spring-flowering planting scheme or where summer-maturing plants can cover the gap they leave. Several species and hybrids are available, all of which bear 2- to 3-inch daisy flowers on slender stems over low, slowly spreading clumps of rounded to heart-shaped, tooth-edged leaves.

Botanists differ about the correct name for *D. cordatum*: you may find it listed as *D. caucasicum*, *D. columnae*, or *D. orientale*. Flowering stems reach 1½ feet in height, each holding aloft a single flower. Varieties 'Finesse' and 'Magnificum' are a bit taller with somewhat larger flowers. Plantain leopard's bane, *D. plantagineum*, is a larger, coarser plant reaching 2½ to 3 feet; its variety 'Excelsum' ('Harpur Crewe') bears branching stems that may exceed 3 feet.

Culture. Set out plants in good, organically enriched soil. Where sum-

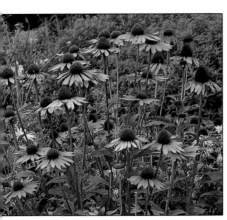

Echinacea purpurea

mers are cool, you can grow leopard's banes in sun; in all regions, woodland-edge conditions are ideal. Give them regular watering while in leaf, at least moderate moisture after they've gone dormant. Divide clumps in early spring about every 3 years.

Good companions. *Brunnera macrophylla, Dicentra, Helleborus, Hosta, Mertensia, Trillium.*

ECHINACEA PURPUREA
Purple coneflower
Compositae

Hardy to: –35°F/–37°C
Exposure: Sun
Water: Moderate
Flowers in: Summer
Colors: Purple, red, pink, white

Here is black-eyed Susan in a different dress. Like *Rudbeckia* flowers, these blossoms are large daisies with dark, beehivelike centers, but the petals are rosy purple instead of yellow. Typically the petals of these 4-inch flowers bend downward from the center, giving flowers a windswept look. But among the various named selections you'll find individuals that have flatter flowers ('Bright Star' is widely sold)—as well as those with petals of pink, rosy red, or white, and centers that range from orange to bronze as well as brownish purple. Dense clumps consist of 4- to 8-inch oval leaves with a sandpaperlike surface. In midsummer, sparsely leafed flowering stems reach 2½ to 4 feet, each usually bearing one flower.

Culture. Purple coneflowers are productive, trouble-free plants that need only a sunny spot in average (but well-drained) soil. In hot-summer regions they'll also succeed in partial shade. Plants are drought tolerant but perform better with moderate watering. After about 4 years, when clumps become crowded, divide them in early spring or autumn.

Good companions. *Achillea, Aster, Chrysanthemum superbum, Gypsophila paniculata, Rudbeckia, Solidago.*

 ## ECHINOPS
Globe thistle
Compositae

Hardy to: –35°F/–37°C
Exposure: Sun
Water: Regular to moderate
Flowers in: Summer
Colors: Blue

These plants are indeed thistle relatives, gussied up to the point of garden value. Leaves are deeply cut, prickly, and up to a foot long—usually green on the surface but gray and woolly underneath. Upright, leafy stems form well-foliaged clumps to about 4 feet high when flowering in midsummer. The distinctive flower heads are spherical, looking like golfball-size pincushions stuck full of tubular, metallic blue blossoms. You'll find globe thistle offered as *E. exaltatus, E. humilis, E. ritro,* or possibly *E. sphaerocephalus.* Whatever name you encounter, you're likely to get a plant that closely resembles the general description, particularly if you select the form 'Taplow Blue' (which may be listed as a form of any of those species). For flower heads of deep, silvery blue on slightly shorter stems, choose 'Blue Globe'. Flowers are good for everlasting arrangements, but you

Echinops ritro

Epimedium youngianum

must cut and dry them, inverted, before the flowers open.

Culture. Given a sunny, warm site, globe thistles thrive in well-drained, average soil with moderate watering; in good soil with plenty of moisture they may grow so robustly as to need staking. Once planted, they can remain in place, undivided, for many years.

Good companions. *Achillea, Gypsophila paniculata, Helenium autumnale, Papaver orientale, Rudbeckia.*

EPIMEDIUM
Epimedium, Barrenwort, Bishop's hat
Berberidaceae

Hardy to: –30°F/–34°C; not suited to mild-winter regions
Exposure: Sun, partial shade, shade
Water: Regular
Flowers in: Spring
Colors: Red, pink, yellow, white

Elegant, neat, polished—and tough—are words that describe the *Epimedium* species and hybrids. All are low growing, making fine border plants or small-scale ground covers. Heart-shaped leaflets are poised on wiry leafstalks, the leaves overlapping to form dense clumps. The year's new growth emerges bronzy pink, becomes green by summertime, and finally turns reddish bronze in autumn; foliage is deciduous or evergreen, depending on the species or hybrid. Small flowers are carried on wiry stems in airy, open spikes—well above the leaves in some kinds, or barely out of the foliage in

Erigeron 'Förster's Liebling'

others. Blossom shape varies from cup-and-saucer formation to just the saucer; flowers of some species have small, columbinelike spurs.

Deciduous *E. grandiflorum* bears the largest flowers: to 2 inches across, in red and violet with prominent white spurs. Named selections include 'Rose Queen', 'Snow Queen', and dark lilac 'Violaceum'. The spiny-leafed plants reach about a foot high. The deciduous hybrid *E. youngianum* produces great numbers of flowers late in the epimedium season, just above the 8-inch clumps of pale green leaves; popular selections are pure white 'Niveum' and mauve pink 'Roseum' (sometimes sold as *E. lilacinum*).

Among the evergreen and nearly evergreen sorts, Persian epimedium, *E. pinnatum*, makes foot-high clumps of broad, glossy leaflets with flowering stems that rise several inches higher. Flowers are soft yellow, though most plants sold actually represent the darker yellow–flowered subspecies *colchicum*. A similar plant is the hybrid *E. versicolor*; most popular is its vigorous light yellow–flowered selection 'Sulphureum'. Short clumps of spiny-edged, red-tinted leaflets characterize the hybrid *E. rubrum*. Numerous white-spurred red flowers appear above its foliage in many-branched sprays.

Culture. Epimediums appreciate a somewhat acid soil with plenty of organic matter. In shaded beds, they associate naturally with shade-loving perennials and shrubs; but if summers are not hot and dry, plants will grow well in full sun as long as moisture is provided. Early in the year, before new growth begins, shear off the last year's foliage (even of the evergreen kinds); this cleanup will reveal all the beauty of new foliage and flowers. You don't need to divide clumps to rejuvenate; but if you want to increase a plant, cut through the clump with a sharp spade and transplant the separated pieces with some soil attached. Do this in autumn or early spring.

Good companions. *Bergenia, Dicentra, Helleborus, Polygonatum, Primula.*

ERIGERON
Fleabane
Compositae

Hardy to: Varies
Exposure: Sun
Water: Moderate
Flowers in: Summer
Colors: Blue, violet, lavender, pink, white

At a casual glance, you could mistake these daisies for their Aster relatives. A closer look would reveal that the flower heads contain threadlike rather than flattened petals. The most widely sold plants are hybrids derived in part from species native to western North America. These hybrids have a bushy habit, with rather narrow, pointed leaves; leafy stems grow to about 2 feet high, bearing clusters of 1½- to 2-inch blossoms. Individual flowers run from single to nearly double, in a pleasing range of soft colors. Violet-blue 'Darkest of All' is widely available; others include semidouble, carmine-pink 'Förster's Liebling' ('Förster's Darling'), light violet 'Strahlenmeer', and pink-blushed white 'Sommerneuschnee' ('New Summer Snow').

Culture. Fleabanes grow best in well-drained light soil. They'll grow in full sun and flower over a long period in regions where summer is cool to mild. In hot-summer areas, they prefer a bit of light shade and have a shorter summer flowering season. Cut plants back after the first flush of flowers to encourage a repeat performance. Divide crowded clumps in early spring.

Good companions. *Gypsophila paniculata, Helenium autumnale, Monarda, Oenothera.*

Eryngium alpinum

ERYNGIUM
Sea holly
Umbelliferae

Hardy to: Varies
Exposure: Sun
Water: Moderate
Flowers in: Summer
Colors: Blue, white

The sea hollies are plants of considerable character: stiff, prickly, almost artificial-looking—and indeed they are good material for everlasting arrangements. All form a rosette of foliage from which rise leafy, branched stems; at the tip of each branch is a cone-shaped flower head sitting on spiny bracts arranged in a starburst pattern. In some kinds the bracts are narrow and jagged, in others broad and deeply cut. Leaves, too, are often lobed or deeply cut and spiny. Silvery gray, steel blue, and sea green are the prevailing colors of flowers, bracts, and foliage.

One of the handsomest species is *E. amethystinum*, which survives to –35°F/–37°C. In its best form, flower heads are steely blue to violet surrounded by broad, spiny, blue-gray bracts. Stems may reach 3 feet high; the foliage is dark green and deeply cut. Plants in commercial circulation, though, may differ in height, size, leaf design, and intensity of color. These are likely to be the hybrid *E. tripartitum*, hardy to –20°F/–29°C: a 2-foot-high plant with thimble-size blue flower heads and dark blue bracts.

E. planum, hardy to –20°F/–29°C, has light blue flower heads that are small and rounded, with narrow and spiky blue-green bracts. Its many-branched stems grow 2 to 3 feet high. Named selections offer white and blue shades; 'Blue Dwarf' grows only to 1½ feet tall. The leaves of *E. bourgatii* are gray-green with white veins, and so deeply cut that the segments are almost threadlike. Small flower heads are silvery blue to greenish, set off by spiky, silvery gray, pinwheel-like bracts. Plants reach about 1½ feet high, are hardy to –20°F/–29°C. Spiny-appearing *E. alpinum* is actually soft to the touch; 1½-inch silvery violet flowers appear on stems to 2½ feet. Plants are hardy to –35°F/–37°C.

Culture. Plants have long taproots, so they need a deep soil. But they prefer a light, sandy or even gravelly soil of no great fertility. These are permanent plants that never need dividing.

Good companions. *Artemisia, Limonium latifolium, Oenothera, Zauschneria.*

EUPATORIUM
Joe-Pye weed
Compositae

Hardy to: –30°F/–34°C
Exposure: Sun, partial shade
Water: Regular
Flowers in: Summer, early autumn
Colors: Purple, lilac, pink

Three species share the name Joe-Pye weed, all of them making hefty, shrublike clumps to 6 feet or more. Massive in size and bulk, they nevertheless are graceful as well—due largely to the tiny blossoms in large, loose clusters that suggest puffs of smoke. Strong,

Eupatorium purpureum

Euphorbia characias wulfenii

upright stems bear whorls of lance-shaped leaves 6 to 12 inches long. In *E. purpureum,* dark green stems and leaves make a backdrop for rosy pink to lilac purple flowers. Purple-mottled stems set apart spotted Joe-Pye weed, *E. maculatum;* in its form 'Atropurpureum', both stems and leaf veins are purple. Hollowstem Joe-Pye weed, *E. fistulosum,* is just that; otherwise, it is similar to *E. purpureum.*

Culture. To enjoy the full magnificence of Joe-Pye weed, give it good, moist soil. It's among the few perennials that will even thrive in boggy soil alongside water. Plants may remain in place for many years, but you can dig and divide for increase in early spring.

Good companions. *Hibiscus moscheutos, Iris* (Louisiana), *Ligularia, Lythrum.*

EUPHORBIA
Spurge
Euphorbiaceae

Hardy to: Varies
Exposure: Sun
Water: Moderate
Flowers in: Spring, summer
Colors: Green, yellow, red

The spurges are an amazingly diverse group of plants, encompassing the familiar holiday poinsettia, the spiny crown-of-thorns, desert-dwelling cactus mimics, and the green-and-white annual snow-on-the-mountain. In many instances, what appear to be flower petals actually are modified leaves (called "bracts") surrounding the insignificant true flowers. The pe-

rennial spurges presented here are, with one exception, a more cohesive group, featuring narrowly oval leaves that surround stems in bottlebrush fashion leading up to clusters of usually cup-shaped "flowers." Note that all spurges have a milky sap that is irritating to eyes and sensitive skin.

The hardiest species, *E. corollata,* will survive to –35°F/–37°C. It also departs from the general description given above. Its slender, branching stems may be a bit floppy in the first few years, but when plants are established they will send out enough stems to form a loose, airy mound to 3 feet high bearing small, willowlike, bluish green leaves. Throughout summer into autumn, plants are a froth of ¼-inch white flowers carried in multibranched sprays giving it the appearance of baby's breath (*Gypsophila paniculata*). In autumn, the leaves turn red.

Orange-red "flowers" and clumps that spread by creeping rhizomes distinguish *E. griffithii,* which is hardy to –20°F/–29°C. Upright, 2- to 3-foot branched stems bear lance-shaped leaves with pink midribs; 'Fireglow' is a selection with brick red bracts.

Four species share the common features of chartreuse to lime green bracts and bluish green foliage. Tallest and most impressive is *E. characias* and its various forms, hardy to 10°F/–12°C. Stems ringed with linear blue-green leaves angle outward then upward, making a shrubby clump to 4 feet high. Topping the stems in late winter to early spring are large, dome-shaped clusters of 1-inch "flowers," each with a dark central eye. The subspecies *E. c. wulfenii* (sometimes sold as *E. veneta*) has broader clusters, the flowers a yellower shade of chartreuse and without dark centers. Its hybrid, *E. martinii,* resembles a 2½-foot version of *E. characias* with bronze-tinted leaves and stems. Flower bracts on these spurges remain attractive for several months. When they fade, cut their stems to the ground; by then, new stems will have grown from the plant's base.

Stems of *E. rigida* (sometimes sold as *E. biglandulosa*) may sprawl a bit at first, then turn upright so that a clump often will be broader than its 1½- to 2-foot height. Narrow-pointed gray-green leaves surround stems up to the

Filipendula purpurea

broad, rounded clusters of greenish yellow bracts produced in late winter or early spring. Bracts fade to pink before stems die; cut out spent stems in favor of new ones that are growing from the base. Plants are hardy to 0°F/ –18°C. For a similar but totally prostrate plant, look for *E. myrsinites*, hardy to –20°F/–29°C. Each of its trailing stems is closely set with broadly oval, stemless, silvery gray leaves; nearly spherical flower clusters are greenish yellow. Like *E. rigida*, the flowering stems are long lasting but should be cut out when bracts fade and new stems have grown in.

Cushion spurge—*E. polychroma*, often sold as *E. epithymoides*—is a popular front-of-the-border plant, forming dense, rounded clumps 1 to 1½ feet high and wide. In spring, flattened clusters of greenish yellow bracts appear at stem ends, nosegay style. The display lasts into summer. In autumn, foliage turns an attractive red shade. Plants are hardy to –30°F/–34°C but do not thrive in Gulf Coast gardens.

Culture. These perennial spurges are an undemanding lot. Though they will accept good garden soil and regular watering (given well-drained soil), they will endure poor soil and scant water—and still look presentable. Consider most of them "permanent" plants, making deep-rooted, tight clumps. Only one—*E. griffithii*—forms a spreading clump that might need to be curbed in time.

Good companions. *Artemisia, Aurinia saxatilis, Limonium latifolium, Linum, Nepeta, Oenothera.*

FILIPENDULA
Meadowsweet
Rosaceae

Hardy to: Varies; not suited to Gulf Coast and Florida
Exposure: Sun, partial shade
Water: Regular
Flowers in: Summer
Colors: Pink, white

With their dense plumes of tiny flowers floating over handsome clumps of large, jagged-lobed leaves, the meadowsweets bear a superficial resemblance to *Astilbe* (see page 53). And like the astilbes, most prefer a moist to constantly damp soil. One immediately obvious difference, though, is size: meadowsweets are generally larger, taller, bolder-textured plants more suited to background positions.

Bright pink queen of the prairie, *F. rubra*, is the most imposing species, growing 6 to 8 feet tall given ample moisture; its selected form 'Venusta' has flowers of darker, purplish pink atop 4- to 6-foot stems. Plants are hardy to –40°F/–40°C. European queen of the meadow, *F. ulmaria*, is a similar, equally hardy species with creamy white flowers on stems to 6 feet tall. More widely grown are two selections with decorative foliage: 'Variegata' has leaves margined in light yellow, while the shade-preferring form 'Aurea' has bright yellow foliage but insignificant flowers. Japanese meadowsweet, *F. purpurea*, grows where temperatures go no lower than –10°F/–23°C. Its broad clumps produce large, maple-like leaves and reddish flower stems to 4 feet that carry plumes of dark cherry pink blossoms. Specialists may offer 'Alba', with white flowers, and 'Elegans', which has white blossoms with red stamens.

Dropwort, *F. vulgaris*, not only has different cultural needs (see below) but differs in other details as well. Foliage is fine textured, fernlike, in low, spreading mounds. Slender stems rise to 2 feet, bearing branched sprays of white blossoms—double, roselike flowers in the slightly shorter selection 'Flore Pleno'. Plants are hardy to –40°F/–40°C.

Culture. Except for dropwort, *F. vulgaris*, the meadowsweets need a good, organically enriched soil and at least regular watering. These are good candidates for pondside planting, where moist soil will be assured. Plant them in full sun where summer is cool and in northern latitudes, in partial shade where summer is warm to hot. Dropwort, in contrast, prefers full sun in all but the warmest regions and will tolerate fairly dry soils—though plants are better-looking with moderate watering.

Good companions. *Astilbe, Hosta, Lobelia cardinalis, Lythrum.*

GAILLARDIA GRANDIFLORA
Gaillardia, Blanket flower
Compositae

Hardy to: –35°F/–37°C
Exposure: Sun
Water: Moderate
Flowers in: Summer
Colors: Yellow, orange, red, bronze

The warmth of summer and the colors of autumn are captured in these showy, easy-to-grow daisies. From early summer into autumn the 3- to 4-inch single or semidouble flowers keep coming on slender stems above clumps of gray-green, dandelionlike, rough-textured foliage. Many flowers display a bicolor combination—typically dark-centered with red, maroon, or bronze petals tipped in yellow. 'Burgundy' offers flowers of solid wine red; blossoms of 'Tokajer' feature orange-yellow petals surrounding a maroon center; 'Yellow Queen' is entirely yellow. The seed-

Gaillardia grandiflora 'Baby Cole'

Gaura lindheimeri

mass, bearing pink buds that open to starry white 1-inch flowers. Each stem opens just a few flowers at a time—a sparse display on young plants but a good show from established clumps. Spent flower stems are not unattractive, but you may want to remove them to prevent widespread self-seeding.

Culture. Gaura needs a deep, well-drained soil—preferably sandy to loam rather than claylike. Heat and drought it takes in stride; it's a top choice for gardens in the semiarid and arid Southwest and West. Plants never need dividing; to gain additional plants, look for volunteer seedlings.

Good companions. Achillea, Artemisia, Cosmos atrosanguineus, Limonium latifolium, Oenothera, Verbena rigida.

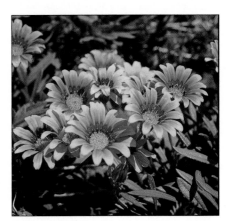

Gazania hybrid

GAZANIA
Gazania
Compositae

Hardy to: 20°F/−7°C; not suited to Gulf Coast and Florida
Exposure: Sun
Water: Moderate
Flowers in: Spring, summer
Colors: Maroon, pink, red, bronze, orange, yellow, cream, white

Gazanias are among the most colorful and varied of the daisy-flowered perennials. Each bloom is a single daisy, 2 to 4 inches across; petals may be one solid color surrounding a yellow center, though many individuals have a contrasting dark ring around the blossom center or a dark center as well. Typically, the flowers open on sunny days, close in late afternoon, and remain closed throughout overcast periods. Plants flower heavily from late spring into summer, and in virtually frostless winters they'll bloom sporadically throughout the year.

Plants sold in nurseries are complex hybrids that are of two growth habits: clump forming and trailing. Among the clump-forming kinds you'll find named selections, named strains, and unnamed plants sold according to particular color or in mixed-color lots. Leaves are long and narrow, generally green on the surface, gray on the underside; margins may be smooth or lobed. Foliage tufts may

reach 6 inches high while flowers rise on individual stems to 10 inches. Popular named hybrids are yellow-and-bronze 'Aztec Queen' and the descriptively named 'Fiesta Red', 'Burgundy', and 'Copper King'. 'Moonglow' has double yellow flowers that remain open at night. Among named strains, Chansonette and Daybreak offer flowers that open early in the day. Mini-strain plants and named selections feature compact, smaller plants.

Trailing gazanias spread by trailing stems to form patches rather than distinct clumps. Leaves generally are more gray or silvery than those of the clumping kinds, and color variety is limited. Named selections offer an extended flowering period. Widely available kinds are orange 'Sunburst', yellow 'Sunglow', and 'Sunrise Yellow', which has dark-centered flowers and green leaves.

Culture. Gazanias aren't particular about soil type. In the desert they may need regular watering, but where heat is less intense moderate watering is adequate. Plants of clumping kinds may decline in vigor after several years; plantings of trailing kinds may become patchy. When this occurs, dig, divide, and replant in early spring. Where winter cold will kill plants, you can take cuttings in autumn and keep them indoors over winter. In regions where they are truly perennial, you can increase favorite plants by cuttings in spring and summer as well.

Good companions. Coreopsis, Iris (bearded), Linum, Lobelia laxiflora, Perovskia, Salvia, Sedum, Senecio.

grown Monarch Strain contains a full range of solid colors and bicolor combinations. In flower, these gaillardias reach about 2½ feet tall. For a front-of-the-border planting, look for red-and-yellow bicolor 'Goblin' or yellow 'Golden Goblin', both of which grow to 1 foot. Even shorter, to about 8 inches, is bright red-and-yellow 'Baby Cole'.

Culture. For good growth and reliable return year after year, set out gaillardias in a well-drained sandy to loam soil. In retentive clay soils, plants may rot over winter. When clumps become crowded or patchy with bare centers, dig, divide, and replant in early spring.

Good companions. Achillea, Coreopsis, Hemerocallis, Linum, ornamental grasses, Solidago.

GAURA LINDHEIMERI
Gaura
Onagraceae

Hardy to: −10°F/−23°C
Exposure: Sun
Water: Moderate
Flowers in: Late spring, summer, autumn
Colors: White

Gaura won't catch your eye from afar, but its delicate appearance, long flowering season, and permanence ensure its popularity. From a carrotlike taproot rise numerous slender stems to form a vase-shaped, shrubby plant 2 to 3 feet high. Narrow leaves set directly on the stems grow to 3 inches long and may be tinted with red. Flower spikes stand above the foliage

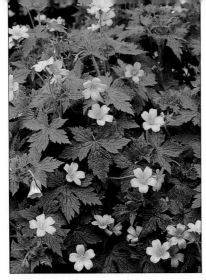

Geranium endressii

GERANIUM
Cranesbill, Geranium
Geraniaceae

Hardy to: –30°F/–34°C, except as noted; not suited to Gulf Coast and Florida
Exposure: Sun, partial shade
Water: Regular
Flowers in: Spring, summer
Colors: Purple, blue, lilac, pink, white

The flashy-flowered, summer-blooming, tender plant called "geranium" is *Pelargonium* (described on page 93). The cranesbills are a less gaudy but profuse group of cold-tolerant plants often referred to as "hardy geraniums." Plant sizes and habits vary—from rounded and bushy to low and spreading—but all have lobed, maple-like to finely cut leaves carried on long leafstalks and five-petaled round flowers about 1 to 1½ inches across. These are rather soft-looking, fine-textured plants that are handsome as border or midrange drifts and as fillers between individuals with contrasting foliage shapes. The lowest-growing kinds are good as small-scale ground covers.

Specialty nurseries offer many species and various named hybrids. Those listed here are among those most frequently offered. *G. endressii* forms 1½-foot dense mounds of deeply cut leaves and pink flowers from spring into fall in mild-summer regions. 'Wargrave Pink' is a selection having warm pink flowers; 'A. T. Johnson' has silvery pink blossoms. The vigorous *G. endressii* hybrid 'Claridge Druce' forms a 1½- to 2-foot mound of gray-green foliage and mauve pink, purple-veined flowers. Two other *G. endressii* hybrids (sometimes listed as *G. riversleaianum*) are spreading plants about 8 inches in height; 'Mavis Simpson' has satiny, light pink flowers over gray-green leaves, while 'Russell Pritchard' is bright magenta with soft green leaves.

Geranium himalayense (*G. grandiflorum*) grows a bit higher than 1 foot, its deeply lobed leaves turning a rich, bright red in autumn; the 2-inch flowers are bright violet-blue with pink to red veins and pinkish red centers. Its double-flowered form 'Plenum' ('Birch's Double') has smaller double flowers of paler lilac-blue. The vigorous but less compact *G. himalayense* hybrid 'Johnson's Blue' is larger in all ways, its flowers an intense violet-blue with red veins; plants are hardy to –20°F/–29°C. Another intense purple-blue flower is *G. magnificum*; plants grow about 1½ feet tall, the deeply cut leaves turning red in autumn.

G. pratense makes a bushy clump 2 to 3 feet high with deeply lobed leaves 3 to 6 inches across. Violet-blue, red-veined flowers 1 to 1½ inches across are typical, but named selections offer variation: 'Mrs. Kendall Clark' is pale gray-blue, 'Galactic' pure white.

G. sanguineum makes a transition between the foregoing taller, bushier types and those that are ground cover or rock garden plants. Purple to crimson flowers come on mounding-spreading plants 1 to 1½ feet tall; the deeply lobed, 2-inch leaves turn bright red in autumn. In the taller range among named selections are rosy magenta 'Cedric Morris' and white 'Album'; low, spreading selections include 'Striatum' ('Lancastriense'), with red-veined, pale pink flowers, and mauve pink 'Glenluce'.

G. cinereum—hardy to –20°F/ –29°C—is a spreading plant to 6 inches high, with deeply cut leaves and inch-wide blossoms; 'Ballerina' has gray-green foliage as a backdrop for dark red-veined, lilac-pink flowers; 'Giuseppi' is an assertive magenta. *G. dalmaticum,* also hardy to –20°F/–29°C, is another 6-inch spreader with red-veined pink blossoms; in autumn, the glossy, lobed leaves become brilliant red-orange. Magenta red *G. macrorrhizum* grows to 12 to 14 inches and spreads by rhizomes into sizable patches; the aromatic, lobed leaves color yellow and red in autumn. For a softer flower color, there is the selection 'Ingwersen's Variety', which has rose pink blossoms. This species has a greater tolerance for heat and dryness. *G. cantabrigiense* is a hybrid of *G. dalmaticum* and *G. macrorrhizum,* with the same spreading growth (to about 8 inches high) that assumes good autumn colors. A typical form bears bright pink blossoms; the selection 'Biokovo' is a pink-shaded white.

Culture. Cool- and mild-summer regions are the best hardy geranium climates, allowing plants to grow in full sun. Where summer is hot, locate plants in filtered sunlight to partial shade. Soil should be moist but well drained. You can leave clumps of most kinds in place for many years before they decline due to crowding. When you need to divide plants, do so in early spring. If you just want to increase a planting, carefully transplant rooted portions from a clump's edge.

Good companions. Alchemilla, Delphinium, Dictamnus albus, Digitalis, Hemerocallis, Lupinus.

GERBERA JAMESONII
Gerbera, Transvaal daisy
Compositae

Hardy to: 15°F/–9°C
Exposure: Sun
Water: Moderate
Flowers in: Summer, autumn
Colors: Red, pink shades, yellow, cream

Gerbera jamesonii

Calling gerberas "daisies" is like calling champagne "grape juice." These are daisies raised to a state of elegance. From clumps of tongue-shaped, lobed, 10-inch leaves rise slim but sturdy stems up to 1½ feet high, each bearing one flawless, slender-petaled, 4- to 5-inch daisy. Colors are pure, unshaded, warm and glowing. The basic flower has a single ring of petals surrounding a prominent central disk, but hybrid forms may have two petal rows, a central ring of short, tufted petals, or may be completely double.

The Blackheart and Ebony Eyes strains have dark-centered flowers; the Double Parade, Dwarf Frisbee, and Happipot strains are compact plants with 7- to 10-inch stems. Heaviest flowering is in early summer and again in autumn, but blooms may come sporadically throughout the year in coastal climates and in autumn through winter into spring in the low desert.

Culture. Gerberas need well-drained soil liberally fortified with organic amendments. Set out plants in partial or light shade in hot- and dry-summer regions. To offset problems with crown rot, be sure to keep the crowns of plants slightly above soil level. For best flowering, fertilize monthly. Give established plants deep watering; then let soil become nearly dry before watering again. Clumps may grow well for a number of years before becoming crowded. When productivity decreases, divide crowded clumps in late winter or early spring.

Good companions. Achillea, Coreopsis, Oenothera, Perovskia, Salvia, Senecio, Sisyrinchium striatum.

Geum quellyon

GEUM
Geum, Avens
Rosaceae

Hardy to: –10°F/–23°C; not suited to Gulf Coast and Florida
Exposure: Sun, partial shade
Water: Regular
Flowers in: Spring, summer
Colors: Red, orange, yellow

The geums bring summery warm, bright colors to the spring garden scene. Blossoms are single to double, ruffly and roselike, carried in airy, branched clusters that stand well above the foliage clumps. Individual plants are informal rosettes of softly hairy, strap-shaped leaves that are elaborately divided to their midribs; established clumps form attractive mounds of foliage slightly more than a foot high in the more robust types.

The largest, showiest geums are selections of *G. quellyon* (also sold as *G. chiloense* and *G. coccineum*). Slender stems lift the open blossom clusters well above the leaves. Named selections include 'Fire Opal' (semidouble orange scarlet), 'Lady Stratheden' (double yellow), 'Mrs. Bradshaw' (double orange-red), 'Princess Juliana' (double copper), and 'Starker's Magnificum' (double copper orange). Retail nurseries often stock plants in cellpacks, labeled by color.

Among shorter geums, *G.* 'Borisii' raises its single orange flowers on foot-high, leafy stalks above a 6-inch foliage mound. The yellowish apricot-flowered hybrid 'Georgenberg' is only slightly taller.

Culture. Set out plants in well-drained, good soil that will be routinely moist through summer. (Plants are somewhat drought tolerant, but their appearance is shabby with little water.) Where summer is cool to mild, you can plant geum in full sun. In hot-summer areas, see that plants receive dappled sunlight or partial shade during the hottest months. When crowded clumps lose vitality, divide them in early spring.

Good companions. Alchemilla, Campanula, Hemerocallis, Hosta, Iris (Siberian).

Gypsophila paniculata 'Bristol Fairy'

GYPSOPHILA PANICULATA
Baby's breath
Caryophyllaceae

Needs lime

Hardy to: –35°F/–37°C; not suited to Gulf Coast and Florida
Exposure: Sun
Water: Regular
Flowers in: Summer
Colors: Pink, white

Airy is the word for baby's breath. The much-branched plants with small or sparse leaves bear a froth of small flowers that seem almost to float in space. Several named selections are available, ranging in height from about 1½ to 4 feet and in flower color from pink to white; most have double or semidouble blossoms. 'Bristol Fairy' is the classic double-flowered, 3-foot-tall white variety; 'Pink Fairy' grows about half as high. Both have individual blossoms about ¼-inch across. 'Perfecta' resembles 'Bristol Fairy' but is more robust, to 4 feet with flowers twice the size. All form billowy, mounded plants. If you cut plants back to remove spent flowers, they may produce a second round of blossoms that will carry on into early autumn. The intricately branched flower sprays are good for fresh arrangements and can easily be dried for everlasting displays.

Culture. Most baby's breaths are long-lived, "permanent" perennials that need a well-drained, deep soil to accommodate their long, carrotlike roots. The name *Gypsophila* indicates a preference for lime, so be sure to incorporate lime into acid soils. To achieve perfectly

Helenium autumnale 'Moerheim Beauty'

Helianthus multiflorus

rounded flowering specimens, you need to support plants; otherwise, they can fall apart in wind, rain, or overhead watering. When stems reach about 1½ feet high, surround the plant with a stake and string "corset" (as shown on page 39) about 2 feet high for the 3- to 4-foot sorts, shorter for smaller kinds. As stems grow they'll spill over the top.

Good companions. *Crambe cordifolia, Echinacea, Echinops, Erigeron, Hemerocallis,* ornamental grasses.

✂ HELENIUM
Sneezeweed
Compositae

Hardy to: −35°F/−37°C
Exposure: Sun
Water: Regular
Flowers in: Summer, autumn
Colors: Yellow, orange, rust, brown

Bright daisies in autumnal tints appear from midsummer into early autumn, a slump period in the garden after the rush of earlier summer-flowering perennials. Each 1- to 2-inch blossom has a nearly spherical yellow or brown center that sits on a wheel of notched petals. A number of named hybrids of *H. autumnale* are available, ranging in height from 2 to about 4 feet, all branching plants with linear leaves. Among them are 'Butterpat', entirely yellow on a 3-foot plant; 'Brilliant', also a 3-footer with dark-centered, rusty orange blossoms; 2- to 3-foot 'Crimson Beauty' (actually bronzy red); and 3-foot, mahogany-colored 'Moerheim Beauty'. The taller sorts

sometimes need staking to remain upright. Or you can pinch the plants during the growing season to promote more branching and compactness; this will delay the start of flowering a bit.

Culture. The sneezeweeds need only average soil, but they do prefer it regularly moist though not boglike. Topnotch performance comes where summers are hot. Because clumps become crowded quickly, dig and divide every 2 to 3 years in spring.

Good companions. *Aster, Chrysanthemum, Echinops, Erigeron, Helianthus, Hemerocallis, Solidago.*

HELIANTHUS
Sunflower
Compositae

Hardy to: Varies
Exposure: Sun
Water: Regular
Flowers in: Summer, autumn
Colors: Yellow

The best-known sunflower is the gigantic, towering kind grown for its seeds. However, there are several perennials of smaller flower and stature that are assets to the summer and early autumn floral scene. Plants are upright with rough-textured oval leaves.

The best-known perennial sunflowers are varieties of *H. multiflorus* (sometimes sold as *H. decapetalus*), which are hardy to −20°F/−29°C. 'Flore Pleno' and 'Loddon Gold' are about 4 and 5 feet tall, respectively, with fully double bright yellow blossoms to 4 inches across. These are the best choices for the tidy garden; other named sorts—and indeed, most other perennial sunflowers—are likely to be invasive spreaders. Swamp sunflower, *H. angustifolius,* is one other well-mannered plant, a 6-footer that bears 2- to 3-inch dark-centered yellow daisies in late summer and early autumn. Plants are hardy to −10°F/−23°C. Despite its common name, it will thrive with regular, even moderate watering.

Culture. Even though sunflowers are natural "survivors," they perform best when given good soil and a regular moisture supply. Plants increase fairly rapidly and should be divided in early

spring about every 3 or 4 years—whenever performance starts to decline.

Good companions. *Aster, Boltonia asteroides, Chrysanthemum, Erigeron, Helenium, Hemerocallis, Sedum, Solidago.*

HELIOPSIS HELIANTHOIDES
False sunflower, Oxeye
Compositae

Hardy to: −30°F/−34°C
Exposure: Sun
Water: Regular to moderate
Flowers in: Summer, autumn
Colors: Yellow

The common name "false sunflower" simply expresses a botanical nicety: in appearance, these plants are as true a sunflower as any of the *Helianthus* individuals described at left. Compared with the sunflowers, they are leafier and bushier, most with roughly hairy,

Heliopsis helianthoides

lance-shaped leaves. Flowers are always yellow or orange-yellow, single to double. Nurseries offer a number of named selections, sometimes listed under *H. h. scabra*, the hairy-leafed subspecies. Semidouble 'Patula', 2 to 3 feet tall, is at the short end of the scale; double 'Gold Greenheart' and 'Golden Plume' ('Goldgefieder') and single 'Karat' normally grow to 4 feet.

Culture. The false sunflowers need the same care as true sunflowers: good soil and regular watering for best appearance. They can wait longer between dividing than sunflowers can; dig, separate, and replant in early spring whenever declining performance indicates crowding. You can also increase a favorite plant from cuttings taken in spring or early summer.

Good companions. *Anthemis, Aster, Chrysanthemum, Delphinium, Helenium, Hemerocallis, Sedum, Solidago.*

HELLEBORUS
Hellebore
Ranunculaceae

Hardy to: Varies; not suited to Gulf Coast and Florida
Exposure: Partial shade, shade
Water: Regular to moderate
Flowers in: Winter, early spring
Colors: Maroon, pink, green, white

The various hellebores are elegant plants, bringing a touch of class to lightly shaded gardens and porcelain-like flowers at a time when few other plants dare to bloom. All bear blossoms fashioned like single roses: five petal-like sepals surround a large cluster of stamens. Compact clumps form mounds of handsome, bold foliage, the leaves consisting of large leathery leaflets grouped together like fingers on an outstretched hand. Christmas rose and Lenten rose form fairly low clumps with leafstalks rising directly from the ground. Corsican hellebore and *H. foetidus* send up leafy stems from the ground, the dome-shaped blossom clusters appearing at the stem tips; after bloom, stems die to the ground just as new stems grow up to replace them.

Christmas rose, *H. niger*, will bloom between December and early spring, depending on winter severity. Each leafless flower stem usually holds one upward-facing blossom to 2 inches across; the color is white at first but turns purplish pink with age. Dark green, lusterless leaves each bear seven to nine leaflets. Plants are hardy to –30°F/–34°C and need winter chill.

Lenten rose, *H. orientalis,* is similar to Christmas rose but differs in details. Flower stems bear a few modified leaves and branched clusters of large flowers that tend to nod toward the ground; colors range from greenish or buff-tinted white through pinkish shades to liver purple, often with dark spots in the centers. Flowering starts in late winter and continues into spring. Leaves are larger, broader, and glossy, with five to eleven leaflets per leaf. Plants are also hardy to –30°F/–34°C, but they will prosper even without subfreezing temperatures.

The misleadingly named *H. foetidus* (it doesn't have an unpleasant, or fetid, odor) boasts the most graceful foliage: seven to nine blackish green, narrow leaflets at the end of each leafstalk. In late winter and early spring, clusters of inch-wide, purple-marked green flowers appear atop the leafy, 1½-foot stems. Plants are hardy to –10°F/–23°C, and when established they are fairly drought tolerant.

Corsican hellebore, *H. lividus corsicus,* is the largest species—almost shrubby when growth is mature. Its leafy stems may rise to 3 feet, each bearing distinctly toothed, light blue-green leaflets in groups of three per leaf. Plants are hardy to –5°F/–20°C. In mild-winter areas, clusters of large, pale chartreuse flowers may appear in

Helleborus orientalis

Hemerocallis hybrids

late autumn; where winter temperatures are lower (yet within its hardiness limit), bloom holds off until early spring. Unlike other hellebores, this one can grow in some sun; established clumps are drought tolerant.

Culture. Although two of the species will withstand some drought when established, all hellebores appreciate rich soil and regular watering. Woodland conditions—medium shade to filtered sunlight with moist soil—are ideal. These are "permanent" perennials, never needing division to maintain vigor. You can divide clumps to gain more plants, but divisions re-establish slowly. The simplest way to increase a planting is to save volunteer seedlings and move them to desired locations while they are small.

Good companions. *Brunnera macrophylla, Dicentra, Digitalis, Doronicum, Epimedium, Polygonatum, Thalictrum.*

HEMEROCALLIS
Daylily
Liliaceae

Hardy to: Varies
Exposure: Sun, partial shade
Water: Regular to moderate
Flowers in: Spring, summer, autumn
Colors: Cream, yellow, orange, red, pink shades, lavender, purple; bicolor combinations

The modern daylily has come a long way from the old dull orange *H. fulva*—an indestructible plant that escaped from cultivation to become a roadside "weed" in eastern North America. In

(Continued on page 78)

Ornamental Grasses

The grasses, it turns out, lead secret garden lives beyond their humdrum roles as lawn and weeds. Ornamental grass species offer distinctive foliage textures to blend and contrast with the more standard flowering perennials; some also provide good autumn foliage color. There are grasses for all aspects: sun or shade, moist or dry soils. None bears flowers in the usual sense of showy, colorful petals, but the heads of tiny flowers (florets) clustered atop slender stems frequently make an attractive display. Flowering season is summer, unless otherwise specified; but many grasses hold their flowering stems well into autumn or even winter.

The best time to both plant and divide ornamental grasses is early spring. At that time, too, tidy up the clumps before new growth begins, removing dead leaves and flowering stems from the previous year.

ARRHENATHERUM elatus bulbosum 'Variegatum'. Bulbous oat grass. *Gramineae*. Hardy to –20°F/–29°C. Silvery white–margined leaves make graceful foliage clumps to about 1½ feet high, the center leaves erect but the outer ones arching in fountainlike sprays. Flowering stems rise to about 3 feet. Clumps spread by rhizomes, which may occasionally need to be curtailed.

Plant bulbous oat grass in sun to partial shade in cool-summer regions; where summers are hot, partial shade will prevent burning of the variegated leaves. Appearance is best in cool seasons and cool climates, with good soil and regular watering. Divide and replant as needed, whenever vigor decreases.

CALAMAGROSTIS acutiflora stricta. Feather reed grass. *Gramineae*. Hardy to –20°F/–29°C. The common name describes its two outstanding characteristics. Reedlike leaves grow upright to about 4 feet, and then in midsummer the vertical flower stems

rising 6 to 7 feet bear feathery, yellowish tan plumes. These remain effective for many months, first turning rust colored and then aging to gray. Clumps expand gradually and remain compact. This is a sterile hybrid, producing no volunteer seedlings.

Feather reed grass prefers good soil and regular watering, but it will grow in soil that is poorly drained and damp.

CAREX. Sedge. *Cyperaceae*. The sedges are not true grasses, but their appearance is decidedly grasslike. Fox red curly sedge, *C. buchananii*, is hardy to –10°F/–23°C. Upright but arching, curly-tipped leaves are rusty bronze and reedlike, 2 to 3 feet tall, making a fine-textured color contrast along other perennials in regularly watered soil. Bowles' Golden sedge, *C. elata (C. stricta)* 'Bowles' Golden', is hardy to –20°F/–29°C. It also has an upright yet fountainlike habit, reaching 2 feet; leaves are brilliant yellow from spring well into summer—before turning green for the remainder of the year. Variegated Japanese sedge, *C. morrowii expallida (C. m.* 'Variegata'), is also hardy to –20°F/–29°C. Shaggy dog–looking plants are foot-high mounds of arching foliage, each leaf white but margined in green. The form 'Aureavariegata' substitutes yellow for white.

These sedges need regular watering and will thrive in the boggy soil of pond and stream margins. In cool-summer regions, they'll grow in full sun; in warmer areas, give them partial shade.

CHASMANTHIUM latifolium. Sea oats. *Gramineae*. Hardy to –20°F/–29°C. Another common name, bamboo grass, paints a better picture of the plant. Broad-leafed blades are set along upright, bamboolike stems that grow 2 to 4 feet high. In summer these terminate in arching flower stems bearing loose spikes of silvery green, oatlike (that is, flattened) flower heads. These remain attractive into autumn,

drying to a straw color. Leaves and stems turn brown in winter and should be cut nearly to the ground before new spring growth begins. Unlike bamboo, clumps increase slowly in girth and are not invasive.

Plant sea oats in full sun where summers are cool, in partial shade in hot-summer climes. Give plants average to good soil and regular watering; divide when vigor and flowering decrease.

FESTUCA. Fescue. *Gramineae*. Hardy to –30°F/–34°C. The fescues make tufted, shaving brush–like clumps of needle-thin foliage. Blue fescue, *F. ovina glauca*, forms steely blue tufts 8 to 12 inches high and about as wide; it is frequently used as a drift plant or small-scale ground cover. *Festuca amethystina* is similar but larger: bluish green *F. a.* 'April Green' reaches 1½ feet. Both species bear slender spikes of florets on stems slightly taller than the foliage.

The fescues tolerate partial shade in all regions and require it where summers are hot. Give them average but well-drained soil. In desert gardens they'll need regular watering, but in other climates they thrive on just moderate irrigation. Eventually clumps will become crowded and decline in vigor, sometimes becoming bare in the centers. At that point, dig clumps, separate them into small divisions, and replant.

HAKONECHLOA macra 'Aureola'. Japanese forest grass. *Gramineae*. Hardy to –30°F/–34°C. In appearance and manner of growth this grass resembles a very small bamboo. Lax, yellow-striped leaves are borne on slender leaning or arching stems that reach about 1½ feet in length. One clump is a low hummock of lush foliage; a drift planting makes a leafy carpet about a foot high.

This forest denizen grows best in cool- to mild-summer regions under woodland conditions: in partial shade and somewhat acid soil that is well drained and enriched with organic matter. Water regularly for best appearance.

HELICTOTRICHON sempervirens. Blue oat grass. *Gramineae*. Hardy to –20°F/–29°C. Picture a triple-size blue fescue (*Festuca ovina glauca*), and you have a clear vision of blue oat grass. Stiff, blue-gray to blue-green, shaving brushlike tufts of foliage grow 2 to 3 feet high. Needle-slim gray stems carry small flowering plumes a bit above the leaves.

Grow blue oat grass in full sun and well-drained soil of average to good quality; give plants moderate to regular watering.

IMPERATA cylindrica 'Rubra' (*I. c.* 'Red Baron'). Japanese blood grass. *Gramineae*. Hardy to 5°F/–15°C. From spring through autumn, this is the most colorful of the grasses. Clumps of upright foliage grow 1 to 2 feet high, the upper half of each leaf blade colored nearly blood red. The color is most intense in full sun and is particularly telling where sunlight can shine through the foliage. Clumps spread slowly and are not invasive.

Give Japanese blood grass average to good soil and moderate to regular watering.

MISCANTHUS sinensis. Eulalia grass. *Gramineae*. Hardy to –20°F/–29°C. Eulalia grass and its named selections form robust, tall clumps good for accent specimens and background planting. Foliage mass usually reaches 5 to 6 feet, and the flowering stems rise another 1 to 3 feet above the leaves. Its foliage turns golden tan in winter.

Maiden grass, *M. s.* 'Gracillimus', has especially narrow, arching, silvery green leaves and loose, feathery, beige flower clusters. Leaves of the selections 'Variegatus' and 'Silberfeil' are broader and have lengthwise white stripes. 'Morning Light' has distinct white margins around its light silvery green leaves. 'Zebrinus' reverses those colors and that arrangement: yellow and green stripes run laterally, across the leaf blades. 'Silver Feather' ('Silberfeder') was selected for its especially fine silvery pink-beige flower plumes. You also have a choice among shorter selections, the leaves of which grow just 3 to 4 feet high. 'Yaku Shima' has fine-textured foliage that becomes red in autumn; 'Arabesque' has especially large flower plumes; and 'Purpurascens' has broader leaves that turn purplish red in late summer.

The eulalia grasses make dense, noninvasive clumps when planted in sun or light shade. Plants will grow in any well-drained soil, given moderate to regular watering.

MOLINIA caerulea 'Variegata'. Purple moor grass. *Gramineae*. Hardy to –20°F/–29°C. Tight clumps of narrow leaves make this another of the shaving brush–style grasses. The bright green leaves are striped cream lengthwise, arching to about 2 feet high. The feathery, cream-colored flower stems rise 2½ to 3 feet, bearing pinkish florets. Throughout winter, the entire plant is a pinkish tan.

As befits a native of the moors (not to be confused with Moorish Spain), this grass prefers a neutral to acid soil, organically enriched and regularly watered. Plant in full sun.

PENNISETUM. Fountain grass. *Gramineae*. Hardiness varies. The fountain grasses are well named, as their narrow leaves form graceful clumps of broadly arching foliage. Above these rise slender stems carrying foxtail-like flower plumes. Hardiest—to –20°F/–29°C—is Chinese pennisetum, *P. alopecuroides*. Dark green leaves form clumps about 3 feet high and wide that produce a showy display of pinkish tan flower plumes from late summer into autumn. Where winter temperatures go no lower than 0°F/–18°C, *P. setaceum* is a popular grass, particularly in drought-tolerant plantings. Clumps are 2-foot-high, broad mounds of narrow leaves, in summer adorned with great numbers of flowering stems brandishing coppery pink to purplish spikes. In mild-winter areas its volunteer seedlings can make it a pest, but in colder regions this is not a problem. The form 'Cupreum' (also sold as *P. s.* 'Rubrum') has bronzed purple foliage and dark flower plumes that do not form seeds.

Give the fountain grasses a full-sun location and, for best appearance, average to good soil. Chinese pennisetum needs regular watering; moderate watering is sufficient for *P. setaceum*.

STIPA gigantea. Giant feather grass. *Gramineae*. Hardy to –10°F/–23°C. When you see this grass in flower, you'll appreciate the accuracy of its name. Tight clumps of fine-textured, arching leaves reach 2 to 3 feet, but above these in summer soar up to 6-foot stems carrying great oatlike heads of yellowish florets that appear to float over the foliage and flutter in every breeze.

This is a grass for full sun and good soil. Give it regular watering, at least while plantings are young; established clumps will grow with regular to only moderate watering.

Calamagrostis acutiflora stricta

the hands of hybridizers, several day-lily species have been interbred for generations to produce a dazzling range of colors and combinations—some soft, others brilliant—on plants that range from foot-high miniatures to 4- and 5-foot specimens. Along with color improvements have come increased petal width and thickness, and the ability for some hybrids to remain open far into the evening or even until the following day. The only part that hasn't been changed is the plant itself. Daylilies are still nearly indestructible and trouble free, while the fountains of linear foliage still recall its old-fashioned name of "corn lily."

Individual daylily blossoms may be lily shaped or chalice shaped, from 3 to 8 inches across in the standard hybrids, about 1½ to 3 inches in the miniature kinds. Specialists offer both single- and double-flowered forms as well as "spiders" with long, narrow, twisted petals. Although each flower lasts just a day, each stem bears numerous buds that give a prolonged display. Flowering starts in mid- to late spring, and by mixing hybrids that flower early, late, and in midseason, you can enjoy a bloom period lasting well over a month. Scattered bloom may occur during summer, then reblooming types will put on a second display in late summer to midautumn.

Culture. Though daylilies have a reputation for toughness and adaptability, they reward any attention beyond the most casual. Where summers are hot and dry, choose a location where plants will get filtered sunlight during the heat of the day. In cool- to mild-summer climates, and where summers are hot yet humid, plants can take full sun; you can plant in partial shade, but bloom production will be reduced. Be aware that in partially shaded plantings, where sunlight comes from a single direction, daylily blossoms will face the sun. For best performance, give plants well-drained soil generously amended with organic matter. Though daylilies will perform with just moderate watering, they are at their best with regular watering from the start of spring growth through summer and into autumn.

Daylily clumps will persist for years without division, but their perfor-mance will flag. For best appearance, divide when crowded, usually after 3 to 6 years. Do this in summer in cool-summer regions and where the growing season is short; where summer is hot, divide in autumn or early spring.

Daylily plants may be evergreen, semievergreen, or deciduous (dormant); catalog descriptions usually give this information for each hybrid. The deciduous types may not be totally successful in frost-free regions, but they are likely to be the hardiest, to about −35°F/−37°C. Evergreen kinds usually need winter protection where temperatures drop below −20°F/−29°C; the semievergreen plants may also benefit from it.

Good companions. Anchusa, Centranthus ruber, Chelone, Chrysanthemum superbum, Delphinium, Dictamnus albus, Gaillardia, Geranium, Gypsophila paniculata, Kniphofia, Lupinus, Paeonia.

HEUCHERA
Coral bells, Alum root
Saxifragaceae

Hardy to: −30°F/−34°C; not suited to Gulf Coast and Florida
Exposure: Sun, partial shade
Water: Regular
Flowers in: Spring, summer
Colors: Red, pink, green, cream, white

Coral bells have been a favorite with generations of gardeners for their good-looking foliage and graceful spikes of flowers. Nearly round to heart-shaped leaves on long leafstalks form low, mounded clumps that gradually spread as the woody rootstocks branch and elongate. Leaves usually have hairy surfaces and may have scalloped edges and attractive dark or silvery mottling. Rising above the foliage in spring through summer come 1- to 2½-foot wiry, branched stalks bearing open clusters of small, bell-shaped blossoms.

The majority of coral bells available are selections of *H. sanguinea* or hybrids of it collectively called *H. brizoides*. Specialists list named varieties; retail nurseries may offer plants identified only by color. The Bressingham Hybrids from England offer the full range of colors and heights.

Heuchera sanguinea

In addition to the *H. brizoides*–type hybrids, several distinct named hybrids are available. 'Palace Purple'—either a hybrid or a selection of *H. micrantha*—forms foot-tall clumps of 3-inch, maplelike leaves of purplish to bronzy red. The tiny pinkish flowers are fairly insignificant. For Pacific Coast dry-summer gardens where winter temperatures remain above 10°F/−12°C, the robust hybrid 'Santa Ana Cardinal' will thrive, producing 2-foot spikes of rosy red flowers over a several-month bloom season.

And finally, crosses between *Heuchera* and related *Tiarella* species have produced several plants cataloged as *Heucherella*. These are similar in culture and hardiness to the *H. brizoides* plants. Low clumps of maplelike, hairy leaves send up wiry spikes of small, starlike (not bell-shaped) blossoms. Light pink 'Bridget Bloom' is the most common representative.

Culture. Where summers are hot and dry, coral bells need partial shade, preferably shade during the afternoon. In other climates, plant in sun. They need only well-drained soil of average fertility. Clumps become crowded in 3 to 4 years, by which time foliage will be clustered at the ends of short, thick, woody stalks. Divide crowded clumps in early spring in cold-winter regions, in autumn where winters are mild. When replanting divisions, set the plant's crown even with the soil surface.

Good companions. Campanula, Iris (bearded), Platycodon, Salvia, Sisyrinchium striatum, Veronica.

HIBISCUS MOSCHEUTOS
Rose-mallow
Malvaceae

Hardy to: –10°F/–23°C
Exposure: Sun, partial shade
Water: Regular
Flowers in: Summer
Colors: Red, pink shades, white

Here is all the splendor of the tropics in a fairly hardy perennial. Really large (6 to 12 inches across) morning-glory–type blossoms begin in early summer and may continue until frost, climate permitting. Large, oval leaves cover upright, shrublike plants that grow 3 to more than 6 feet in height. For specific colors, look for named selections such as 'Lord Baltimore' (red) and 'Lady Baltimore' (pink with red center). Fine seed strains that produce plants of assorted colors include 'Southern Belle' and 2-foot-tall 'Disco Belle'.

Culture. Plenty of water is the key ingredient in rose-mallow culture. Plant in good soil and mulch plants to conserve moisture; avoid windswept locations where flowers will burn and plants lose moisture rapidly. In regions where summer is typically both hot and dry, give plants partial shade to prevent wilting. Tall stems die to the ground each winter and are replaced by new growth in spring. Clumps increase in size gradually but do not need to be divided for rejuvenation.

Good companions. *Aruncus dioicus*, *Astilbe*, *Eupatorium*, *Iris* (Louisiana), *Lythrum*.

Hibiscus moscheutos

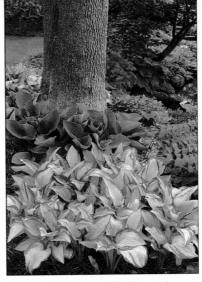

Hosta sieboldiana and *H. fortunei*

HOSTA
Hosta, Plantain lily, Funkia
Liliaceae

Hardy to: –35°F/–37°C; needs some winter chill
Exposure: Partial shade, shade
Water: Regular
Flowers in: Summer
Colors: Violet, lavender, white

Hostas do put on a bit of a floral display, but the flowers pale in comparison to the exceptionally handsome and varied foliage. To fully appreciate the tremendous variety of leaf size, shape, and color among *Hosta* species, named selections, and hybrids, you'll need to consult a specialist's catalog or visit a well-stocked nursery. Leaves may be lance shaped, heart shaped, oval, or nearly round, carried at the ends of leafstalks that rise from the ground and radiate from the center of a clump; leaves overlap to form symmetrical, almost shingled foliage mounds. Depending on the individual, leaf texture may be smooth, quiltlike, or puckery, while the surface may be glossy or dusted with a grayish, plumlike bloom; margins may be smooth or gracefully waved. Leaf colors range from light to dark green to chartreuse, gray, and blue. You'll also find combinations of colors, including variegations with white, yellow, or cream.

Plant sizes include diminutive hostas that grow no higher than 3 to 4 inches as well as showpiece plants that reach 3 feet high and wide. Bell-shaped to lilylike flowers are borne—outward facing or drooping—on spikes that barely top the foliage in some kinds or extend well above it in others.

While specialists offer a dazzling array of choices, a few widely available, tried-and-true hostas are good and inexpensive choices for the neophyte.

H. fortunei may be, in fact, an ancient hybrid affiliated to *H. sieboldiana* (below). Many named selections are sold, offering a wide range of foliage color from gray-green to yellow-green to variegated. Typical leaves are oval, up to 1 foot long; flowers are lilac.

H. lancifolia (*H. japonica*) is the aptly named narrow-leafed plantain lily. The dark green, 6-inch leaves are lance shaped, their bases tapering into long leafstalks. Foliage mounds to about a foot; lavender, outward-facing flowers come on 2-foot spikes.

H. plantaginea (*H. p.* 'Grandiflora', *H. subcordata*) has glossy bright green leaves up to about 10 inches long, broadly oval with parallel veins and a quilted surface. Foliage mounds rise to 2 feet. Its 4-inch white flowers are notably fragrant, rising just above leaves on short spikes. 'Honeybells' (lavender flowers) and 'Royal Standard' (white flowers) are hybrids that have fragrant blossoms on taller stems.

H. sieboldiana (*H. glauca*) is a classic giant. Blue-green, broadly heart-shaped leaves may reach 15 inches long, displaying a puckered surface; established clumps may reach 3 feet high. In contrast, the pale lavender flowers are small and carried on spikes that barely clear the impressive leaves. Selected forms include 'Elegans', which has the typical foliage covered in a blue-gray "bloom," and 'Frances Williams' ('Gold Edge', 'Gold Circle'), which features a broad, irregular yellow leaf edge.

H. undulata is, for good reason, known as the wavy-leafed plantain lily. Narrowly oval, 8-inch leaves have undulating margins that produce a rather lively foliage clump to 1½ feet high. Light lilac flowers appear on 3-foot spikes. The typical leaf has a creamy white center stripe, the balance of the leaf being green. Named selections offer variations that include 'Erromena' (all green) and 'Albomarginata' or 'Silver Rim' (green center with white edge).

H. ventricosa (*H. caerulea*) is called "blue plantain lily"—not for its foli-

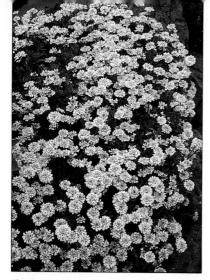
Iberis sempervirens

age, but for the violet-blue blossoms that appear on 3- foot stems above 2-foot foliage mounds. Deep green leaves are broadly heart shaped, up to 8 inches long, with glossy and deeply veined surfaces. In the form 'Aureomarginata' ('Variegata'), each leaf is edged in creamy white.

H. 'Gold Standard' features broadly heart-shaped leaves of greenish yellow edged in green—the foliage mounding to 3 feet.

Culture. Hostas are easy to grow in regions where frosty or freezing winters are followed by humid summers. In the cool humidity of the Northwest and Pacific Coast, you can grow most hostas in sun as well as shade. But where summers are hot, choose a location in at least partial shade. In general, plants with considerable white or yellow in their leaves are the most sun sensitive. Hostas in sun will be more compact than in shade and will produce more flowers; shade-grown plants may grow taller as well as larger. You'll get the most luxuriant growth when you plant hostas in good, organically enriched soil and fertilize them during the growing season. Be sure plants are kept moist.

Foliage collapses and withers in autumn frost, grows anew in spring. Slugs and snails are constant foliage enemies, especially to new growth as it unfurls. These are "permanent" plants that remain vigorous without division; in fact, clumps become more beautiful as they grow larger. To increase a favorite hosta, carefully remove plants from a clump's perimeter.

Good companions. *Alchemilla mollis, Anemone hybrida, Astilbe, Campanula, Dicentra, Polygonatum, Thalictrum.*

IBERIS SEMPERVIRENS
Evergreen candytuft
Cruciferae

Hardy to: −30°F/−34°C; not suited to Gulf Coast and Florida
Exposure: Sun
Water: Moderate to regular
Flowers in: Spring
Colors: White

This old-fashioned border plant will smother itself with 2-inch clusters of sparkling white flowers from early to late spring. Even when not in bloom, plants are good-looking: densely foliaged with glossy, narrow, dark green leaves. Typical plants are 8 to 12 inches high and twice as wide, but named strains include short and compact 'Little Gem' and low, wide- spreading 'Purity'. 'Snowflake' offers larger flowers and broader leaves on a plant that may reach 1 foot high and spread to 3 feet; it will flower at intervals throughout the year where summer and winter temperatures are mild.

Culture. Give evergreen candytuft good, well-drained soil and a full-sun location (except in hot-summer regions, where plants need a bit of shade). In all regions, set out plants in early spring; autumn planting is possible in mild-winter areas. After the main flowering burst, cut or shear back plants to encourage compactness. You can start new plants from summer cuttings; use these to replace old plants as they decline.

Good companions. *Armeria maritima, Aurinia saxatile, Dianthus, Heuchera, Iris* (bearded), *Phlox subulata, Veronica*

IRIS
Iris
Iridaceae

Hardy to: Varies
Exposure: Sun, partial shade
Water: Regular
Flowers in: Spring, early summer, autumn
Colors: All colors; many multicolor combinations

Mention the name *Iris* and most people will think of the tall, showy, bearded irises that are mainstays of the midspring flower display. But though these may be the most widely planted irises, they constitute only part of a highly diverse group of plants.

Despite their considerable differences, all irises have similar foliage and the same basic flower structure. Plants are composed of swordlike leaves that overlap each other to form a flat fan of foliage. All blossoms have three true petals (called "standards") and three petal-like sepals (called "falls"). Standards may be upright, arching, or flaring to horizontal; falls range from flaring to drooping. Flower types fit into two broad groups: bearded, with a caterpillarlike ridge of hairs on each fall, and beardless, which have no such hairs.

Bearded irises

Among bearded irises you'll find a dazzling array of flower colors and color combinations. Irises of this type are separated into the four main classes outlined below. Except for the aril and arilbred irises, all bearded irises need the same basic care outlined under "Bearded iris culture."

Tall bearded irises (TB). The tall bearded irises (called simply "TBs" by fanciers) bloom in midspring, bearing large, broad-petaled blossoms on branching stems that reach 2½ to 4 feet high. Types designated as *reblooming* or *remontant* will flower again in summer, autumn, or winter— depending on the individual hybrid, the climate in which it is growing, and the cultural encouragement it receives.

Median and dwarf irises. Flowers of these irises resemble those of the tall beardeds but on a smaller scale; stems and foliage are smaller as well. *Median* is a collective term for the first four types listed below; the miniature dwarfs are in a class by themselves.

Border bearded irises (BB). These are segregates from tall bearded breeding, growing 15 to 28 inches tall with foliage and flowers in proportion to the reduced height.

Miniature tall bearded irises (MTB). These have the same height range as

Iris 'Gala Madrid' (tall bearded hybrid)

the border beardeds, but this group is characterized by pencil-slim stems, rather narrow and short foliage, and relatively tiny flowers just 2 to 3 inches wide. Bloom time is the same as for the tall and border beardeds, though the color range is more limited. Usually these MTBs have more stems per clump than the average tall bearded.

Intermediate bearded irises (IB). Modern intermediates are hybrids of tall beardeds and standard dwarf kinds (below). Flowers are 3 to 5 inches wide, carried on 15- to 28-inch stems. Their flowering period starts 1 to 3 weeks before the tall bearded season; some individuals bloom a second time in autumn. (This group also comprises a number of similar-ancestry antique sorts, including the old "common purple" and "graveyard white" irises that flower in early spring.)

Standard dwarf bearded irises (SDB). Most modern members of this group were developed from a cross of tall bearded varieties with a miniature dwarf species from central Europe. Bloom time is even earlier than that of the intermediates. Plants produce a profusion of 2- to 3-inch-wide flowers in a wide range of colors and patterns; stems reach 10 to 15 inches tall.

Miniature dwarf bearded irises (MDB). These are the shortest of bearded irises, growing just 2 to 10 inches tall when in flower. Typically they bear a wealth of flowers in a great variety of colors; blooms are often a bit large in proportion to the rest of the plant. Well-grown, established clumps can become cushions of flowers—attractive in foreground plantings and in rock gardens.

Aril and arilbred irises. The word "exotic" might have been coined especially for the aril species, which take their name from the collarlike white cap (the *aril*) on their seeds. These irises comprise two groups, Regelia and Oncocyclus; both are native to arid regions of the Near East and central Asia.

Oncocyclus irises typically feature 4- to 7-inch-wide domed or globe-shaped flowers with a base color of gray, silver, lavender, gold, or maroon. In many types the petals are intricately veined and dotted with darker hues. Stems are short, usually reaching no more than 1 foot; leaves are narrow, ribbed, and often sickle shaped.

Regelia irises have smaller and more vertical blossoms than the oncocyclus types, but the base colors and contrasting veining often are in brighter shades (though *I. hoogiana* is pure blue), often with a lustrous sheen. Flower stems may reach 1½ to 2½ feet high; narrow, ribbed leaves are usually linear. Hybrids between Oncocyclus and Regelia irises are called Oncogelias.

All the pure aril irises have strict cultural needs: perfect drainage, alkaline soil, and a hot, dry summer dormant period. Oncocyclus types are the most particular; regelias and oncogelias are relatively more adaptable. All are hardy to about –20°F/–29°C.

Arilbred irises are hybrids between aril types and tall or median bearded irises. Many named hybrids are sold, varying in the amount of aril "blood" in their ancestries; in general, those with more aril in their background have a more exotic appearance. Many arilbreds are nearly as easy to grow as tall beardeds, needing only the addition of lime to acid soil and a bit of extra attention to drainage.

Bearded iris culture. All bearded irises demand good drainage. As long as rhizomes don't sit in saturated soil, they'll grow well in soils that range from sandy to claylike. If you must grow irises in heavy clay soil, plant them in a raised bed or a raised planting area so that soil will not remain moist for long around the rhizomes.

In cool-summer climates, bearded irises must have full sun from spring through autumn. But where summers are hot, plants may appreciate a bit of afternoon filtered sunlight or high shade. Be judicious, though: too much shade seriously cuts down on flowering and interferes with the necessary summer ripening of rhizomes. None succeeds in Gulf Coast and Florida gardens.

Plant rhizomes from early summer through midautumn—in July or August in cold-winter climates, in September or October where summer temperatures are high and winters fairly mild. Set rhizomes with their tops just beneath the soil surface. After planting, water well to settle the soil and start root growth; thereafter, water sparingly until you see by new growth that plants have taken hold. Then water regularly unless rain or freezing weather intercedes. If weather turns hot after planting, shade the newly planted rhizomes to prevent sunscald and subsequent rot.

From the moment growth starts in late winter or early spring, water plants regularly until about 6 weeks after flowers fade (increases and buds for the following year are formed during the immediate postbloom period). During summer, established plantings can get by on less frequent watering—as little as every other week in warm climates, as seldom as monthly where summers are cool. In cold-winter climates, where temperatures will drop below about –15°F/–26°C, give plantings protection (see page 40) just after the ground freezes.

Clumps become crowded after 3 or 4 years, causing the number of stems and quality of flowers to decrease. When this occurs, dig and divide clumps at the best planting time for your climate.

Beardless irises

Only two characteristics are common to all irises in this broad category: the lack of a beard on the falls, and roots that are more fibrous than fleshy. The following four hybrid groups are the most widely sold of the beardless types.

Japanese irises. Hardy to about –20°F/–29°C, these are derived from *I. ensata* (formerly *I. kaempferi*). Japanese irises are graceful, moisture-loving plants that, grown under ideal con-

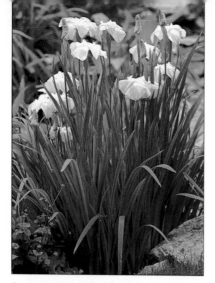

Japanese iris hybrid

ditions, will bear the largest flowers among irises. The narrow, upright leaves, each with a distinct midrib, are reminiscent of rushes. Above the foliage clumps, on stems up to 4 feet high, float 4- to 12-inch flowers. Blooms are fairly flat, either single (standards small and distinct in appearance from falls) or double (standards and falls of about equal size, shape, and markings). Colors include white and all shades of purple, violet, blue, and pink; light-colored flowers often are intricately marked, veined, or striped. Flowering begins in late spring and extends into early summer in some areas.

Japanese irises must have rich, acid soil and copious amounts of nonalkaline water from the time growth begins until the blooming period ends. Grow them at pond edges or in large containers of soil sunk halfway to the rim in the water of a pond or pool. If you water plants liberally, they'll also succeed in garden beds—preferably in loam to clay soil, liberally amended with organic matter.

Where summers are cool, plant in full sun; in warm- to hot-summer regions, choose a spot that receives high or dappled afternoon shade. Plant rhizomes 2 inches deep in autumn or spring. When clumps become crowded (as indicated by declining performance), divide them in late summer or early autumn; replant rhizomes immediately.

Louisiana irises. Hardy to about 0°F/−18°C, the progenitors of this group are three or more species native to swamps and moist lowlands primarily along the Gulf Coast. Though

the species come from regions of fairly mild winters, some hybrids have been successful as far north as South Dakota. Louisiana iris leaves are long, linear, and unribbed; graceful, flattish blossoms are carried on 2- to 5-foot stems. The range of flower colors and patterns is nearly as extensive as that found among the tall bearded kinds.

These irises will thrive in rich, well-watered garden soil as well as at pond margins and in shallow water; both soil and water should be neutral to acid. Full sun is best in cool- and mild-summer areas, but where summer heat is intense, choose a spot that will receive light afternoon shade. Plant rhizomes ½ to 1 inch deep in late summer. Where ground freezes in winter, give plants winter protection (see page 40). Louisiana irises form large rhizomes that will make for crowded plantings in a year or two if not spaced 2 or more feet apart. When a clump or planting becomes overcrowded—easily within 3 to 4 years—dig and divide in late summer. Replant divisions immediately or hold them in a bucket of water so roots will not dry out.

Siberian irises. Hardy to about −30°F/−34°C, the most widely sold members of this group are named hybrids derived from *I. sibirica* and *I. sanguinea*, two species found in moist meadows in parts of Europe and Asia. Both species and their hybrids have narrow, almost grasslike deciduous foliage and reed-thin flower stems. Depending on the individual hybrid, leaf length ranges from 1 to 3 feet, stem height from about 14 inches to 4 feet. In midspring, each stem bears two to five blossoms with upright standards and flaring to drooping falls. Colors include violet, purple, lavender, wine, pink, blue, and white; several hybrids are light yellow.

Plant Siberian irises in early spring or late summer in cold-winter regions, in autumn where summers are hot and winters mild to moderate. Choose a location in sun (or light afternoon shade where summers are hot) in good, neutral to acid soil; set rhizomes 1 to 1½ inches deep. Although these irises will thrive in ordinary perennial beds with regular watering, they will truly flourish if you can water them gener-

ously from the moment growth begins in spring until about a month after flowering has finished. Dig and divide infrequently, in late summer or early autumn, only when old clumps begin to show hollow centers.

Spuria irises. Hardy to about −30°F/−34°C, the spurias are nearly identical in flower form to florists' Dutch irises. The older members among the spuria group have a color range limited to white, yellow, and blue, but modern hybrids offer a greatly expanded range that includes blue, lavender, gray, orchid, tan, bronze, brown, purple, earthy red, and nearly black, often with a prominent yellow spot on the falls. Flowers are held closely against 3- to 6-foot flower stems; narrow, dark green leaves grow upright 3 to 4 feet.

Plant these irises in late summer or early autumn, setting rhizomes an inch deep in a full-sun location with good soil. When growth begins in spring, water plants regularly until flowering ceases. Most spurias need very little water during summer but will accept regular watering if soil does not remain soggy. Give plants winter protection (see page 40) where temperature drops below −20°F/−29°C. Divide plantings only when they show by declining performance that they are overcrowded; do this in late summer or early autumn.

Siberian iris hybrids

Kniphofia uvaria

KNIPHOFIA
**Poker plant, Torch-lily,
Red-hot poker**
Liliaceae

Hardy to: −10°F/−23°C, except as noted
Exposure: Sun
Water: Regular to moderate
Flowers in: Late spring, summer, autumn
Colors: Orange, yellow, cream, pink shades

With thick, fountainlike clumps of coarse, grassy foliage, poker plants strike a distinctive note among the multitude of broad-leafed plants. But these bold clumps become even more prominent when spearlike flowering spikes rise above the leaves, bearing thick bottlebrush-style "torches" of drooping, tubular flowers.

The old-fashioned red-hot poker, *K. uvaria*, makes a hefty clump bearing 4- to 6-foot blossom spikes; flowers at the bottom of clusters are yellow, those toward the top orange-red. Modern hybrids include this color combination but also come in solid colors as well as pastel bicolors; some are shorter plants, just 1½ to 3 feet tall. The exact flowering period depends on the individual hybrid: some are late spring blooming, whereas others display themselves in early or midsummer. Three-foot *K. galpinii* has clumps of fairly erect foliage and clear orange "torches" in early to midautumn; plants are hardy to 0°F/−18°C. Specialty growers may carry hybrids or selections of this species that flower in summer.

Culture. Poker plants tolerate considerable heat and some drought, but they are much more attractive and productive if those conditions are moderated.

Set plants in good, well-drained soil; be sure soil won't be overly damp in winter. Give them regular to moderate watering during the growing season. In hottest, driest regions, pick a location in partial shade; in milder climates, full sun is better. Wherever winter temperatures drop to 0°F/−18°C or below, tie the foliage over the clump to protect the growing points. Where winter chill is not an issue, cut old foliage to the ground in mid- to late autumn. Clumps will grow undisturbed for many years; you can consider them among the "permanent" perennials. If you need to increase a plant, carefully dig and remove young plants from a clump's edge.

Good companions. *Achillea, Agapanthus, Anchusa, Boltonia asteroides, Gypsophila paniculata, Hemerocallis, Nepeta.*

LIATRIS
Gayfeather
Compositae

Hardy to: −35°F/−37°C
Exposure: Sun
Water: Regular to moderate
Flowers in: Summer
Colors: Rosy purple, white

Although the plant family name reveals that gayfeathers are kin to all the daisies, it is difficult to imagine a more undaisylike appearance. From clumps of narrow, almost grassy foliage rise leafy stems topped by foxtail-like spikes of small, bright flowers with prominent stamens. Unlike most plants that bear flowers clustered in terminal spikes, these flowers first open at the top of the spike rather than at the base.

Perennials specialists offer several similar species that differ mainly in height. Tallest is Kansas gayfeather, *L.*

Liatris spicata

pycnostachya, which reaches 4 to 5 feet; purplish pink is the normal color, but the selection 'Alba' has white flowers. At 3 to 4 feet, *L. scariosa* carries its flowers in looser, more open spikes than do the other species; 'White Spires' is a fine white-flowered selection. Of all the gayfeathers, this one most demands good drainage. The most widely available species, *L. spicata* (sometimes sold as *L. callilepis*), also offers the shortest plants. Wild plants may grow to 4 feet, but nurseries usually offer 2-foot 'Kobold', which has flowers of a particularly bright rosy lilac. A white-flowered form, 'Alba', reaches about the same height.

Culture. The gayfeathers have thick, almost tuberous roots that need a well-drained soil, especially one not sodden in winter. Otherwise, they'll grow well in just moderately fertile or "average" soils. Though plants are drought tolerant, the best performance comes with moderate to regular watering. Clumps will persist for many years before performance declines from overcrowding. When division is needed—for rejuvenation or just for increase—do it in spring.

Good companions. *Achillea, Chrysanthemum superbum, Coreopsis, Echinacea, Gypsophila paniculata,* ornamental grasses.

LIGULARIA
Ligularia
Compositae

Hardy to: −30°F/−34°C, except as noted; not suited to Gulf Coast and Florida or to dry-summer regions
Exposure: Partial shade
Water: Regular
Flowers in: Summer
Colors: Yellow, orange

(Continued on page 86)

Ligularia stenocephala

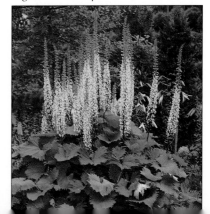

Herbs As Perennials

Not to be overlooked among Perennials on Parade are a number of plants more commonly thought of as herbs. Their ornamental value lies not just in flowers: all are attractive plants and many have foliage that is pleasantly aromatic on warm days. A few of these plants are culinary herbs, but most have had other herbal uses in the past or are simply grown "for tradition's sake" in contemporary herb gardens. Though some become shrublike as they mature, none is truly woody.

FOENICULUM vulgare purpureum. Bronze fennel. *Umbelliferae.* Hardy to –20°F/–29°C. Because it seeds itself prolifically (if seed heads are not removed), common green-leafed fennel has become a roadside weed in mild regions. But the plant is undeniably attractive, and this variant's foliage adds a high note of brownish purple to the garden composition. An established clump contains numerous vertical stems up to 6 feet high, their leaves intricately divided into threadlike segments that give an ostrich plume effect. Small yellow flowers at stem tips are borne in flat-topped clusters; cut them off to prevent unwanted volunteer seedlings. Stems die back in autumn, but new growth from the ground replaces them in spring. Plant in full sun, in well-drained, average soil. Fennel is drought tolerant but will also take moderate watering. This taprooted plant never needs dividing and cannot be transplanted. When vigor declines after a number of years, replace with a new seedling plant. Fennel seed is a key ingredient in some Italian cuisines, and the leaves have a pleasant anise flavor.

HYSSOPUS officinalis. Hyssop. *Labiatae.* Hardy to –30°F/–34°C. Narrow, pleasantly aromatic leaves clothe a bushy plant 1½ to 2 feet high. Throughout summer and into autumn it bears spikes of small blue-violet blossoms—never a dramatic show, but al-

ways pleasant. Some searching may turn up selections with flowers of white, pink, and lavender. Hyssop is a good, rather fine-textured "filler" plant, needing full sun, moderate to regular watering, and well-drained, average soil. Cut plants back by about half in early spring; start new plants from summer cuttings to replace established plants declining in vigor.

Lavandula stoechas 'Otto Quast'

LAVANDULA. Lavender. *Labiatae.* Hardiness varies. English lavender, *L. angustifolia* (sometimes sold as *L. officinalis, L. spica,* or *L. vera*) is the source of the beloved lavender fragrance. Plants are hardy to –10°F/–23°C. Shrubby growth is clothed in linear to almost needlelike 2-inch, gray to gray-green leaves. Small flowers are grouped in dense spikes that project well above the plant on slim stems; flowering starts in late spring to early summer and lasts for a month or more. The basic species may reach 3 to 4 feet high and wide, but you can find smaller variants such as 1½-foot-tall 'Hidcote', with violet-blue flowers, and foot-tall 'Munstead', which opens its dark lavender flowers several weeks earlier than the others. 'Jean Davis'

features nearly white flowers on a compact 1½-foot-high plant.

Spanish lavender, *L. stoechas,* is hardy to about 0°F/–18°C. Leaves are gray and narrow, to 1 inch long, on spreading plants that reach 1½ to 3 feet high and flower in midspring to early summer. Small violet flowers appear in dense, pine conelike spikes that are topped by conspicuous "rabbit ears" of purple bracts. 'Otto Quast' ('Quasti') and 'Royal Pennant' have especially showy flowers.

French lavender, *L. dentata,* is hardy to about 10°F/–12°C. Dense, billowy plants to 3 feet high have gray-green, square-toothed leaves. Lilac purple flowers, borne over a long spring-summer period, resemble Spanish lavender but with less showy bracts.

The lavenders thrive in average to poor but well-drained soil, though not in the humid lower South. Plant them in full sun and water them moderately. To keep plants compact, shear them after flowering or cut them back in early spring just as growth begins. When plants decline, start new plants from summer cuttings.

PHLOMIS. *Labiatae.* Hardiness varies. These sage relatives offer a display of yellow flowers in late spring and early summer on plants with coarse-textured, bold foliage. Jerusalem sage, *P. fruticosa,* is hardy to 0°F/–18°C. Shrubby, branching plants reach 4 feet high, the stems bearing opposing pairs of woolly, gray-green, 4-inch leaves; inch-long bright yellow flowers are clustered in tight, ball-shaped whorls toward stem ends. Cut back lightly after first flowering to encourage a repeat bloom, and then cut back plants in autumn or early spring by about a third to keep them shapely. *P. russelliana* is a clump-forming plant hardy to –20°F/–29°C. Heart-shaped to arrow-shaped 8-inch leaves make a foliage mound about a foot high. From it rise branched, leafy, flowering stems about 3 feet high, bearing tiered whorls of soft yellow flowers. After blossoms have finished, the flowering stems remain decorative (climate permitting) throughout autumn and winter.

Plant both *Phlomis* species in full sun. Plants tolerate drought and poor (but well-drained) soil, but appearance improves if they are given at least average soil and moderate watering. You can start new plants of Jerusalem sage from summer cuttings; increase *P. russelliana* by division in early spring.

RUTA graveolens. Rue. *Rutaceae.* Hardy to –20°F/–29°C; short lived in Gulf Coast and Florida. Rue foliage is especially good-looking: like maidenhair fern, it's a soft bluish green. Though it's aromatic, the aroma produced by brushing against it is sometimes called unpleasant. Shrubby, rounded plants grow 2 to 3 feet high and wide; clusters of ½-inch greenish yellow flowers make a substantial show in spring and then form seed capsules that have some decorative value when dry. 'Jackman's Blue' is a smaller plant selected for its blue-gray foliage color; 'Variegata' features creamy white foliage variegation and will come true from seed. Leaves can cause a skin rash in susceptible individuals.

Rue will take regular watering but is also drought tolerant. Plant it in full sun, in well-drained, good to average soil. Cut plants back in early spring to encourage bushiness; start new plants from cuttings in late spring or summer.

SALVIA officinalis. Garden sage. *Labiatae.* Hardy to –10°F/–23°C. This is culinary sage, useful in the kitchen as well as attractive in the garden. Oval leaves to 2 inches long cover a shrubby plant to 2 feet high and 3 feet across. In mid- to late spring, stems elongate into upright flowering spikes that bear tiered clusters of inch-long, violet-blue blossoms. Typical leaves are gray-green with a corrugated texture, but several foliage variants are commonly

available. 'Icterina' has green leaves variegated with chartreuse to yellow; 'Tricolor' foliage is basically gray-green with irregular white margins, but new growth is tinged purple, so that the white portions appear to be pink; 'Purpurascens' is soft wine purple in new foliage that ages to green (though its stems remain purple).

Although garden sage is fairly drought tolerant, plants look better with moderate watering. Plant in full sun, in average to poor, well-drained soil. Cut back plants after flowering to keep them shapely, then cut back by about half in early spring. You can start new plants from spring and summer cuttings; use them to replace old plants with reduced vigor.

SANTOLINA chamaecyparissus. Lavender cotton. *Compositae.* Hardy to –10°F/–23°C. Although it's frequently used as a small-scale ground cover in many mild regions, amenable lavender cotton will make a spreading, front-of-the-border accent plant or an ankle-high pathway-edging hedge. Plants are low, spreading, frothy mounds of gray-white foliage—each very narrow, inch-long leaf finely divided into feathery segments. Left to its own devices, a plant will spread outward, its stems arching upward; stems root as they spread, so a clump will gradually extend its coverage unless checked occasionally. In late spring to early summer, plants are covered with buttonlike, half-inch yellow flowers: daisies without petals. Specialists list several named selections. 'Edward Bowles' has gray-green leaves and light yellow flowers; 'Nana' and 'Compacta' are smaller plants that otherwise resemble the species.

Lavender cotton will grow in nearly any soil; plants are short lived in the lower South. Moderate watering is best, though plants are quite drought tolerant. Shear or cut back plants after flowering to maintain compactness; cut back unkempt plants in early spring.

Ruta graveolens 'Jackman's Blue'

Cuttings root easily in spring and summer, but rooted stems will usually supply the need for new plants.

THYMUS citriodorus. Lemon thyme. *Labiatae.* Hardy to –30°F/–34°C. Tiny oval leaves pack a pungent, sweetly lemony punch when bruised or crushed and can be used for a hint of lemon in cooking. Wiry-stemmed plants are densely foliaged, mounding as high as 1 foot and spreading wider. In spring, rounded heads of tiny, rosy lavender blossoms nearly obscure the foliage. Two variegated-leaf forms are the most widely grown: 'Aureus' has bright green leaves edged in cream; 'Argenteus' has leaves of grayed green margined in white.

Lemon thyme grows best in well-drained soil with moderate watering. Plant in full sun where summers are cool to mild; give it a bit of afternoon shade in hot-summer regions. Shear or cut back plants to restrict spread and maintain compactness. Replace plants when they decline in vigor after several years. Stems will self-layer, usually ensuring a few replacement plants, but cuttings also root easily in spring and summer.

If you can offer organically rich soil, plenty of moisture, and some degree of shade, the ligularias will reward you with bold clumps of handsome foliage, usually topped by spikes or clusters of bright daisy flowers. Leaves make a dramatic garden statement, usually heart shaped to nearly circular in outline and a foot or more across. Leaf margins may be strongly toothed, waved, or deeply dissected, somewhat like fancy-leafed Japanese maples.

Of the generally available species and hybrids, *L. dentata* is distinct in bearing its flowers in flattened clusters. Stems reach 3 to 5 feet above 2-foot clumps of nearly round, wavy leaves. The selection 'Desdemona' has green leaves that are purple underneath, supported by purple leafstalks; flowers are orange. 'Othello' is similar but a bit shorter and less infused with purple.

Upright spikes of flowers characterize the following ligularias. The *L. dentata* hybrid 'Gregynog Gold' carries its yellow-orange flowers on conical spikes that may reach 6 feet, over heart-shaped, tooth-edged leaves. Also with deeply toothed, heart-shaped leaves, *L. stenocephala* bears slender, graceful spires of yellow flowers held aloft on dark stems. Five-foot 'The Rocket' is either a selection or hybrid of *L. stenocephala*. Dark, 6-foot stems and slender spikes of yellow flowers also describe *L. przewalskii*, but its deeply lobed and cut leaves set it apart. The giant groundsel, *L. wilsoniana*, features broadly triangular leaves and 5- to 6-foot flower spikes that are thicker and more compact than those of the preceding species. Plants are hardy to −20°F/−29°C.

Leopard plant, *L. tussilaginea*, differs from the others in a number of details. Its thick leaves are almost rubbery in texture, kidney shaped to nearly round in overall outline but with angled edges; each leaf rises from the ground on a 1- to 2-foot leafstalk. Yellow daisies come in few-flowered clusters just above the foliage. Plants are hardy to 0°F/−18°C, though leaves will be killed to the ground at 20°F/−7°C. The most common selection, 'Aureo-maculata', has deep green leaves irregularly spotted creamy white, like paint spatters on a dark

drop cloth. Specialists may offer other decorative-foliage forms.

Culture. Ligularias are good choices for pond- or streamside in a wooded setting and for damp, north-shaded exposures. Plants will grow in sunny beds, but sunlight will wilt the leaves even when soil is moist. In cool-summer regions, though, where fog and gray days screen the sun's intensity, you may succeed with ligularias in full-sun locations. Set out plants in spring, in soil liberally enriched with organic matter. You can leave clumps undisturbed for many years. Be sure to control slugs and snails, which can ravage the foliage display.

Good companions. *Aruncus dioicus, Cimicifuga, Eupatorium, Iris* (Louisiana), *Lobelia cardinalis.*

LIMONIUM LATIFOLIUM
Sea lavender, Statice
Plumbaginaceae

Hardy to: −35°F/−37°C; not suited to Gulf Coast and Florida
Exposure: Sun
Water: Moderate
Flowers in: Summer
Colors: Lavender

The common name sea lavender well expresses the flower color and the plant's ability to thrive under coastal conditions, but something like "summer cloud" would be more alluring and descriptive. A clump of oblong, 10-inch leaves growing in an informal rosette is a striking contrast to the

Limonium latifolium

Linaria purpurea

many-branched, somewhat flattened spray of tiny flowers that floats above the leaves like a haze of lavender baby's breath. On an established plant, this cloud of blossoms may reach 2 feet high and 3 feet across. Flowers have a papery texture and can be dried for use in everlasting arrangements.

Culture. Despite its delicate appearance, this is a tough plant that needs only well-drained, average soil. Sea lavender is drought tolerant, but for impressive flower production, give it moderate to regular watering. Plants can remain in place indefinitely.

Good companions. *Eryngium, Euphorbia, Gaura lindheimeri, Lobelia laxiflora, Nepeta, Oenothera.*

LINARIA PURPUREA
Toadflax
Scrophulariaceae

Hardy to: −20°F/−29°C
Exposure: Sun
Water: Moderate
Flowers in: Summer
Colors: Purple, pink

Toadflax won't grab your attention from across the garden, but you'll come to appreciate its filmy charm if you plant it in small drifts or as a mixer among more assertive plants. Even though each plant is a bushy 2 to 3 feet tall, there is an air of slenderness or verticality about it: gray-green leaves are very narrow, stems are upright, and atop the stems are slender spikes of small flowers that look like tiny snapdragons. Flowers of the basic species are lilac purple with a small orange spot, but the widely available selection 'Canon Went' exchanges purple for soft pink.

Culture. Soil for toadflax should drain easily but doesn't need to be highly fertile or constantly moist. If you want to increase your planting, you can remove rooted portions from a clump's edge.

Good companions. *Cosmos atrosanguineus, Nepeta, Oenothera, Sedum, Stachys lanata.*

LINUM
Flax
Linaceae

Hardy to: –10°F/–23°C; not suited to Gulf Coast and Florida
Exposure: Sun
Water: Moderate
Flowers in: Spring, summer
Colors: Blue, yellow, white

The perennial flaxes are filmy plants that add a wildflowerlike charm to the planting scheme. Each bright blossom lasts just a day (and remains closed in overcast weather), but a seemingly endless supply of buds keeps the display going for many weeks. Five overlapping petals form a circular flower about an inch across; these flowers are liberally scattered over much-branched plants with narrow, short leaves.

Among blue-flowered flaxes, you have two choices; both grow 1½ to 2 feet high. *Linum perenne* has a somewhat longer flowering period, start-

Linum perenne with *Lychnis coronaria*

ing in spring and continuing through late summer; there is also a white-flowered form. The white-eyed blue flowers of *L. narbonense* are larger, reaching 1½ inches across, and come mainly in summer. Good named selections such as 'Six Hills' are sometimes available. Golden flax, *L. flavum,* is compact and shrubby, up to 15 inches high, flowering in spring and into summer. The selection 'Compactum' makes a 6-inch tuffet for the front of the border.

Culture. Flax culture is simplicity itself. Good soil drainage is more important than fertility; sandy soil to loam is best. Plants may not last more than 3 or 4 years, but it is easy to keep a new supply coming from cuttings taken in early summer. One species, *L. perenne,* will keep you supplied with a crop of volunteer seedlings.

Good companions. *Coreopsis, Euphorbia, Gaillardia, Gazania, Oenothera.*

LIRIOPE
Lily turf
Liliaceae

Hardy to: –10°F/–23°C
Exposure: Partial shade, shade
Water: Regular to moderate
Flowers in: Summer
Colors: Violet, lavender, white

Like hostas, these plants are grown primarily for their attractive foliage. With neat, fountainlike clumps of glossy, grassy leaves, the lily turfs are popular border plants, small-scale ground covers, and accent clumps, especially in Oriental-style gardens. They're equally at home in the humid Southeast and dry-summer West. Small flowers come in tight spikes atop vertical stems—protruding above the foliage in some kinds, mingled among the leaves in others.

Big blue lily turf, *L. muscari,* is the most widely grown. Its leaves may be ½ inch wide and up to 2 feet long, arching over to form clumps about 1½ feet high. Small, dark violet flowers in midsummer resemble those of grape hyacinth and appear just above the foliage or partly hidden within it. Nurseries offer a number of named selections. 'Lilac Beauty' is identical

Liriope muscari 'Variegata'

except for its lighter violet flowers, while 'Monroe White' drops color altogether. 'Majestic' is, appropriately, a bit taller growing, with foliage in more open clumps; violet flowers come in flattened sprays that resemble cockscombs. The mid-lavender flowers of 'Christmas Tree' are carried in narrowly triangular spikes, wider at the bottom and coming to a point at the tip.

Several *L. muscari* selections offer variegated foliage. 'Variegata' has yellow-edged leaves that become entirely green in their second year; leaves reach 1 to 1½ feet long, making a shorter foliage mound above which the spikes of violet flowers show well. 'Silvery Sunproof' is more upright, with longer leaves that are yellow-striped at first, later fading to white; lilac flowers show above the foliage. 'Gold Banded' retains a yellow margin on its dark green leaves. 'John Burch' reverses the variegation pattern, each dark green leaf having a greenish yellow center stripe; flowers in cockscomb clusters extend above the leaves. 'Silvery Midget' makes an 8-inch plant with lavender flowers; some leaves are variegated with white.

The plant sometimes sold as *L. gigantea* is usually the closely related *Ophiopogon jaburan,* hardy to 10°F/–12°C. Its dark green leaves will reach 2 or even 3 feet long and ½ inch wide. Clusters of small, nodding white flowers appear in summer, partly hidden in the leaves; the round, metallic blue fruits that follow are ornamental. 'Vittatus' has white-striped leaves that mature to solid green.

(Continued on next page)

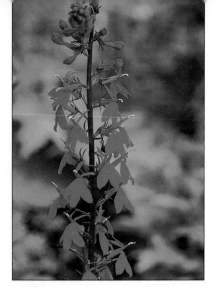

Lobelia cardinalis

...Liriope

Culture. Unless summer temperatures are cool, plant lily turf in filtered sunlight to full shade. Plants need well-drained soil; even though they're somewhat drought tolerant, they'll be most attractive with regular watering. Watch for slugs and snails, which can disfigure foliage. Clumps will thrive undisturbed for many years; if you need to divide for increase, dig and separate clumps in early spring.

Good companions. *Acanthus mollis, Anemone hybrida, Hosta, Polygonatum, Tricyrtis.*

LOBELIA
Lobelia
Lobeliaceae

Hardy to: Varies; moisture-loving kinds need some winter chill
Exposure: Sun to partial shade, except as noted
Water: Regular, except as noted
Flowers in: Summer
Colors: Red, blue, violet, orange

If you know only the low, spreading annual *Lobelia erinus*, these very different perennial relatives will come as a surprise. Several moisture-loving species and hybrids feature low foliage clumps from which rise 3- to 4-foot stems bearing narrow spires of bright blossoms. One other species spreads extensively from underground stems and will tolerate drought.

Best known of the moisture-loving lobelias is cardinal flower, *L. cardinalis*, hardy to –40°F/–40°C. Rosettes of bright green, lance-shaped leaves send up 3- to 4-foot leafy spikes that bear brilliant red, 1½-inch flowers. Specialists may offer selections with flowers of pink or white. Hybrids of cardinal flower and a similar Mexican species have flaming scarlet flowers set off by rich, reddish purple foliage; plants are hardy to –30°F/–34°C. 'Bees' Flame' is the most widely sold of these hybrids.

The great blue lobelia (or blue cardinal flower), *L. siphilitica*, is similar in appearance to *L. cardinalis*, growing a bit shorter, with its vivid blue to blue-purple flowers carried in tighter spikes. Plants are hardy to –30°F/–34°C. Hybrids between this species, cardinal flower, and perhaps other lobelias may be offered as *L. vedrariensis*, *L. gerardii*, or *L. speciosa*. Many of these have flowers of glowing purple produced on stems 2½ to 3 feet high; in some individuals, the foliage is tinged with purple or bronze.

The Mexican native *L. laxiflora* differs from the previous species and hybrids in nearly all details. Plants are hardy to 10°F/–12°C, each clump spreading by underground stems to form a large colony in time; in well-watered gardens it can become invasive. Upright stems may reach 2 feet high, somewhat sparsely clothed in very narrow, dark green leaves and topped by loose clusters of tubular orange-red flowers for 2 months or longer. Plants are drought tolerant and need only moderate watering to thrive.

Culture. In nature, these lobelias grow in moist meadows and in near-boggy pondside locations. Transported to the garden, they still need continually moist soil, cardinal flower having the highest demand for wetness. Great blue lobelia is the most amenable to more ordinary conditions, given regular watering. For best results with any of these moisture-loving kinds, plant in a retentive soil liberally amended with organic matter. In cool-summer climates they will grow in full sun; where summer is warm to hot, plant in partial to light shade or where they'll have morning sun and afternoon shade. Plants are not long lived but can be maintained by dividing clumps every year or two right after flowering, saving and replanting the most vigorous young divisions. You can also take stem cuttings just after flowering or even layer the stems. Where soil is wet enough, plants may produce volunteer seedlings that will give an ongoing supply of fresh plants. Where winter temperatures reach –10°F/–23°C or lower, protect plants with a thick, noncompacting winter mulch.

Good companions. (For moist soil) *Filipendula, Iris* (Louisiana, Siberian), *Ligularia, Trollius;* (for dry soil) *Convolvulus mauritanicus, Limonium latifolium, Linum.*

LUPINUS
Lupine
Leguminosae

Hardy to: –30°F/–34°C; not suited to hot-summer regions
Exposure: Sun
Water: Regular
Flowers in: Spring, early summer
Colors: Blue, purple, pink, red, orange, yellow, cream, white

The glorious perennial lupines suggest Victorian perennial borders and romantic cottage-garden plantings, yet today's lupines are derived from the Russell Hybrids developed early in the 20th century. A typical plant of these lupines is a bushy clump of attractive foliage, each leaf resembling in size and shape an outstretched hand. Vertical flower spikes may reach 4 to 5 feet tall, the sweet pea–shaped blossoms densely encircling the upper portion of the spike. Besides the wide array of solid-color flowers available, there also are numerous lovely bicolor combinations. Smaller versions for

Lupinus Russell Hybrids

front-of-the-border planting include Little Lulu and Minarette strains, which reach only about 1½ feet.

Culture. Lupines attain best development with the least coddling in regions where summers are fairly cool. This includes parts of the West Coast, Pacific Northwest, New England, the northern tier of states and adjacent southern Canada, and higher elevations in mountains of the South that escape the steamy lowland heat. Humidity plus heat is a greater enemy than dry heat; in dry-summer, warm areas, you may achieve some success if you plant lupines in filtered sunlight to partial shade and see that plants are always moist.

Plant lupines in well-drained, neutral to acid soil, well prepared and enriched with organic matter. A mulch helps provide the even moisture and coolness they prefer. Set out plants in spring. Lupines are rather short lived and may need to be revitalized or replaced after several years. You can raise new plants from spring cuttings, and you can divide established clumps in spring. Easiest of all, though, is to start with new seedling plants.

Good companions. *Alchemilla mollis, Geranium, Hemerocallis, Iris* (bearded), *Papaver orientale, Thalictrum.*

LYCHNIS
Campion, Catchfly
Caryophyllaceae

Hardy to: −35°F/−37°C, except as noted; not suited to Gulf Coast and Florida
Exposure: Sun
Water: Regular to moderate
Flowers in: Summer
Colors: Red, orange, magenta, pink, white

The campions are not dramatic plants, but their brightly colored flowers are hardly subtle. These are old-fashioned border perennials, valued—like their relatives *Dianthus* (pinks)—for easy culture as well as plentiful color.

Maltese cross, *L. chalcedonica,* features broadly rounded clusters of vibrant red, ¾-inch flowers; each of the five segments is shaped like the arms of a Maltese cross. Upright stems 2 to

Lychnis coronaria

3 feet high are clothed in pairs of upward-pointing, lance-shaped leaves. Its slightly less hardy hybrid *L. arkwrightii* offers larger, broader-petaled flowers of orange-red, beautifully complemented by bronzed purple foliage, on a plant up to 1½ feet high. For both *L. chalcedonica* and *L. arkwrightii,* divide crowded clumps in early spring.

Another similar campion is *L. haageana,* which may have flowers of red, orange, salmon, or white carried in clusters of two or three blossoms. Its stems reach 1½ feet high, clothed in green leaves; plants die down shortly after flowering ceases. Plants are short lived, so should be replaced every few years by new, seed-grown plants.

Crown-pink, *L. coronaria,* offers a change of pace in both color and aspect. Oblong, 4-inch leaves are gray-white with a surface like felt, carried in rosettes that form low clumps. Rising above the leaves come many-branched, gray-white stems to 2½ feet high, bearing 1-inch-wide circular flowers of vibrant magenta. There is a form with pure white flowers as well as a rare selection with magenta-eyed white blossoms. Plants last just a few years, but prolific seeding ensures that a new crop is always available.

German catchfly, *L. viscaria,* may also be listed under its old name, *Viscaria vulgaris.* In contrast to the other campions, this has clumps of linear, almost grasslike leaves to 5 inches long. Slender, sticky stems reach about 1 foot high, bearing loose clusters of ½-inch, five-part flowers in bright pink. Specialists may offer selections with flow-

ers of white, various pink shades, and magenta as well as the double bright pink 'Splendens Flore Pleno'. Divide crowded clumps in early spring.

Culture. All the campions need well-drained soil. Three species—*L. chalcedonica, L. arkwrightii,* and *L. haageana* are best in good soil with regular watering. Average soil and moderate to regular watering suit *L. viscaria,* while *L. coronaria*—through it will grow well under ordinary garden conditions—will also flourish in poor soil with just moderate watering.

Good companions. *Armeria, Catananche caerulea, Coreopsis, Dianthus, Oenothera, Verbascum.*

LYTHRUM SALICARIA
Purple loosestrife
Lythraceae

Hardy to: −35°F/−37°C
Exposure: Sun, partial shade
Water: Regular
Flowers in: Summer
Colors: Purple, magenta, pink

Gracefully wiry stems clothed in willowlike leaves offer wands of color from midsummer to early autumn, when each stem bears a terminal spike of showy blossoms. Despite its legitimate claim to beauty, moisture-loving purple loosestrife is scorned (even feared!) as a weed, able to seed itself prolifically in wild marshland where it competes seriously with the native flora. Many states, in fact, forbid its planting. However, gardeners anywhere may safely grow the named se-

Lythrum salicaria

lections, most of which appear to be sterile hybrids.

Heights vary among the named selections, but each forms a bushy mound that can function as a flowering shrub. Under favorable conditions, *L. salicaria* will bear its showy magenta flowers on stems to 5 feet tall. 'Morden's Pink' tones down the color to a clear pink on a 3-foot plant. 'Morden's Gleam' reaches 4 feet with carmine red blossoms; 'Dropmore Purple' features rich violet blossoms atop 3-foot stems; and 'Rose Queen' presents its clear pink flowers on stems 2 to 2½ feet high. Dark pink 'Happy' reaches just 1½ feet.

Culture. Although purple loosestrife occurs naturally in damp soil, it will accept garden conditions that range from damp to moderately dry. For best appearance, strike a happy medium: good, organically enriched soil and regular watering. Clumps may remain in place for many years; if you need to divide a crowded clump, do so in early spring. To increase a favorite plant, take stem cuttings in summer.

Good companions. *Eupatorium, Filipendula, Iris* (Japanese, Louisiana, Siberian), *Trollius.*

MACLEAYA CORDATA
Plume poppy
Papaveraceae

Hardy to: –30°F/–34°C
Exposure: Sun, partial shade
Water: Regular
Flowers in: Summer
Colors: White

Though a poppy by name and family, this plant shows no obvious kinship to its more familiar relatives. Unlike Oriental, Iceland, and California poppies, which are prized for their bright, showy blossoms, plume poppy is valued more for its foliage. And you get plenty of that: plants may grow to 8 feet high and 3 feet across, the upright stems bearing deeply lobed grayish green leaves with silvery undersides, each up to 12 inches across. Loose, plumelike flower clusters appear at stem tips, bearing tiny, petal-less flowers that make a pleasant display with their numerous white stamens.

Macleaya cordata

Plume poppy makes hefty clumps that spread gradually. Another species, *M. microcarpa,* is a similar plant that spreads rapidly to the point of being invasive. Its tiny flowers have fewer stamens of a soft buff color, while the selected form 'Coral Plume' is a pleasing warm pink.

Culture. Give plume poppy good soil and regular watering to support its large foliage mass. In cool-summer regions it will take full sun; in warm to hot areas, plant where it will be partly shaded. Because of its size and vigor, plume poppy can crowd out or overshadow many smaller plants. Use it as though it were a specimen shrub, or at least give it the company of other sizable plants. You can divide clumps for increase in early spring.

Good companions. *Kniphofia,* ornamental grasses; shrubs.

MALVA
Mallow
Malvaceae

Hardy to: Varies
Exposure: Sun, partial shade
Water: Regular
Flowers in: Summer
Colors: Pink, red, white

The *Malva* species, along with their close relatives *Sidalcea,* offer hollyhock-like blossoms on truly perennial plants. None is as tall or large as hollyhock, but profuse bloom more than compensates for the size difference.

Two *Malva* species are widely sold. Hollyhock mallow, *M. alcea,* is hardy to –30°F/–34°C. Bushy plants reach 3 to 4 feet high, bearing rounded, lobed leaves and saucer-shaped, 2-inch pink blossoms toward the ends of stems. Nurseries usually carry the selection

Malva alcea

'Fastigiata', which flowers throughout summer into autumn on strongly upright, narrow plants. Musk mallow, *M. moschata,* will endure winters down to –40°F/– 40°C. Plants reach about 2½ feet and are more rounded than hollyhock mallow, the leaves finely cut into numerous threadlike segments. Two-inch satin-textured flowers appear along stems and in clusters at the tips; soft pink is the basic color, but 'Alba' has blossoms of pure white.

Checkerbloom or prairie mallow, *Sidalcea malviflora,* is hardy to –20°F/ –29°C. Specialists offer a number of named selections or hybrids that look like hollyhocks scaled down to 2½ to 4 feet. From low clumps of rounded, lobed leaves rise strongly upright stems bearing smaller leaves divided into fingerlike segments and topped by spires of 1- to 2-inch saucer-shaped flowers. 'Elsie Heugh' is an old favorite, in soft pink with fringed petals. Other good clear pink shades include 'Rose Queen' (among the tallest at 4 feet), 'Loveliness', and 'Sussex Beauty'; 'Brilliant' is deep rose verging on red.

Culture. All the mallows are at their best in regions where summer is cool to mild. In hot-summer areas, the *Malva* species are the better bet, particularly *M. moschata;* be sure to locate plants where they'll receive light shade during the heat of the day. Plant in good, well-drained, organically enriched soil. The *Malva* species are rather short lived but are easy to raise from seed; volunteer seedlings often provide replacement plants. The *Sidalcea* selections are longer-lasting plants that can be divided for increase in early spring.

Good companions. *Artemisia, Centranthus ruber, Cosmos atrosanguineus, Delphinium, Platycodon grandiflorus.*

MERTENSIA
Bluebells
Boraginaceae

Hardy to: −35°F/−37°C; needs some winter chill; not suited to Gulf Coast and Florida
Exposure: Partial shade, shade
Water: Regular
Flowers in: Spring
Colors: Blue

Although their garden presence is ephemeral, the bluebells are cherished as a charming harbinger of spring. Like their forget-me-not relatives, they present clear blue blossoms—nodding and rather bell shaped—timed to coincide with daffodils, trilliums, bleeding hearts, azaleas, and others in the vanguard of the season.

Virginia bluebells, *M. virginica*, is the more commonly available of two North American species. Broadly oval, bluish green leaves form loose clumps that send up leafy flowering stems 1½ to 2 feet tall bearing 1-inch, trumpet-shaped flowers in pendant clusters. Buds are usually pink to lavender, but blossoms open out a clear blue. Chiming bells or mountain bluebells, *M. ciliata*, may grow to 3 feet under favorable conditions, its slightly smaller flowers bearing fringed petal margins. Both species begin to go dormant soon after flowering has finished. Virginia bluebells will have died down completely by midsummer; chiming bells will remain green longer if you keep it well watered. Grow these bluebells where their demise won't leave a gap in your planting scheme, or plant them where their positions will be covered over by foliage of other perennials (*Hosta*, for example) that leaf out later.

Culture. Organically enriched soil and dappled sun to light shade are ideal bluebell conditions. Plants need ample

Mertensia virginica

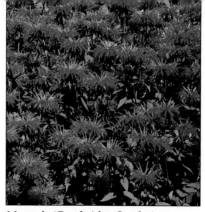

Monarda 'Cambridge Scarlet'

moisture from the time growth begins until they finish flowering; after entering dormancy their water need decreases a bit, though soil should not be allowed to go dry. Clumps may remain in place indefinitely. Volunteer seedlings may supply additional plants, though you can can dig and divide for increase in early autumn.

Good companions. *Dicentra, Doronicum, Hosta, Primula, Pulmonaria, Trillium, Trollius.*

MONARDA DIDYMA
Bee balm, Oswego tea
Labiatae

Hardy to: −30°F/−34°C; needs some winter chill; not suited to Gulf Coast and Florida
Exposure: Sun, partial shade
Water: Regular
Flowers in: Summer
Colors: Violet, red, pink, white

Crush or rub a leaf and you'll instantly sense bee balm's kinship with mint. In fact, its leaves steeped in water make a refreshing minty tea. Spreading clumps of lance-shaped, 6-inch leaves send up numerous well-foliaged, branching stems, each tip crowned with one or two whorls of tubular, two-lipped flowers. Stems reach 2½ to 4 feet tall, the height depending on the individual named selection. Catalogs carry a number of named sorts—selections of *M. didyma* or hybrids of it with the less showy, rather gaunt *M. fistulosa*. Soft rose 'Croftway Pink' and brilliant 'Cambridge Scarlet' are time-tested favorites. Others are 'Violet Queen', 'Prairie Night', and 'Blue Stocking' (violet); 'Adam', 'Gardenview Scarlet', 'Kardinal', 'Mahogany', and 'Prairie Fire' (red); and 'Snow White'.

Culture. In good, organically enriched soil and with liberal watering, bee balm will grow vigorously. Plants will tolerate some dryness between waterings, but under those conditions performance diminishes and mildew susceptibility increases. In cool- to mid-summer regions, give plants full sun; in hotter areas, partial shade will be more satisfactory. Rapid increase calls for dividing clumps every 2 to 3 years in early spring.

Good companions. *Alchemilla mollis, Chrysanthemum superbum, Delphinium, Erigeron, Filipendula, Hemerocallis, Lythrum.*

NEPETA
Catmint
Labiatae

Hardy to: −35°F/−37°C; not suited to Gulf Coast and Florida
Exposure: Sun
Water: Regular to moderate
Flowers in: Spring, summer
Colors: Blue

Planted at the edge of a sunny path, the catmints will furnish a refreshing blue to lavender haze over a long period starting with the midspring perennials. Loose spikes of small, clustered blossoms cover the billowy plants, which are dense and usually broader than tall. Gray-green foliage is pleasantly aromatic: each textured leaf is oval to almost arrow shaped and ¾ to 1½ inches long. Cats find these plants nearly as enticing as their close relative, catnip (*N. cataria*).

Several catmints are sold, varying mainly in size. Most widely available are plants of the hybrid *N. faassenii*, which reach 1 to 2 feet high in flower. This is a sterile hybrid that produces no volunteer seedlings. Named selections include 'Dropmore', which car-

(Continued on page 94)

Nepeta faassenii

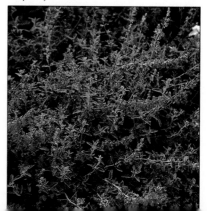

Mild-Winter Specialties

Gardeners who live where frost is rare or light may yearn for Minnesota-quality peonies or New England–style astilbes. But the mild-winter regions provide congenial conditions for a number of fine perennials that are, at best, tender container plants where freezes are the norm. The following plants are standard perennial landscape fare where temperatures remain above the stated limits.

CHRYSANTHEMUM frutescens. Marguerite. *Compositae*. Hardy to 20°F/ –7°C; not suited to Gulf Coast and Florida. This fast–growing daisy is frequently planted as a flowering shrub. Bushy, mounding growth can reach 4 feet high and wide in a matter of a few months, becoming a plant densely clothed in coarsely cut green leaves and dotted with 2½-inch daisies. The most typical marguerite has single white daisy flowers with yellow centers, but you can also find named selections with double white flowers and with single or double blossoms in cream, yellow, and pink. 'Silver Leaf' has small, single white flowers and gray-green foliage.

Plant marguerites in fairly light, well–drained soil in full sun. Water regularly. Cut back plants lightly and frequently to maintain bushiness, encourage rebloom, and limit size. In early spring you can cut them back fairly heavily, but not to totally leafless, woody stems: these may not sprout new growth. Individual plants last just a few years; start replacements from spring and summer cuttings.

DIETES. Fortnight lily. *Iridaceae*. Hardy to 15°F/–9°C. These southern hemisphere iris relatives offer both attractive flowers and year-round foliage. Individual plants are fans of narrow, irislike leaves, and a clump gives much the same effect as some ornamental grasses. Wiry, branching flower stalks carry flat, six-segmented flowers; each blossom lasts just one day, but the flowering period extends from spring well into summer—even, in periodic bursts, through autumn and winter in the mildest areas. The most widely planted is *D. vegeta (D. iridioides);* in flower it reaches 4 feet, bearing irislike 3-inch white flowers, three segments of which have a brown-purple spot surrounded by an orange ring. Its flower stalks last for several years. Blossoms of *D. bicolor* are about 2 inches across, circular in outline, and light yellow with pea-size brown spots on three segments. Foliage and stalks reach 3 to 3½ feet high; flowering stems last just one year.

Fortnight lilies grow and flower best in full sun but will take some light shade in hot-summer areas. Give them average to good soil and moderate to regular watering; plants are drought tolerant, but performance does decline in drought conditions. Divide overgrown clumps in autumn or winter.

EURYOPS pectinatus. *Compositae*. Hardy to 20°F/–7°C; not suited to Gulf Coast and Florida. Like marguerite *(Chrysanthemum frutescens)*, this is a shrubby daisy, but the plant has a stiffer appearance. Rapid growth gives you a mounded, spreading plant 3 to 6 feet tall. Yellow 2-inch daisies flower most of the year (most profusely in late winter and spring) against a background of finely divided gray-green leaves. 'Viridis' has green foliage.

Plants need excellent drainage but are not particular about soil quality. Plant in full sun and give moderate watering. Cut back in late spring or early summer to maintain compactness and limit size. Start new plants from spring and summer cuttings.

FELICIA amelloides. Blue marguerite. *Compositae*. Hardy to 20°F/ –7°C. These shrublike daisies are indefatigable flower factories from spring through autumn. Bright blue, yellow-centered daisies appear individually at ends of wiry stems that protrude from the foliage mass of inch-long oval, rough-textured leaves.

Bushy, mounding plants grow rapidly to about 1½ feet high and up to 4 feet across. Named selections feature dark blue flowers ('George Lewis', 'Midnight', 'Rhapsody in Blue') and large flowers to 3 inches ('San Gabriel', 'San Luis', 'Santa Anita'). Medium blue 'Jolly' grows just a foot high, while the compact-growing, medium blue 'Astrid Thomas' has flowers that remain open at night. There's also a white-flowered selection as well as a less vigorous blue-flowered form with creamy variegated leaves.

Give blue marguerite well-drained, average soil and full sun. Remove spent flowers to promote ongoing bloom; cut back large plants heavily in late summer to rejuvenate and restore compactness. Propagate from cuttings of new growth in late spring and summer.

LIMONIUM perezii. Statice, Sea lavender. *Plumbaginaceae*. Hardy to 25°F/ –4°C. Because small nursery plants grow rapidly, this statice can be used as a summer annual where winters are cold. But especially in mild- winter gardens with some coastal influence, this is a reliable perennial with a bloom season that can stretch from midspring into autumn. Clumps consist of broad, wavy-edged leaves to 1 foot long—a good foliage accent throughout the year. Wiry stems can reach 2 to 3 feet tall on established plants, branching freely in their upper portions to carry large, airy clusters of small purple-and-white, papery-textured flowers.

Plant in average, well-drained soil; for best appearance, water moderately.

NIEREMBERGIA hippomanica violacea. Dwarf cup flower. *Solanaceae*. Hardy to 15°F/–9°C. From midspring through summer, these low, spreading plants produce a seemingly endless succession of violet-blue flowers. A study in fine texture, the much-branched stems are clothed in short, needlelike leaves that make a filmy backdrop for the inch-wide, broadly cupped blossoms. 'Purple Robe' is a widely sold selection; white-flowered kinds are also available.

Where summers are cool to mild, plant dwarf cup flower in full sun. In most hot-summer regions, give plants a bit of shade during the hottest afternoon hours; in the desert, plant in filtered sun or light shade. Plants need good soil and regular watering. Trim back after flowering to promote new growth, compactness. When performance declines after several years, replace with new nursery plants.

PELARGONIUM. Geranium. *Geraniaceae*. Hardy to 28°F/−2°C. These tender geraniums are far more familiar to mild-climate gardeners than are the related hardy geraniums described on page 72. Three types are widely grown out-of-doors all year in frost-free areas: Martha Washington geraniums or pelargoniums *(P. domesticum)*, common geranium *(P. hortorum)*, and ivy geranium *(P. peltatum)*. And where frost is a threat, all make excellent container plants (see page 29).

Martha Washington geraniums are shrubby plants to 3 feet or more in height and width; their rounded to heart-shaped leaves, 9 to 4 inches across, have fluted edges. Clusters of 2-inch azalealike flowers come in spring and summer; colors include white, pink, red, purple, and lavender shades, the petals often having velvety dark blotches toward their bases. Common geraniums also reach about the same dimensions, but leaves and stems are soft and hairy. Individual flowers—single or double—are smaller than those of the Martha Washington types, but clusters may be larger and fuller; flowers come in red, magenta, pink shades, orange, and white. Some fancy-leafed selections feature variously patterned leaves, including "zoned" foliage, in which green, red, and cream or white are arranged in a pattern of concentric circles.

In contrast to those two types, ivy geraniums are trailing plants used as a ground cover and in containers where stems can spill over the edges. Moderate-size clusters of 1-inch flowers (single or double) may be red, white, lavender, pink, or bicolor. Leaves are thick and glossy, somewhat ivylike; some kinds are variegated in white or yellow.

Give all the tender geraniums light, well-drained soil and moderate watering; let soil dry to about an inch deep before watering thoroughly. Where summer temperatures are hot, plant in filtered sunlight, light shade, or at least shade during the hottest hours of the day. To promote bushiness in the two shrubby kinds, pinch off growing tips periodically. In late winter or early spring, just as growth starts, prune plants back to at least half their size. Spring and summer cuttings root easily. Tobacco or geranium budworm can be a serious summer pest on the two shrubby kinds, consuming flower buds and ruining the color display.

PHORMIUM tenax. New Zealand flax. *Agavaceae*. Hardy to 15°F/−9°C. In terms of foliage, the New Zealand flaxes resemble giant irises: each plant is a fan of swordlike leaves, and plants huddle together in tight clumps. The species may reach 10 feet high, its dark flowering stems rising several feet above the foliage and bearing branched sprays of tubular red to yellow 2-inch flowers. Named selections offer variations in both foliage color and plant size. In the original, large-size form, you can find plants with bronze or red-purple leaves or with green leaves striped creamy white. Smaller kinds include 6-foot 'Sundowner' (green, pink, and cream leaves), 5-foot 'Maori Sunrise' (pink and green leaves), 4-foot 'Maori Maiden' (pink and green), 'Dark Delight' (maroon), 'Yellow Wave' (yellow and green), and 2-foot 'Tiny Tim' (yellow and bronzy green).

New Zealand flax grows best where summers are cool to mild. In hot-summer areas, plants need light shading during the heat of the day;

Limonium perezii

selections with pink and cream leaves are especially susceptible to sunburn. Plant in average, well-drained soil and water moderately. Clumps may remain in place indefinitely.

SALVIA. Sage. *Labiatae*. Hardiness varies. Mexican bush sage, *Salvia leucantha*, is on the borderline between perennial and shrub, functioning as a graceful shrub in the landscape. Plants are arching mounds 3 to 4 feet high and wide, with white-felted stems and sage green, lance-shaped leaves. Long flower spikes begin to open in late summer and continue well into autumn. Each small white flower is surrounded by a showy, fuzzy, purple calyx; a few color variations exist, particularly one with purple flowers. Plants are hardy to 25°F/−4°C. Mexican bush sage thrives in well-drained, average to poor soil, in full sun with moderate water. In early spring, cut last year's stems to the ground; start new plants from spring cuttings, or remove rooted stems from a clump's perimeter.

Bog sage, *S. uliginosa*, will take regular or moderate watering. Its upright stems reach 6 feet tall, bearing sprays of sky blue, white-marked blossoms. Plants are hardy to 10°F/−12°C.

Oenothera tetragona

...Nepeta

ries longer flower spikes of rich blue blossoms, and white-flowered 'Snowflake'. 'Six Hills Giant' may also be an *N. faassenii* selection, but it is larger in all ways, growing 2 to 3 feet tall. The parent of the *N. faassenii* group, *N. mussinii*, is smaller in both foliage and lavender flowers than the hybrids but makes a pleasant show on foot-high plants. It sets seed, so it will usually provide seedling plants as a plus.

Culture. Few plants are easier to grow than the catmints. Just give them well-drained, average soil in a warm, sunny position. If you shear off spent flowering spikes, cutting plants back about halfway, you'll induce a repeat performance. In early spring, just as growth begins, cut out last year's growth to make way for new stems. You can divide clumps then for increase, though it's also easy to start new plants from spring and summer cuttings.

Good companions. *Asclepias tuberosa, Belamcanda chinensis, Centranthus ruber, Coreopsis, Euphorbia, Iris* (bearded), *Limonium latifolium, Verbena.*

OENOTHERA
Sundrops, Evening primrose
Onagraceae

Hardy to: −20°F/−29°C, except as noted; not suited to Gulf Coast and Florida
Exposure: Sun
Water: Moderate
Flowers in: Summer
Colors: Yellow, pink, white

The appealingly named sundrops and evening primroses provide a great bounty of bright blossoms over a long summer period in return for little care. Four broad, silky petals compose each bowl-shaped flower. Some species display their blossoms during the day, but many of the evening primrose kinds open as sun wanes in the afternoon and close the following morning.

Showiest of the yellow-flowered species is *O. missourensis*, the Ozark sundrop. It forms a sprawling plant with stems that turn upward to about 9 inches, bearing narrow, velvety leaves to 5 inches long. Flowers are surprisingly large for the plant—3 to 5 inches across—and open, evening primrose–fashion, in the afternoon. The other commonly available yellow sundrops is variously cataloged as *O. tetragona, O. fruticosa*, or possibly *O. f. youngii*. The two species—*O. tetragona* and *O. fruticosa*—differ in small details. What is offered under these names is a shrubbier plant to 2 feet high with broader, shiny leaves about 3 inches long and day-blooming flowers to 1½ inches across. Stems and flower buds are reddish brown. Good named selections include 'Fyrverkeri' ('Fireworks'), with purple-tinted foliage, and larger-flowered 'Sonnenwende' ('Solstice').

If you locate plants where their invasiveness won't interfere with other plants, the Mexican evening primrose *O. berlandieri* (*O. speciosa childsii*) will, despite its common name, give you an amazing quantity of 2-inch rose pink blossoms during the day. Plants are hardy to −10°F/−23°C and will colonize rapidly, sending up slender 10- to 15-inch stems bearing narrow, 3-inch leaves; 'Woodside White' has totally white blossoms, while 'Siskyou' is a less aggressive, shorter plant to about 8 inches in height. If plants are cut back after the first flowering, they'll deliver a second burst of bloom. White evening primrose, *O. speciosa*, is a taller, coarser, rampantly spreading edition of the Mexican evening primrose; flowers open white and age to pink.

Culture. Tolerant of drought and poor soil, the sundrops and evening primroses need at best only well-drained

Paeonia hybrid

soil and moderate watering. To rejuvenate crowded plantings or obtain increase, divide in autumn in mild regions, in early spring where winter is cold. You can also start new plants from spring cuttings.

Good companions. *Asclepias tuberosa, Belamcanda chinensis, Centranthus ruber, Coreopsis, Euphorbia, Iris* (bearded), *Limonium latifolium, Verbena.*

PAEONIA
Peony
Paeoniaceae

Hardy to: −50°F/−46°C; needs some winter chill; not suited to Gulf coast and Florida
Exposure: Sun
Water: Regular
Flowers in: Late spring
Colors: Red, pink, cream, white

Herbaceous peonies are old-fashioned perennial favorites, cherished for their spectacular late-spring blossoms that momentarily divert attention from the beauty of their foliage. Each spring, new shoots rise from below the ground and develop into rounded shrublike clumps of especially handsome large leaves divided into numerous segments. Then from round buds at the stem tips come the impressive blossoms: silk or satin textured, up to 10 inches across.

The "traditional" peonies are fully double, like pompons, but there are semidouble and entirely single flowered sorts plus the Japanese and anemone types, which have one or two rows of petals surrounding a conspicuous fluff of petaloid stamens. Peony specialists list countless named hybrids with flowers that range in color from the darkest red through endless pink variations on to white and cream. Plant heights range from 2 to 4 feet. Flowering extends from 4 to 6 weeks, with hybrids that bloom early, midseason, and late.

Culture. A well-planted, well-located peony can remain undisturbed indefinitely. Start with well-drained soil, dig it deeply, and incorporate plenty of organic matter in advance of the usual late summer or early autumn planting period. (In some parts of the West, peony roots are available in earliest spring.) If your soil is highly acid, add lime. Choose a location in full sun, sheltered from strong winds that can topple the bloom-heavy stems. However, where spring bloom season is hot and dry, choose only early-flowering hybrids and plant them where they'll be lightly shaded in the afternoon. Even in windless spots, the double-flowered kinds may need staking to remain upright; the metal hoop support and metal link stakes illustrated on page 39 are popular peony supports.

Planting depth is critical—overly deep planting eliminates flowering—and depends on your climate. In warmer-winter regions, position the growth buds ("eyes" at the top of the roots) just below the soil surface—no deeper than 1 inch. This will give plants the benefit of as much winter chill as your climate offers. In colder regions, where winter chill is guaranteed, plant so that growth buds are 1½ to no more than 2 inches deep. In marginally cold areas (as in parts of California and the South), the nearly single Japanese types will consistently perform better.

One disease problem to guard against is botrytis blight: flower buds turn brown, fail to open, and foliage and stems become brown-spotted. If this occurs, cut off and destroy infected parts, spray plant with benomyl, then spray again the following spring before buds show color.

Good companions. *Chrysanthemum superbum, Hemerocallis, Iris* (bearded, Siberian), *Lupinus.*

Papaver orientale hybrid

PAPAVER ORIENTALE
Oriental poppy
Papaveraceae

Hardy to: –40°F/–40°C; needs some winter chill; not suited to Gulf coast and Florida
Exposure: Sun, partial shade
Water: Regular to moderate
Flowers in: Late spring
Colors: Red, orange, pink shades, white

Flamboyant Oriental poppies are guaranteed attention getters, their bowl-shaped flowers of silky petals easily reaching 8 inches across. A typical flower contains four to six broad, wavy-edged petals, each with a dark blotch at its base; the prominent seed capsule and stamens at the flower's center are also of the same contrasting darkness. The original Oriental poppies were a neon-bright orange or red with black centers, but among the many named hybrids are pastel shades and white flowers (some with colored petal edges), flowers with lighter centers that lack dark petal bases, as well as the shimmering orange and red kinds. Clumps of finely divided, very hairy leaves mound to about 2 feet high, sending up leafy flower stalks that reach 3 to 4 feet tall, depending on the individual variety. Soon after flowering finishes, the entire plant dies down to the ground, the leaves emerging again in early autumn and remaining in a small tuft over winter.

The recently developed Minicaps hybrids have blossoms much like the traditional Oriental poppies but flower profusely over a longer season because they set no seeds. Flowers range from pale pink to bright red, with and without dark centers. Plants come in three sizes: dwarf (1 to 2 feet), standard (2 to 4 feet), and tall (4 to 6 feet).

Culture. Oriental poppies need well-drained soil and really flourish if the soil is deeply dug and some organic matter incorporated. In cool- to mild-summer regions the plants will take full sun; where summer is hot, give them light shade during the heat of the day. Plants need regular water while growing and flowering, less when dormant (they're actually rather drought tolerant then). In mild-winter regions, plant with 1 inch of soil covering; where soil freezes in winter, plant 3 inches deep. You can leave clumps in place for many years. If you need to divide for increase or to reduce crowding, do so in late summer. New plants may sprout from any portion of cut root you leave in the ground.

Good companions. *Achillea, Artemisia, Coreopsis, Euphorbia corollata, Gypsophila paniculata, Iris* (bearded), *Verbena rigida.*

PENSTEMON
Penstemon, Beard tongue
Scrophulariaceae

Hardy to: Varies; not suited to Gulf Coast and Florida
Exposure: Sun, partial shade
Water: Regular to moderate
Flowers in: Spring, summer
Colors: Blue, purple, red, pink, white

(Continued on next page)

Penstemon gloxinioides

Although penstemons are not long-lived perennials, they offer so much color over a long period that they're worth the trouble of periodic replacement. Fortunately, new plants are easy to start from cuttings or by layering, so you can always have backups ready to plant out. Several species and hybrids are available; they vary both in hardiness and in their tolerance of humid heat. In general, the West and Southwest offer the most congenial conditions.

Bushy plants consist of generally upright stems with glossy, narrow, pointed leaves. Bright, clear-colored flowers come in loose spikes, each blossom tubular with a flaring mouth; flowers may be a solid color, but many feature a light-colored or white throat with decorative spotting. The best bet for regions with humid summers is also the hardiest species: *P. barbatus* will take temperatures to –30°F/–34°C and needs some winter chill for best performance. The species features inch-long flowers on a somewhat sprawling plant to 3 feet high, but you're more likely to locate selected forms and hybrids. Pink-flowered 'Rose Elf', scarlet 'Prairie Fire', and purple 'Prairie Dusk' all grow about 2 feet tall.

Hybrids derived from several Mexican species are nearly foolproof color producers in regions with fairly mild winters (to 15°F/–9°C) and dry summers. Wine red 'Garnet' and light pink 'Evelyn' are loosely upright to about 2 feet with narrow leaves and spikes of slender-tubed flowers. More readily available are the hybrids known as border penstemons (*P. gloxinioides*). Flowers have broader tubes to 2 inches long on shrubby plants 2 to 3 feet high. Nurseries may offer seed-raised plants of mixed colors or named selections such as 'Holly's White', 'Huntington Pink' (soft rose and white), 'Firebird' (red), and 'Midnight' (purple). A West Coast specialty is *P. heterophyllus purdyi*, commonly sold in nurseries as 'Blue Bedder'. Stems are inclined to sprawl, then turn upward 1 to 1½ feet; flowers range from lavender to intense sky blue. Plants are hardy to about 0°F/–18°C.

Culture. These penstemons are easy to grow in average soil provided that drainage is good; overmoist soil can prove fatal—especially soggy soil during winter. Where summer is hot, give plants a bit of shade during the heat of the day. In all areas, early spring is a good planting time; in mild-winter regions, you can set out young plants in autumn. If you cut back plants after a burst of flowers has finished, they'll flower again on new growth. Plants are productive for about 3 to 4 years; replacement plants are easy to start and grow quickly to flowering size.

Good companions. *Artemisia, Coreopsis, Echinacea, Gypsophila paniculata, Nepeta, Oenothera, Scabiosa caucasica.*

PEROVSKIA
Russian sage
Labiatae

Hardy to: –20°F/–29°C; needs some winter chill
Exposure: Sun
Water: Moderate
Flowers in: Late spring, summer
Colors: Blue

In the shimmering heat of summer, you'll appreciate the cool blue haze of Russian sage. Shrubby clumps contain numerous upright, gray-white stems clothed in gray-green foliage; lower leaves are 2 to 3 inches long and deeply cut, but they become smaller and merely toothed as they ascend the stems. Each stem terminates in a widely branched spray of small lavender-blue blossoms that seem to float over the foliage. Mature clumps may reach 3 to 4 feet high and wide. Russian sage is usually sold as *Perovskia atriplicifolia* but plants in

Perovskia with *Coreopsis verticillata*

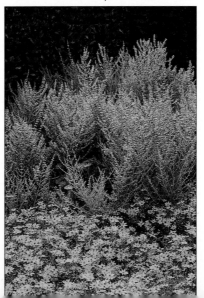

circulation are probably hybrids of that species and *P. abrotanoides*. 'Blue Spire' and lighter-colored 'Blue Haze' are named selections.

Culture. Russian sage will grow in soils that are sandy, rocky, or of generally low fertility as well as in regular garden soil. Its only real need is for good drainage. This is a "permanent" perennial that can remain in place indefinitely. Cut plants nearly to the ground in early spring, leaving just one or two pairs of growth buds on each vigorous stem. To increase a planting you can take cuttings in summer, or you may be able to find and dig up a rooted stem near the edge of a clump.

Good companions. *Achillea, Artemisia, Coreopsis, Limonium latifolium, Oenothera, Sedum, Zauschneria.*

PHLOX
Phlox
Polemoniaceae

Hardy to: Varies; needs some winter chill
Exposure: Sun, partial shade
Water: Regular, except as noted
Flowers in: Spring, summer
Colors: Blue, purple, red, salmon, pink, white

Vivid color is a phlox trademark, and by choosing different species and hybrids you can have a bright display from spring into autumn. Perennial phloxes separate into two rather distinct groups. One contains several low-growing species that flower in spring, their spreading plants good for foreground or ground cover planting. The second group contains the summer-blooming border phloxes and their allies; these are upright plants 2 to 4 feet tall, bearing their showy flowers in dense terminal clusters.

Despite their different growth habits, all phlox flowers are alike in composition: a slender tube flares out to a flat flower, circular in outline, with five segments. In the low-growing species, the segments may be distinctly separate, giving a star or pinwheel appearance; the tall phloxes usually have segments that overlap, making each blossom a full circle.

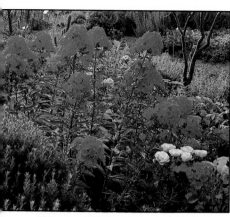
Phlox paniculata

Two of the low-growing species and one hybrid are similar and have similar cultural needs; all are hardy to –35°F/–37°C. Sweet William phlox, *P. divaricata*, is a spreading plant to about 1 foot high, its slender and sticky stems clothed in 2-inch elliptical leaves. Loose clusters of lavender-blue 1-inch flowers appear as early as tulip time in spring and continue for 6 weeks or more. Selected color forms are available, including 'Fuller's White' and darker blue *P. d. laphamii*. The plants of creeping phlox, *P. stolonifera*, also spread but generally remain under 1 foot in height. The slightly larger flowers come in smaller clusters, also appearing. with the spring bulbs. Nurseries usually offer named color selections such as 'Blue Ridge', 'Bruce's White', and 'Pink Ridge'. The hybrid 'Chattahoochee'—presumably derived from *P. d. laphamii*—forms a foot-tall spreading mound that is covered in midspring by maroon-eyed lavender-blue flowers 1 inch across. All the low-growing phloxes described above prefer light shade, except in cool-summer regions, where they will grow in sun. Plant them in well-drained, organically enriched soil.

Moss pink, *P. subulata*, is another low-growing species popular as a foreground specimen and also used as a small-scale ground cover. Creeping stems clothed in ½-inch, needlelike leaves form spreading mats to 6 inches high. During a month-long flowering period starting in late spring, plants are smothered in ¾-inch blossoms; colors include lavender-blue, white, and some fairly neon shades of pink through magenta to violet. In contrast to other low-growing kinds, moss pink prefers full sun in all but the hottest-summer regions. Give it a light, well-drained soil and moderate watering. Plants are hardy to –30°F/–34°C.

The tall phloxes have been a summer garden mainstay for generations. Their colors range from white, lavender, and soft pink through intense shades of salmon orange, magenta, red, maroon, and purple. Many feature a contrasting spot of color in the center of each flower. Plants are hardy to –30°F/–34°C. Beginning in early summer, you can choose 3- to 4-foot *P. carolina* and *P. maculata*. Nurseries offer named selections which may be assigned to either species. Whatever their exact ancestry, these plants have glossy, lance-shaped leaves to 4 inches and blossom clusters that are elongated and nearly cylindrical. Pure white 'Miss Lingard' is a classic; others include 'Alpha' (rose pink, darker eye), 'Omega' (white, purple eye), and 'Rosalinde' (lilac pink). Foliage of these phloxes is more resistant to mildew and mites than is that of the other tall phloxes.

Following these early kinds and reaching a peak in midsummer come the named selections and hybrids of *P. paniculata*, commonly known as border or summer phlox. Compared with the earlier-flowering tall kinds, these plants have somewhat larger, duller green leaves, while the blossoms are carried in dense, dome-shaped or pyramidal clusters. Stems reach 2½ to 4 feet or more, depending on the particular selection. Specialists carry a great number of named selections, including ones that come into bloom before midsummer and others that extend the flowering into early autumn.

Culture. The low-growing phloxes are less particular about climate and conditions than are the tall kinds. Their needs are outlined above; all can be divided for increase in early spring.

Tall phloxes need regular attention if they are to look good and remain healthy. They're at their best where summer is cool to mild; in hot-summer regions, give them a bit of shade during the heat of the day and be sure to mulch soil to maintain moisture and coolness. Prepare the soil well: they need good drainage, good fertility, and plenty of organic matter. Keep plants well watered during the growing season. The *P. paniculata* selections in particular are susceptible to powdery mildew and spider mites, either or both of which may need control during the season. To lessen the chances of mildew, plant where air circulation is good; avoid crowding plants close together or planting next to walls and hedges. A clump will send up numerous stems, but you should cut out all but four to six of the strongest. This will not only aid air circulation but will promote superior-quality blossoms. Cut off the spent flower heads; this may encourage a second flowering from side shoots and will prevent seed setting and a subsequent crop of inferior volunteer seedlings. Divide clumps every 2 to 4 years, replanting only strong rooted sections from the perimeters of the clumps. Where winter is severe, do this in early spring; in milder regions, you may also divide in autumn.

Good companions. (For tall kinds) Aster, Chrysanthemum, Monarda, Physostegia virginiana, Platycodon grandiflorus.

PHYSOSTEGIA VIRGINIANA
False dragonhead, Obedient plant
Labiatae

Hardy to: –35°F/–37°C
Exposure: Sun, partial shade
Water: Regular
Flowers in: Summer, early autumn
Colors: Pink, white

(Continued on next page)

Physostegia virginiana 'Vivid'

False dragonhead takes pink shades and white from mid- to late summer into early autumn, a time of year when the garden is dominated by warm colors. Spreading clumps send up stems of toothed, lance-shaped leaves to 5 inches long, each stem topped by a tapering spike of snapdragonlike blooms. Each flower, if twisted or pushed out of position, will remain in place, hence the name "obedient plant." The most usual flower color is a bright bluish pink, but there are named selections that feature flowers in a softer rose pink, rosy red, and white. 'Variegata' carries the typical cool pink blossoms on a plant with foliage strikingly variegated in creamy white. The usual height of most selections is 2 to 3 feet; bright rose pink 'Vivid' flowers at about 18 inches high.

Culture. False dragonheads grow best in good soil with plenty of moisture, though they will put on a reduced show in soil of lesser quality or given less water. Under their preferred conditions, plants tend to spread rapidly and will need to be divided and replanted every 2 to 3 years in early spring.

Good companions. *Anemone hybrida, Aster, Chrysanthemum, Erigeron, Phlox paniculata, Scabiosa caucasica.*

PLATYCODON GRANDIFLORUS
Balloon flower
Campanulaceae

Hardy to: –35°F/–37°C; not suited to Gulf coast and Florida
Exposure: Sun, partial shade
Water: Regular
Flowers in: Summer
Colors: Blue, pink, white

Star-shaped, 2-inch flowers like wide-open *Campanula* bells open from nearly round, balloonlike buds that, with gentle thumb-and-forefinger pressure, you can pop open. Flowers are carried on slender stalks at the ends of upright stems clothed in broadly oval, 3-inch leaves. With some searching, you may find named selections with flowers of different colors, in differing heights ranging from foot-high dwarfs

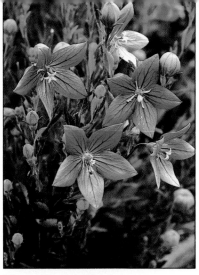

Platycodon grandiflorus

to nearly 3 feet, and with double blossoms. The bushy plants begin to flower in early summer and will continue for 2 months or more if you remove spent blossoms.

Culture. Best conditions for balloon flower are a well-prepared, fairly light, well-drained soil. Where summers are hot, plant in light shade or filtered sunlight; in cooler regions, locate plants in full sun. Stems die in autumn and new growth appears quite late the next year; mark a plant's location to avoid damaging it before it makes its appearance. This is a deep-rooted "permanent" plant, unless gophers, who consider it a delicacy, get to it.

Good companions. *Astilbe, Campanula, Heuchera, Hosta, Malva.*

POLYGONATUM
Solomon's seal
Liliaceae

Hardy to: –30°F/–34°C; not suited to Gulf Coast and Florida
Exposure: Partial shade, shade
Water: Regular
Flowers in: Spring
Colors: Greenish white

The Solomon's seals are studies in elegance. Gradually spreading clumps send up stems that grow upright for a distance and then bend outward; on either side of the arching stems appear broadly oval leaves arranged in nearly horizontal planes. Where leaves join stems, pairs or clusters of small bell-shaped flowers hang beneath the stems on threadlike stalks; small blue-

black berries may form after flowering. Leaves and stems turn bright yellow in autumn before they die down. Nurseries don't all agree on the botanical names for these plants—one species may travel under two or more names. For garden purposes, size is the chief difference among available kinds.

Small Solomon's seal, *P. biflorum*, bears 4-inch leaves on stems that grow to 3 feet; flowers are usually in pairs or threes. A bit shorter, at 2 to 3 feet, *P. odoratum* 'Variegatum' offers leaves cleanly margined in creamy white and carried on stems that are a contrasting dark red until fully grown. Flowers are individual or in pairs. For an ankle-high clump or small ground cover, choose the plant sold as *P. falcatum*, or dwarf Japanese Solomon's seal. At the other end of the size scale rises *P. commutatum* (sometimes sold as *P. canaliculatum*), which carries 7-inch leaves on stems normally reaching 4 to 5 feet in height; pendant flowers come in groups of two to ten.

Culture. Although Solomon's seals grow best in moist, organically rich soil—typical woodland conditions—they will perform moderately well in drier soils and even when competing with tree roots. These are "permanent" plants that can remain in place without dividing for rejuvenation. If you want to dig for increase, remove rhizomes from a clump's edge in early spring.

Good companions. *Alchemilla mollis, Astilbe, Bergenia, Epimedium, Helleborus, Hosta, Liriope.*

Polygonatum odoratum 'Variegatum'

Potentilla nepalensis

POTENTILLA
Cinquefoil
Rosaceae

Hardy to: Varies; not suited to Gulf Coast and Florida
Exposure: Sun
Water: Regular
Flowers in: Summer
Colors: Yellow, orange, red, pink, white

Roses and strawberries may seem unlikely relations, but their kinship comes together in the cinquefoils. Over foliage that suggests strawberry leaves appear clusters or sprays of small, wild-roselike blossoms.

Two Himalayan species—*P. atrosanguinea* and *P. nepalensis*—have produced named selections and hybrids that form a group of similar, colorful individuals with hairy leaves either green or silvery gray. These are hardy to −20°F/−29°C. Plants may reach 1½ feet high and spread wider; individually they may be a bit floppy, but planted in groups for mutual support they put on a better show. Among the most widely sold are *P. atrosanguinea* 'Gibson's Scarlet', with green foliage and brilliant red blossoms; *P. nepalensis* 'Miss Willmott', with red-centered cherry pink flowers and green leaves; and the hybrids 'William Rollison', semidouble orange and yellow over green foliage, and 'Yellow Queen', with brassy yellow double flowers and gray leaves.

Narrower leaflets and more upright stems distinguish *P. recta*, hardy to −35°F/−37°C. The dark green foliage is a good backdrop for the inch-wide, single yellow flowers. Nurseries usually offer the selection *P. r.* 'Warrenii', a more compact grower with bright, clear blossoms.

Culture. The cinquefoils present no cultural difficulties. Give them average to good, well-drained soil; in cool climates, just moderate watering will suffice. If you want to increase a plant, you can dig and divide in early spring or early autumn; *P. r.* 'Warrenii' will give you volunteer seedlings.

Good companions. *Belamcanda chinensis, Coreopsis, Dictamnus albus, Hemerocallis, Salvia, Sisyrinchium striatum.*

PRIMULA
Primrose
Primulaceae

Hardy to: −20°F/−29°C, except as noted; most need some winter chill; not suited to Gulf Coast and Florida
Exposure: Partial shade
Water: Regular
Flowers in: Late winter, spring, summer
Colors: All colors; many multicolor combinations

If the word "primrose" evokes images of an English woodland in spring, you have a good impression of the conditions many of these plants prefer. There is a great number of primrose species and countless selections, named hybrids, and hybrid strains; specialists have organized the species into 34 sections: groups of species that strongly resemble each other (and frequently hybridize with one another) and that usually have the same cultural needs. But those primroses of fairly easy garden culture are fewer in number and can be divided roughly into two categories: those that grow easily under ordinary garden conditions, and those that need abundant moisture—even boggy soil. Most of these latter, however, still need the "primrose conditions" described here under "Culture."

All primrose plants form rosettes of leaves above which the flowers are borne in one of three ways: on individual stems, in clusters at ends of

Primula polyantha 'Gold Lace'

stems, or in tiered clusters up the stems. An individual flower is circular in outline but composed of five equal lobes, each of which is more or less indented at its apex (sometimes so deeply that each flower appears to have ten parts). Some primroses begin flowering in mid- to late winter in mild climates; most blossom some time in spring; and a very few will be in bloom in early summer.

Primroses that grow under ordinary garden conditions. The most familiar of these "easy" primroses are the polyanthus primroses, hybrids of *P. polyantha*. These plants are the most adaptable of all primroses, thriving even in mild-winter regions. Flowering plants of these (especially the Pacific Giants strain) are mass marketed in small pots each year in winter and spring. Tongue-shaped leaves can reach 8 inches long and resemble romaine lettuce; yellow-centered flowers appear in terminal clusters on stocky, 8- to 12-inch stems, with individual flowers reaching up to 2 inches across. Colors include everything but black and true green, the tones ranging from soft to bright. The hybrid 'Gold Lace', with gold-edged mahogany petals and large yellow center, belongs to this group.

Two other species are similar to, but smaller than, the polyanthus types. English primrose, *P. vulgaris*, bears its light yellow, fragrant flowers on individual stems held above 6-inch clumps of leaves shaped like canoe paddles. Garden strains of this species may have two or three flowers to a stem in a range of colors that includes red, pink, blue, cream, white, and brownish shades as well as yellow; some strains include double flowers. The Barnhaven strain is especially fine, predominantly in soft colors. (Any Barnhaven primrose is superior, bred for beauty and vigor.) The Juliana primroses—hybrids of *P. juliae*—are shorter, smaller, broader-leafed editions of polyanthus primroses in nearly as broad a color range. Retail nurseries usually offer mixed-color assortments or unnamed plants in flower; you may find individual named hybrids, such as wine-red 'Wanda', cataloged by perennials and primrose specialists.

As a floral departure, *P. denticulata* displays its ½-inch flowers in dense, ball-shaped clusters atop foot-high stems. With good reason, it is sometimes referred to as the "drumstick primrose." Colors are lavender-blue, pink, and white; flowering starts in earliest spring. Leaves resemble those of polyanthus primroses, but at flowering time they are only about half the latter's mature size. They will grow under standard garden conditions but will also take nearly as much dampness as the moisture lovers described below. Plants are hardy to −30°F/−34°C.

Primula sieboldii departs from the polyanthus type in several ways. Downy, wrinkled leaves are carried on slender leafstalks, each leaf arrow shaped with a distinctly scalloped margin. In late spring, slender stems 4 to 8 inches high bear clusters of phloxlike flowers; to the basic lilac shade, hybrid strains add white, pink, and purple blossoms. Foliage dies down soon after flowering finishes, enabling the then-dormant plants to endure hotter summers better than other primroses.

Primroses that need damp soil.

Quite a few primroses thrive in soil that could be called poorly drained, provided it also contains plenty of organic matter. Prominent among these moisture lovers are 2 of the 34 sections: Candelabra (Proliferae), and Sikkimensis. Species and hybrids in these groups are good candidates for stream- and pond-side planting as well as for any lightly shaded spot that re-

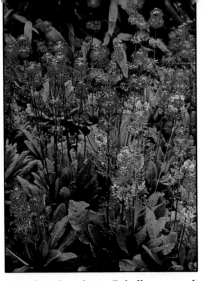

Primula pulverulenta, P. bulleyana, and *P. bullesiana*

mains damp. To grow them in more standard situations, choose a medium to heavy (loam to claylike) soil, add generous amounts of organic matter, and water plants faithfully.

Candelabra primroses are considerably larger than the previous kinds, some forming clumps to 2½ feet across and sending up stems as high as 3 feet. Flowers appear in tiered whorls around the stem; the lowest tier opens first, just above the leaves; then, as the stalk elongates, successive whorls come into flower. The most widely available is *P. japonica*, a 2½-foot plant when in flower, with 9-inch tongue-shaped leaves. Colors include purple, red, pink, and white; 'Miller's Crimson' is a standard dark red selection. Where garden conditions are favorable, plants will self-sow prolifically. Reddish purple *P. beesiana* is a similar species; its hybrid *P. bullesiana* includes pink, cream, and lavender shades. A similar species, except in being 50 percent larger, is *P. pulverulenta*; blossoms are purple-eyed red to magenta, though the Bartley strain offers shades of pink and salmon. If you want to add yellow color to your planting, look for *P. bulleyana* and *P. helodoxa*.

The Sikkimensis primroses are noted for their late flowering—in early summer—and fragrance. Bell-shaped flowers come in clusters atop sturdy stems but are gracefully nodding rather than upright. Yellow *P. sikkimensis* forms clumps of oblong, stalked leaves from which rise 1½-foot stems that carry up to 24 flowers apiece. *P. florindae* grows about twice as tall, bearing up to 60 blossoms in each cluster;

the basic color is yellow, but hybrids come in orange and red as well. This species will grow in several inches of water, provided there is enough movement to prevent stagnation.

Culture. Primrose species come from woodlands and moist meadows, frequently from climates that are cool and humid. This combination of moist, organically rich soil and cool, humid air constitute ideal "primrose conditions." It is no wonder that these plants flourish in the Pacific Northwest, much of the British Isles, and New Zealand. You can work with your soil to bring it up to primrose standards, but climate is a larger obstacle. The more summer heat you have, the more protection from direct sun you should provide. In cool-summer regions—foggy, overcast, or cool due to high latitude—many primroses may prosper in nearly full-sun locations. But in sunnier climes, only morning sunshine will work; filtered or dappled sunlight and high shade will be the preferred exposures. In less-than-perfect situations, try the rugged polyanthus primroses and Juliana hybrids and the heat-tolerant, summer-dormant *P. sieboldii*. Where winter chill is negligible or lacking, rely on the polyanthus hybrids.

Primrose plants form tight clumps that in time will need to be divided when performance declines. Divide crowded clumps right after flowering finishes.

Good companions. *Aquilegia, Dicentra, Epimedium, Mertensia, Polygonatum.*

PULMONARIA
Lungwort
Boraginaceae

Hardy to: −35°F/−37°C, except as noted; not suited to Gulf Coast and Florida
Exposure: Shade
Water: Regular
Flowers in: Spring
Colors: Blue, pink, red, white

A planting of lungworts isn't likely to stop traffic. But their quiet charm is endearing, and their low growth and preference for shade mark them as highly useful in moist gardens.

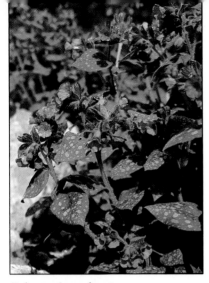

Pulmonaria saccharata

Broadly oval to lance-shaped hairy leaves form rosettes or clumps close to the ground; many kinds have leaves attractively dappled with gray or silver. Flowering stems bear smaller leaves beneath the nodding clusters of funnel- or trumpet-shaped blossoms. After flowering finishes, plants produce more leaves from their bases. If you keep plants well watered, foliage will remain ornamental throughout the growing season.

Blue lungwort, *P. angustifolia*, typically has bright blue flowers that open from pink buds; plants grow 8 to 12 inches high, bearing dark green, unspotted foliage. Specific-color selections include light blue 'Azurea' and intensely deep blue 'Johnson's Blue'. Pale green, unspotted leaves are one distinguishing feature of 1- to 2-foot *P. rubra*, hardy to −20°F/−29C. Its very early flowering and coral red blossom color also set it apart. 'Redstart' is a superior selection.

For beautifully spotted leaves, Bethlehem sage, *P. saccharata*, offers a choice of several variations. This is a taller plant—12 to 18 inches—with blue flowers and silvery-spotted leaves, but specialists usually offer named selections. 'Mrs. Moon' and 'Margery Fish' have pink flowers that mature to blue; 'Janet Fisk' has similar flowers carried above heavily marbled leaves; 'Sissinghurst White' gives a totally green-and-white display; 'Roy Davidson' (with narrower foliage) and 'E. B. Anderson' have sky blue flowers. Jerusalem cowslip, *P. officinalis*, features heart-shaped, mottled leaves on a 12- to 18-inch plant; red-toned

buds open to lilac-blue blossoms, though the selection 'Rubra' has rosy red flowers. Long narrow leaves and upright stems distinguish *P. longifolia*; flowers are dark blue to violet.

Culture. Lungworts need a well-drained but always moist soil; liberally incorporate organic matter into the soil they'll occupy. Plant them in partial to full shade, as leaves will temporarily wilt in sunlight even though soil is moist. These are good plants for small ground cover patches and along woodland garden paths, especially under deciduous trees and shrubs. Crowded clumps will need dividing after a number of years; do so in early autumn and keep newly set plants well watered.

Good companions. *Dicentra, Hosta, Mertensia, Polygonatum, Primula.*

ROMNEYA COULTERI
Matilija poppy
Papaveraceae

Hardy to: −10°F/−23°C; not suited to humid-summer regions
Exposure: Sun
Water: Regular to little
Flowers in: Late spring, summer
Colors: White

Romneya coulteri

Dramatic, shrublike Matilija poppy is a strong candidate for the title of "largest perennial." Established plants send up stout, gray-green stems to 8 feet or more, bearing variously lobed, almost oaklike leaves of the same color. Leaf size varies from nearly hand size at the bases of strong shoots to 2 to 3 inches long toward stem tips and on weakest growth. Flowers come on upper portions of major stems, each blossom 8 to 10 inches wide and composed of (usually) six crepe-papery white petals surrounding a large central cluster of yellow stamens. Two named selections are found in the nursery trade; both may be hybrids between the species and the slightly different *R. c. trichocalyx*. 'White Cloud' has petals of a randomly crumpled texture; petals of 'Butterfly' appear to be pleated lengthwise.

Culture. Matilija poppy is also a contender for "easiest to grow." Simply plant it (it's available only in containers) then water until established. After that, a plant can be self-sufficient. Plants will grow in any kind of soil, from heavy to gravelly; with good drainage, they'll take regular garden watering even though established plants (in any soil) tolerate extreme drought. Prolific root sprouting, especially in light soils, puts Matilija poppy in the invasive category. Though you can contain plants by vigilantly pulling up wayward shoots, it's better to choose a location where their spreading tendency may be an advantage—or at least not a drawback. This is a good perennial for planting in background "garden fringe" areas, on dry hillsides, and along rural drives.

Stems will last for several years but begin to look shabby—with much spindly branching—before they die. To keep plants looking neat, cut all stems back to about 6 inches in late autumn or winter; new growth will quickly build up in spring. This is a "permanent" perennial. If you want to gain more plants, the simplest way is to dig up rooted shoots and pot them until they form good root systems. The best time to do this is late autumn through winter.

Good companions. *Artemisia, Baptisia australis, Centranthus ruber*, ornamental grasses, *Salvia*.

Rudbeckia

RUDBECKIA
Coneflower
Compositae

Hardy to: –35°F/–37°C
Exposure: Sun
Water: Regular
Flowers in: Summer, autumn
Colors: Yellow

The wild forms of these sunny daisies—black-eyed Susan, coneflower, golden glow—may be familiar in many parts of the North American countryside as field and roadside plants. But those often rangy and rampant wildflowers have been tamed by plant breeders, resulting in several fine, easy-to-grow garden ornaments. The common name reflects the flower's center: typically dark and raised in a cone or beehive shape.

For a typical black-eyed Susan–type flower—yellow orange petals surrounding a dark central cone—look for *R. fulgida sullivantii* 'Goldsturm'. Clumps of broadly lance-shaped, hairy leaves send up branching, leafy stems 2 to 2½ feet tall, the clump becoming a mass of 3-inch daisies for many weeks. Some nurseries offer plants of Goldsturm Strain; these are raised from seed of 'Goldsturm' and will vary from it a bit in color, size, and foliage.

Two other widely available coneflowers offer variations on the yellow daisy theme. Both are usually listed as selections of *R. nitida*, though it is more likely that they are allied with *R. laciniata*. 'Herbstsonne' ('Autumn Sun') is an impressive background daisy, sending stems of green-centered flowers to about 6 feet high. In contrast, 'Goldquelle' grows to a more modest 2½ to 3½ feet tall and features fully double flowers. If you encounter true *R. laciniata*—usually as its selected double-flowered form 'Hortensia' ('Golden Glow')—be aware that this is an aggressive spreader that grows to about 6 feet tall and that may need support.

Culture. You'll get abundant bloom over a long period with little fussing. Give coneflowers average to good soil and moderate to regular watering. To maintain good performance, you'll need to divide clumps every 2 to 4 years in early spring.

Good companions. *Achillea, Artemisia, Echinacea purpurea, Echinops, Helenium, Gaillardia grandiflora, Nepeta,* ornamental grasses, *Salvia, Sisyrinchium striatum.*

SALVIA
Sage
Labiatae

Hardy to: Varies
Exposure: Sun
Water: Moderate
Flowers in: Summer
Colors: Purple, blue, white

Many sages are noted for their aromatic foliage, and most are cherished for the cool blue tones they bring to the summer garden scene. Mild-winter gardeners have a wide choice among fairly tender perennial sages; see page 93 for an account of these. Where sub-freezing winter temperatures are the norm, the following kinds are reliable.

The most widely planted hardy perennial sage is *S. superba,* tolerant of winter temperatures down to –20°F/–29°C but not of Gulf Coast humidity. Low, dense plants of green, lance-shaped leaves produce upright spikes of small flowers reaching 1½ to 2½ feet, depending on the particular selection. A drift of these plants creates a very vertical—and very colorful—picture. 'Ostfriesland' ('East Friesland'), with vibrant purple flowers, and 'Mainacht' ('May Night'), in deep indigo blue, are classic choices;

Salvia farinacea

perennials specialists may also offer other selections in different blues. After the first flush of flowering, cut stems back to encourage a repeat performance.

Mealy-cup sage, *S. farinacea,* is hardy only to 10°F/–12°C, but is often grown as an annual in colder climates. Rounded plants are somewhat shrubby, reaching about 3 feet high, with lance-shaped, gray-green leaves and spikes of ½-inch flowers. Retail nurseries frequently stock plants: 'Blue Bedder' and 'Victoria' are popular blue-flowered selections, while 'White Porcelain' and 'Silver White' offer all-white blossoms. Blue sage—*S. azurea grandiflora* (sometimes sold as *S. pitcheri*)—will be hardy to –20°F/–29°C. This is an upright and more open plant—to 5 feet high, with narrow leaves and bright blue blossoms in elongated spikes from midsummer into autumn. You can counteract a tendency to ranginess and topheaviness if, early in the growing season, you cut or pinch back stems to encourage branching.

A different growth habit distinguishes *S. pratensis* (sometimes sold as *S. haematodes)* from the previous species. Wrinkled, 6-inch leaves form a loose rosette on the ground; from this rise branched stems to 3 feet bearing spikes of lavender blue, 1- to 2-inch flowers shaped like an open parrot's beak. Flowering may begin in late spring and continue into midsummer. Plants are hardy to –20°F/–29°C but usually last only a few years; replace played-out plants as needed with new seedlings.

Culture. Other than needing good drainage, the sages are not demanding. Moderately fertile soil and moderate watering will keep them healthy and vigorous. You can increase *S. superba* by division in early spring. With *S. azurea grandiflora* you can remove rooted segments from clumps in early spring or take cuttings later in the season. Start new plants of *S. farinacea* from spring and summer cuttings; *S. pratensis* is easy to start from seed.

Good companions. *Achillea, Coreopsis, Gazania, Gerbera jamesonii, Heuchera, Potentilla, Rudbeckia.*

Scabiosa caucasica

Sedum 'Autumn Joy'

SCABIOSA CAUCASICA
Pincushion flower
Dipsacaceae

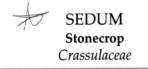

Hardy to: –35°F/–37°C; not suited to Gulf Coast and Florida
Exposure: Sun, partial shade
Water: Regular
Flowers in: Summer
Colors: Blue, white

A sprinkling of protruding stamens looking like pins in a pincushion were the inspiration for this flower's name. Each blossom is actually a compound head of two types: marginal flowers produce the circle of petals, and the central "cushion" contains tiny tubular blooms. The entire affair reaches 2 to 3 inches across, carried up to 2 feet on a flexuous, knitting-needlelike stem. Foliage clumps consist of long, narrow leaves; stem leaves are deeply cut. Seed-raised plants will offer a range of blue and lavender shades plus white; good flowers come from the strain called House's Hybrids or House's Novelty Mixture. For specific colors, you can buy named selections including blue 'Fama', lavender 'Clive Greaves', and white 'Miss Willmott'.

For gardens in hot-summer, mild-winter portions of the Southwest, the similar *S. columbaria* is a better choice. Flowers are in blue and lavender shades, white, and light pink; leaves are gray green and deeply cut.

Culture. Well-drained soil is a prerequisite for success with pincushion flower; plants are particularly sensitive to wet soil over winter. Best

growth comes in sandy to loam soils, enriched with organic matter and amended with lime if the pH is particularly acid. Plants of *S. caucasica* perform best in regions with cool to mild summers, where they appreciate full-sun positions. In warmer areas, give plants filtered sunlight or light shade during the hottest part of the day. During the bloom season, remove spent blossoms to prolong the flowering period. When clumps show a decline in performance, divide them in early spring.

Good companions. *Achillea* 'Moonshine', *Diascia, Geranium, Malva, Penstemon, Sisyrinchium striatum.*

SEDUM
Stonecrop
Crassulaceae

Hardy to: –35°F/–37°C
Exposure: Sun
Water: Moderate
Flowers in: Summer, autumn
Colors: Pink, white

The undemanding stonecrops are fleshy-leafed, succulent plants that provide good foliage contrast in a perennials planting, in addition to a pleasant floral display. There is a world of different ground-hugging stonecrops for rock garden and ground cover planting, but of larger sorts for general garden beds, the following are the top choices. All bear tiny, star shaped blossoms grouped together into flat-topped clusters. Leaves are oval, rubbery tex-

tured, and usually have blunt-toothed or scalloped margins.

As its name suggests, *S. maximum atropurpureum* has something purple about it—in this case the stems and leaves, which emerge purplish gray then mature to maroon. The somewhat lax stems reach 1½ to 2 feet, bearing late summer clusters of pinkish red blossoms. In *S.* 'Ruby Glow' the stems are red and the bluish green foliage is red tinted. Stems reach about 12 inches but tend to sprawl from the weight of the broad clusters of pink blossoms that age to a darker tone. A presumed hybrid between the two, *S.* 'Vera Jameson', has dusky plum red leaves on arching stems to about 8 inches high. Its late-summer flowers are dusty rose.

Most familiar of these larger stonecrops is *S. spectabile*. In early spring the dormant clumps initiate growth, sending up gradually elongating stems of sea green leaves to form a dome-shaped mound of foliage 1½ to 2 feet tall. In late summer, stem tips bear broad, flat-topped clusters of pink blossoms; named selections include carmine red 'Meteor', rosy red 'Brilliant', and white 'Star Dust'. 'Variegata' has pink flowers but ivory cream leaves irregularly margined in green. *Sedum* 'Autumn Joy'—sometimes listed as a selection of *S. telephium*—is similar to the *S. spectabile* group, its 1½- to 2-foot stems bearing broad and somewhat rounded flower clusters in late summer. The flowers emerge pink but age to coppery pink and finally to rust, remaining attractive (though dried) throughout autumn and into winter.

(Continued on next page)

Senecio cineraria

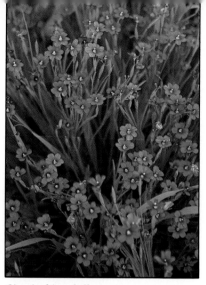

Sisyrinchium bellum

...Sedum

Culture. Stonecrops want a well-drained soil but are not particular about fertility or quality. When clumps become so crowded that quality decreases, divide them in early spring. In addition to dividing, you can increase plants easily from stem cuttings during late spring and early summer.

Good companions. *Anthemis, Artemisia, Aster, Belamcanda chinensis, Dictamnus albus, Gazania, Helianthus, Linaria, Stachys lanata.*

SENECIO CINERARIA
Dusty miller
Compositae

Hardy to: 10°F/–12°C
Exposure: Sun
Water: Moderate
Flowers in: Summer
Colors: Yellow

Many plants are called "dusty miller"; this one, like its *Artemisia* relatives, is grown for its nearly white, deeply cut foliage. (The heads of small, yellow daisies are inconsequential and even detracting.) Felt-textured leaves are deeply cut into round- or blunt-tipped lobes, the entire plant dense and bushy at about 2 feet tall. The silvery filigreed foliage is a refreshing contrast among green-leafed perennials, especially good-looking with those having soft pink, mauve, blue, cream, and white flowers.

Culture. This dusty miller will thrive in a variety of soils, from good to fairly nutrient poor—as long as drainage is

good. Pinch or lightly cut back plants during the growing season as needed to maintain compactness; cut back established plants more heavily in early spring. Plants will decline after several years, becoming sparse and woody, but it is easy to obtain a supply of new plants from spring and summer cuttings.

Good companions. *Agapanthus, Belamcanda chinensis, Gaura lindheimeri, Gazania, Gerbera jamesonii, Sedum, Sisyrinchium striatum, Verbena.*

SISYRINCHIUM
Blue-eyed grass
Iridaceae

Hardy to: 0°F/–18°C
Exposure: Sun, partial shade
Water: Regular
Flowers in: Spring, summer
Colors: Yellow, cream, blue, white

These iris relatives show the relationship in their fans of narrow, swordlike leaves. But the flowers are far from irislike—each is flat and circular in outline, with six segments. These are good plants for foliage contrast with other perennials, forming fairly low, dense clumps. One species offers a showy floral display; the other two have a less assertive, wildflowerlike charm.

The Chilean *S. striatum* offers the largest plant and most conspicuous flowers. Grayish green leaves may reach 2 feet long by 1 inch wide; old leaves become black rather than brown. In spring to early summer, flowering stems rise 2 to 2½ feet bearing 1-inch, creamy yellow blossoms set close to the stems. If you leave spent flowers to form seed capsules, you'll get a sizable crop of volunteer seedlings the following year. Plants are hardy to 0°F/–18°C.

Two similar species from Pacific coastal North America may be sold by native plant specialists. Yellow-eyed grass, *S. californicum*, and California blue-eyed grass, *S. bellum*, are similar plants with narrow leaves 8 to 12 inches tall and slender, flattened stems that rise above the foliage. Flowers are slightly less than an inch across and bright yellow in yellow-eyed grass but purple, blue, or occasionally white in

blue-eyed grass. Both species will grow in moist soil as well as under regular garden conditions.

Culture. Set out plants in ordinary garden soil. Although regular watering is best, plants will endure short periods of drought. Clumps seldom need dividing unless you need to remove portions for increase. Volunteer seedlings usually provide a surplus for enlarging a planting.

Good companions. *Aquilegia, Artemisia, Coreopsis, Heuchera, Potentilla, Rudbeckia, Sedum, Senecio.*

SOLIDAGO & SOLIDASTER
Goldenrod
Compositae

Hardy to: –30°F/–34°C
Exposure: Sun, partial shade
Water: Moderate
Flowers in: Summer, autumn
Colors: Yellow

Gardeners in the Midwest and East may snub goldenrods because they are familiar roadside "weeds," but that fact doesn't diminish their beauty in the garden. Their flowering, which starts in mid- to late summer and extends into autumn, gives the landscape a shot of fresh color when many other perennials are on the wane.

For garden use there are, in fact, named hybrids that are less aggressive and less wild-looking than the native species. All form clumps of upright, unbranched stems clothed in lance-shaped leaves. At stem tips ap-

Solidago

Stachys lanata

Stokesia laevis

pear multibranched flower sprays containing countless yellow blossoms, each of which is a tiny daisy. Heights vary from about 1 foot to 3 feet or more. The widely available hybrids are 3-foot 'Goldenmosa', which starts flowering in midsummer, and 1½-foot later-blooming 'Cloth of Gold'.

For softer yellow flowers on a goldenrod-type plant, there is *Solidaster luteus*—a hybrid of goldenrod and a perennial aster. The 2-foot plant resembles goldenrod, but the late-summer flower sprays contain larger blossoms like small, primrose yellow asters. Unlike the generally self-supporting goldenrods, these need staking to remain upright.

Culture. Goldenrods are good plants for garden margins where soil is of lesser quality and watering may be spotty, though they'll grow quite well under good conditions, too. Plan to divide and replant clumps about every 3 to 4 years, in early spring.

Good companions. *Aster, Boltonia asteroides, Chrysanthemum, Echinacea purpurea, Gaillardia grandiflora, Helenium, Helianthus,* ornamental grasses.

STACHYS
Betony
Labiatae

Hardy to: –30°F/–34°C
Exposure: Sun, partial shade; not suited to Gulf Coast and Florida
Water: Moderate
Flowers in: Late spring, summer
Colors: Pink, lilac, violet

Among the betonies is one of the favorite gray-leafed perennials. Lamb's ears, *S. lanata* (sometimes sold as *S. byzantina* or *S. olympica)*, is widely grown as both accent plant and small-scale ground cover. Its 6-inch, elliptical (ear-shaped) leaves are thick and gray green but covered by a feltlike coating of silvery white, woolly hairs. One plant will quickly spread into a clump, the stems rooting where they touch soil and the leaves rising about 1 foot high under best conditions. Wooly white stems rise to 18 inches, bearing short spikes of pinkish lilac flowers. Floral display is pleasant but not showy, and spent stems should be removed to maintain good appearance. If you prefer nothing but foliage, look for the flowerless selection 'Silver Carpet'.

Two other betonies are quite different from lamb's ears but similar to one another. The larger of the two, *S. grandiflora* (sometimes sold as *S. macrantha* or *Betonica grandiflora)* forms dense clumps of stalked, heart-shaped green leaves, each one textured, hairy, and with scalloped margins. Slender stems rise above leaves to 1½ or 2 feet, bearing tiered whorls of showy, purplish pink flowers. Specialists offer the selected forms 'Superba' and 'Robusta'. Common betony, *S. officinalis,* has elongated rather than heart-shaped leaves and small lilac-pink flowers in more closely spaced whorls on 1½- to 2-foot stems.

Culture. The betonies are undemanding perennials, content with average to even poor soil and moderate water-

ing. The two green-leafed species are better with a bit of shade in hot-summer regions; lamb's ears will tolerate light shade but doesn't require it. Divide and replant lamb's ears in spring whenever patches show bare spots or vigor decreases. The other betonies need less frequent division—only when performance declines.

Good companions. *Armeria maritima, Dianthus, Diascia, Linaria, Perovskia, Salvia, Sedum, Verbena.*

STOKESIA LAEVIS
Stokes' aster
Compositae

Hardy to: –20°F/–29°C
Exposure: Sun
Water: Regular to moderate
Flowers in: Summer, autumn
Colors: Blue, pink, white

Ease of care and a long flowering season are two qualities that recommend Stokes' aster. Flowers are reminiscent of both annual aster and cornflower, each 3 to 4 inches across and emerging from prickly bracts. Loose clusters of blossoms appear over mounding clumps of linear leaves throughout summer in cold-winter regions, well into autumn where winter is milder. In frost-free regions they can bloom intermittently throughout the year, if you keep removing spent flowers. On established clumps, flowering stems can reach 1½ to 2 feet high. Blue is the basic color, ranging from pale to fairly deep in seed-raised plants. Named selections include spe-

Thalictrum aquilegifolium

cific blue shades as well as pink and white. Most widely available are the clear light blue 'Blue Danube' and tinted white 'Silver Moon'.

Culture. Give plants average, well-drained soil and regular to moderate watering, depending on drainage. Roots will not tolerate excessive moisture; the more retentive a soil is, the less often you should water. Plants are especially sensitive to soil wetness in winter. In time clumps will become crowded and performance will decline. At that point, divide clumps in early spring.

Good companions. *Achillea, Coreopsis, Lychnis coronaria, Oenothera, Salvia, Stachys lanata.*

THALICTRUM
Meadow rue
Ranunculaceae

Hardy to: –20°F/–29°C; most need some winter chill; not suited to Gulf Coast and Florida
Exposure: Sun, partial shade
Water: Regular
Flowers in: Late spring, summer
Colors: Purple, lilac, yellow, white

The delicate, filmy meadow rues show several similarities to their columbine relatives: fernlike, graceful foliage that's often blue-green in color, and a preference for woodland edge situations. Two points of difference, though, are size and flower shape. Meadow rues are generally larger than columbines, the leafy flower stems rising 2 to 6 feet high, depending on the species. Their many-branched, open flower clusters carry numerous small blossoms, each with four segments and a prominent cluster of stamens.

Early-blooming *T. aquilegifolium* reaches 2 to 3 feet in height, bearing flowers that appear to be nothing but puffs of fluffy stamens. Rosy lilac is the typical color, though white and purple selections exist. Five-foot *T. speciosissimum* has similar blossoms, but the color is lemon yellow. Other species have flowers consisting of four or five petal-like sepals and a central tuft of stamens. The intricately branched flowering stems of *T. rochebrunianum* rise to 5 feet, bearing a cloud of small blossoms with lilac sepals and yellow stamens. 'Lavender Mist' is a superior selection.

Plants sold as *T. dipterocarpum* and *T. delavayi* belong to the same species, though there is disagreement about which is the proper name. Plants and flowers are similar to *T. rochebrunianum*, growing 4 to 5 feet high when in bloom, but flowers may have darker lilac to violet sepals. This is the only meadow rue really successful in mild-winter regions. In the selection 'Hewitt's Double', the stamens have been converted to lilac, petal-like segments.

Culture. The meadow rues thrive in good, well-drained, organically enriched soil. Light shade or dappled sunlight is good anywhere; in cool-summer regions, plants will take full-sun positions. Divide clumps in early spring every 4 to 5 years.

Good companions. *Aconitum, Bergenia, Digitalis, Helleborus, Hosta*

TRADESCANTIA ANDERSONIANA
Spiderwort
Commelinaceae

Hardy to: –20°F/–29°C
Exposure: Sun, partial shade
Water: Regular
Flowers in: Late spring, summer
Colors: Purple, blue, pink, lilac, white

Out of flower, a spiderwort clump might be mistaken for some sort of grass. Individual stems look like small corn plants, bearing arching, straplike leaves on either side. Clump height may reach 2 feet, with clusters of flower buds appearing atop each stem. Three broad petals comprise each 1½-inch flower, which is triangular in outline. An individual blossom lasts just one day, but a seemingly limitless number of buds promises a long bloom season. Nurseries offer a number of named selections, sometimes cataloged as *T. virginiana*, a species that is an ancestor of these hybrids.

Culture. Spiderworts appreciate plenty of water and an organically enriched soil, but the soil itself can be anything from sand to clay. The plants are nearly abuseproof, though, and will survive under much less than ideal conditions. As summer progresses, clumps often become leggy or sprawling; when this happens, cut plants nearly to the ground. They will bounce back, sometimes giving a second show of flowers. To increase a favorite plant, dig and divide in early spring.

Good companions. *Chelone, Digitalis, Filipendula, Iris* (Louisiana, Siberian), *Lythrum, Trollius.*

Tradescantia andersoniana

TRICYRTIS
Toad lily
Liliaceae

Hardy to: 0°F/−18°C
Exposure: Partial shade, shade
Water: Regular
Flowers in: Summer, autumn
Colors: Purple, lavender, white

The overused description "orchidlike" actually conveys some of the unusual beauty of toad lily blossoms. Each flower contains three petals and three sepals, arranged in starlike fashion; rising from the center is a column of decorative stamens and styles. In most species and selections, the background flower color is elaborately spotted in some shade of purple. Upright to arching stems bear broadly oval leaves that clasp the stems; flowers appear at leaf bases and in terminal clusters.

The most widely sold species, *T. hirta*, has softly hairy leaves on arching stems to 3 feet high. Flowers are white to pale lilac, densely peppered with purple; 'White Towers' and 'Alba' have unspotted pure white blossoms. The plant sold as *T.* 'Miyazaki' also has arching stems reaching about 3 feet high. Its leaves are narrower, lance shaped, and smooth, while the white flowers are spotted in lilac.

Tricyrtis hirta

Upright stems and flowers mostly in terminal clusters distinguish *T. formosana*. Stems reach 2 to 2½ feet, bearing glossy leaves that are mottled with darker green. Brown to maroon buds open white to pale lilac densely speckled with purple. The selection 'Amethystina' has lavender-blue, white-throated blossoms spotted in dark red. This is the earliest-blooming toad lily, the flowers appearing in mid- to late summer.

Culture. Toad lilies are woodland plants that appreciate an organically enriched, well-drained but moist soil. *T. formosana* will spread in time by underground stems into broad patches; the other toad lilies remain in more discrete clumps. You seldom need to divide clumps, but if you want to increase a plant you can carefully dig and remove rooted pieces from a clump's perimeter. Plants often self-sow, giving you an abundance of volunteer seedlings.

Good companions. *Helleborus, Hosta, Liriope, Trillium.*

TRILLIUM
Wake robin, Trillium
Liliaceae

Hardy to: Varies; needs some winter chill; not suited to Gulf Coast and Florida
Exposure: Partial shade, shade
Water: Regular
Flowers in: Spring
Colors: White, purple

Elegant trilliums are one of spring's harbingers, flowering in the dappled sunlight beneath bare and newly leafed branches. Plant parts are in groups of three: a whorl of three leaves tops a short stem, and nestled in the whorl is a three-petaled flower backed by three green sepals. Most trilliums reach 1 to 1½ feet when in flower; plants go dormant in mid- to late summer.

Many trillium species occur in eastern and western North America; native plant specialists will list regional species, well adapted within their native areas. Of the more generally available kinds, the eastern native *T. grandiflorum* bears the classic broad-petaled white flower to 3 inches across;

Trillium ovatum

as blossoms age they become pink and nod toward the ground. Its selection 'Roseum' is pink from start to finish. A complete departure is 'Flore Pleno'; its double white blossoms give it a gardenialike appearance. Plants are hardy to −40°F/−40°C. Mottled leaves and narrow, upright maroon petals characterize another eastern native, *T. sessile*, hardy to −30°F/−34°C.

Both the eastern species have near-counterparts from the western part of the continent. *Trillium ovatum (T. californicum)* resembles *T. grandiflorum* but with narrower white petals and flowers that remain upright. It will take winter temperatures down to −20°F/−29°C. Flowers of *T. chloropetalum* can range from greenish yellow to maroon, but the petals are rather narrow and upright, in the manner of *T. sessile*, and each flower sits directly on a collar of three 6-inch, mottled leaves. Plants are hardy to −10°F/−23°C.

Culture. Give all trilliums organically enriched soil that is deep and well drained but always moist. Plants are permanent, never needing division; clumps gradually increase in size and beauty over the years.

Good companions. *Doronicum, Hosta, Mertensia, Polygonatum, Primula, Pulmonaria.*

TROLLIUS
Globeflower
Ranunculaceae

Hardy to: –30°F/–34°C
Exposure: Sun, partial shade
Water: Regular
Flowers in: Late spring, summer
Colors: Yellow, orange

Where you can provide the abundant moisture they need, the various globeflowers will offer brilliant blossoms on good-looking, well-behaved plants. From clumps of finely cut, rather celerylike leaves rise 2- to 3-foot-tall stems that terminate in yellow to orange blossoms, often roundly cupped to globe shaped. Some globeflowers begin flowering in spring, others in summer; blooming can be prolonged if you remove spent flowers.

For a "classic" globular blossom on an early-flowering plant, choose butter yellow *T. europaeus* 'Superbus', a 2-foot selection that begins flowering in midspring. The various hybrids listed under *T. cultorum* present their globular flowers from late spring into summer. 'Lemon Queen' is a soft yellow, blossoming on 2-foot stems; 'Etna' is an orange 3-footer; 'Golden Monarch' is canary yellow, growing to 2½ feet. Plants listed as *T. ledebourii* are probably *T. chinensis* instead. Flowers are not globular but consist of an outer set of broad, cupped petals and a central cluster of upright, narrow ones. The most widely available is *T. c.* 'Golden Queen', with large yellow-orange flowers on 2- to 3-foot stems in summer.

Trollius europaeus

Culture. Moisture is the key to globeflower success. In regular garden beds, liberally amend soil with organic matter and water regularly. If you have continually damp ground near a pond or stream, globeflowers should thrive there. In all but cool-summer regions, locate plants in filtered sun to partial or light shade. In time, when clumps decline in vigor or thin out at the centers, divide and replant in late summer or early autumn.

Good companions. *Iris* (Japanese, Siberian), *Lobelia cardinalis* and *siphilitica*, *Lythrum*, *Mertensia*, *Tradescantia andersonii*.

VERBASCUM
Mullein
Scrophulariaceae

Hardy to: –20°F/–29°C
Exposure: Sun
Water: Moderate
Flowers in: Late spring, summer
Colors: Purple, pink, yellow, white

Like delphiniums and foxgloves, the mulleins bring a strongly vertical accent to the landscape. From a rosette of large, broad leaves rises a spire closely set with nearly flat, rather ruffled flowers circular in outline and about 1 inch across. Both foliage and stems are often covered in woolly hairs. Some mulleins send up a single vertical stem, while others produce a branched spike; heights range from 2 to 5 feet. Many species are short lived or strictly biennial, plants dying after the flowers set seed. The following mulleins are reliably perennial.

Hybrids of purple mullein, *V. phoeniceum*, offer flowers in colors other than purple. Sometimes cataloged as the Cotswold Hybrids, these reach 3 to 5 feet tall depending on the individual. 'Pink Domino' is a good deep rose pink to 3½ feet; 'Royal Highland' is a 5-foot purple flower. Other selections include flowers in white, yellow, and warm pink. In *V. chaixii*, bold clumps of woolly, gray-green leaves send up dark, unbranched, 3-foot stems of red-centered light yellow flowers. Its form 'Album' substitutes white petals for yellow.

Verbascum chaixii 'Album'

Culture. All the mulleins are tough and undemanding plants: give them a well-drained, not-too-rich soil, and grow them on the dry side. Cut off spent flowering spikes: it may induce a second flowering from new stems and will prevent seed setting, which can result in numerous volunteer plants. Raising seedling plants is the easiest way to increase a planting, though seedlings of hybrids won't reproduce the parents. The hybrid selections must be increased from root cuttings or by carefully separating rooted young rosettes from the clump.

Good companions. *Achillea*, *Artemisia*, *Limonium latifolium*, *Lychnis coronaria*, *Oenothera*, *Verbena rigida*.

VERBENA
Verbena, Vervain
Verbenaceae

Hardy to: 10°F/–12°C
Exposure: Sun
Water: Moderate
Flowers in: Spring, summer
Colors: Purple, lavender, pink, white

The following two truly perennial verbenas have several admirable qualities. They flower over a long period, they're not particular about having first-rate soil, and they will thrive on moderate amounts of water. Both perform best where summers are sunny and warm. (The familiar bedding verbenas, *V. hybrida* and *V. peruviana*, are

Verbena rigida

VERONICA
Veronica, Speedwell
Scrophulariaceae

Hardy to: –30°F/–34°C; not suited to Gulf Coast and Florida
Exposure: Sun, partial shade
Water: Regular
Flowers in: Late spring, summer
Colors: Purple, blue, pink, white

The upright veronicas (there are also a number of ground cover types) refresh the summer garden scene with their cool colors presented in unmistakable fashion. The individual flowers are starlike and tiny—perhaps ¼-inch across—but they are closely packed in tapering spikes that rise like candles above shrubby clumps of narrow, pointed leaves. Midsummer is prime veronica time, though some will begin as early as late spring, particularly in mild-winter regions.

Catalog shopping for veronicas can be a bit confusing. A few species may be listed under two (or more) names, and named individuals may appear listed under different species. From the gardener's standpoint, it is simplest to avoid trying to sort out name assignments (most named selections are hybrids) and to make choices based simply on a plant's stated height and the color of its flowers and foliage.

The tallest veronicas are violet-blue *V. longifolia* and a few of its derivatives, which may reach 4 feet. But the majority of available veronicas fall in the 1½- to 2½-foot range.

Very glossy, dark green oblong leaves and dark blue blossoms distinguish 2- to 3-foot *V. grandis holophylla.* In *V. longifolia subsessilis,* the larger deep blue flowers rise to about the same height above narrow, green, toothed leaves. Similar is *V. spicata,* though its blossom spikes are a bit shorter, growing to just about 1½ feet. For foliage variety, low-growing *V. incana* offers gray-white, felted leaves that combine well with the 1½-foot spires of violet-blue blossoms.

Named selections, usually hybrids, offer an assortment of blue shades as well as white, pink, and a pink so dark as to be called red. Pink 'Barcarole'

Veronica 'Blue Charm'

and 'Minuet' grow 1 to 1½ feet high, showing grayish foliage inherited from *V. incana.* Probable derivatives of *V. spicata* include white 'Icicle', medium blue 'Blue Charm', dark blue 'Blue Peter', violet-blue 'Sunny Border Blue', and pinkish red 'Red Fox'. In flower, these plants reach about 1½ feet high, though 'Blue Peter' and 'Sunny Border Blue' are inclined to grow a bit taller.

A tendency to sprawling or lax growth and shorter flower spikes separate *V. latifolia* from the previous species and hybrids. Best known is 'Crater Lake Blue', which bears appropriately vivid, medium blue blossoms about 1 foot tall when in flower. This will flower earlier than most veronicas and will repeat the process if you cut off spent blossom spikes from the first flowering.

Culture. The veronicas need only average soil with good drainage. In hot-summer regions they'll appreciate light shade or filtered sunlight during the hottest hours. Remove flower spikes as they finish blooming; this not only keeps the plant neat but also encourages further flowering on secondary spikes. When clumps show declining vigor, dig and divide them in early spring or early autumn. You can increase a plant from cuttings in spring and summer.

Good companions. Coreopsis, Diascia, Geranium, Heuchera, Iberis sempervirens, Malva, Sedum.

perennial in the mildest regions, but even there they are usually grown as annuals and replaced each year.)

The shorter of the two perennial species, *V. rigida,* reaches 1 to 1½ feet. Its small, circular flowers are carried in tight clusters on branching sprays at the ends of stiff, upright stems clothed in narrow, toothed leaves with a sandpapery texture. Plants spread fairly rapidly by underground stems, forming dense drifts that flower from mid- or late spring until frost. The basic flower color is a shade between lavender and purple, but the selection 'Lilacina' is pale lilac; 'Alba' is white. *Verbena bonariensis* also features small, circular flowers in tight clusters, but in this species the stems reach 4 to 6 feet tall, branching near the tops, so that the violet blossoms seem almost to float in air. Dark green leaves are narrow and toothed, each plant forming a foliage clump to 1½ feet in height.

Culture. Growing verbenas is no challenge, as long as you plant them where soil won't be continually moist. You can divide *V. rigida* for increase; it may become slightly invasive, giving you plenty of surplus plants if you remove shoots from the outsides of clumps. *Verbena bonariensis* will seed itself if you leave a few spent flowering stems; the volunteer seedlings will provide you with an ongoing supply of new plants.

Good companions. Achillea 'Moonshine', *Artemisia, Gaura lindheimeri, Nepeta, Sedum, Senecio, Zauschneria.*

Viola odorata

Zauschneria californica

VIOLA ODORATA
Sweet violet
Violaceae

Hardy to: −10°F/−23°C
Exposure: Partial shade, shade
Water: Regular
Flowers in: Early spring
Colors: Purple, blue, pink, white

Sweet violets are among the first flowers to assure gardeners that spring is coming. An established violet patch will, in fact, remain colorful for over a month—a veritable sheet of color for most of that time. And sweet they are. Most selections exude the legendary violet fragrance, making them candidates for the first bouquet of the year. Plants are just 4 to 8 inches tall, and an individual plant consists of a clump of long-stalked, nearly round leaves. Flowers come on stems just long enough to rise above the foliage. Plants grow like strawberries, sending out runners that root and produce new plants. Because of their low stature and spreading nature, violets make excellent small-scale ground covers beneath deciduous shrubs and trees.

'Royal Robe' is the most widely available "classic" sweet violet, with rich purple flowers and an intense fragrance. But perennials specialists offer other named sorts with flowers in light to dark blue, pink, lilac, and white. A small group of hybrids, the Parma violets, features very double and powerfully fragrant blossoms on plants hardy to about 10°F/−12°C. Colors range from deep violet 'Marie Louise' through lavender to white.

Culture. Where summers are cool, you can plant violets in full-sun locations; but the hotter the summer the more shade they'll need. Plant sweet violets in good soil liberally enriched with organic matter. You can dig and separate plants in early spring for increase; with faster-growing selections, you may need to periodically curb the spread by removing the clump's perimeter. Spider mites can be a pest in summer.

Good companions. *Doronicum, Helleborus, Hosta, Polygonatum, Pulmonaria, Trillium.*

ZAUSCHNERIA
California fuchsia
Onagraceae

Hardy to: 0°F/−18°C
Exposure: Sun
Water: Moderate
Flowers in: Summer, autumn
Colors: Red, orange, pink, white

If the word "fuchsia" brings to mind elegant pendant flowers, you'll be misled. Like their distant relatives the true fuchsias, these plants do offer a lavish display of bright blossoms, but the 1- to 2-inch flowers are carried in a near-horizontal position, each one tubular but flaring into an unequally lobed trumpet. Most individuals have red or orange flowers, and many have gray or silvery foliage; growth varies from upright and shrublike to low and spreading. The species hail from western North America and are best within their broad native range, where summer rains are scant to nonexistent and heat is not accompanied by humidity. Their best landscape use is among plantings of natives and other drought-resistant plants or at the fringes of cultivated areas. Plants spread by underground stems and can be mildly invasive.

A bit of name confusion in the trade is the result of botanical examination and revision. (Some botanists now classify all Zauschnerias as *Epilobium.*) It is, therefore, better to make choices based on a plant's catalog description or its appearance—which may not accord logically with the name attached to it! The tallest plants—shrubby, mostly upright to about 2 feet—belong to *Z. californica* and its forms. Some have very linear gray-green leaves and narrow-mouthed orange flowers. Plants with *arizonica* in the name have oval green leaves and larger orange-red blossoms; some plants labeled *Z. californica latifolia* may also fit this description.

Lower-growing types include other plants labeled *Z. californica latifolia,* which may also be listed as *Z. septentrionalis* and *Z. latifolia* 'Etteri'. Generally these are spreading plants that remain under 1 foot tall, their lance-shaped leaves green to gray. Green-leafed 'Solidarity Pink' is a surprisingly soft, warm pink among the strident oranges and reds, of which 'Glasnevin' ('Dublin') is a good scarlet-flowered selection. A spreading to ground-hugging plant, *Z. cana* (*Z. californica microphylla*) has linear silver-gray leaves and scarlet flowers.

Culture. Poor soil—low in nutrients, rocky, even shallow—is no obstacle to California fuchsia. But it doesn't object to better conditions, and will improve in appearance if planted in soil that has at least been well dug. In well-drained soil, moderate watering over summer is sufficient; in heavy soils, stretch out the watering intervals. You can start new plantings from rooted segments of established clumps in the spring.

Good companions. *Achillea filipendulina, Ceratostigma plumbaginoides, Eryngium, Gaura lindheimeri, Lobelia laxiflora, Oenothera, Perovskia, Verbena.*

Index

Mail-Order Sources for Perennials

Andre Viette Farm & Nursery
Route 1, Box 16
Fisherville, VA 22939

Bluestone Perennials
7213 Middle Ridge Road
Madison, OH 44057

Busse Gardens
Route 2, Box 238
Cokato, MN 55321

Canyon Creek Nursery
3527 Dry Creek Road
Oroville, CA 95965

Carroll Gardens
P.O. Box 310
Westminster, MD 21157

Fieldstone Gardens, Inc.
620 Quaker Lane
Vassalboro, ME 04989

Kurt Bluemel Inc.
2543 Hess Road
Fallston, MD 21047

Lamb Nurseries
101 East Sharp Avenue
Spokane, WA 99292

Milaeger's Gardens
4838 Douglas Avenue
Racine, WI 53402

Perpetual Perennials
1111 Upper Valley Pike
Springfield, OH 45504

Surry Gardens
P.O. Box 145
Surry, ME 04684

Wayside Gardens
1 Garden Lane
Hodges, SC 29695

White Flower Farm
Litchfield, CT 06759

Combined Index

A comprehensive index to both *Annuals* and *Perennials* appears on the following pages. You will also find individual book indexes on pages 95 and 96 of *Annuals* and on pages 111 and 112 of *Perennials*.

Well-prepared soil helps ensure a colorful display of annuals like this bed of pansies (Viola), stock (Matthiola), *sweet alyssum (Lobularia),* petunias, and carnations (Dianthus).

Trouble-free yarrow (Achillea) is a favorite perennial; Galaxy series hybrids offer varied colors on 2-foot stems.

DARROW WATT

NORMAN A. PLATE

Combined Index

Combined Index